MW00811282

POLITICAL PHILOSOPHY IN THE TWENTY-FIRST CENTURY

POLITICAL PHILOSOPHY IN THE TWENTY-FIRST CENTURY

ESSENTIAL ESSAYS

EDITED BY

Steven M. Cahn

The City University of New York Graduate Center

AND

Robert B. Talisse

Vanderbilt University

WESTVIEW PRESS

A Member of the Perseus Books Group

Westview Press was founded in 1975 in Boulder, Colorado, by notable publisher and intellectual Fred Praeger. Westview Press continues to publish scholarly titles and high-quality undergraduate- and graduate-level textbooks in core social science disciplines. With books developed, written, and edited with the needs of serious nonfiction readers, professors, and students in mind, Westview Press honors its long history of publishing books that matter.

Copyright © 2013 by Westview Press

Published by Westview Press,
A Member of the Perseus Books Group

All rights reserved. Printed in the United States of America. No part of this book may be reproduced in any manner whatsoever without written permission except in the case of brief quotations embodied in critical articles and reviews. For information, address Westview Press, 2465 Central Avenue, Boulder, CO 80301.

Find us on the World Wide Web at www.westviewpress.com.

Every effort has been made to secure required permissions for all text, images, maps, and other art reprinted in this volume.

Westview Press books are available at special discounts for bulk purchases in the United States by corporations, institutions, and other organizations. For more information, please contact the Special Markets Department at the Perseus Books Group, 2300 Chestnut Street, Suite 200, Philadelphia, PA 19103, or call (800) 810-4145, ext. 5000, or e-mail special.markets@perseusbooks.com.

Designed by Brent Wilcox

Library of Congress Cataloging-in-Publication Data
Political philosophy in the twenty-first century : essential essays / edited by Steven M. Cahn, Robert B. Talisse.
p. cm.
Includes bibliographical references and index.
ISBN 978-0-8133-4690-8 (pbk. : alk. paper)—
ISBN 978-0-8133-4691-5 (e-book)
1. Political science—Philosophy—History—21st century. I. Cahn, Steven M. II. Talisse, Robert B. III. Title: Political philosophy in the 21st century.
JA83.P5629 2012
320.01—dc23

2012009753

10 9 8 7 6 5 4 3 2 1

CONTENTS

PREFACE

The publication in 1971 of John Rawls's *A Theory of Justice* inspired a resurgence of writing in political philosophy, focused primarily on the nature of justice. By the early 1990s, however, Rawls and others began to explore related concepts, including equality, liberty, public justification, citizenship, democracy, and international relations. Indeed, in the early years of the twenty-first century, political philosophy has grown less concerned with the ideas of Rawls himself and has developed in ways he did not anticipate and might have rejected. This collection offers influential and accessible examples of such recent work.

We thank Elizabeth Anderson, Thomas Christiano, John Christman, and Philip Pettit, who edited their previously published articles for use in this collection. We also wish to express our appreciation to our editor, Kelsey Mitchell, the production staff at Westview Press, and editorial assistant Andrew Forcehimes.

Introduction: The Rawlsian Background

ROBERT B. TALISSE

The publication of John Rawls's *A Theory of Justice* (TJ) in 1971 (and revised in 1999) resulted in a renaissance of political philosophy. The impact of his thought is evident throughout the influential, contemporary articles collected here, and so as a background to them, we offer a brief sketch of Rawls's thought and some of the controversies it has inspired.

For most of the twentieth century, systematic political philosophy lay nearly moribund. The reigning conception of social justice derived from utilitarian sources. Utilitarianism maintains that "pleasure" or "satisfaction" is the only intrinsic good, and consequently that individual actions and social policies are morally right only in the degree to which they maximize satisfaction across an entire population. Rawls opposes utilitarianism, but he nonetheless provides a succinct and accurate encapsulation of the view: "The main idea [of utilitarianism] is that society is rightly ordered, and therefore just, when its major institutions are arranged so as to achieve the greatest net balance of satisfaction summed over all the individuals belonging to it" (TJ, 20).

The intuitive appeal of utilitarianism is hard to deny. Yet it is important to note that on the utilitarian conception of justice, normative questions of social policy are answerable in terms of descriptive social scientific data. A question concerning whether a proposed policy should be adopted is simply a matter of whether the policy reasonably can be expected to generate a greater amount of satisfaction across the population than any of its realizable rivals. This question is one for social scientists, not philosophers. Hence utilitarianism puts political philosophy out of business; with utilitarianism in place, distinctively philosophical theorizing about social questions is irrelevant.

Thus Rawls's first task in developing his theory of justice is to demonstrate a *need* for such a theory. Accordingly, early in *A Theory of Justice* and in many of his early essays, he offers arguments to the effect that, despite its predominance, utilitarianism is an inadequate account of justice for two reasons. First, he argues that since on the utilitarian view "the precepts of justice are derivative from the one end of attaining the greatest net balance of satisfactions," there is "in principle" no reason that "the greater gains of some should not compensate for the lesser losses of others; or why the violation of the liberty of a few may not be made right by a greater good shared by many" (1967, 131). In other words, utilitarianism cannot countenance a sufficiently robust set of individual rights; it cannot acknowledge that "each member of society has an inviolability founded on justice which even the welfare of society cannot override," and that a "loss of freedom for some is not made right by a greater sum of satisfactions enjoyed by many" (1967, 131). More generally, Rawls argues that "[utilitarianism] is incapable of explaining the fact that in a just society the liberties of equal citizenship are taken for granted, and the rights secured by justice are not subject to political bargaining" (1967, 131).

Second, Rawls argues that because utilitarianism requires us to maximize the total sum of satisfactions in society, it can make no distinction between different *distributions* of the same amount of satisfaction; all that matters is *how much* satisfaction is produced, not how it is distributed. According to the utilitarian, a state of affairs in which great satisfaction is provided to a relatively small sector of the population is morally equivalent to a state of affairs in which the same degree of satisfaction is distributed more equally. Rawls insists that certain distributions of satisfaction are *unfair*, granting to some individuals *undeserved* benefits or burdens.

Given these failings of utilitarianism, Rawls concludes, "we shall have to look for another account of the principles of justice" (1967, 131). Interestingly, in crafting an alternative theory, Rawls looks back to the social contract tradition that utilitarianism had largely displaced. Rawls writes, "What I have attempted to do is to generalize and carry to a higher order of abstraction the traditional theory of the social contract as represented by Locke, Rousseau, and Kant. . . . Indeed, I must disclaim any originality for the views I put forward. The leading ideas are classical and well known" (TJ, xviii).

His positive view of justice, which he calls Justice as Fairness, begins with a recognizably contractarian device. We are asked to imagine hypothetical "parties" in an "original position" who are "free and rational" and "concerned to further their own interests" (TJ, 10). These parties are given the task of choosing "in one joint act" a conception of justice that will "assign basic rights and duties," "determine the division of social benefits," "regulate all further agreements," and "specify the kinds of social cooperation that can be entered into and the forms of government that can be established" (TJ, 10). Unlike the traditional social contract theories, which employ the idea of a contract in a state of nature as a means to explain the origin of states and their authority, Rawls has his parties deliberating not about whether to form a state but about the nature of justice itself. Rawls explains, "Justice as fairness begins . . . with one of the most general of all choices which persons might make together, namely, with the choice of the first principles of a conception of justice which is to regulate all subsequent criticism and reform of institutions. Then, having chosen a conception of justice, we can suppose that they are to choose a constitution and a legislature to enact laws, and so on, all in accordance with the principles of justice initially agreed upon" (TJ, 11–12).

The agreement made in the original position establishes "once and for all" (TJ, 11) the first principles of justice. Consequently, the deliberations are monumental: the agreement reached in the original position will affect all persons in society, including the descendants of the parties to the original agreement. A classic objection to social contractarianism contends that the original agreement will simply reflect the will of the naturally powerful or those most clever and persuasive or those best informed; hence, it is charged, the original agreement cannot be rightly said to be free—the weak will be subjected to the strong.

Rawls meets this traditional challenge by introducing into his original position the "veil of ignorance" (TJ, 11), which deprives the parties of information of their personal interests, desires, and capacities. Hence in the original position, "no one knows his place in society, his class position or social status, nor does any one know his fortune in the distribution of natural assets and abilities, his intelligence, strength, and the like" (TJ, 11).

The veil of ignorance corrects "the arbitrariness of the world" (TJ, 122) insofar as it guarantees that "no one is advantaged or disadvantaged in the choice of principles by the outcome of natural chance or the contingency of social circumstances" (TJ, 11). Although Rawls stipulates that the parties in the original position are rational and self-interested, the veil nullifies "the effects of specific contingencies which put men at odds and tempt them to exploit social and natural circumstances to their own advantage" (TJ, 118). Thus in the original position none of the parties is "in a position to tailor principles to his advantage" (TJ, 120–121). Consequently, whatever conception of justice that is chosen is "the result of a fair agreement" (TJ, 11).

We now can see the essential principle driving Rawls's view. Justice as Fairness is based on the fundamental intuition that the connection between social justice and fairness is so *essential* that justice *simply is* that which would emerge from an agreement reached by rational and self-interested agents from behind the veil of ignorance. Thus Rawls's contractarianism differs from traditional social contract theory. Rawls is not offering a historical or anthropological explanation of how societies came to be; rather he is proposing what philosophers call a "thought experiment" about justice. The original position provides a theoretical vantage point from which to *think* about justice, and so to evaluate competing conceptions of justice. The veil of ignorance represents the kinds of constraints on our thinking about justice that we think it reasonable to impose; more specifically, we think that someone who proposes principles of social justice that are intentionally designed to favor his own preferences and talents is not properly thinking about justice. Thinking about justice requires that we take the kind of impartial or objective standpoint represented in the veil of ignorance. In short, the original position "best expresses the conditions that are widely thought reasonable to impose on the choice of principles" (TJ, 105). It collects together "into one conception a number of conditions on principles that we are ready upon due consideration to recognize as reasonable" (TJ, 19). Consequently, "one or more persons can at any time enter [the original] position, or perhaps better, simulate the deliberations of this hypothetical situation, simply by reasoning in accordance with the appropriate restrictions" (TJ, 119).

But is *rational choice* possible from behind a veil of ignorance? If the veil blocks all information pertaining to one's preferences, goals, talents, desires, and projects, how then can one rank the different proposals for principles of justice? Certainly such a ranking, and eventual choice, requires a standard by which the proposals can be evaluated. Yet any relevant standard would seem to involve knowledge of the kind of information the veil is supposed to block. Hence it would seem that the choice in the original position must come to nothing but an *arbitrary selection* or a *guess* (TJ, 123). In short, what *motivates* the choice in the original position?

Rawls meets this difficulty by stipulating that the parties in the original position appeal to what he calls the "thin" theory of the good. Rawls supposes that the parties recognize that there is a set of "primary goods" that "normally have a use whatever a person's rational plan of life" (TJ, 54). Primary goods, then, are all-purpose resources "that every rational man is presumed to want" (TJ, 54), "no matter what else he wants" (TJ, 79). Among the primary goods are "rights, liberties, and opportunities, and income, and wealth" and the social bases for "self-respect" (TJ, 54). Any rational agent in the original position can be assumed to "prefer more primary goods rather than less" (TJ, 123). "With more of these goods men can generally be assured of greater success in carrying out their intentions and in advancing their ends, whatever these ends may be" (TJ, 79).

Thus rational deliberation and choice are possible in the original position—the veil of ignorance blocks information of one's *personal* desires, objectives, and talents, but it does not block information about the kinds of preferences one has as a rational agent. Rawls concludes, "Thus even though the parties are deprived of information about their particular ends, they have enough knowledge to rank the alternatives. They know that in general they must try to protect their liberties, widen their opportunities, and enlarge their means for promoting their aims whatever these are. Guided by the thin theory of the good . . . their deliberations are no longer guesswork. They can make a rational decision in the ordinary sense" (TJ, 123).

Finally, Rawls imagines that his parties are presented with a list of conceptions of justice (TJ, 107), including a number of traditional ones such as utilitarianism, egoism, and Rawls's own. The parties are "presented with this list and required to agree unanimously that one conception is best among those enumerated" (TJ, 106). We know that various parties will seek to maximize their share of the primary goods, but this observation leaves open the question of how the parties will compare the various proposals. Suppose that on one conception of justice an extremely small minority enjoys an enormous share of the primary goods, and on another the primary goods are distributed roughly equally. Which option is a more worthy of choice in the original position?

Rawls argues that rational parties in the original position concerned to maximize their share of the primary goods would follow the choice strategy known among decision theorists as *maximin*. According to the maximin strategy, we "rank alternatives by their *worst* possible outcome: we are to adopt the alternative the worst outcome of which is superior to the worst outcomes of the others" (TJ, 133); in other words, we *max*imize the *min*imum position in society. Rawls contends that the parties would not assume a winner-take-all strategy of ranking highest the conception in which the best off are better off than in any alternative option (what may be called *maximax*), nor would they adopt a strategy according to which the preferred option is the one in which the average person is better off than on any other scheme (what may be called *maximid*). Instead rational parties will imagine themselves in the worst possible position and select the conception of justice in which the worst off is best off.

To sum up, on Rawls's view the question of social justice is simply the question of what conception of justice would be chosen by rational and self-interested parties in the original position. Any conception of justice that for obvious reasons would *not* be chosen may be dismissed as unjust. With this principle in place we are now in position to turn from Rawls's way of framing the question to his positive account of justice.

The bulk of *A Theory of Justice* is devoted to demonstrating the worthiness in the original position of a conception of justice consisting of exactly two prioritized principles. Here is Rawls's final formulation of them:

> **First Principle of Justice**
> Each person is to have an equal right to the most extensive total system of equal basic liberties with a similar system of liberty for all.
>
> **Second Principle of Justice**
> Social and economic inequalities are to be arranged so that they are both: (a) to the greatest benefit of the least advantaged . . . , and (b) attached to offices and positions open to all under conditions of fair equality of opportunity. (TJ, 266)

Rawls's first principle is known as the "equal liberty principle." The parts of the second, (a) and (b), are referred to in turn as the "difference principle" and the "equal opportunity principle."

Rawls contends that the parties in the original position would unanimously agree to the following prioritization of these principles: the equal liberty principle has priority over the second principle of justice, and the equal opportunity principle has priority over the difference principle. Accordingly, liberty cannot be sacrificed for social and economic gains (TJ, 55) and equality of opportunity cannot be sacrificed for distributions that benefit the least advantaged.

How each of these principles is to be interpreted is a matter of much dispute (see the essays in Part I, Equality, and Part II, Justice). Here I try to provide a noncontroversial elaboration of the difference principle.

The difference principle stipulates that certain kinds of social and economic inequalities are consistent with, even required by, justice. Hence Rawls is not a strict egalitarian. Nor, however, is he a typical laissez-faire capitalist—the difference principle calls for distributive efforts that go beyond the standard free-market mechanisms. The hand of Rawlsian distribution is not invisible: the difference principle calls for government intervention within the social and economic order. Specifically, the difference principle bids governments to eliminate any inequality that is not to the advantage of the worst off. Allen Buchanan has provided a good example of how the difference principle may be applied:

> Suppose that large-scale capital investment in a certain industry is required to raise employment and to produce new goods and services. Suppose that by raising employment and producing these new goods and services such capital investment will ultimately be of great benefit to the least advantaged members of the society. Suppose in particular that such capital investment, if it can be achieved, will greatly increase the income prospects of the least advantaged through employing many who are not now employed and by raising the wages of those who are already employed. Suppose, however, that individuals will not be willing to undertake the risks of this large-scale capital investment unless they have the opportunity to reap large profits from the enterprise, should it succeed. In such a case, tax advantages for capital investment and lowered taxes on profits might provide the needed incentives for investment. (1980, 11)

Under such conditions the difference principle would require the suggested tax policies. They would involve an unequal distribution of the economic tax burden, but by stipulation this inequality works to the advantage of the worst off and so is just.

A Theory of Justice has generated a mountain of critical work. Philosophers generally sympathetic to Rawls's two principles have criticized Rawls for his contractarian methodology. Among the earliest of these critics is Thomas Nagel. In his review of *A Theory of Justice*, Nagel questions the value of framing the question of justice in terms of choice in the original position. Nagel writes, "The egalitarian liberalism which [Rawls] develops and the conception of the good on which it depends are extremely persuasive, but the original position serves to model, rather than to justify them. . . . I believe Rawls's conclusions can be more persuasively defended by direct moral arguments for liberty and equality" (1973, 15).

Nagel's suggestion is that Rawls has described the original position so as to ensure that his favored principles would be chosen. While Nagel accepts Rawls's principles, he wants also a "direct" argument for their justice. In an essay included in this volume (Chapter 1), Ronald Dworkin offers such a "direct" argument for a liberal conception of justice.

Robert Nozick, by contrast, rejects Rawls's views of distributive justice. In his *Anarchy, State, and Utopia* (1974), Nozick claims that individual liberty, which is rooted in a robust conception of the right to private property, precludes the kind of redistributive scheme inherent in Rawls's difference principle. Nozick argues that proper respect for individual liberty requires us to think of distributive justice as a primarily *historical* matter—that is, how holdings are acquired determines whether they are held justly. If an individual gains holdings without committing an act of injustice (such as violating a contract or stealing), then the distribution is just. Therefore any redistributive project would constitute an assault on individual liberty and hence be unjust.

Nozick couches his argument in a famous example involving then-world-famous basketball player Wilt Chamberlain (1974, 160–162). Nozick asks us to imagine that at the beginning of a given day the Rawlsian difference principle is realized: there are no inequalities that are not to the benefit of the least well-off in society. Call this Rawlsian initial distribution of goods D1. Now imagine that Wilt Chamberlain decides to play basketball and allow people to watch him play on the condition that each gives him a dollar. Many people pay for this privilege, and thus Chamberlain becomes richer than many others. Call this new distribution D2. The Rawlsian must contend that D2 is unjust because it involves inequality that is to the benefit of Wilt Chamberlain, not the worst off. But Nozick asks, since the move from D1 to D2 involved no act of injustice (the people freely decided that watching Chamberlain was worth a dollar), how could D2 be unjust? To insist, as the Rawlsian does, that justice requires restoring D1 is, according to Nozick, to violate liberty.

Another line of criticism, often characterized as "communitarian," comes from those who challenge Rawls's view at a more fundamental level. In his book *Liberalism and the Limits of Justice* ([1982] 1998), Michael Sandel charges that Justice as Fairness presupposes a demonstrably false philosophical conception of the self. According to Sandel, the construct of the original position commits Rawls to the view that the self is essentially an asocial *chooser* of its ends and purposes. In other words, Sandel argues that Justice as Fairness presumes that "what is most essential to our personhood is not the ends we choose but our capacity to choose them" (1998, 19). Such a conception disallows the view that certain commitments, projects, traditions, and relations are *constitutive* of our identities, not detachable baggage that may be peeled away by the veil of ignorance. The image of the asocial individual unencumbered by and independent of social relatedness has long been a target of criticism.

In his second major work, *Political Liberalism* (PL, 1993, expanded edition in 2005), Rawls launches a revised version of Justice as Fairness, one that does not so much answer the objections occasioned by *A Theory of Justice* as *subverts* them. Note that the criticisms sketched above share the common premise that one's political theory derives from deeper philosophical premises concerning the nature of the self or the normative value of liberty. Rawls characterizes such theories as "comprehensive." The views of John Locke, Immanuel Kant, Thomas Jefferson, and John Stuart Mill fit neatly into this category, because they attempt to derive the principles of their political philosophies from more basic claims about human nature, God, natural right, and so forth.

In *Political Liberalism*, Rawls rejects the project of providing a "comprehensive" political theory. He instead promotes what he calls a "political" theory of liberal democracy. A *political* theory does not look to philosophical premises for support but rather "deliberately stays on the surface, philosophically speaking" and "look[s] to avoid philosophy's longstanding problems" (PL, 10). Thus instead of defending the conception of the self against Sandel's objections or responding to Nozick's contention that liberty trumps all or providing Nagel with direct arguments for his principles, Rawls leaves such philosophical concerns behind and introduces a new conception of the architecture of liberal political theory. A political liberalism begins with the "tradition of democratic thought" (PL, 18) and the "public culture" of society: it does not rest on philosophical theories but draws from the "shared fund of implicitly recognized basic ideas and principles" of contemporary democratic states (PL, 9). Whereas Justice as Fairness had been cast in *A Theory of Justice* as a comprehensive theory, it is presented in *Political Liberalism* as a "political" theory.

Note that in his "political" reformulation of Justice as Fairness, Rawls retains much of the substance and content of his original theory. For example, the two principles of justice remain as before, as do the original position and the veil of ignorance. The difference, which is considerable, is the *justification* offered for these concepts. As Sandel argues in his critique of Rawls, a metaphysical conception of the human self appears to lurk within Rawls's conception of the original position. In response, Rawls explicitly declares that Justice as Fairness is "political not metaphysical."

The fundamental idea behind Rawls's shift to political liberalism is what he calls "the fact of reasonable pluralism" (PL, 36). Rawls notes that in any free society, citizens hold a plurality of comprehensive philosophical, religious, and moral views, and that many of these, though incompatible, will be equally reasonable. Rawls writes, "Under political and social conditions secured by the basic rights and liberties of free institutions, a diversity of conflicting and irreconcilable—and what is more, reasonable—comprehensive doctrines will come about and persist if such diversity does not already obtain" (PL, 36).

This pluralism is thus "not an unfortunate condition of human life" (PL, 37) but rather the "long-run outcome of the work of human reason under enduring free institutions" (PL, 129). Reasonable pluralism is a "permanent feature" of a free society (PL, 37).

The fact of reasonable pluralism entails what Rawls calls the "fact of oppression" (PL, 37), which he characterizes thus:

> [A] continuing shared understanding on one comprehensive religious, philosophical, or moral doctrine can be maintained only by the oppressive use of state power. If we think of political society as a community united in affirming one and the same comprehensive doctrine, then the oppressive use of state power is necessary for political community. In the society of the Middle Ages, more or less united in affirming the Catholic faith, the Inquisition was not an accident; its suppression of heresy was needed to preserve that shared religious belief. (PL, 37)

The fact of oppression applies equally to comprehensive philosophical doctrines: "The same holds, I believe, for any reasonable comprehensive philosophical and moral doctrine, whether religious or nonreligious. A society united on a reasonable form of utilitarianism, or on the reasonable liberalisms of Kant and Mill, would likewise require the sanctions of state power to remain so" (PL, 37).

Given the facts of reasonable pluralism and oppression, we can see why Rawls rejects the project of formulating a comprehensive liberal theory. Recall that such a theory attempts to derive the fundamental principles of liberal political philosophy from some set of more basic philosophical premises, invoking philosophical, religious, and moral claims. According to reasonable pluralism, however, all citizens cannot be reasonably expected to agree on such basic premises. Because a fundamental principle of any liberal democratic political theory is that state power is legitimate only when exercised with the consent of the people, no state based on a philosophical, religious, or moral doctrine can be fully liberal. Any such state will require coercion and oppression to hold its grounding premises in place among the citizenry. Hence only a political liberalism can provide a public conception of justice for a liberal society.

Political liberalism overturns the tradition of political philosophy, reconstructing its very task. Whereas traditional theorists have sought a philosophical, religious, or moral foundation for the fundamental commitments of liberal democracy, Rawls contends that "the question the dominant tradition has tried to answer has no answer: no comprehensive doctrine is appropriate as a political conception for a constitutional regime" (PL, 135). The alternative task Rawls sets for political theory is to answer the following question: "How is it possible for there to exist over time a just and stable society of free and equal citizens, who remain profoundly divided by reasonable religious, philosophical, and moral doctrines?" (PL, 4)

One answer imagines proponents of the divided doctrines endorsing the liberal state as a matter of power-balancing compromise, what Rawls calls a "modus vivendi" agreement. In such circumstances, citizens view society as a livable compromise between what they see as the best possible arrangement (namely, a state based solely upon their own comprehensive doctrine) and the worst arrangement (namely, a state based solely upon a comprehensive doctrine opposed to their own). Hence under this modus vivendi, each citizen sees the liberal state as at best a second-best political order, and for this reason, Rawls argues that a modus vivendi liberal democracy will be unstable. He illustrates this point with an example from the sixteenth-century contest between Catholicism and Protestantism: "Both faiths held that it was the duty of the ruler to uphold the true religion and to repress the spread of heresy and false doctrine. In such a case the acceptance of the principle of toleration would indeed be a mere modus vivendi, because if either faith becomes dominant, the principle of toleration would no longer be followed" (PL, 148).

Rawls insists that the stability of a liberal democracy requires a deeper commitment on the part of the citizens than exists in a modus vivendi. He contends that if a liberal democracy is to be stable, its political conception of justice and principal institutions must be endorsed by what Rawls calls an "overlapping consensus" (PL, 142). In that case, citizens see the conception of justice and major political institutions as an appropriate reflection of *their own* comprehensive doctrines in the political sphere. Thus Rawls sees his political liberalism as a "module" that "fits into and can be supported by various reasonable comprehensive doctrines that endure in a society regulated by it" (PL, 12). He explains further, "An overlapping consensus, therefore, is not merely a consensus on accepting certain authorities, or on complying with certain institutional arrangements, founded on a convergence of self- or group-interests. All those who affirm the political conception start from within their own comprehensive view and draw on the religious, philosophical, and moral grounds it provides" (PL, 147).

Hence a politically liberal conception of justice that is the focus of an overlapping consensus is stable because it is endorsed by citizens in a way that gives them reason to uphold its principles regardless of the balance of power among their respective doctrines; citizens endorse the political conception of justice "for its own sake" and "on its own merits" (PL, 148). The stability of a politically liberal democratic state does not rely upon compromise and bargaining, nor does it rest on deep agreements across society on a single philosophical doctrine. Instead, stability comes from citizens endorsing the political conception of justice and the basic political institutions *from within* a plurality of reasonable comprehensive doctrines. Consequently, in a politically liberal democracy each citizen endorses the state, but each gives such endorsement for different reasons drawing from different comprehensive doctrines.

A fundamental feature of any liberal democratic theory is that the state needs to *justify* its actions and policies to those citizens affected by them. The idea of an overlapping consensus places strict constraints on the kind of justification the state can offer. Given reasonable pluralism, the state cannot justify its policies by appealing to specific theological or philosophical principles. Similarly, discourse among citizens concerning essential issues of basic justice must be conducted in terms that do not favor or presuppose any particular comprehensive view. Rawls therefore countenances a "public domain" in which "public reason" operates, where reasoning makes no appeal to the comprehensive doctrines over which reasonable citizens will disagree. Rawls explains:

> This means that in discussing constitutional essentials and matters of basic justice we are not to appeal to comprehensive religious and philosophical doctrines—to what we as individuals or members of associations see as the whole truth—nor to elaborate economic theories of general equilibrium. As far as possible, the knowledge and ways of reasoning that ground our affirming the principles of justice and their application to constitutional essentials and basic justice are to rest on plain truths now widely accepted, or available to citizens generally. (PL, 224–225)

The idea of public reason establishes an ideal of politically liberal citizenship. In a politically liberal society, citizens try "to explain to one another . . . how the principles and policies they advocate and vote for can be supported by the political values of public reason." Citizens hence are "ready to listen to others" (PL, 217) and "meet others halfway" (PL, 157) when disagreements arise. Hence political liberalism, and the consequent idea of public reason, entails a conception of civic duty and civility in political discussion (PL, 217).

This feature of political liberalism has struck many as objectionable, tending to exclude the concerns, reasons, and perspectives of disadvantaged or marginalized persons. Others have argued that public reason trivializes deep moral and religious convictions of citizens, which cannot be disowned in discussions of basic justice. Some have objected on the grounds that Rawls's conception of public reason renders many of Martin Luther King's speeches unreasonable, along with much of Lincoln's case for abolition. In response to such criticisms, Rawls offers a further clarification of his position in his 1997 essay "The Idea of Public Reason Revisited" (later Part IV in the revised expanded edition).

Rawls's work has been the subject of extensive commentary and criticism, but the essays contained in this volume, while presuming some acquaintance with Rawls's thought, discuss a variety of other theoretical and practical issues that have been the focus of debate in recent political philosophy. This introduction has aimed to sketch the Rawlsian commitments that form the background to contemporary political philosophy.

Works Cited

Buchanan, Allen. 1980. "A Critical Introduction to Rawls' Theory of Justice." In *John Rawls' Theory of Social Justice*, edited by H. Gene Blocker and Elizabeth Smith. Athens: Ohio University Press.

Nagel, Thomas. 1973. "Rawls on Justice." Reprinted in *Reading Rawls*, edited by Norman Daniels. New York: Basic Books.

Nozick, Robert. 1974. *Anarchy, State, and Utopia*. New York: Basic Books.

Rawls, John. [1967] 1999. "Distributive Justice." Reprinted in *John Rawls: Collected Papers*, edited by Samuel Freeman. Cambridge, MA: Harvard University Press.

________. [1971] 1999. *A Theory of Justice*. Rev. ed. Cambridge, MA: Harvard University Press.

________. [1993] 2005. *Political Liberalism*. Expanded ed. New York: Columbia University Press.

________. [1997] 2005. "The Idea of Public Reason Revisited." Reprinted in John Rawls, *Political Liberalism*. Expanded ed. New York: Columbia University Press.

Sandel, Michael. [1982] 1998. *Liberalism and the Limits of Justice*. Cambridge: Cambridge University Press.

Part I

EQUALITY

Many political theorists hold that government should respect the equality of all citizens, or in other words, treat all citizens as equal. But what does treating all citizens as equal actually mean?

Ronald Dworkin contends that government should show equal regard for the life of each citizen and that this principle requires government to distinguish between differences among people based on individual choice and differences based on chance. Dworkin holds that government should not allow citizens' fates to be determined by chance, so he proposes a scheme by which resources are distributed by means of an auction and an insurance market. Elizabeth Anderson rejects Dworkin's approach, arguing that equality demands institutions and norms that enable citizens to stand in certain social relationships to one another. Thus according to Anderson, equality is primarily a democratic social ideal involving the rejection of hierarchy and oppression, and only secondarily a set of principles by which resources are to be distributed. Kok-Chor Tan, like Dworkin, holds that equality requires equal distribution of social goods and burdens. He also agrees with Dworkin that government should recognize a difference between chance and choice. Furthermore, Tan holds that equality requires that society's institutions avoid distributing benefits and burdens on the basis of individual traits not of individuals' own choosing.

READING

1

Equality

RONALD DWORKIN

Philosophy and Shame

Poverty makes an odd subject for reflective philosophy; it seems fit only for outrage and struggle. In most of the rich countries the distance between the comfortable and the poor is unconscionably great; in some, including the United States, the distance increases relentlessly. In these circumstances academic political philosophy must seem artificial and self-indulgent. Theories of distributive justice almost inevitably urge radical reform in the advanced capitalist communities in which they are most avidly studied. But the practical possibility of anything like the reform they recommend is remote. Left-of-center politicians struggle, with at most moderate success, to achieve incremental gains for those at the bottom, and the best politics is politics that does not ask more than the comfortable majority is willing to give. The gap between theory and politics is particularly great and depressing in racially or ethnically diverse communities; majorities continue to be reluctant to help poor people who are markedly different from them.[1] It is nevertheless important to continue to trouble the comfortable with argument, especially when, as I believe is now the case, their selfishness impairs the legitimacy of the politics that makes them comfortable. At a minimum they must not be allowed to think that they have justification as well as selfishness on their side.

Theories of distributive justice are highly artificial in a further and different way. They rely heavily on the furniture of fantasy: fictitious ancient contracts, negotiations among amnesiacs, insurance policies that will never be written or sold. John Rawls imagines people negotiating terms of an original political constitution behind an opaque curtain that hides from each what he really is, thinks, and wants. I imagine desert-island auctions that might take months to complete. This second kind of artificiality is inevitable, however. If we are to reject politics as the final arbiter of justice, we must supply something else to define what justice requires, some other way of showing what equal concern and respect really do demand. Given our complex and deeply unfair economic structure, with its own dense history, it is difficult to do this without heroically counterfactual exercises. It would be worse than pointless, however, for political philosophers to describe angelic societies that actual human beings could not even approach. Or to suppose that our own communities could be improved only by an actual completely fresh start: by a voluntary return to a state of nature or an isolated island with convenient veils or bidding chips at hand. A useful theory of distributive justice must show which of the minimal steps we can actually take now are steps in the right direction.[2] If philosophers build ivory towers, they must set some Rapunzel at the top so that we can, slowly, climb higher. The economist Amartya Sen has criticized what he calls the "transcendentalist" theories of justice offered by Rawls and others, including me, for their exclusive concern with "one-shot" achievements of perfection and their corresponding neglect of comparative judgments of actual political systems. His criticism is unfounded, but it would be damning if accurate.[3]

False Conceptions

Laissez-Faire

Coercive government is legitimate only when it attempts to show equal concern for the fates of all those it governs and full respect for their personal responsibility for their own lives. (Edwin Baker had reservations about this claim even at that abstract level.)[4] Because we know that moral truth cannot be bare truth, we must seek an interpretation of those two demands that produces not conflict but mutual reinforcement. One interpretation of the first requirement is popular among political conservatives and would indeed avoid conflict. This denies that the distribution of material resources is a proper function of government at all. On this view, government treats people with equal concern simply by allowing them all the freedom they need to work, buy and sell, save or spend, as they themselves can and think best. Their wealth would then be very unequal, because some people are much more talented in production and management than others, wiser in investment and more frugal in spending, and some inevitably have better luck than others. But that is not the doing of government and therefore cannot be taken to signal any lack of equal concern for those who fail, any more than the fact that most runners lose a race signals a lack of concern for the losers by the race organizers.

This popular argument is silly because it assumes that government can be neutral about the results of the economic race. In fact, everything the government of a large political community does—or does not do—affects the resources that each citizen has and the success he achieves. Of course, his resources and success are also a function of many other variables, including his physical and mental abilities, his past choices, his luck, the attitudes of others toward him, and his power or desire to produce what others want. We might call these his personal economic variables. But the impact of these personal variables on his actual resources and opportunities must in every case also depend on the political variables: on the laws and policies of the communities in which he lives or works.

A community's laws and policies constitute its political settlement. Tax laws are of course central to a political settlement, but every other part of the law belongs to that settlement as well: fiscal and monetary policy, labor law, environmental law and policy, urban planning, foreign policy, health care policy, transportation policy, drug and food regulation, and everything else. Changing any of these policies or laws changes the distribution of personal wealth and opportunity in the community, given the same choices, luck, capacities, and other personal variables of each person. So we cannot avoid the challenge of equal concern by arguing that the resources an individual has depend on his choices, not government's choices. They depend on both. The political settlement, which is under the community's control, fixes the opportunities and consequences of choice for each individual for each of the sets of choices about education, training, employment, investment, production, and leisure he might make, and for each of the events of good or bad luck he might encounter. It is a clumsy evasion to say that a laissez-faire policy, which simply means one set of laws rather than another, is not the act of government.

The footrace analogy reveals the weakness of the claim that government can be neutral about distribution. Properly designed races are not neutral: they are rigged so that people with particular skills are more likely to win. That kind of rigging is not bias; it treats people as equals because they are assumed to share that sense of the purpose of the enterprise. But the point of living together in legitimate political communities subject to the principles of dignity is not to identify and reward any particular set of skills, qualities, or luck, so laws that will predictably have that result may well be biased.

Utility

That observation might suggest a different strategy for defending laissez-faire government, however. On this view, the point of government is to identify and reward productive skill, not as an end in itself but in order to make the community more prosperous overall. We can put that claim more formally in the vocabulary of utilitarianism: we treat each person as an equal by valuing his pleasure (or happiness or welfare or success) equally in choosing policies that will increase the aggregate of pleasure (or one of those other commodities) in the community as a whole. Utilitarianism has been and remains an influential position in political theory. But it offers an unpersuasive interpretation of equal concern. Parents would not show equal concern for all their children if they spent their entire available budget educating only those who were likely to earn heavily in the market. That would not treat the success of each child's life as equally important. Concern for a large group of persons is not the same thing as concern for its members one by one. Yes, an aggregation strategy values happiness or welfare or some other interpretation of utility no matter in which person it resides. But that is concern for a commodity, not for a person.

Welfare

These two responses to the challenge of equal concern—that the distribution of resources is not the business of government, and that government's goal should be to maximize some aggregate good—have at least this virtue: they recommend policies that respect people's individual responsibility for their own lives. But neither offers a reasonable conception of what it is to treat people with equal concern. Now we should notice a group of theories that fail in the opposite way. These aim to make people equal in welfare or well-being or capability according to some conception of what counts as well-being or what opportunities or capabilities are important.

They aim, for example, at making people equally happy or giving priority to the least happy, all as tested by some happiness Geiger counter. Or they aim to make people equally successful in their own lights. Or equal in their opportunities for achieving happiness or well-being.[5] Or equal in their overall capabilities.[6] But people disagree about what happiness is, and they value happiness differently: some are ready, even anxious, to sacrifice happiness for other goals. They also disagree in their views about what makes their lives successful: some have much more ambitious—and expensive—plans than others. So they also differ, for both these reasons, in their view about what they need by way of opportunities to be happy or what capabilities are more important than others. If a community set out to make people equal in any of these welfare commodities, then it would necessarily be imposing on everyone its collective judgment of what lives are good and how to live well. It would annihilate personal responsibility even more fundamentally in another way, moreover: it would aim to ensure that people were equal in the designated welfare commodity no matter what choices they had made or risks they had run. Personal responsibility would count for almost nothing.

We must try to avoid both these errors; we need a theory of distributive justice that satisfies both of our two principles. The welfare-based theories of the last paragraph show that we can do that only if we choose, as our basic metric, not people's happiness or opportunities or capabilities for achieving happiness but some test for equality that is as shorn of assumptions about welfare or well-being as possible. We must concentrate on resources, not welfare, and we must distinguish between personal and impersonal resources. Someone's personal resources are his physical and mental capacities; his impersonal resources consist in his wealth, measured as abstractly as possible. Only impersonal resources can be measured without welfare assumptions, and only these can be distributed through economic transactions and redistributed through taxation or other government programs. We must aim, as a first approximation, to make members of our political community equal in those material resources. That goal might seem perverse, because it aims to make people equal in what they value only as a means.[7] Reasonable people want resources not for their own sake but for their ability to make lives better or better lived. But that is the point. A community that respects personal ethical responsibility must concentrate on a fair distribution of means when it fixes its political settlement. It must leave the choice of ends to its citizens one by one.[8]

Equality of Resources

The Envy Test

What political settlement, seeking what distribution of resources, fits our two principles taken together? I have proposed a fantasy answer.[9] Imagine people shipwrecked on an empty island with diverse natural resources. They are each given an equal number of clamshells as bidding tokens, and they compete in an auction for individual ownership of the island's resources. When the auction finally ends, and everyone is satisfied that he has used his clamshells most efficiently, the following "envy" test will necessarily be satisfied. No one will want to trade his bundle of resources for anyone else's bundle, because he could have had that other bundle in place of his own if he had so wanted. Because the result is an envy-free distribution in that sense, the strategy treats everyone with equal concern. Each person understands that his situation reflects that equal concern: his wealth is a function of what others want as well as what he wants. The strategy also respects the personal responsibility of each bidder for his own values. He uses his clamshells to acquire the resources that he deems best suited to the life he deems best. He is limited in designing that life by what he discovers are the choices of others, and therefore of what he can have available for whatever life he designs. His choices are not limited by any collective judgments about what is important in life, but only by the true opportunity costs to others of what he chooses. (I discuss the nature of true opportunity costs and their role in establishing a theory of justice, together with Samuel Freeman's comments on that role, in a note.)[10]

The fantasy distribution respects both our principles: it provides attractive conceptions of both equal concern and full respect. But you and I are not shipwrecked passengers on a newly discovered and abundantly stocked island. How far and in what way can we be guided by this fantasy in the very different situation of modern economies? The story has an immediate negative lesson. A command or socialist economy in which prices, wages, and production are set collectively by officials would be a very imperfect realization of our values. The decisions of a command economy are collective; they reflect a collective decision about what ambitions, and hence which resources, are best suited to a good life. A free market is not equality's enemy, as is often supposed; rather, it is indispensable to genuine equality. An egalitarian economy is a basically capitalist economy.

That bald claim must, however, quickly be qualified in two crucial ways. First, it is essential to the justice of the island auction that the price someone pays for what he acquires reflects the true opportunity cost to others of his acquiring it, but actual markets in capitalist economies are often corrupted in ways that defeat that condition. Regulation is therefore often needed to perfect the freedom or efficiency of a market: to protect it against distortions of monopoly or externality. These distortions include (as we have recently come to learn) exaggerated risk in search of exaggerated profit when the risk falls largely on those who took no part in the decision and would have little share in any gain. Climate impact is another important example of distortion: because the market cannot easily be structured to reflect the opportunity costs of energy consumption now to future generations, extra-market regulation seems necessary. These adjustments to a free market do not contradict the spirit of this understanding of equal concern; on the contrary, they enforce that understanding by better matching people's resources to the true opportunity cost of what they do or consume.

The second qualification is very different and must occupy us at some length. The fantasy auction scheme shows equal concern, I said, because the result satisfies the envy test I described. What each islander has is fixed by his own choices, given the choices others make from an equal base. When the auction is finally over, however, and the islanders begin their economic lives, the envy test soon fails. They plant, manufacture, and consume using the resources they acquired in the auction, and they enter into transactions with one another, each trading to improve his situation. Some of the differences this activity generates reflect their choices—to consume rather than save, to rest rather than work, or to produce poetry that others do not much want rather than corn, which is popular. The envy test is still met in spite of these differences if we apply that test over time: people's resources continue to be sensitive to their choices. But other differences do corrupt the envy test. Some islanders do not have much talent to produce what the markets value or they fall sick or they make responsible investments that nevertheless fail. They then have fewer resources with which to build a life, not as a consequence of, but in spite of, the choices they have made. Now the envy test fails because their resources do not depend, after all, only on their choices. The market is no longer egalitarian.

Ex Ante or Ex Post?

How should we respond? Runners in a fair race are equally placed, all at the starting line, before the race begins. They are ex ante equal. But they are not equally placed after the race has been run: ex post one has beaten the others. Which is the right temporal focus for justice? Does equal respect require trying to satisfy the envy test, so far as we can, ex ante, before the impact of transactions and luck? Or ex post, after those events have run their course? A government committed to ex post equality undertakes, so far as this is possible, to bring citizens who lack market skills to the same economic level as those with more skills and to restore those who have fallen ill or suffered handicaps to the position they would otherwise have occupied. A government that aims at ex ante equality, on the other hand, responds differently. It aims that its citizens face these contingencies in an equal position—in particular, that they have an opportunity to buy appropriate insurance against low productive talent or bad luck on equal terms.

At first blush ex post compensation might seem the more appropriate goal. People who are unemployed or who are badly injured or crippled and who receive only what an insurance policy might pay by way of compensation remain in a much worse position than others. Insurance payments typically do not compensate fully, and for some instances of bad luck—terrible physical disability—they fall sickeningly short of restoring people to their prior position. So long as the community can improve the situation of someone who has been a victim of bad luck, then equal concern might seem to require that it do that. In fact, however, the ex post approach, even so far as it is possible, is a very poor understanding of equal concern. The ex ante approach is better.

Investment luck, very broadly understood, is an important reason that people's income and wealth differ. You and I study financial charts with equal care and make equally intelligent though different choices. Your stocks thrive and mine wither; you are rich and I am poor, and this is only because your luck has been better than mine. But if our political community undertook to erase this consequence of luck, it would undermine the responsibility each of us exercised; if it made our investment choices pointless in that way, we would cease to invest. Many of the most important decisions we make are also investment decisions whose consequences turn on luck: any educational or training decision might be undermined by unforeseeable technological shifts that make our particular training useless, for instance. If the community aimed to ensure that our fate in no way depended on how any such investment gambles fare—if it guaranteed that we are equal in wealth, whether or not our choice of career turned out to be suited to our tastes or talents or market conditions—it would end by crippling our own responsibility for our choices. So any plausible version of an ex post approach would have to draw a distinction between investment and other forms of luck and rule out the former as a ground for redistribution.

That distinction would be difficult to draw. But ex post compensation would be not a reasonable goal, even if restricted to noninvestment luck. Any community that undertook to spend all it could to improve the position of its blind or crippled members, for example, until further expenditure would not even marginally benefit them, would have nothing left to spend on anything else, and the lives of all other citizens would be miserable in consequence.[11] That policy would reflect no one's actual priorities, including the antecedent priorities of the victims of terrible accidents. If the choice had been up to them before they were injured, they would not have spent everything they had to buy the best possible accident insurance policy, because they would not have thought, given the odds, that it made sense to compromise their lives in every other respect to secure the most expensive possible insurance. The ex post compensation approach to bad luck is irrational.

It remains wrong even if we apply it to erase the consequences, not of bad luck as ordinarily understood, but only of the bad genetic luck of not having talents prized in the contemporary market. If the community restores people to a condition of equal wealth, no matter what choices they make about work and consumption, then, as I said, it destroys rather than respects this dimension of responsibility. But there is no way fully to erase the consequences of differences in talent without adopting that foolish remedy. It is impossible in principle, not simply practically impossible, to distinguish the consequences of choice and capacity across the range of economic decision, because preference and capacity interact in both directions. Our preferences both shape the talents we are disposed to develop and are shaped by the talents we believe we have. So we cannot separate choice from genetic luck in what might seem the most direct way: by making sure, ex post, that people's wealth reflects only the former and no tinge of the latter.

Equal concern does indeed require that a community compensate in some way for bad luck. But we need an understanding of compensation that is compatible with the right respect for individual responsibility, and we must therefore seek an ex ante approach. This aims, as I said, to situate people equally as they face both economic decisions and the contingencies that hedge those decisions. An economic market for investment, wage, and consumption is a crucial step toward that equality, because it allows people's decisions to carry costs or gain rewards that are measured by the impact of those decisions on other people. But we need a further step: we need to place people in the position they would have occupied if they had been, at a point before the decisions and events that shaped their lives began, equally able to protect themselves against these different dimensions of bad luck through appropriate insurance. That step unfortunately requires the kind of fantasy speculation that I referred to earlier. For of course it is impossible that people could ever be equally able to insure in any real insurance market, certainly impossible before their genetic luck begins, because before that point they do not even exist.

Hypothetical Insurance

We must return to our island. Now we notice that insurance is among the resources auctioned. Some islanders undertake to insure others, in competition with other insurers, at market clamshell rates. When the auction ends, ex ante equality has been preserved and future transactions maintain it. How does this expanded story help us? It teaches us the importance of the following hypothetical question: What level of insurance against low income and bad luck would people in our own actual community buy if the community's actual wealth were equally divided among them, if no information were available that would lead anyone or any insurer to judge that he was more or less at risk than others, and if everyone otherwise had state-of-the-art information about the incidence of different kinds of bad luck and the availability, cost, and value of medical or other remedies for the consequences of that bad luck?

We can sensibly speculate about answers to that question from information readily available about what kinds of insurance insurers actually do offer and people actually do buy. Of course, there must be a large range of uncertainty in any answer we give. We cannot specify any particular coverage level that we can be confident any specific number of people would buy under the fanciful counterfactual conditions we imagine. But that need not be our aim. We can try to identify a top coverage level at which we can sensibly assume that most people in our community would have chosen to insure, given what we know about their needs and preferences, and given the premium structure that that coverage would require. We cannot answer even that question with any pretense to exactitude. But we can dismiss some answers as plainly too low. We can identify a coverage level such that it would be foolish for most people, given their preferences as we can ascertain them, not to buy coverage at that level.

We can then insist that our officials use at least that coverage level as a guide to redistributive programs of different kinds. We might aim to collect from the community, through taxes, an amount equal to the aggregate premium that would have been paid for universal coverage at that level and then distribute, to those who need it, services, goods, or funds that match what that coverage would have provided them in virtue of their bad luck. We would fund unemployment and low-wage insurance, medical care insurance, and social security for people in retirement in that way. It is important to notice that by hypothesis any community can afford the programs that this insurance scheme describes; those programs would not be irrational in the way those mandated by a goal of ex post compensation would be. On the contrary, because the programs the scheme identifies reflect reasonable assumptions about the overall preferences of the community over risk and insurance, a government that did not provide them would fail in its economic responsibilities.

Paternalism?

Our overall ambition, remember, is to provide a scheme of distributive justice that satisfies both principles of dignity. It might now be objected that the hypothetical insurance scheme I just summarized offends the second principle because it is, in effect, mandatory. (Arthur Ripstein offers this objection and another concern.)[12] The scheme assumes that most citizens would have purchased insurance at least at the coverage levels and for the premiums it stipulates. But perhaps some would not, and taxing those citizens under the scheme (or indeed, awarding them benefits under it) is therefore, according to this objection, a paternalistic imposition of a supposedly reasonable choice upon them.

The point calls for further explanation, but the objection is not yet well framed. Paternalism means imposing a decision on someone supposedly for his own good but contrary to his own sense of what that is. The hypothetical insurance scheme makes assumptions, on the contrary, about what citizens' preferences would have been in circumstances very different from those anyone has actually encountered. It is no more paternalistic to assume, for any individual, that he would have chosen to buy the insurance at what we judge to be a level at which most people would have insured than it would be to suppose that he would not have bought that insurance and to treat him accordingly.

So the scheme is not paternalistic. But it is probabilistic. No one can sensibly think or argue that he would not have made the decision we assume most people would have made. The counterfactuals are too deep for any such individualized judgment; the scheme's claims can only be statistical. But he can rightly say that he might not have made it. That fact presents an issue not of paternalism but of fairness. We can treat individual citizens on either of two assumptions, and it seems fair to treat them, lacking any information to the contrary, as if each would have done what we judge most would have done.

This is our justification. We aim to charge people the true opportunity costs of their choices. Though we must rely on actual markets in production and wage, we must supplement and correct those markets in a variety of ways. In particular we must try to eliminate the effects of bad luck and other misfortunes by judging what a more comprehensive and fairer market would have revealed as the opportunity costs of provision against those misfortunes. We must make probabilistic counterfactual assumptions in that exercise, to be sure. But that seems fairer than the alternatives, which are either to leave the misfortunes uncorrected or to choose some level of redistributive transfer payments through politics guided only by raw reactions of fairness that have no ground in theory and are likely to be stingy in practice. We choose the hypothetical insurance device, even though it requires rough judgments of probability, as more faithful to the overall opportunity costs conception of fairness. That is the best we can do to show equal concern and the right respect for individual responsibility. Our overall interpretive project endorses a redistributive scheme modeled on hypothetical insurance assumptions for that reason. (Amartya Sen offers a number of further objections to the hypothetical insurance scheme.)[13]

Laissez-Faire Again

That completes my summary sketch of a design for a political settlement that merges equal concern by government and personal responsibility for citizens. (I have elsewhere described in much more detail the tax structure that this exercise would generate and the social programs it would justify.)[14] But we must take care not to confuse our ex ante approach, which features ex ante compensation, with a different ex ante approach—misleadingly called equality of opportunity—that is popular among political conservatives. This holds that we show equal concern by letting the chips fall where they may; it allows no redistribution of market rewards and insists those who have bad luck must bear it themselves. This is just a form of the laissez-faire doctrine I mentioned at the outset of this discussion. Proponents say that laissez-faire rewards individual responsibility. But people with little market talent or bad luck can reply that it does not show equal concern, because a different economic arrangement is available that also satisfies the requirements of individual responsibility and that shows more appropriate concern for them.

Equality of resources, understood as I have described it, may reward qualities of productive intelligence, industry, dedication, shrewdness, or contribution to the wealth of others. But that is not its aim. It does not even suppose that these are virtues; it certainly does not suppose that a life earning more money is a better or more successful life. It presumes only that we treat people with equal concern when we allow each to design his own life, aware that his choices will have, among other consequences, an impact on his own wealth. However, it is crucial to this understanding that the character and degree of that impact reflect the effect his choices have on the fortunes of others: the cost to others, in lost opportunities for themselves, of the various decisions he has made.

Notes

1. See Eduardo Porter, "Race and the Social Contract," *New York Times*, March 31, 2008.

2. See my *Sovereign Virtue: The Theory and Practice of Equality* (Cambridge, MA: Harvard University Press, 2000), chap. 3.

3. Sen says that his recent book, *The Idea of Justice* (Cambridge, MA: Harvard University Press, 2009), marks an important "departure" from standard theories of justice—he cites, among others, John Rawls's and my own work—that are concerned only to describe ideally just institutions and are therefore of no use in guiding the comparative judgments we must make in the real and very imperfect world. But Rawls's two principles of justice are tailor-made for the comparative real-world judgments Sen has in mind. There is, in fact, an astronomically extensive literature of philosophers, political scientists, economists, lawyers, and even politicians applying Rawls's theories to actual concrete political controversies. (A

sample can be harvested by typing "Rawls" and the name of any particular controversy into a Google search.) In my own case, Sen may not have taken full account of my discussion "Back to the Real World," in Chapter 3 of *Sovereign Virtue*, which describes in some detail how the abstract theory of justice I defend in that book can be used to justify comparative judgments about improvements in justice. Nor of the entire Part II—half—of *Sovereign Virtue*, which is devoted, as that book's subtitle promises, to the "practice" rather than the "theory" of equality. I discuss there, again in some detail, the application of the general theory of Part I of that book to practical improvement on present policies in the fields of taxation, health care, racial justice, genetic policy, abortion, euthanasia, freedom of speech, and the regulation of elections. I have also tried to explain practical consequences of my views in general journals, particularly the *New York Review of Books*.

Sen's own work in developmental economics has been enormously important and useful. His views on the causes of famine have been particularly influential. He has brought a wealth of Eastern, particularly Indian, history, literature, and philosophy to the attention of Western readers; his latest book is particularly rich in such information. However, *The Idea of Justice* does not support Sen's claim of a departure in normative political philosophy. In fact he offers less help in real-world judgment than do the theories he means to depart from. His comments on particular political issues are either uncontroversial—he condemns slavery—or noncommittal. He appeals to a variety of standards for comparative judgment of existing structures, but at far too abstract a level to be useful in comparative judgment. He endorses the spirit of Adam Smith's "impartial observer" test, which recommends the decisions that an ideal and impartial judge would reach. But that test, unless construed in a utilitarian way, lacks bite; it does not tell us what theory a beneficent spectator would deploy to decide issues now controversial. Sen says that policy should focus (though not exclusively) on promoting equality in what he calls "capabilities" (see the discussion of "capabilities" in note 6 below). But he concedes the wide variations in people's rankings of the importance of these capabilities and does not recommend any way of choosing among these rankings in the face of serious disagreement. He believes that free democratic discussion among ideally public-spirited citizens would be helpful to comparative judgment. He does not say how this thought is helpful in real communities that include a great many followers of, say, Sarah Palin. It is not helpful, in the world of real politics, only to call for due consideration of a large variety of factors that everyone concedes relevant without also offering some overall scheme to suggest how these different factors should be weighted in a practical decision about a controversial issue.

4. Baker's ambitious and impressive article was completed just before his tragic death (C. Edwin Baker, "In Hedgehog Solidarity," in *Symposium: Justice for Hedgehogs: A Conference on Ronald Dworkin's Forthcoming Book* [special issue], *Boston University Law Review* 90, 2 [April 2010] [hereafter BU]: 759). He believed, contrary to my own opinion, that citizens need have no more concern for their fellow citizens when they act together in politics than they need have when they act as individuals. Politics, he thought, should be understood as a competitive activity in which each citizen works to advance his own values and goals by winning a collective political decision to create an ethical environment he approves. There are losers as well as winners in this competition. Political majorities must be tolerant of minorities: they must not coerce them to embrace the majority's values or otherwise violate their liberty or other rights. But majorities need not otherwise refrain from using politics to shape the community to their own convictions about good lives. They need not try to be neutral out of concern for those who disagree with them.

Baker also disagreed with me, in a parallel way, about democracy. He agreed on the need for what I call a partnership conception of that ideal. But he thought that I favor an "epistemic" interpretation of partnership in which the community's role is limited to identifying and enforcing a correct theory of distributive and political justice, while he favored a "choice" interpretation in which majorities choose the values that define the community as a whole. "This alternative sees people in the partnership as trying to convince each other about, and as acting as a partnership to pursue, ethical ideals. It treats equality of respect, not equality of concern, as the sovereign virtue." He thought that conceiving of citizens as "reason-giving" partners in "communicative action" as well as in competition with one another allows us to provide a more secure basis for principles of justice than a view like mine is able to provide. He adopted Jurgen Habermas's view that people in conversation commit themselves to certain principles, and that it is these commitments that identify justice for them.

It will be helpful in considering his views to distinguish two questions. First, do the members of a coercive political community have an obligation when they design an economic structure to treat the fate of each citizen as equally important? Second, are they obliged not to adopt laws that can be justified only by assuming the truth of ethical ideas controversial within the community? This chapter answers the first question: yes. Though Baker denied the need for equal concern, I am not sure he actually meant to disagree. I think he rather associated equal concern with a "yes" answer to the second question. There is nothing in his picture of a choice democracy that would suggest that a majority should not have equal concern for the fate, as distinct from the values, of all fellow citizens.

Turn to the second question. Baker believed that the majority in a choice democracy should have the power to select texts for public education that reflect their values and to establish a particular religion as official. I believe he underestimated the coercive power of that kind of control. (See my *Is Democracy Possible Here? Principles for a New Political Debate* [Princeton, NJ: Princeton University Press, 2006]). Baker's version of tolerance would not in fact encourage the "reason-giving" he hoped for among citizens. On the contrary, a majority confident of its power to choose public school textbooks would have little reason to try to explain itself to those left out. For a frightening contemporary example, see Russell Shorto, "How Christian Were the Founders?" *New York Times*, February 11, 2010. The conception of liberty I describe in Chapter 17, which allows the ethical environment to be set organically, so far as possible, through individual choices one by one rather than by collective action, provides much more incentive for conversation aimed at persuasion.

5. Richard Arneson, "Equality and Equal Opportunity for Welfare," *Philosophical Studies* 56 (1989): 77–93; G. A. Cohen, "On the Currency of Egalitarian Justice," *Ethics* 99 (1989): 906–944.

6. See my *Sovereign Virtue*, 301–303. In his *Inequality Reexamined* (Cambridge, MA: Harvard University Press, 1992), Amartya Sen describes the "capabilities" that should figure in such a calculation to include capacities to bring about "being happy, having self-respect, taking part in the life of the community, and so on" (39). These seem to be welfarist notions, though I offered in those pages an alternative characterization. In *The Idea of Justice* Sen adds that "happiness does not generate obligations in the way that capability must do" (271), but it is not plain whether this judgment is meant to change his earlier opinion.

7. Sen, *The Idea of Justice*, 265.

8. See "Ronald Dworkin Replies," in *Dworkin and His Critics*, edited by Justine Burley (Maiden, MA: Blackwell, 2004), 340ff.

9. I describe the story summarized here in much greater detail, and consider its implications for tax and other political policy, in *Sovereign Virtue*, chap. 2.

10. Freeman suggests, in the course of a very instructive essay, that an ambition to charge people the true opportunity costs of their choices in work and consumption cannot help us

to fix a theory of justice in distribution because what we take true opportunity costs to be depends on which such theory we have already assumed (Samuel Freeman, "Equality of Resources, Market Luck, and the Justification of Adjusted Market Distributions," BU 90, 2 [April 2010]: 921n41). If we decide that a utilitarian scheme is most fair, for instance, then we will think that the true opportunity costs of a person's choices are those fixed by the price system that best promotes utility. If we think some other theory of justice superior, we will take true opportunity costs to be those set by prices in an economic system that enforces that other theory. So even if we assume that asking someone to pay the true opportunity costs of his choices respects his responsibility for his own life, we cannot draw any conclusion from that assumption about which theory of justice is best.

However, the conception of equality of resources described in the text uses the idea of opportunity costs at a more basic level. Any defensible interpretation of equal concern supposes that no one in a political community is initially entitled to more resource than anyone else; it asks whether any reason consistent with that assumption justifies an economic system in which some prosper more than others. Utilitarians, Rawlsians, and other theorists offer such reasons: that treating people with equal concern requires maximizing their average welfare or protecting the situation of the worst-off group or something of the sort. They then offer models of economic systems that these different assumptions would justify, and, as Freeman says, any such model carries with it its own distinct calculation of the true opportunity costs of one person's choices to others'. Equality of resources, on the other hand, offers the idea of a fair distribution of opportunity costs, not as derivative from other reasons for allowing deviation from flat equality but as itself a reason for deviating and limiting the scope of such deviation. It defines true opportunity costs recursively as those measured by prices in a market in which all have equal resources and in which insurance against risks of different sorts is marketed on equal terms. The yield of that market then structures, through taxation and redistribution, future markets in which prices set true opportunity costs. So the ambition to make people responsible for their choices is at work in that conception of distributive justice right from the start.

11. See the discussion in *Sovereign Virtue*, chaps. 8 and 9.

12. I recommend Ripstein's account of my views about distributive justice. See his essay "Liberty and Equality," in *Ronald Dworkin*, edited by Arthur Ripstein (Cambridge: Cambridge University Press, 2007), 82. He cites the mandatory character of the insurance scheme as an objection (103). He also comments that though the insurance scheme is designed to separate tastes from handicaps, it actually assumes that distinction, because it does not suppose that people can insure against having expensive tastes. I did not intend the scheme to help make that distinction, which I assumed could be made independently through what I described as an identification test. A taste is not a handicap for an agent who does not wish not to have it. See my "Ronald Dworkin Replies," in *Dworkin and His Critics*, 347S. See also my "Sovereign Virtue Revisited," *Ethics* 113 (October 2002): 106, n8ff.

It is worth noting here, however, that the insurance scheme does operate to enforce the distinction through the phenomenon of moral hazard. Insurers will not insure against a risk whose cultivation is under the control of the insured and cannot be assumed to be undesirable to him. Nor will they insure, except at extravagant premium, against a risk when it would be expensive and particularly difficult to prove that its cultivation was not desired and not under the insured's control. This is not just a convenient side effect of the insurance scheme. It reflects the connection between that scheme and the view of judgmental responsibility defended in Chapter 10.

I also recommend another thoughtful discussion of the mandatory-insurance objection in the course of a detailed and careful study of equality of resources: Alexander Brown, *Ronald*

Dworkin's Theory of Equality: Domestic and Global Perspectives (Basingstoke, UK: Palgrave Macmillan, 2009). Brown's study has the great virtue of discussing the role of that conception of equality in global justice, which, as he notices, I have so far not taken up.

13. Sen discusses the hypothetical insurance strategy at some length in *The Idea of Justice*, 264–268. I can best respond through the inelegant vehicle of a list. (1) He discusses comments I made in an earlier book about his "capability" approach. See *Sovereign Virtue*, 299–303. He denies that this approach is welfarist. I offered reasons that it could easily be so interpreted: see the discussion of "capabilities" in note 6 above. (2) He says of the alternative interpretation I offered—that the capabilities approach "is only equality of resources in a different vocabulary" (*Sovereign Virtue*, 303)—that even if that were so, the capabilities approach would be superior because it identifies what is finally important rather than focusing on resources, which, as I have conceded, are mere means. But first, though some people might deem capabilities important for their own sake (that is also true of resources: some people value them as sources of freedom even if they do not use them), others will value them only so far as they can use them to lead lives they find desirable. Like resources, most capabilities, for most people, are only instrumental. Second, as I have several times said in a variety of places, it doesn't follow from the fact that sensible people value resources as means to better lives that government should aim to make people equal not in resources but in the goodness of their lives. This chapter argues that any such program would impair personal responsibility. (3) Sen's remaining comments are specifically about the insurance strategy. He says that an insurance market cannot reflect relative disadvantage. That seems incorrect, for reasons Adam Smith made plain. In deciding how much coverage to buy against unemployment or low wage or disability, people will naturally take into account not only their absolute need but also how they would fare relative to others in different situations. (4) Sen next says that the insurance device supposes individuals acting as "atomistic operators" rather than as part of a process of "public reason." But the insurers I imagine can have the benefit of as much public and private discussion as a flourishing community will generate, as well as the benefit of a shared culture that reflects different strands of opinion. They must finally decide for themselves, but that hardly means that they must decide in an isolation chamber. (5) He declares that my focus "in common with other transcendental institutionalist approaches, is on getting to perfectly just institutions (in one step)" (266). That is wrong; see the discussion of Sen's claim in note 3 above. (6) He says that I take for granted the "existence, uniqueness and efficiency of perfectly competitive market equilibria, which he needs for his institutional story to be entirely unproblematic" (267). He doesn't say why I need this unreal assumption, and I have denied that I do. See, e.g., *Sovereign Virtue*, 79; "Sovereign Virtue Revisited"; *Is Democracy Possible Here?*, 115; as well as this and the preceding paragraphs of this text. (7) He concludes, reluctantly, that I betray "institutional fundamentalism" and "innocence" in my assumption that fixing just institutions will solve all human problems, and in my pretense, as he sees it, that the hypothetical insurance scheme has "imperial powers" (267–268). But I disavow any such assumption or pretense. The insurance scheme plays a role in the more complex integrated theory of justice described here. It does nothing "one shot." It offers advice about marginal gains in distributive justice in imperfect communities, and it takes into account the wisdom of flexible insurance policies that can be adjusted to reflect changes in circumstances and ambitions, and also the need sometimes to temper justice with compassion. See my "Sovereign Virtue Revisited."

14. *Sovereign Virtue*, part II.

READING

2

What Is the Point of Equality?

ELIZABETH S. ANDERSON

If much recent academic work defending equality had been secretly penned by conservatives, could the results be any more embarrassing for egalitarians? Consider how much of this work leaves itself open to classic and devastating conservative criticisms. Ronald Dworkin defines equality as an "envy-free" distribution of resources.[1] This feeds the suspicion that the motive behind egalitarian policies is mere envy. Philippe Van Parijs argues that equality in conjunction with liberal neutrality among conceptions of the good requires the state to support lazy, able-bodied surfers who are unwilling to work.[2] This invites the charge that egalitarians support irresponsibility and encourage the slothful to be parasitic on the productive. Richard Arneson claims that equality requires that, under certain conditions, the state subsidize extremely costly religious ceremonies that its citizens feel bound to perform.[3] G. A. Cohen tells us that equality requires that we compensate people for being temperamentally gloomy or for being so incurably bored by inexpensive hobbies that they can get fulfilling recreation only from expensive diversions.[4]

These proposals bolster the objection that egalitarians are oblivious to the proper limits of state power and permit coercion of others for merely private ends. Van Parijs suggests that to fairly implement the equal right to get married, when male partners are scarce, every woman should be given an equal tradable share in the pool of eligible bachelors and have to bid for whole partnership rights, thus implementing a transfer of wealth from successful brides to compensate the losers in love.[5] This supports the objection that egalitarianism, in its determination to correct perceived unfairness everywhere, invades our privacy and burdens the personal ties of love and affection that lie at the core of family life.

Those on the left have no less reason than conservatives and libertarians to be disturbed by recent trends in academic egalitarian thought. First, consider those whom recent academic egalitarians have singled out for special attention:

beach bums, the lazy and irresponsible, people who can't manage to entertain themselves with simple pleasures, religious fanatics. Thomas Nagel and Gerald Cohen give us somewhat more sympathetic but also pitiable characters in taking stupid, talentless, and bitter people to be exemplary beneficiaries of egalitarian concern.[6] What has happened to the concerns of the politically oppressed? What about inequalities of race, gender, class, and caste? Where are the victims of nationalist genocide, slavery, and ethnic subordination?

Second, the agendas defined by much recent egalitarian theorizing are too narrowly focused on the distribution of divisible, privately appropriated goods, such as income and resources, or privately enjoyed goods, such as welfare. This neglects the much broader agendas of actual egalitarian political movements. For example, gay and lesbian people seek the freedom to appear in public as who they are without shame or fear of violence, the right to get married and enjoy benefits of marriage, to adopt and retain custody of children. The disabled have drawn attention to the ways the configuration of public spaces has excluded and marginalized them, and campaigned against demeaning stereotypes that cast them as stupid, incompetent, and pathetic. Thus, with respect to both the targets of egalitarian concern and their agendas, recent egalitarian writing seems strangely detached from existing egalitarian political movements.

What has gone wrong here? I shall argue that these problems stem from a flawed understanding of the point of equality. Recent egalitarian writing has come to be dominated by the view that the fundamental aim of equality is to compensate people for undeserved bad luck—being born with poor native endowments, bad parents, and disagreeable personalities, suffering from accidents and illness, and so forth. I shall argue that in focusing on correcting a supposed cosmic injustice, recent egalitarian writing has lost sight of the distinctively political aims of egalitarianism. The proper negative aim of egalitarian justice is not to eliminate the impact of brute luck from human affairs, but to end oppression, which by definition is socially imposed. Its proper positive aim is not to ensure that everyone gets what they morally deserve, but to create a community in which people stand in relations of equality to others.

The theory I shall defend can be called "democratic equality." In seeking the construction of a community of equals, democratic equality integrates principles of distribution with the expressive demands of equal respect. Democratic equality guarantees all law-abiding citizens effective access to the social conditions of their freedom at all times. It justifies the distributions required to secure this guarantee by appealing to the obligations of citizens in a democratic state. In such a state, citizens make claims on one another in virtue of their equality, not their inferiority, to others. Because the fundamental aim of citizens in constructing a state is to secure everyone's freedom, democratic equality's principles of distribution neither presume to tell people how to use their opportunities nor attempt to judge how responsible people are for choices that lead to unfortunate outcomes. Instead, it avoids bankruptcy at the hands of the imprudent by limiting the range of goods provided collectively and expecting individuals to take personal responsibility for the other goods in their possession.

What Is the Point of Equality?

It is helpful to recall how egalitarian political movements have historically conceived of their aims. What have been the inegalitarian systems that they have opposed? Inegalitarianism asserted the justice or necessity of basing social order on a hierarchy of human beings, ranked according to intrinsic worth. Inequality referred not so much to distributions of goods as to relations between superior and inferior persons. Those of superior rank were thought entitled to inflict violence on inferiors, to exclude or segregate them from social life, to treat them with contempt, to force them to obey, to work without reciprocation, and to abandon their own cultures. These are what Iris Young has identified as the faces of oppression: marginalization, status hierarchy, domination, exploitation, and cultural imperialism.[7] Such unequal social relations generate, and were thought to justify, inequalities in the distribution of freedoms, resources, and welfare. This is the core of inegalitarian ideologies of racism, sexism, nationalism, caste, class, and eugenics.

Egalitarian political movements oppose such hierarchies. They assert the equal moral worth of persons. This assertion does not mean that all have equal virtue or talent. Negatively, the claim repudiates distinctions of moral worth based on birth or social identity—on family membership, inherited social status, race, ethnicity, gender, or genes. There are no natural slaves, plebeians, or aristocrats. Positively, the claim asserts that all competent adults are equally moral agents: everyone equally has the power to develop and exercise moral responsibility, to cooperate with others according to principles of justice, to shape and fulfill a conception of their good.[8]

Egalitarians base claims to social and political equality on the fact of universal moral equality. These claims also have a negative and a positive aspect. Negatively, egalitarians seek to abolish oppression—that is, forms of social relationship by which some people dominate, exploit, marginalize, demean, and inflict violence upon others. Diversities in socially ascribed identities, distinct roles in the division of labor, or differences in personal traits, whether these be neutral biological and psychological differences, valuable talents and virtues, or unfortunate disabilities and infirmities, never justify the unequal social relations listed above. Nothing can justify treating people in these ways, except just punishment for crimes and defense against violence. Positively, egalitarians seek a social order in which persons stand in relations of equality. They seek to live together in a democratic community, as opposed to a hierarchical one. Democracy is here understood as collective self-determination by means of open discussion among equals in accordance with rules acceptable to all. To stand as an equal before others in discussion means that one is entitled to participate, that others recognize an obligation to listen respectfully and respond to one's arguments, that no one need bow and scrape before others or represent themselves as inferior to others as a condition of having their claim heard.[9]

Contrast this democratic conception of equality with equality of fortune. First, democratic equality aims to abolish socially created oppression. Equality of fortune aims to correct what it takes to be injustices generated by the natural order. Second, democratic equality is what I shall call a relational theory of equality: it views equality as a social relationship. Equality of fortune is a distributive theory of equality: it conceives of equality as a pattern of distribution. Thus, equality of fortune regards two people as equal so long as they enjoy equal amounts of some distributable good—income, resources, opportunities for welfare, and so forth. Social relationships are largely seen as instrumental to generating such patterns of distribution. By contrast, democratic equality regards two people as equal when each accepts the obligation to justify their actions by principles acceptable to the other, and in which they take mutual consultation, reciprocation, and recognition for granted. Certain patterns in the distribution of goods may be instrumental to securing such relationships, follow from them, or even be constitutive of them. But democratic egalitarians are fundamentally concerned with the relationships within which goods are distributed, not only with the distribution of goods themselves. This implies, third, that democratic equality is sensitive to the need to integrate the demands of equal recognition with those of equal distribution.[10] Goods must be distributed according to principles and processes that express respect for all. People must not be required to grovel or demean themselves before others as a condition of laying claim to their share of goods. The basis for people's claims to distributed goods is that they are equals, not inferiors, to others.

This gives us a rough conception of equality. How do we derive principles of justice from it? Our investigation of equality of fortune has not been completely fruitless: from its failures, we have gleaned some desiderata for egalitarian principles. First, such principles must identify certain goods to which all citizens must have effective access over the course of their whole lives. Some goods are more important from an egalitarian point of view than others, within whatever space of equality is identified as of particular concern for egalitarians. And starting-gate theories, or any other principles that allow law-abiding citizens to lose access to adequate levels of these goods, are unacceptable. Second, egalitarians should be able to justify such guarantees of lifetime accessibility without resorting to paternalism. Third, egalitarian principles should offer remedies that match the type of injustice being corrected. Private satisfactions cannot make up for public oppression. Fourth, egalitarian principles should uphold the responsibility of individuals for their own lives without passing demeaning and intrusive judgments on their capacities for exercising responsibility or on how well they have used their freedoms. Finally, such principles should be possible objects of collective willing. They should be capable of supplying sufficient reasons for citizens acting together to collectively guarantee the particular goods of concern to egalitarians.

Let us take up the last desideratum first. The determination of what can or must be collectively willed has been the traditional task of social contract theory. In liberal democratic versions of social contract theory, the fundamental aim of the state is to secure the liberty of its members. Since the democratic state is nothing more than citizens acting collectively, it follows that the fundamental obligation of citizens to one another is to secure the social conditions of everyone's freedom.[11] Because libertarians also embrace this formula, it might be thought to lead to inegalitarian implications. Instead of repudiating this formula, democratic equality interprets it. It claims that the social condition of living a free life is that one stand in relations of equality with others.

This claim might seem paradoxical, given the prevailing view that represents equality and freedom as conflicting ideals. We can see how it is true by considering the oppressive relationships that social equality negates. Equals are not subject to arbitrary violence or physical coercion by others. Choice unconstrained by arbitrary physical coercion is one of the fundamental conditions of freedom. Equals are not marginalized by others. They are therefore free to participate in politics and the major institutions of civil society. Equals are not dominated by others; they do not live at the mercy of others' wills. This means that they govern their lives by their own wills, which is freedom. Equals are not exploited by others. This means they are free to secure the fair value of their labor. Equals are not subject to cultural imperialism; they are free to practice their own culture, subject to the constraint of respecting everyone else. To live in an egalitarian community, then, is to be free from oppression to participate in and enjoy the goods of society, and to participate in democratic self-government.

Egalitarians thus differ from libertarians in advocating a more expansive understanding of the social conditions of freedom. Importantly, they view private relations of domination, even those entered into by consent or contract, as violations of individual freedom. Libertarians tend to identify freedom with formal, negative freedom: enjoying the legal right to do what one wants without having to ask anyone else's permission and without interference from others. This definition of freedom neglects the importance of having the means to do what one wants. In addition, the definition implicitly assumes that, given the material means and internal capacity to do what one wants, the absence of interference from others is all one needs to do what one wants. This ignores the fact that most of the things people want to do require participation in social activities, and hence communication and interaction with others. One cannot do these things if others make one an outcast. A libertarian might argue that freedom of association entails the right of people to refuse to associate with others on any grounds. Yet a society embodying such an unconditional right hardly needs physical coercion to force others to obey the wishes of those with the power to exclude others from participation in social life. The same point applies to a society in which property is so unequally distributed that some adults live in abject dependence on others, and so live at the mercy of others. Societies that permit the creation of outcasts and subordinate classes can be as repressive as any despotic regime.

Equality in the Space of Freedom: A Capabilities Approach

Amartya Sen has proposed a better way to understand freedom. Consider the states of being and doing that constitute a person's well-being: a person can be healthy, well nourished, physically fit, literate, an active participant in community life, mobile, happy, respected, confident, and so forth. A person may also care about other states of being and doing that reflect her autonomous ends: she may want to be outgoing, raise children, practice medicine, play soccer, make love, and so forth. Call such states *functionings.* A person's *capabilities* consist of the sets of functionings she can achieve, given the personal, material, and social resources available to her. Capabilities measure not actually achieved functionings, but a person's freedom to achieve valued functionings. A person enjoys more freedom the greater the range of effectively accessible, significantly different opportunities she has for functioning or leading her life in ways she values most.[12] We can understand the egalitarian aim to secure for everyone the social conditions of their freedom in terms of capabilities. Following Sen, I say that egalitarians should seek equality for all in the space of capabilities.

Sen's capability egalitarianism leaves open a large question, however: *Which* capabilities does society have an obligation to equalize? Some people care about playing cards well, others about enjoying luxury vacations in Tahiti. Must egalitarians, in the name of equal freedom, offer free card-playing lessons and state-subsidized vacations in exotic lands? Surely there are limits to which capabilities citizens are obligated to provide one another. We should heed our first desideratum: to identify particular goods within the space of equality that are of special egalitarian concern.

Reflection on the negative and positive aims of egalitarianism helps us meet this requirement. Negatively, people are entitled to whatever capabilities are necessary to enable them to avoid or escape entanglement in oppressive social relationships. Positively, they are entitled to the capabilities necessary for functioning as an equal citizen in a democratic state. While the negative and positive aims of egalitarianism overlap to a large extent, they are not identical. If functioning as an equal citizen were all that egalitarians cared about, they could not object to forced clitoridectomy, by which men control women's sexuality in private relations. But egalitarians also aim at abolishing private relations of domination, and therefore support the functionings needed for individual sexual autonomy. If having the capabilities needed to avoid oppression were all that mattered, then egalitarians would not oppose discrimination among the relatively privileged—for example, the glass ceiling for female executives. But egalitarians also aim at enabling all citizens to stand as equals to one another in civil society, and this requires that careers be open to talents.

Democratic equality thus aims for equality across a wide range of capabilities. But it does not support comprehensive equality in the space of capabilities. Being a poor card player does not make one oppressed. More precisely, the social order can and should be arranged so that one's skill at cards does not determine one's status in civil society. Nor is being a good card player necessary for functioning as a citizen. Society therefore has no obligation to provide free card lessons to citizens. Democratic equality satisfies the first desideratum of egalitarian theory.

Consider further the capabilities that democratic equality does guarantee to citizens. Let us focus on the capabilities necessary for functioning as an equal citizen. Citizenship involves functioning not only as a political agent—voting, engaging in political speech, petitioning government, and so forth—but participating as an equal in civil society. Civil society is the sphere of social life that is open to the general public and is not part of the state bureaucracy in charge of the administration of laws. Its institutions include public streets and parks; public accommodations such as restaurants, shops, theaters, buses and airlines; communications systems such as broadcasting, telephones, and the Internet; public libraries; hospitals; schools; and so forth. Enterprises engaged in production for the market are also part of civil society, because they sell their products to any customer and draw their employees from the general public. One of the important achievements of the civil rights movement was to vindicate an understanding of citizenship that includes the right to participate as an equal in civil society as well as in government affairs. A group that is excluded from or segregated within the institutions of civil society, or subject to discrimination on the basis of ascribed social identities by institutions in civil society, has been relegated to second-class citizenship, even if its members enjoy all of their political rights.

So, to be capable of functioning as an equal citizen involves the ability not just to effectively exercise specifically political rights, but also to participate in the various activities of civil society more broadly, including participation in the economy. And functioning in these ways presupposes functioning as a human being. Consider, then, three aspects of individual functioning: as a human being, as a participant in a system of cooperative production, and as a citizen of a democratic state. To be capable of functioning as a human being requires effective access to the means of sustaining one's biological existence—food, shelter, clothing, medical care—and access to the basic conditions of human agency—knowledge of one's circumstances and options; the ability to deliberate about means and ends; the psychological conditions of autonomy, including the self-confidence to think and judge for oneself; freedom of thought and movement. To be capable of functioning as an equal participant in a system of cooperative production requires effective access to the means of production, access to the education needed to develop one's talents, freedom of occupational choice, the right to make contracts and enter into cooperative agreements with others, the right to receive fair value for one's labor, and recognition by others of one's productive contributions. To be capable of functioning as a citizen requires rights to political participation, such as freedom of speech and the franchise, and also effective access to the goods and relationships of civil society. This entails freedom of association, access to public spaces such as roads, parks, and public accommodations including public transportation, the postal service, and telecommunications. This also entails the social conditions of being accepted by others, such as the ability to appear in public without shame, and not being ascribed outcast status. The freedom to form relationships in civil society also requires effective access to private spaces, since many such relationships can only function when protected from the scrutiny and intrusions of others. Homelessness—that is, having only public dwelling—is a condition of profound unfreedom.

Three points should be made about the structure of egalitarian guarantees in the space of freedom or capabilities. First, democratic equality guarantees not actual levels of functioning, but effective access to those levels. Individuals are free to choose to function at a lower level than they are guaranteed. For example, they might choose to join a religious group that discourages political participation. Moreover, democratic equality can make access to certain functionings—those requiring an income—conditional upon working for them, provided that citizens have effective access to those conditions—they are physically capable of performing the work, doing so is consistent with their other duties, they can find a job, and so forth. Effective access to a level of functioning means that people can achieve that functioning by deploying means already at their disposal, not that the functioning is unconditionally guaranteed without any effort on their own part. Thus, democratic equality is consistent with constructing the incentive systems needed for a modern economy to support the production needed to support egalitarian guarantees in the first place.

Second, democratic equality guarantees not effective access to equal levels of functioning but effective access to levels of functioning sufficient to stand as an equal in society. For some functionings, equal citizenship requires equal levels. For example, each citizen is entitled to the same number of votes in an election as everyone else. But for other functionings, standing as an equal does not require equal levels of functioning. To be capable of standing as an equal in civil society requires literacy. But in the U.S. context, it does not require literacy in any language other than English, or the ability to interpret obscure works of literary theory. Democratic equality does not object if not everyone knows a foreign language, and only a few have a Ph.D.-level training in literature. In other countries, multilingual literacy might be required for equal standing.

Third, democratic equality guarantees effective access to a package of capabilities sufficient for standing as an equal over the course of an entire life. It is not a starting-gate theory in which people could lose their access to equal standing through bad option luck. Access to the egalitarian capabilities is also market-inalienable: contracts whereby individuals irrevocably transfer their fundamental freedoms to others are null and void.[13] The rationale for establishing such inalienable rights might seem difficult to grasp from the point of view of the rights holder. Why shouldn't she be free to trade some of her egalitarian-guaranteed freedoms for other goods that she prefers? Isn't it paternalistic to deny her the freedom to trade?

We can avoid this thought by considering the point of view of the obligation holder. The counterpart to an individual's inalienable right to the social conditions of her freedom is the unconditional obligation of others to respect her dignity or moral equality. Kant would put the point as follows: every individual has a worth or dignity that is not conditional upon anyone's desires or preferences, not even the individual's own desires. This implies that there are some things one may never do to other people, such as to enslave them, even if one has their permission or consent. Contracts into slavery or servitude are therefore invalid. In basing inalienable rights on what others are obligated to do rather than on the rights bearer's own subjective interests, democratic equality satisfies the second desideratum of egalitarian theory: to justify lifetime guarantees without resorting to paternalism.

One advantage of the capabilities approach to equality is that it allows us to analyze injustices in regard to other matters besides the distribution of resources and other divisible goods. One's capabilities are a function not just of one's fixed personal traits and divisible resources, but also of one's mutable traits, social relations and norms, and the structure of opportunities, public goods, and public spaces. Egalitarian political movements have never lost sight of the whole range of targets of egalitarian assessment. For example, feminists work to overcome the internal obstacles to choice—self-abnegation, lack of confidence, and low self-esteem—that women often face from internalizing norms of femininity. Gays and lesbians seek the ability to publicly reveal their identities without shame or fear, which requires significant changes in social relations of contempt and hostility, and changes in norms of gender and sexuality. The disabled aim to reconfigure public spaces to make them accessible and adapt work situations to their needs, so that they can participate in productive activity. No mere redistribution of divisible resources can secure the freedoms these groups seek.

Of course, democratic equality is also concerned with the distribution of divisible resources. It requires that everyone have effective access to enough resources to avoid being oppressed by others and to function as an equal in civil society. What counts as "enough" varies with cultural norms, the natural environment, and individual circumstance. For example, cultural norms and climate influence what kind of clothing one needs to be able to appear in public without shame and with adequate protection from the elements. Individual circumstances, such as disabilities, influence how much resources one needs to function as an equal. People without use of their legs may need more resources—wheelchairs, specially adapted vans—to achieve mobility comparable to that of ambulatory persons. Equality in the space of capabilities may therefore demand an unequal division of resources to accommodate the disabled.[14] What citizens ultimately owe one another are the social conditions of the freedoms people need to function as equal citizens. Because of differences in their internal capacities and social situations, people are not equally able to convert resources into capabilities for functioning. They are therefore entitled to different amounts of resources so that they can enjoy freedom as equals.

Suppose we abstract from the fact that people have different internal physical and mental capabilities. Would democratic equality demand that external resources be divided equally from the start, as equality of fortune holds? There is no reason to think so. The capabilities relevant to functioning as a human being, as a participant in the system of social cooperation, and as an equal citizen do not include all functionings or all levels of functioning. To function as a human being, one needs adequate nutrition. To eat without being relegated to a subhuman status, one needs access to sources of nutrition besides pet food or the dumpster. But to be able to function as a dignified human being, one does not need the quantity or quality of food intake of a gourmet. Democratic equality therefore requires that everyone have effective access to adequate nutrition, as well as sources of nutrition that one's society considers dignified—fit for consumption in social gatherings. It does not require that everyone have the resources needed for an equal opportunity to function as a gourmet. It therefore does not require criteria for equality of resources that depend on the morally dubious idea that the distribution of resources should be sensitive to considerations of envy.

Participation as an Equal in a System of Cooperative Production

So far we have considered what citizens are obligated to provide one another. But how are such things to be produced, and by what means and principles shall they be distributed? In stressing the concept of obligation, democratic equality heads off the thought that in an egalitarian society everyone somehow could have a right to receive goods without anyone having an obligation to produce them. Democratic equality seeks equality in the capability or effective freedom to achieve functionings that are part of citizenship, broadly construed. For those capable of working and with access to jobs, the actual achievement of these functionings is, in the normal case, conditional on participating in the productive system. Contrary to Van Parijs's view, citizens do not owe one another the real freedom to function as beach bums. Most able-bodied citizens, then, will get access to the divisible resources they need to function by earning a wage or some equivalent compensation due to them on account of their filling some role in the division of labor.

In deciding principles for a just division of labor and a just division of the fruits of that labor, workers are to regard the economy as a system of cooperative, joint production.[15] I want to contrast this image of joint production with the more familiar image that invites us to regard the economy as if it were a system of self-sufficient Robinson Crusoes, producing everything all by themselves until the point of trade. By "joint production," I mean that people regard every product of the economy as jointly produced by everyone working together. From the point of view of justice, the attempt, independent of moral principles, to credit specific bits of output to specific bits of input by specific individuals represents an arbitrary cut in the causal web that in fact makes everyone's productive contribution dependent on what everyone else is doing. Each worker's capacity to labor depends on a vast array of inputs produced by other people—food, schooling, parenting, and the like. It even depends on workers in the recreation and entertainment industries, since enjoyment of leisure activities helps restore energy and enthusiasm for work. In addition, the productivity of a worker in a specific role depends not only on her own efforts, but also on other people performing their roles in the division of labor. Michael Jordan could not make so many baskets if no one kept the basketball court swept clean. Millions of people could not even get to work if public transportation workers went on strike. The comprehensiveness of the division of labor in a modern economy implies that no one produces everything, or indeed anything, they consume by their own efforts alone. In regarding the division of labor as a comprehensive system of joint production, workers and consumers regard themselves as collectively commissioning everyone else to perform their chosen role in the economy. In performing their role in an efficient division of labor, each worker is regarded as an agent for the people who consume their products and for the other workers who, in being thereby relieved from performing that role, become free to devote their talents to more productive activities.

In regarding the economy as a cooperative venture, workers accept the demand of what G. A. Cohen has defined as the principle of interpersonal justification:[16] any consideration offered as a reason for a policy must serve to justify that policy when uttered by anyone to anyone else who participates in the economy as a worker or a consumer. The principles that govern the division of labor and the assignment of particular benefits to the performance of roles in the division of labor must be acceptable to everyone in this sense. To see how interpersonal justification works within the context of the economy considered as a system of cooperative, joint production, consider three of the cases equality of fortune gets wrong: disability compensation for workers in dangerous occupations, federal disaster relief, and dependent caretakers with their children.

Eric Rakowski argues that workers who choose particularly dangerous occupations, such as farming, fishing, mining, forestry, firefighting, and policing, have no claims to medical care, rehabilitation, or compensation if they are injured on the job.[17] Since they engage in these occupations by choice, any bad fortune they suffer on the job is a form of option luck, the consequences of which must be born by the worker alone. Cohen's test invites us to consider how persuasive this argument is when uttered to the disabled workers by the consumers who eat the food, use the metal and wood, and enjoy the protection from fire and crime that these workers provide. These consumers are not free to disclaim all responsibility for the bad luck that befalls workers in dangerous occupations. For they commissioned these workers to perform those dangerous tasks on their own behalf. The workers were acting as agents for the consumers of their labor. It cannot be just to designate a work role in the division of labor that entails such risks and then assign a package of benefits to performance in the role that fails, given the risks, to secure the social conditions of freedom to those who occupy the role. The principle "let us be served by occupations so inadequately compensated that those in them shall lack the means necessary to secure their freedom, given the risks and conditions of their work" cannot survive the test of interpersonal justification.

Similar reflections apply to those who choose to live and work in areas prone to particularly severe natural disasters, such as residents near the San Andreas Fault. Rakowski argues that such residents should be excluded from federal disaster relief because they live there by choice.[18] But they live there because other citizens have, through their demand for California products, commissioned them to exploit the natural resources in California. To deny them federal disaster relief is to invoke the rejected principle above. Economists may object that, on balance, it may not be efficient to continue production in a particular region, and that disaster relief, in subsidizing the costs of living in disaster-prone regions, perpetuates a costly error. However, if, on balance, citizens decide that a region should be designated uninhabitable, because the costs of relief are too high, the proper response is not to leave its residents in the lurch but to designate their relief toward helping them relocate. Citizens are not to be deprived of basic capabilities on account of where they live.[19]

The case of non-wage-earning dependent caretakers and children might seem to fall outside the purview of society as system of cooperation. But this is to confuse the economy with the market sector.[20] Non-wage-earning dependent caretakers contribute to production in at least three ways. First, most engage in household production—cleaning, cooking, and so forth—which services, if not performed, would have to be hired out. Second, they raise the future workers of the economy and help rehabilitate the sick and injured ones so that they can return to work. Third, in discharging the obligations everyone has to dependents, considered as human beings, and the obligations all family members have toward their dependent kin, they relieve others of such responsibility and thereby free them to participate in the market economy. Fathers would not be so productive in the market if the non-wage-earning or part-time working mothers of their children did not relieve them of so much of their responsibility to engage in direct caretaking.[21] The principle "let us assign others to discharge our caretaking obligations to dependents, and attach such meager benefits to performance in this role that these caretakers live at our mercy" cannot survive interpersonal justification either. Dependent caretakers are entitled to enough of a share of their partner's income that they are not vulnerable to domination and exploitation within the relationship. This principle supports Susan Moller Okin's proposal that paychecks be split between husband and wife.[22] If this is not sufficient to eliminate caretakers' vulnerability in domestic partnership, a case can be made for socializing some of the costs of dependent care through a child-care (or elder-care) subsidy, as is common in western Europe. Ultimately, full equality may not be achievable simply through the redistribution of material resources. Equality may require a change in social norms by which men as well as women would be expected to share in caretaking responsibilities.[23]

Against the proposal to socialize the costs of dependent care, Rakowski insists that children are entitled only to resources from their parents, not from others. Even if they will provide benefits to others when they grow up and participate in the economy, it is unjust to make people pay for benefits they never asked for, and in any event most of those benefits will accrue to other family members.[24] If the economy consisted of isolated, economically self-sufficient family groups, as in a primitive hunter-gatherer society, one could see Rakowski's point. But in a society with an extensive division of labor, his assumptions make no sense. As long as one doesn't plan to commit suicide once the next generation enters the workforce, one can't help but demand the labor services of future generations. Moreover, most of what people produce in a market economy is consumed by non-family members. In regarding the whole society as a system of cooperation that jointly produces the economy's entire output, democratic equality acknowledges everyone's profound mutual dependency in modern society. It rejects the atomistic norm of individual self-sufficiency as based on a failure to recognize the dependency of wage earners on the work of those whose labor is not for sale. In adjusting entitlements to account for the fact that adults have moral responsibilities to take care of dependents, democratic equality also rejects equality of fortune's reduction of moral obligations to expensive tastes and its consequent guarantee of equality only to egoists. Democratic equality says that no one should be reduced to an inferior status because they fulfill obligations to care for others.

The conception of society as a system of cooperation provides a safety net through which even the imprudent are never forced to fall. It provides that no role in the productive system shall be assigned such inadequate benefits that, given the risks and requirements of the job, people could be deprived of the social conditions of their freedom because they have fulfilled its requirements. Society may not define work roles that amount to peonage or servitude, nor, if it can avoid it, pay them so little that an able-bodied person working full-time would still lack basic capabilities.[25] One mechanism for achieving a decent minimum would be a minimum wage. A minimum wage need not raise unemployment if low-wage workers are given sufficient training to make them more productive or if the higher wage induces employers to supply their workers with productivity-enhancing tools. Benefits could also be attached to work by other means, such as socially provided disability and old-age pension schemes, and tax credits for earned income. Democratic equality also favors a qualified entitlement to work on the part of willing, able-bodied adults. Unemployment insurance is a poor substitute for work, given the central importance of participation in productive activity to living life as an equal in civil society. So is "workfare" if, as is typically the case in the United States, it means forcing people to engage in make-work for aid while depriving them of the dignity of a real job with a real wage.

It is instructive to consider what democratic equality says to those with low talents. Equality of fortune would offer compensation to those with low talents, precisely because their innate inferiority makes their labor so relatively worthless to others, as judged by the market. Democratic equality calls into question the very idea that inferior native endowments have much to do with observed income inequalities in capitalist economies. The biggest fortunes are made not by those who work but by those who own the means of production. Even among wage workers, most of the differences are due to the fact that society has invested far more in developing some people's talents than others and that it puts very unequal amounts of capital at the disposal of each worker. Productivity attaches mainly to work roles, not to individuals. Democratic equality deals with these facts by stressing the importance of educating the less advantaged and by offering firms incentives to increase the productivity of low-wage jobs through capital investment.

Moreover, in regarding society as a system of cooperation, democratic equality has a less demeaning rationale than equality of fortune for state interventions designed to raise the wages of low-wage workers. Society need not try to make the impossible and insulting judgment of whether low-wage workers are there by choice or by the fact that their meager native endowments prevent them from getting better work. Instead, it focuses on appreciation for the roles that low-wage workers fill. In performing routine, low-skill tasks, these workers free other people to make more productive uses of their talents. Those occupying more productive roles owe much of their productivity to the fact that those occupying less productive roles have freed them from the need to spend their time on low-skill tasks. Fancy corporate executives could not cut so many lucrative deals if they had to answer their own telephone calls. Such reflections express appreciation for the ways that everyone benefits from the diversity of talents and roles in society. They also undermine the thought that workers at the top make a lopsided contribution to the social product and thereby help motivate a conception of reciprocity that would squeeze the gap between the highest- and lowest-paid workers.

Would democratic equality support a wage-squeezing policy as demanding as John Rawls's difference principle? This would forbid all income inequalities that do not improve the incomes of the worst off.[26] In giving absolute priority to the worst off, the difference principle might require considerable sacrifices in the lower middle ranks for trifling gains at the lowest levels. Democratic equality would urge a less demanding form of reciprocity. Once all citizens enjoy a decent set of freedoms, sufficient for functioning as an equal in society, income inequalities beyond that point do not seem so troubling in themselves. The degree of acceptable income inequality would depend in part on how easy it was to convert income into status inequality—differences in the social bases of self-respect, influence over elections, and the like. The stronger the barriers against commodifying social status, political influence, and the like, the more acceptable are significant income inequalities.[27] The moral status of free-market allocations is strengthened the more carefully defined is the domain in which these allocations have free rein.

Democratic Equality, Personal Responsibility, and Paternalism

Democratic equality guarantees effective access to the social conditions of freedom to all citizens, regardless of how imprudently they conduct their lives. It does not deprive negligent or self-destructive citizens of necessary medical care. It does not discriminate among the disabled depending on how much they can be held responsible for their disability. Under democratic equality, citizens refrain from making intrusive, moralizing judgments about how people ought to have used the opportunities open to them or about how capable they were of exercising personal responsibility. It need not make such judgments, because it does not condition citizens' enjoyment of their capabilities on whether they use them responsibly. The sole exception to this principle concerns criminal conduct. Only the commission of a crime can justify taking away a person's basic liberties and status as an equal in civil society. Even convicted criminals, however, retain their status as equal human beings, and so are still entitled to basic human functionings such as adequate nutrition, shelter, and medical care.

One might object to democratic equality on the grounds that all these guarantees invite personal irresponsibility, just as critics of equality have long suspected. If people are going to be bailed out of the situations they get into because of their own imprudence, then why act prudently? Egalitarians must face up to the need to uphold personal responsibility, if only to avoid bankrupting the state. There are two general strategies for doing so. One is to insure only against certain causes of loss: to distinguish between the losses for which people are responsible and those for which they are not, and to indemnify individuals only against the latter. This is the approach of luck egalitarianism, which leads to Poor Law thinking, and intrusive and disrespectful judgments of individuals. The second strategy is to insure only against the losses of certain types of goods: to distinguish between guaranteed and unguaranteed types of goods within the space of egalitarian concern, and to insure individuals only against the loss of the former. This is the approach of democratic equality.

Democratic equality does not indemnify individuals against all losses due to their imprudent conduct. It only guarantees a set of capabilities necessary to functioning as a free and equal citizen and avoiding oppression. Individuals must bear many other losses on their own. For example, a person who smokes would be entitled to treatment for resulting lung cancer, regardless of their degree of responsibility for smoking. But she would not be entitled to compensation for the loss of enjoyment of life brought about by her confinement in the hospital and reduced lung capacity, for the dread she feels upon contemplating her mortality, or for the reproach of her relatives who disapprove of her lifestyle. Individuals thus have plenty to lose from their irresponsible conduct, and therefore have an incentive to behave prudently. Luck egalitarianism can't take advantage of this incentive structure, because it indemnifies individuals against the loss of all kinds of goods (kinds of resources or sources of welfare) within its space of egalitarian concern. It therefore must resort to moral judgments about the cause of loss in order to promote individual responsibility.

Democratic equality has two further strategies for promoting individual responsibility. First, it offers equality in the space of capabilities, which is to say opportunities or freedoms. Individuals still have to exercise responsible agency to achieve most of the functionings effective access to which society guarantees. In the typical case of an able-bodied adult, for instance, access to a decent income would be conditioned on responsible performance of one's duties in one's job, assuming a job was available.

Second, most of the freedoms that democratic equality guarantees are prerequisites to exercising responsible agency. Responsible agency requires real options, awareness of these options, deliberative skills, and the self-respect needed to trust one's own judgment. Democratic equality guarantees the education needed to know and deliberate about one's options, and the social bases of self-respect. Moreover, people will do almost anything to secure what they need to survive. In ensuring effective access to the means of subsistence through legitimate routes, democratic equality prevents the criminal behavior that would be spurred by a society that let people fall below subsistence or that deprived people of dignified legitimate means of subsistence. It also avoids the powerful incentives to deny personal responsibility that are built into equality of fortune, because it ensures that people will always have legitimate means at their disposal to get access to their basic capabilities without having to resort to deception about their role in getting into their predicament.

It might be objected that democratic equality, in guaranteeing such goods as medical care to all, still requires an objectionable subsidy of irresponsible behavior. Why should prudent nonsmokers have to pay more for universal health insurance, because so many fools choose to smoke? If the costs of some particularly dangerous activity are high, and if the activity is not performed in one's capacity as a participant in the productive system, then justice permits a tax on that activity to cover the extra costs of medical care for those injured by engaging in it. A tax on each pack of cigarettes, adjusted to cover the medical costs of treating smokers, would force smokers to absorb the extra costs of their behavior.

If it is just to force smokers to absorb these costs ex ante, why isn't it equally just to force them to absorb these costs ex post, as some luck egalitarians hold? John Roemer's plan does this by discounting the medical subsidy people are entitled to according to their degree of personal responsibility.[28] Besides entangling the state in intrusive moralizing judgments of personal responsibility, Roemer's plan leaves people vulnerable to such a deprivation of their capabilities that they cannot function as an equal. This is unjust. By making smokers pay for the costs of their behavior ex ante, democratic equality preserves their freedom and equality over the course of their whole lives.

It might be objected that democratic equality, in guaranteeing a specific set of capabilities to citizens, paternalistically violates the freedom of citizens and violates the requirement of liberal neutrality among conceptions of the good. Suppose a smoker would prefer to have cheaper cigarettes than to be provided medical care? Shouldn't citizens be free to choose what goods they prefer to have? Thus, citizens should be entitled to the welfare equivalent of medical care and not be forced to consume medical care at the cost of other things they might prefer. This line of thought supports equality in the space of opportunities for welfare, rather than in capabilities for equal citizenship.

These objections fail to appreciate the distinction between what people want and what other people are obligated to give them. The basic duty of citizens, acting through the state, is not to make everyone happy but to secure the conditions of everyone's freedom. In securing for citizens only the capabilities they need to function as equal citizens, the state is not declaring that these capabilities are more important for individual happiness than some others that they might prefer. It leaves individuals free to decide for themselves how useful or important are the goods that the state guarantees to them. It guarantees certain capabilities to citizens not because these are the most important ones as judged from the standpoint of the best conception of the good, but because these are the ones citizens are obligated to provide one another in common.

But why can't any given citizen waive his right to guaranteed health care in return for its welfare equivalent? Citizens can, with justice, refuse to provide what any individual regards as the welfare equivalent of health care. As Thomas Scanlon has stressed, the fact that someone would rather have help in building a temple to his god than to be decently fed does not generate a greater claim on others to subsidize his temple than to ensure his access to adequate nutrition.[29] Furthermore, the obligation to provide health care is unconditional and can't be rescinded, even with the permission of the person to whom the obligation is owed. We are not permitted to abandon people dying by the side of the road just because they gave us permission to deny them emergency medical care.[30]

One might object that democratic equality fails to respect neutrality among competing conceptions of the good. Some citizens will find the capability sets guaranteed them far more useful than others. For example, those whose conception of the good involves widespread participation in civil society will find their good more fully secured by democratic equality than those who prefer to lead their lives in insular religious cults. Democratic equality is therefore biased in favor of certain conceptions of the good.

This objection misunderstands the point of neutrality. As Rawls has stressed, given the fact the people hold conflicting conceptions of the good, liberal states need some basis for judging claims of justice that does not rest on partisan views of the good. The point of view of citizens acting collectively—the political point of view—does not claim authority in virtue of promoting the objectively best or most important goods but in virtue of being a possible object of collective willing. Neutral goods are the goods we can reasonably agree to collectively provide, given the fact of pluralism.[31] Thus, the capabilities citizens need to function as equals in civil society count as neutral goods for purposes of justice not because everyone finds these capabilities equally valuable, but because reasonable people can recognize that these form a legitimate basis for making moral claims on one another.[32] By contrast, reasonable persons need not recognize the desire to build a temple to their god as a legitimate basis for a claim to public subsidy. A person who does not worship that god could reasonably object to the state taxing her to subsidize someone else's involuntarily expensive religious desires.

Consider now what equality of fortune and democratic equality have to say to the person who decides, prudently or imprudently, not to purchase health insurance for himself. According to equality of fortune, there are two options. One is to allow the person to decline health insurance and abandon him if he needs emergency care. The other is to tell him, "You are too stupid to run your own life. Therefore, we will force you to purchase health insurance, because we know better than you what is for your own good." Democratic equality passes no judgment on whether it would be prudent or imprudent for any given individual to purchase health insurance. It tells the person who would not purchase insurance for himself, "You have a moral worth that no one can disregard. We recognize this worth in your inalienable right to our aid in an emergency. You are free to refuse this aid once we offer it. But this freedom does not absolve you of the obligation to come to the aid of others when their health needs are urgent. Since this is an obligation we all owe to our fellow citizens, everyone shall be taxed for this good, which we shall provide to everyone. This is part of your rightful claim as an equal citizen." Which rationale for providing health insurance better expresses respect for its recipients?

The Disabled, the Ugly, and Other Victims of Bad Luck

According to democratic equality, the distribution of nature's good or bad fortune is neither just nor unjust. Considered in itself, nothing in this distribution calls for any correction by society. No claims to compensation can be generated by nature's effects alone. This may seem an unduly harsh doctrine. Does it not leave the congenitally disabled, ugly, and stupid out in the cold, even though they do not deserve their sorry fates?

Democratic equality says no. Although the distribution of natural assets is not a matter of justice, what people do in response to this distribution is.[33] People may not make the possession of a disability, repugnant appearance, or low intelligence the occasion for excluding people from civil society, dominating them, beating them up, or otherwise oppressing them. In a liberal democratic state, all citizens are entitled to the social conditions of their freedom and standing as equals in civil society, regardless of handicap, physical appearance, or intelligence.[34] Moreover, these conditions are sensitive to variations in people's circumstances, including their disabilities. People who can't walk are entitled to accommodation in civil society: to wheelchairs, ramps on public buildings, and so forth. However, these conditions are not sensitive to variations in people's tastes. Everyone has an entitlement to the same package of capabilities, whatever else they may have, and regardless of what they would prefer to have. Thus, if a person who needs a wheelchair to get around has an involuntarily expensive taste for engaging in particular religious rituals, and would prefer having this taste satisfied to having a wheelchair, democratic equality does not substitute a subsidy for her rituals for the wheelchair. For individuals need to be able to move around civil society to have equal standing as citizens, but they do not need to be able to worship in particularly expensive ways in order to function as equals.

Richard Arneson objects to this distinction between disabled people and people with involuntarily expensive tastes. For disabilities are just another kind of involuntarily expensive taste. It's not the disabled individual's fault that it costs more for her to get around in a wheelchair than it takes ambulatory people to make the same journey. Once we see that it is the involuntariness of the costs of her tastes that entitles her to special subsidy, one must allow people with other involuntarily expensive tastes to make equal claims on behalf of their preferences. Arneson claims that only an illegitimate perfectionist doctrine—the claim that mobility is intrinsically more important than worship—can support discrimination between the disabled and those with other involuntarily expensive tastes.[35]

Democratic equality takes no stand on what goods individuals should value more when they are thinking only of their own interests. It provides the social conditions for equal citizenship, and not the conditions for equal ability to fulfill the demands of one's gods, because citizens are obligated to provide the first and are not obligated to provide the second. Arneson argues that capabilities are diverse, and the resources available to provide them scarce. Some trade-offs among capabilities must therefore be accepted. Some index is therefore needed to rank the importance of different capabilities. If one rejects perfectionist doctrines, the only basis for constructing an index of capabilities is subjective, based on the importance to the individual of having that capability.[36]

Against Arneson, democratic equality follows Scanlon in insisting that the weight that a citizen's claim has on others depends solely on the content of her interest and not on the importance she places on it in her own conception of the good.[37] In some cases, the weight of an interest can be determined by considering its impact on a person's standing as an equal in society. Some deprivations of capabilities express greater disrespect than others in ways any reasonable person can recognize. From a public point of view, it is more disrespectful to deny a person in a wheelchair access to the public schools than it is to deny her access to an amusement park ride that only accommodates the walking. This is true even if she'd rather go through the Fun House than learn how to read. In other cases, where the concepts of equal standing and respect don't yield a determinate answer to how capabilities should be ranked, the ranking may legitimately be left up to democratic legislation. Even here, voters are not to ask themselves what priorities they give to different capabilities for citizenship in their private choices, but what priorities they want the state to assign to these different capabilities, given that these goods shall be provided in common. The answers to the questions are likely to diverge, if only because many capabilities are more valuable to others than to their possessors. Most people gain much more from other people's freedom of speech than from their own.[38]

It might be argued that democratic equality is still too harsh to those who are disabled through bad brute luck. It would not compensate them for all of the miseries they face. For example, democratic equality would ensure that the deaf have equal access to civil society, but not that they be compensated for the loss of the pleasures of hearing itself. Yet the lives of the deaf are less happy for lacking these pleasures, and should be compensated on that account.

It is useful to ask what the deaf demand on their own account, in the name of justice. Do they bemoan the misery of not being able to hear, and demand compensation for this lack? On the contrary, like the disabled more generally, they resent being cast as poster children for the abled to pity, because they do not want to have to cast their claims as appeals to the condescending benevolence of kindly patrons. Many deaf people identify as part of a separate Deaf community that repudiates the intrinsic choiceworthiness of hearing itself. They insist that sign language is just as valuable a form of communication as is speech and that the other goods obtainable through hearing, such as appreciation of music, are dispensable parts of any conception of good. One needn't pass judgment on the intrinsic choiceworthiness of hearing to appreciate the rhetorical uses of denying it: the Deaf want to cut the hearing down to size, to purge the arrogant assumption of the hearing that the lives of the Deaf are somehow less worth living. They want to make claims on the hearing in a manner that expresses the dignity they see in their lives and community, rather than in a manner that appeals to pity for their condition.[39] They do this by denying that their condition, considered in itself, is anything to be pitied.

Equality of fortune, despite the fact that it considers the treatment of the disabled as a core case, has difficulty with such ideas. This is due to the fact that it relies on subjective measures of welfare or of the worth of personal assets. Subjective measures invite all the wrong thoughts on the part of the abled. Van Parijs's criterion of undominated diversity allows the disabled to make claims of justice regarding their disability only if everyone regards their condition as so wretched that everyone would prefer being someone else. This test asks the abled to take the horror they feel upon imagining that they had a disability as their reason for compensating the disabled. To regard the condition of the disabled as intrinsically horrible is insulting to the disabled people who lead their lives with dignity. Arneson's criterion of equal opportunity for welfare implies that as long as the disabled have equal chances for happiness, they have no claims to special accommodation. Survey research shows that the disabled experience the same range of happiness as the abled.[40] Thus, by Arneson's criterion, it is all right to exclude the disabled from public life because they are happy enough without being included.

Subjective measures of people's condition generate either pity for the disabled or reluctance to consider their claims of justice. The way to escape this dilemma is to take seriously what the disabled are actually complaining about. They do not ask that they be compensated for the disability itself. Rather, they ask that the social disadvantages others impose on them for having the disability be removed. "The inequality of people mobilizing in wheelchairs . . . manifests itself not in the inability to walk but in exclusion from bathrooms, theaters, transportation, places of work, [and] life-saving medical treatment."[41] Democratic equality can handle this distinction. It demands, for instance, that the disabled have good enough access to public accommodations that they can function as equals in civil society. To be capable of functioning as an equal does not require that one's access be equally fast, comfortable, or convenient, or that one get equal subjective utility from using public accommodations. There may be no way to achieve this. But the fact that, with current technology, it takes an extra minute to get into city hall does not compromise one's standing as an equal citizen.

Democratic equality thus supports the use of objective tests of unjust disadvantage. Such tests fit the claims of justice that the disabled make on their own behalf. For example, what the Deaf find objectionable is not that they can't hear, but that everyone else has rigged the means of communication in ways that leave them out of the conversation. One can detect this injustice without investigating anyone's preferences or subjective states. The test for a satisfactory remedy is equally objective. The Americans with Disabilities Act, for example, embodies an objective standard of accommodation. "Rather than speculating on how the *subjective personal response* of unimpaired agents would be transfigured by the onset of physical or mental impairment, this standard calls for projecting how *objective social practice* would be transformed were unimpaired functioning so *atypical* as to be of merely marginal importance for social policy."[42] The act asks us to imagine how communications in civil society would be arranged if nearly everyone were deaf, and then try to offer to the deaf arrangements approximating this.

The objective standards of injustice and remedy proposed by democratic equality have several advantages over those proposed by equality of fortune. They match the remedy to the injustice: if the injustice is exclusion, the remedy is inclusion. Democratic equality does not attempt to use private satisfactions to justify public oppression. Objective standards do not insultingly represent the disabled as deserving aid because of their pitiful internal condition. They locate the unjust disadvantage of disability in the way others treat the disabled. Democratic equality also does not assimilate the disabled to the situation of those suffering from involuntarily expensive tastes. Having a disability is not like being so spoiled that one can't help wanting expensive toys.

Should other victims of bad brute luck be treated like the handicapped? Equality of fortune thinks so—it extends its concern to the ugly, the stupid, and the untalented as well. Democratic equality does not pass judgment on the worth of people's native endowments, and so has nothing special to say to the stupid and the untalented. Instead, it focuses on the productive roles that people occupy in recognition of the fact that society attaches economic benefits to performance in a role rather than to the possession of talent in itself. Democratic equality requires that sufficient benefits be attached to performance in every role so that all workers can function as equals in society. Talent brings noneconomic advantages as well, such as the admiration of others. Democratic equality finds no injustice in this advantage, because one doesn't need to be admired to be able to function as an equal citizen. As justice requires, most residents of modern democracies live in a state of civilization where the attainment of honor is not a condition of enjoying basic freedoms. In places where this is not so, such as certain tough inner-city neighborhoods, it is clear that the injustice lies not in the fact that some individuals are unfortunately born with lower native endowments of courage, but that the social order is arranged so that only those willing to display uncommonly high degrees of ruthlessness can enjoy personal security.

What about the ugly? Are they not entitled to compensation for their repugnant appearance, which makes them so unwelcome in social settings? Some luck egalitarians would view this bad luck as calling for a remedy, perhaps in the form of publicly subsidized plastic surgery. Democratic equality refuses to publicly endorse the demeaning private judgments of appearance that are the basis of such claims to compensation. Instead, it asks whether the norms based on such judgments are oppressive. Consider a birth defect, affecting only a person's appearance, that is considered so abhorrent by current social norms that people tend to shun those who have it. Since the capability to participate in civil society as an equal citizen is a fundamental freedom, egalitarians demand that some remedy be provided for this. But the remedy need not consist in plastic surgery that corrects the defect. An alternative would be to persuade everyone to adopt new norms of acceptable physical appearance, so that people with the birth "defect" were no longer treated as pariahs. This is not to call for the abolition of norms of beauty altogether. The norms need only be flexible enough to deem the person an acceptable presence in civil society. They need not entitle such a person to claim equal beauty to others, since successful functioning as a contestant in a beauty pageant, or as a hot prospect for a Saturday night date, is not among the capabilities one needs to function as an equal citizen.

By directing attention to oppressive social norms of beauty, democratic equality avoids the disparaging scrutiny of the ugly through the lens of the oppressive norms themselves. This lets us see that the injustice lies not in the natural misfortune of the ugly but in the social fact that people shun others on account of their appearance. To change the person rather than the norm insultingly suggests that the defect lies in the person rather than in society. Other things equal, then, democratic equality prefers altering social norms to redistributing material resources in response to the disadvantages faced by the unsightly. Of course, other things are often not equal. It may be very difficult and costly to change prevailing norms of beauty that cruelly dictate who cannot appear in public without provoking shock and rejection. The liberal state can't do too much in this regard without overstepping its proper bounds; thus, this task must be delegated mainly to egalitarian social movements, which vary in their abilities to transform social norms. Under these conditions the better option may well be to supply the plastic surgery. Democratic equality, in focusing on equality as a social relationship rather than simply as a pattern of distribution, at least enables us to see that we have a choice between redistributing material resources and changing other aspects of society to meet the demands of equality.

Democratic Equality and the Obligations of Citizens

Democratic equality refocuses egalitarian theorizing in several ways. It conceives of justice as a matter of obligations that are not defined by the satisfaction of subjective preferences. This ensures that people's rights do not depend on arbitrary variations in individual tastes and that people may not claim rights without accepting corresponding obligations to others. Democratic equality applies judgments of justice to human arrangements, not to the natural order. This helps us see that people, not nature, are responsible for turning the natural diversity of human beings into oppressive hierarchies. It locates unjust deficiencies in the social order rather than in people's innate endowments. Instead of lamenting the human diversity of talents and trying to make up for what is represented as innate deficiencies in talent, democratic equality offers a way of conceiving and harnessing human diversity so that it benefits everyone and is recognized as doing so. Democratic equality conceives of equality as a relationship among people rather than merely as a pattern in the distribution of divisible goods. This helps us see how egalitarians can take other features of society besides the distribution of goods, such as social norms, as subject to critical scrutiny. It lets us see how injustices may be better remedied by changing social norms and the structure of public goods than by redistributing resources. And it allows us to integrate the demands of equal distribution and equal respect, ensuring that the principles by which we distribute goods, however equal resulting patterns may be, do not in fact express contemptuous pity for the beneficiaries of egalitarian concern. Democratic equality thus offers a superior way to understand the expressive demands of justice—the demand to act only on principles that express respect for everyone. Finally, in refocusing academic egalitarian theorizing, democratic equality holds out the promise of reestablishing connections with actually existing egalitarian movements. It is not a moral accident that beach bums and people who find themselves slaves to their expensive hobbies are not organizing to make claims of justice on behalf of their lifestyles. Nor is it irrelevant that the disabled are repudiating forms of charity that appeal to pity for their condition and are struggling for respect from others, not just handouts. Democratic equality helps articulate the demands of genuine egalitarian movements in a framework that offers some hope of broader appeal.

Notes

1. Ronald Dworkin, "What Is Equality? II. Equality of Resources," *Philosophy and Public Affairs* 10 (1981): 283–345, at 285.

2. Philippe Van Parijs, "Why Surfers Should Be Fed: The Liberal Case for an Unconditional Basic Income," *Philosophy and Public Affairs* 20 (1991): 101–131.

3. Richard Arneson, "Equality and Equal Opportunity for Welfare," in *Equality: Selected Readings*, edited by Louis Pojman and Robert Westmoreland (New York: Oxford University Press, 1997), 231.

4. G. A. Cohen, "On the Currency of Egalitarian Justice," *Ethics* 99 (1989): 906–944, at 922–923, 930–931.

5. Philippe Van Parijs, *Real Freedom for All* (Oxford: Clarendon Press, 1995), 127.

6. Thomas Nagel, "The Policy of Preference," in his *Mortal Questions* (Cambridge: Cambridge University Press, 1979), 91–105.

7. Iris Marion Young, *Justice and the Politics of Difference* (Princeton, NJ: Princeton University Press, 1990).

8. John Rawls, "Kantian Constructivism in Moral Theory," *Journal of Philosophy* 77 (1980): 515–572, at 525. The use of "equally" to modify "moral agents" might seem otiose. Why not just say that all competent adults are moral agents? Egalitarians deny a hierarchy of types of moral agency—e.g., any theory that says there is a lower type of human only able to follow moral commands issued by others and a higher type able to issue or discover moral commands for themselves.

9. Elizabeth Anderson, "The Democratic University: The Role of Justice in the Production of Knowledge," *Social Philosophy and Policy* 12 (1995): 186–219. Does this requirement mean that we must always listen patiently to those who have proven themselves to be stupid, cranky, or dishonest? No. It means that (1) everyone must be granted the initial benefit of the doubt, (2) a person can be ignored or excluded from discussion only on demonstrated grounds of communicative incompetence or unwillingness to engage in fair discussion, and (3) reasonable opportunities must be available to the excluded to demonstrate their communicative competence and thereby win back a place in the conversation.

10. Nancy Fraser, "From Redistribution to Recognition? Dilemmas of Justice in a 'Post-socialist' Age," in her *Justice Interruptus* (New York: Routledge, 1997), 11–39; Axel Honneth, *The Struggle for Recognition*, translated by Joel Anderson (Cambridge: Polity Press, 1995).

11. Christine Korsgaard, "Commentary on G. A. Cohen and Amartya Sen," in *The Quality of Life*, edited by Martha Nussbaum and Amartya Sen (Oxford: Clarendon Press, 1993).

12. Amartya Sen, *Inequality Reexamined* (Cambridge, MA: Harvard University Press, 1992), 39–42, 49.

13. Margaret Radin, "Market Inalienability," *Harvard Law Review* 100 (1987): 1849–1937. A person might have to forfeit some of her market-inalienable freedoms, however, if she is convicted of a serious crime.

14. Sen, *Inequality Reexamined*, 79–84.

15. I shift from talk of "citizens" to talk of "workers" in part because the moral implications of regarding the economy as a system of cooperative production cross international boundaries. As the economy becomes global, we are all implicated in an international division of labor subject to assessment from an egalitarian point of view. We have obligations not only to the citizens of our country but to our fellow workers, who are now found in virtually every part of the globe. We also have global humanitarian obligations to everyone, considered simply as human beings—to relieve famine and disease, avoid fomenting or facilitating aggressive warfare, and the like. Alas, I do not have the space to consider the international implications of democratic equality.

16. G. A. Cohen, "Incentives, Inequality, and Community," in *Equal Freedom*, edited by Stephen Darwall (Ann Arbor: University of Michigan Press, 1995), 348.

17. Eric Rakowski, *Equal Justice* (New York: Oxford University Press, 1991), 79.

18. Ibid.

19. What about rich people who build their vacation homes in disaster-prone areas? They haven't been commissioned by others to live there, nor does it seem fair to force taxpayers to insure their luxurious estates. Democratic equality cannot allow even unproductive citizens to lose everything, but it does not indemnify them against all their losses either. It only guarantees sufficient relief to get them back on their feet, not to shod them in luxurious footwear. If even this relief seems too expensive, an egalitarian state can forbid people from inhabiting disaster-prone areas, or tax people who do to cover the excess costs of disaster relief. What it may not do is let them live there at their own risk and then abandon them in their hour of need. Such action treats even the imprudent with impermissible contempt.

20. Marilyn Waring, *If Women Counted* (San Francisco: HarperCollins, 1990).

21. Joan Williams, "Is Coverture Dead?" *Georgetown Law Journal* 82 (1994): 2227–2290, at 2227.

22. Susan Moller Okin, *Justice, Gender, and the Family* (New York: Basic Books, 1989), 180–182,

23. Nancy Fraser, "After the Family Wage: A Postindustrial Thought Experiment," in *Justice Interruptus*, 41–66.

24. Rakowski, *Equal Justice*, 153.

25. It might be thought that poor societies cannot afford even basic capabilities for all workers. However, Sen's studies of the standard of living in India and China show that even extremely poor societies can supply an impressive set of basic capabilities—decent nutrition, health, literacy, and the like—to all of their members if they apply themselves to the task. See, e.g., Amartya Sen, *Commodities and Capabilities* (Amsterdam, the Netherlands: North-Holland, 1985).

26. John Rawls, *A Theory of Justice*, rev. ed. (Cambridge, MA: Harvard University Press, 1999), 75–78.

27. Michael Walzer, *Spheres of Justice* (New York: Basic Books, 1983); Mickey Kaus, *The End of Equality* (New York: Basic Books, 1992).

28. John Roemer, "A Pragmatic Theory of Responsibility for the Egalitarian Planner," in his *Egalitarian Perspectives* (Cambridge: Cambridge University Press, 1994), 179–196.

29. Thomas Scanlon, "Preference and Urgency," *Journal of Philosophy* 72 (1975): 655–669, at 659–660.

30. This point is entirely distinct from the right to refuse medical care. It is one thing for an individual to exercise the right to refuse medical care when offered, quite another for others to refuse to offer medical care when needed.

31. John Rawls, *Political Liberalism* (New York: Columbia University Press, 1993).

32. Peter De Marneffe, "Liberalism, Liberty, and Neutrality," *Philosophy and Public Affairs* 19 (1990): 253–274, at 255–258.

33. Rawls, *A Theory of Justice*, 102.

34. Some exceptions would have to be made for those so severely mentally disabled or insane that they cannot function as agents. In addition, children are entitled not immediately to all of the freedoms of adults, but to the social conditions for the development of their capacities to function as free and equal citizens.

35. Richard Arneson, "'Liberalism, Distributive Subjectivism, and Equal Opportunity for Welfare," *Philosophy and Public Affairs* 19 (1990): 158, 187, 190–194.

36. Arneson, "Equality and Equality of Opportunity for Welfare," 236–237.

37. Scanlon, "Preference and Urgency," 659.

38. Joseph Raz, "Rights and Individual Well-Being," in his *Ethics in the Public Domain* (Oxford: Clarendon Press, 1994), 52–55.

39. Owen Wrigley, *The Politics of Deafness* (Washington, DC: Gallaudet University Press, 1996), discusses the potentials and problems of reconceiving disability (being deaf) as community (being Deaf) after the manner of identity politics.

40. Anita Silvers, "Reconciling Equality to Difference: Caring (f)or Justice for People with Disabilities," *Hypatia* 10 (1995): 30–55, at 54n9.

41. Ibid., 48.

42. Ibid., 49.

READING

3

A Defense of Luck Egalitarianism

KOK-CHOR TAN

Luck egalitarianism offers one grounding reason for why distributive equality matters (see, for example, the work of Richard J. Arneson, G. A. Cohen, and Ronald Dworkin).[1] For luck egalitarians, the idea of the moral equality of persons requires that each person take responsibility for her choices and assume the costs of these choices. Conversely, it holds that no one should be worse off just because of bad luck. For some luck egalitarians, the aim of a distributive principle is to counter the effects of luck on persons' opportunity for well-being (Arneson and, in a qualified way, Cohen); for others, the aim is to mitigate the effects of luck on the social distribution of goods and resources among persons (Dworkin). But however different luck egalitarians work out its implication, the intuitive idea that they all share is that persons should not be disadvantaged or advantaged simply on account of bad or good luck. As Cohen writes, "There is injustice in distribution when the inequality of goods reflects not such things as differences in the arduousness of different people's labors, or people's different preferences and choices with respect to income and leisure, but myriad forms of lucky and unlucky circumstance."[2] Put another way, distributive justice should be fundamentally choice-sensitive but luck-insensitive. This distinction between luck and choice is basic to the luck egalitarian position, and for convenience I will refer to it as the luck/choice principle.

A competing account of the value of equality may be broadly labeled "democratic equality" (see, for example, Elizabeth Anderson, Samuel Scheffler, Samuel Freeman, and John Rawls).[3] Democratic equality holds that the goal of a distributive principle is not so much to mitigate the effects of luck on people's life prospects as to establish and secure the requisite social relations that membership in a democratic society entails. Democracy presupposes an ideal of reciprocity between citizens, which I will refer to as "democratic reciprocity." Among other things, democratic reciprocity holds that citizens may support and impose on each other only those economic, social, and political institutional arrangements that all can reasonably accept. Because a social arrangement that allows for excessive economic and social inequalities between citizens will not be one that all can reasonably accept, democratic reciprocity must require (among other things) the regulation of such inequalities among citizens via a distributive principle. On this reading, distributive equality matters because of the underlying commitment to democratic reciprocity among members of a democratic order. The motivating aim of a distributive principle is to ensure that the gap between rich and poor does not exceed that permitted by the ideal of democratic reciprocity.[4]

It is important to note that the difference between luck egalitarianism and democratic equality is not that the former relies on the luck/choice distinction and the latter not at all. The defining difference is in how each invokes this distinction and the purpose for which it is invoked. For example, Rawls makes use of this distinction, as evinced by his well-known remarks that distributive justice is concerned with "contingencies" that affect persons' life prospects and that the distribution of goods in society should not be affected by factors that are "arbitrary from the moral point of view."[5] Yet this does not make Rawls a luck egalitarian because the luck/choice principle does not motivate his commitment to distributive equality. The commitment to equality is motivated by the ideal of democratic reciprocity in the way explained above. The luck/choice distinction is only subsequently appealed to by Rawls for the purpose of working out what the commitment to distributive equality entails, but it plays no role in explaining why such a commitment exists.[6] Luck egalitarianism, on the other hand, relies on the luck/choice principle to motivate the commitment to distributive equality. This is one important feature of luck egalitarianism that I will elaborate on below. The crucial difference between luck egalitarianism and democratic equality is properly appreciated only if we treat each to be responding specifically to the question "Why does distributive equality matter?"

There is a certain intuitive appeal to the luck egalitarian ideal that persons should not be disadvantaged simply because of bad luck. After all, if we accept the premise that individuals are equal moral agents, then it seems to follow that individuals can be held responsible only for outcomes that are due to their own choices but not for those due to circumstances over which they exercise no personal agential control. In recent debate, however, democratic egalitarians have argued that this intuitiveness of luck egalitarianism is only illusory, that on further investigation luck egalitarianism is in fact a rather implausible account of distributive equality. I will look at two classes of objections that stand out.

One line of objection is that luck egalitarianism has morally absurd implications.[7] Three types of cases are commonly forwarded to support this claim: one is that the luck/choice principle implies that persons suffering severely due to unwise choices of their own have no claim to social assistance at all; another is that luck egalitarianism has to treat all natural misfortunes as matters of justice and so matters for which persons should be socially compensated, which is absurd; the third is that luck egalitarianism, when it provides assistance to a person who has suffered bad luck, does so by disparaging the worth of that person's life.

The other class of criticism is that luck egalitarians have a mistakenly individualistic understanding of equality. In taking the central goal of distributive equality to be that of mitigating the effects of luck on people's life options, luck egalitarians, unlike democratic egalitarians, fail to appreciate the social dimension of equality and that the point of distributive equality is to ensure that persons are able to relate to each other as social equals.[8] The concern of distributive equality, which luck egalitarians allegedly miss, is not how persons fare individualistically with respect to their own good or bad luck, but how they stand in relation to each other as members of a just social order.

In defense of luck egalitarianism, I will argue that once the limited domain, the special subject matter, and specific justificatory purpose of luck egalitarianism are properly identified, these objections are deflected. I first outline an account of luck egalitarianism with respect to these features (section I); then I elaborate further on these features by addressing the objections that luck egalitarianism is morally implausible (section II) and wrongly asocial (section III). I conclude by highlighting the ways in which my account of luck egalitarianism, even as it departs from some extant accounts, is still significantly a luck egalitarian position (section IV).

No doubt a complete defense of luck egalitarianism will have to address other possible objections, as well as, very importantly, clarify its key idea of luck versus choice. Luck egalitarians are well aware of this, and there is a lively ongoing debate among luck egalitarians on what luck is and how to place the cut between luck and choice.[9] But for the purpose of getting the luck egalitarian position off the ground, there is sufficient agreement among egalitarians in general concerning the typical cases with which distributive justice is concerned as to whether luck or choice is determinant. For instance, most egalitarians would accept that a person who is worse off because she freely squandered opportunities presented to her is worse off due to her choice, whereas a person who is made worse off because of an unexpected illness or accident that she could not have reasonably avoided is worse off on account of bad luck. Or, to take another example, most egalitarians accept that the social class into which one is born is a matter of luck, whereas the offices or positions one acquires through ambition and hard work under conditions of fair equal opportunity can be credited to personal choice and effort. Moreover, it seems to me any plausible egalitarian theory must make use of the luck/choice distinction at some point in its account of distributive justice. It is hard to imagine a defensible theory of distributive justice, particularly one predicated on the capacity of individuals to make decisions and to take responsibility for these decisions, as liberal conceptions are, that does not recognize the difference between matters over which persons can exercise some meaningful choice and those that are beyond their control. As noted above, even though Rawls is not a luck egalitarian in that the mitigation of luck is not what motivates his egalitarian project, he nonetheless invokes the luck/choice distinction at a later stage in the construction of his theory of distributive justice. The philosophical responsibility to further refine and develop the luck/choice distinction is therefore not borne by luck egalitarians alone.

Still, since luck egalitarians take the luck/choice principle to be fundamental to their position, they have a special responsibility to make more precise the divide between choice and luck. I do not deny this. My twofold objective is to clarify other important features of luck egalitarianism that are less well examined, and to motivate continuing study and development of the luck egalitarian position by defending it against objections that it is deeply implausible, objections that, if left to stand, would render moot any effort at refining and developing the luck/choice principle.

I

I.A. Its Domain: Distributive Justice

First, concerning its operational domain, luck egalitarianism should be seen strictly as an account of *distributive justice*, or more precisely as a response to the question of why *distributive equality* matters. It should not be seen to be speaking for an account of justice broadly conceived, let alone an account of the whole of morality. Questions of distributive egalitarian justice are distinct from questions of assistance or rescue, and luck egalitarianism need not attempt to provide answers to questions about the conditions under which a person who is lacking urgent and basic needs is entitled to social assistance or rescue. Instead of claiming such a broad domain, luck egalitarianism should, and can, claim for itself a more limited domain of application. Its purpose is to explain and justify why distributive equality with respect to economic goods and burdens, over and above those that persons need for basic subsistence, is required as a matter of justice.

A social order in which all members' basic and urgent needs are accounted for will still have to decide how fairly to distribute social and economic resources among its members beyond what their basic needs demand. This is the distinct question of distributive justice, and in a productive social order it remains a morally salient one even when persons' basic needs are met, for there are fairer and less fair ways of distributing available economic benefits. Limiting luck egalitarianism to the domain of distributive justice therefore does not trivialize it. A theory of distributive justice aims to justify a particular distributive assignment, and egalitarian distributive justice will set limits on the inequalities between agents that would be admissible. As an account of distributive justice, luck egalitarianism is primarily concerned with this question, and it is only with regard to the distribution of resources in the space above the threshold of basic needs that the luck/choice principle is meant to take effect.[10] This does not mean that luck egalitarianism regards the provision of basic needs as morally insignificant. To the contrary, luck egalitarians can accept, as most egalitarians do, that the fulfillment of basic needs takes precedence over the commitment to distributive equality.[11] It only means that their luck/choice principle is not meant to provide guidance for cases involving basic needs.

This division of moral domains (for example, between that of distributive justice and that of humanitarian assistance) I am assuming is neither eccentric nor arbitrary, but is in fact a commonly accepted idea in contemporary moral philosophy. To take an example, Rawls in *The Law of Peoples* makes the distinction within his theory of international justice between the duty of assistance and the duty of distributive justice, each motivated by different considerations. The former (which he endorses) has as its target that of ensuring that all societies are able to support decent institutions of their own, and hence ceases when that threshold is met; the latter (which he rejects) seeks to regulate economic inequalities between societies and is thus ongoing.[12] Likewise, Thomas Nagel assumes a similar division when he argues that global justice includes a global duty of humanitarian assistance but not a global duty of distributive justice.[13] My point is that, assuming such a division, luck egalitarianism can be understood to apply only within the domain of distributive justice. Indeed, as we will see below, it is advantageous to understand the domain of luck egalitarianism in this limited way.

I.B. Its Subject Matter: Institutions Not Nature

Rawls writes that natural facts in themselves are neither just nor unjust; what is just or unjust is "the way the basic structure of society makes use of these natural differences and permits them to affect the social fortune of citizens, their opportunities in life, and the actual terms of cooperation between them."[14] On this view, social justice is principally concerned with the basic structure of society, that is, its main political and social institutions, and does not deal directly with natural facts as such. Luck egalitarianism, in my view, can and should accept this important point about the subject matter of social justice. Luck egalitarianism ought not to be in the business of mitigating all natural contingencies (due to luck) that people face. As an aspect of social justice, luck egalitarianism is only concerned with how institutions deal with such natural contingencies. Its goal is to ensure that institutions are not arranged so as to convert a natural trait (a matter of luck) into actual social advantages or disadvantages for persons. So only those natural contingencies that have such an institutional input fall within the scope of luck egalitarianism.

As a simple illustration, it is purely a matter of luck whether one is born with blue or brown eyes. Normally in our society, this contingency in itself does not raise questions of justice because our social institutions are not such that the color of one's eyes determines one's life opportunities. It follows that arbitrariness of eye color is not the sort of luck that exercises luck egalitarians. If, counterfactually, social institutions are designed such that persons with brown eyes are favored with more opportunities or resources and those with blue eyes discriminated against, a matter of luck has become a matter of justice. This is not, however, because one's eye color in itself is a matter of luck that demands the attention of luck egalitarians, but rather because institutions have, in this counterfactual, turned this natural fact into a matter of (in)justice. Luck egalitarians can sensibly say, in this imagined case, that the luck of people's eye color is a matter of justice and demand that institutions be reformed such that this natural fact does not disadvantage or advantage people. But they say this, again, because of how existing institutions are treating this contingency.[15]

Thus, it is the justice of institutions that remains the primary objective of luck egalitarians in that institutions should not be designed in ways that turn natural facts about persons into social advantages or disadvantages for them. This institutional focus is still a luck egalitarian position because it is fundamentally concerned with how institutions respond to matters of luck.

How broadly should we understand institutionally generated advantages and disadvantages? Do these include, say, the good luck of having good parents and the converse, the bad luck of having bad parents? The key here would be whether societal institutions are designed such that a person's luck with regard to her familial background affects her life prospects compared with others. In a society in which there is no decent and mandated public education (and assuming therefore that the educational prospects of its children are determined and limited very much by their particular familial culture and resources), and yet that is also set up such that persons with better education are better positioned to compete for better-paying jobs, the luck of familial background effectively results in social advantages or disadvantages for persons that are institutionally generated. This sensitivity to how the luck of family background affects persons' options significantly in a society governed by competitive market institutions is one reason that luck egalitarians would call for public education and other policies to ensure equality of opportunity in the public domain. Generalizing from the above example, I believe that given the wide and interconnecting reach of social institutions, many of the typical cases of social and economic inequalities that exercise egalitarians can be revealed to have an underlying institutional explanation.[16]

I.C. Its Justificatory Role: Why Distributive Equality Matters

Luck egalitarianism is specifically a response to the question "Why does distributive equality matter?" It is important to recognize that this is a distinct question from the questions "Equality of what?" and "How to distribute?"[17] Luck egalitarians are not forced to say, for example, that it is equality of welfare that is fundamental (which has to do with "Equality of what?"). This might be a tempting (though false) inference, because its concern with making up for a person's bad luck may suggest to its critics that luck egalitarianism is ultimately about making everyone equally happy within the constraints of their free choice, or making everyone feel equally lucky. But a luck egalitarian could just as well be concerned specifically that the social and economic resources that people have to pursue their ends not be distributed as luck dictates.[18] It is a further and distinct question as to whether luck egalitarians should be welfare egalitarians of some stripe or resource egalitarians, and so on. As mentioned in the opening of this essay, understanding luck egalitarianism specifically as a response to the question of "why equality matters" underscores what is really distinctive about it as compared to democratic equality.

To put the above comments in a more general way, the luck/choice principle of luck egalitarianism offers a grounding principle for distributive equality and not a substantive principle of distributive equality. By a substantive principle, I mean the implemented distributive principle that formulates the requirements of distributive justice. It specifies how to distribute what. To illustrate, Rawls's difference principle is a substantive principle (in my sense) in that it specifies how to distribute (that is, choose that arrangement that maximizes the situation of the worst off) and presumes a common metric of equality (that is, primary goods like income and wealth). The ideal of democratic reciprocity under democratic equality, in contrast, provides the grounding principle that motivates the commitment to equality that the difference principle is designed to meet. This grounding principle (which holds that equality matters because the gap between rich and poor cannot be greater than what reasonable persons in a reciprocal relationship can accept) does not by itself specify how to distribute what; the substantive principle does that. Similarly, under luck egalitarianism, the luck/choice principle provides the motivating grounds for a commitment to distributive equality. It holds that some distributive egalitarian commitment matters in order to regulate the impact of luck on a person's life chances via the interventions of institutions. This would in turn require the construction and implementation of some distributive principle to specify the form and content of that commitment. But this substantive principle is not given immediately by the luck/choice principle itself. Rather, it would have to be worked out through further interpretation of the luck/choice ideal, as well as considerations of the different candidates for the metric of equality on their own merits.[19]

Understanding luck egalitarianism to be primarily a grounding principle for distributive equality is important, as mentioned earlier, because it allows us to see what is really distinctive about it. Moreover, as we will see later, some of the challenges against the plausibility of luck egalitarianism mistakenly read it as a substantive principle of distributive equality and thereby unwarrantedly deride it for not doing what it is not meant to do.

Let me summarize the three features of the luck egalitarian position sketched out above. (a) Luck egalitarianism is an account of distributive justice and not the whole of justice or morality, and the luck/choice principle is meant to apply only within the special domain of distributive justice. (b) Its subject matter is the basic structure of society; its aim is to ensure that social institutions do not convert matters of luck into social advantages or disadvantages for persons. (c) Luck egalitarianism provides a grounding principle for distributive equality and is not itself the substantive distributive principle. That is, luck egalitarianism addresses the question "Why does distributive equality matter?," but it does not specify by itself how and what to distribute. I will elaborate more on these features of luck egalitarianism by addressing the objections against it in the next two sections.

II

I turn first to the criticism that luck egalitarianism is morally implausible. I will consider in turn the three cases put forward in defense of this charge. Along the way, I will take the opportunity to note how my account of luck egalitarianism differs from, but I believe improves on, some influential standard accounts.

II.A. Indifferent to the Severe Suffering of the Imprudent

According to critics, because of its luck/choice principle, luck egalitarianism is indifferent to the suffering of people whose plight is due to their own poor choices. But surely, the objection goes, a person who is in dire straits because of her own unwise choice is still entitled to rescue or assistance from the rest of society. People should not be left to perish just because of their imprudence. As Scheffler notes, "Most people do not insist, as a general matter, that someone who makes a bad decision thereby forfeits all claims to assistance."[20]

But my account of luck egalitarianism evades this objection. The objection attributes to luck egalitarianism a more spacious operative moral domain than luck egalitarians need to claim. Luck egalitarianism is an account of the grounds of distributive equality, and nothing about luck egalitarianism so understood rules out other moral considerations in favor of assisting or rescuing persons in dire straits. The luck/choice principle provides guidance for how resources and goods above the basic minimum people need are to be assigned, but it can defer to other principles when the case at hand falls under the domain of basic needs. Assuming a division of moral domains, luck egalitarians can easily accept arguments based on, say, basic rights: that persons deprived of basic needs retain a principled claim to assistance in spite of their own bad choices. These basic right considerations do not clash with the luck/choice principle that persons are to be held responsible for their choices because they apply within different domains.

In short, there are moral reasons for assisting persons in distress that are distinct from considerations of distributive justice. Principles of basic rights or human decency can require that a person deprived of basic needs be rescued or assisted, even if the deprivation was due to her own imprudence. The luck/choice principle, designed for the domain of distributive justice, does not kick in here to oppose considerations in favor of rescue.[21]

Thus, the objection that luck egalitarians neglect the imprudent in need of rescuing rests on a category mistake of sorts. It mistakenly applies the luck egalitarian principle to a category of cases (for example, cases of urgent and basic needs) to which it is not designed to apply. Not surprisingly, then, the principle is easily (but wrongly) shown to result in absurdity. The reductio objection has to invoke cases of severe deprivation (that luck egalitarians allegedly neglect) in order to demonstrate the alleged absurdity. Yet precisely because of this, the objection misses the target entirely. By shifting the discussion from that of distributive justice to that of basic needs, it changes the subject.

It is in fact curious that democratic egalitarians do not think that an *analogous reductio ad absurdum* could be turned against them. Critics of democratic equality can charge that democratic equality is counterintuitive because it is not responsive to the severe suffering of nonmembers of a democratic order. For instance, it seems compelled to say that foreigners deprived of basic needs are not entitled to any assistance at all from us since we do not stand in reciprocal democratic relation with them. To avoid this embarrassing implication, democratic egalitarians too must presuppose some division of moral domains, and stake the democratic equality principle only within the domain of distributive justice. They must accept something along the lines that although distributive equality commitments apply only among members of a democratic order, there are obligations based on other moral principles to meet the humanitarian needs of all persons.

It is true that some luck egalitarians give the impression that they intend the luck/choice principle to have a general across-the-board application, consequently implying that society has no obligation at all to persons suffering severely because of their own bad choices.[22] To be sure, this "hard-line" version of luck egalitarianism (as Anderson labels it[23]) concedes that luck egalitarianism allows for the withholding of any assistance from people in dire straits because of their poor choices, and accepts the onerous burden of explaining why this is not an absurdity. My contention is that it is not necessary for any luck egalitarian to assume this burden, nor should any want to. The core of the luck egalitarian doctrine and its distinctiveness as an account of the point of distributive equality can be preserved even as we confine the luck/choice principle to the domain of distributive justice (thus evading the charge of absurdity). Luck egalitarianism can be constructively interpreted in this more morally modest way without losing its important distinctiveness as an account of why distributive equality matters.

My account also deals with the problem of severe deprivation differently from Dworkin's luck egalitarianism. Dworkin, responding specifically to Scheffler's challenge, argues that on his egalitarian theory, people "deprived of urgent needs" because of their own decisions would not be left out in the cold, pace Scheffler, because "equal concern requires that everyone be given the benefit of a hypothetical insurance regime that would meet the 'urgent needs' [Scheffler] has in mind."[24] That is, rational and prudent individuals would want to insure themselves against being deprived of urgent needs (even as a result of their own poor choices), and so a just society should replicate the distributive allocation of an imaginary society in which persons have the means and option of taking out such an insurance policy. Thus, for Dworkin, a society has the collective responsibility to provide for persons thus deprived, and so contra Scheffler, a society regulated by luck egalitarian principles does not leave makers of bad choices to their dire fates.

As is clear, Dworkin responds to Scheffler's objection not by limiting the domain of the luck/choice principle (as my account does) but, on the contrary, by showing how the luck/choice principle, aided by his ideal of a hypothetical insurance market, can justify social support for the severely deprived unwise chooser. While Dworkin's approach has the advantage of unity—his luck egalitarianism aims to account for both cases of distributive justice and basic needs—its success turns on the success of his argument that his hypothetical insurance scheme can provide coverage for persons' basic needs even when the deprivation is due to personal choice.

Yet Dworkin's argument is contentious on his own terms, it seems to me, because on Dworkin's own understanding and description of the hypothetical insurance market, it is not obvious that persons will indeed have the benefit of such a policy. Though it is, plausibly, rational and prudent for persons to want to take up an insurance coverage against severe deprivation regardless of past choice, it is doubtful that it would be rational and prudent for any insurance provider to offer such a coverage, for this policy effectively guarantees the basic needs of persons with no consideration whatsoever of their personal conduct. Such coverage would be either too costly for insurance providers to offer, or, if insurance providers were to offer this coverage without loss, its premiums would be too high for the average rational person to want to purchase.

Considerations of what insurance policies providers in the hypothetical insurance market would find profitable and prudent to offer are hugely important to Dworkin's theory of egalitarian justice, for they are appealed to in order to set the upper limits on the levels of coverage that are available to individuals in his imaginary world. For example, in the hypothetical insurance market, there can be no policy guaranteeing a person a "movie star's wage" and no policy for "highly speculative and marginal" health care because, Dworkin argues, such policies will either be too expensive for rational persons to want to buy or too unprofitable for providers to want to sell.[25] Because these kinds of coverage would not be available for any rational person to purchase in the hypothetical insurance market, individuals in the real world will have no claim against society for such guarantees. Analogously, one can argue that an insurance policy guaranteeing people their basic needs without regard for their habitual conduct would not be available under Dworkin's hypothetical insurance market, and so in the real world individuals cannot have any claim against society to cover their basic needs without regard for their own past conduct. His insurance scheme, invented originally for the purpose of protecting persons against bad luck, cannot be extended to protect persons against their own detrimental bad choices, and hence does not successfully deflect Scheffler's challenge. My account of luck egalitarianism, even if not all-encompassing in the way that Dworkin's aspires to be, is able immediately and economically to deflect Scheffler's objection by appealing noncontroversially to the background division of moral domains and limiting the luck/choice ideal to the domain of distributive justice.[26]

II.B. Must Compensate for All Natural Misfortunes

Consider, next, the charge that luck egalitarianism is absurdly in the business of compensating individuals for any of their natural deficiencies. For example, Anderson argues that luck egalitarians will have counterintuitively to compensate ugly people who find their bad looks distressing, "perhaps in the form of publicly subsidized plastic surgery."[27]

But luck egalitarianism need not be committed to this kind of absurdity. First, as mentioned, luck egalitarianism is not necessarily a welfarist position. So just because a person scores poorly on a welfare scale because of his (real or perceived) bad luck of, say, being born ugly does not mean that luck egalitarians must compensate him for his lower welfare. A luck egalitarian who is an egalitarian about resources, for instance, will not be fazed by the person's ugliness so long as that person does not get less than his fair share of resources on account of his ugliness. So, at best, the objection strikes only luck egalitarians who are also welfare egalitarians.

In addition, a luck egalitarian need not be a resource egalitarian to escape this charge of absurdity.[28] There is a more generic point about luck egalitarianism that immunizes it against this charge independently of how luck egalitarians understand the currency of distributive equality. As mentioned, luck egalitarianism is not in the business of correcting for every natural misfortune that comes along; rather it can accept the institutional approach to social justice. Accordingly, what luck egalitarianism is concerned with is how institutions deal with matters of luck, not with luck per se. A person who is ugly may truly be unlucky, but luck egalitarians have nothing to say about this unless it were the case that social institutions were such that ugly people were in fact put at a social disadvantage.

We accept Anderson's intuition that it would be absurd to compensate people who are ugly because, or so we hope in any case, ordinary ugliness is not a natural trait that institutions in our society turn into actual social disadvantage for persons. Such people may be less happy, but this is not necessarily an issue of justice for distributive egalitarians. It would indeed be absurd if society were obliged to provide those who deem themselves ugly with publicly funded plastic surgery. On the other hand, our consideration of the matter would surely change if it were the case that society did disadvantage ugly people. In this case, luck egalitarians would take ugliness as a concern of justice and this would be far from absurd. They would want institutions and social norms about appearances to be reformed (through education, legislation); or if (counterfactually) social institutions could not help disadvantaging somewhat people perceived to be ugly, then they would want existing institutions to be supplemented by additional arrangements to compensate the ugly for their institutionalized disadvantage. Under this scenario, a matter of natural luck has, because of institutional intervention, become a matter of actual disadvantage and luck egalitarians would, and not absurdly so, be exercised by this, because of how institutions or background norms are treating this brute natural fact, and not because of people's ugliness per se. Yet this is still a staunchly luck egalitarian position because the concern is with how institutions handle the natural fortunes or misfortunes of persons.

Unlike Arneson's version of luck egalitarianism, which explicitly "*rejects* the idea that nature is not the concern of social justice,"[29] my account holds that it is how institutions handle nature that is the concern of social justice. On my approach, it is not "the natural fact that people are susceptible to disease, accident, and natural catastrophe" that social justice is concerned with, pace Arneson,[30] but the fact that social institutions are (often) designed such that diseases, accidents, or natural catastrophes translate into significant disadvantages for persons. It is not, for example, the fact that a coastal city has been unluckily devastated by a hurricane that is unjust; what is unjust is the lack of appropriate governmental anticipation, response, and reaction to the situation, which is an institutional failing.[31] My version of luck egalitarianism, which ties natural facts to institutions, preserves the attractive central intuition of luck egalitarians, like Arneson's, that the social disadvantages faced by, say, the unfortunate disabled person constitute an objectionable social injustice. Pace Arneson, however, the locus of this injustice lies not in nature or the cosmic order but in institutions—that is, in what institutions make of people's disabilities. My account, by maintaining an institutional focus, advantageously sidesteps the charge that luck egalitarians absurdly treat the natural order as a subject of social justice while preserving the core intuition of luck egalitarianism: namely, that persons should not be socially disadvantaged because of bad luck.

Some luck egalitarians will object that by limiting the range of luck egalitarian concerns to those cases of bad luck that have converted by institutions into advantages or disadvantages for persons, I have rendered luck egalitarianism insensitive to instances of bad luck that most luck egalitarians would find intuitively troubling.[32] But this challenge will have to present a case of bad luck that has no institutional influence but that is also not so devastating to the unlucky person such that it falls under the domain of basic needs, on the one side, and on the other, that is intolerable enough that egalitarians should be moved by it. For example, even if we can say that a person who has been unluckily blinded is now at a serious disadvantage independently of any institutional cause, my institutional account of justice can nonetheless accept that this person ought to be assisted on humanitarian grounds.

One might offer an example of a less debilitating misfortune, say, that of a person who is unluckily slightly shortsighted and so is at a slight disadvantage compared to others with normal sight. It is plausible, or at least grantable, that this person's disadvantage is not due to any institutional input; and it is plausible to hold that his misfortune is not so severe as to demand humanitarian assistance. So is my institutional luck egalitarian view defective because it seems unable to address this and other similar types of natural bad luck? Not necessarily, I would argue, for we have to ask, Is the slight handicap so intolerable that any egalitarian view that cannot account for it is thereby obviously flawed? In the case of shortsightedness, for instance, I do not think that it is immediately counterintuitive from the perspective of distributive justice to say that a society has no obligation of justice to provide corrective eyeglasses for people (who are not legally blind but simply have less than perfect eyesight). Now if it were the case that the afflicted person would go blind without special care, humanitarian considerations for assisting her would kick in. But it is far from obvious that the bad luck of having marginally poorer eyesight than others in society must entail some form of special social compensation, when eyeglasses are not so prohibitively expensive such that they would be out of reach for persons with the resources or opportunities that they ordinarily would have in an otherwise just society.

Indeed, finding a case of a disadvantage arising from bad luck that is preinstitutional, but that is not so severe as to tip over into the domain of basic needs and yet bad enough to intuitively move egalitarians may be harder to do than it seems. Still, I am prepared to grant that there might be such cases (so I am not denying that such cases can exist, but I am suggesting that they are possibly exceptions rather than the rule). Ultimately, the question for luck egalitarians proposing a transinstitutional approach (as I will call the approach that says natural bad luck in itself can be a matter of justice) is this: What is the alternative? Even if my institutional account leaves certain cases of bad luck outside the purview of justice (because there is no identifiable institutional cause), it seems to me preferable over transinstitutional approaches because the latter will have a hard time evading the Anderson-type challenge that luck egalitarians have to be absurdly compensating persons for all of their natural misfortunes.[33] In other words, the trade-off is between an institutional account like mine that potentially ignores some cases of bad luck but is immune to Anderson-type objections, on the one side, and, on the other, a transinstitutional approach that aspires to cover all instances of bad luck (independently of institutional influence) but precisely because of this also stands exposed to Anderson-type objections. Given that Anderson's objection would fatally convict luck egalitarianism of absurdity if it were to hit the mark, my institutional approach seems preferable overall.

II.C. Disrespectful of Victims of Bad Luck

Finally, consider the worry that luck egalitarianism is disrespectful of victims of bad luck. According to this worry, when luck egalitarians come to the aid of the unfortunate, the motivating premise is that the victim is living a life that is less worthwhile (due to her misfortune). Rather than expressing equal respect for persons, this reflects some kind of contempt, pity, or disrespect for the unlucky.[34]

From the preceding paragraphs, we have a ready response to this challenge. The objection falsely assumes that luck egalitarians must necessarily be egalitarians about welfare, and so has to impute to the unlucky a life that is going so poorly (perhaps even in spite of her own perception) as to be less worthy. If luck egalitarianism takes the form of a resource egalitarian position, however, then it need not make such judgments about the quality of a person's life. Rather, its concern is with persons' legitimate resource entitlements. Conceived as a form of resource egalitarianism, luck egalitarianism's central point is that persons' legitimate resource entitlement, as this is determined institutionally, should not be distorted by good or bad luck. This commitment to secure for persons their legitimate entitlements is a mark of equal respect for persons rather than a show of disrespect or contempt.

More fundamentally, the objection treats luck egalitarianism as if it were merely a theory of remedial justice, as about giving handouts and compensation to the unlucky. For example, Freeman argues that a basic problem with luck egalitarianism is that it is only a principle of redress and hence is a "truncated conception" of distributive justice. Distributive justice, Freeman notes, aims to regulate the background norms and rules of society that determine ownership and rightful entitlements; yet the luck/choice principle does not appear to do any of this but functions only to reallocate resources or goods from the lucky to the less lucky.[35] If luck egalitarianism were indeed only a principle of compensation or redress, a form of reallocation to the unlucky to help her weather her bad luck, one can understand why critics would think that it risks undermining the self-worth and self-respect of the unlucky recipients of assistance. It would seem that the assisted is not getting her due as a matter of distributive justice but is simply getting some aid out of compassion in light of her unlucky circumstance.

On the institutional account, however, luck egalitarianism is by design concerned with the institutional norms and background rules of society that establish who owns what. On the institutional reading, luck egalitarians do not want persons' distributive entitlements to be determined by institutions that assign resources to individuals according to natural and arbitrary facts about them. For example, institutions should not be structured such that persons born into wealth continue to gain social advantages, or that persons born disabled are socially disadvantaged because of certain institutional barriers. This is fundamentally a distributive concern and not merely a concern with redress. It is a commitment toward securing what Rawls refers to as "background justice," that is, the justness of "the background social framework within which the activities of associations and its individuals take place."[36] Thus luck egalitarianism does not judge an unlucky person's life to be less worthy and then proceed to compensate her for her poorer life out of pity, much less out of contempt. Rather it seeks to determine (and to protect) persons' rightful entitlements as a matter of justice. A just distributive arrangement, on its view, should reflect persons' efforts and choices but not their good or bad luck. Pace Freeman, the realization of this luck egalitarian commitment must require addressing all the complex questions of institutional design and background justice that Freeman rightly says distributive justice is concerned with, including "the specification of property rights and permissible economic relations, control of capital, limits on concentration of wealth, permissible uses of property" and so on.[37] Any reallocation of resources to the unlucky (who are disadvantaged under a given institutional arrangement) is really a case of adjusting the distributive assignment to better meet what justice antecedently requires.

The claim that luck egalitarianism only offers a principle of redress not only neglects the possibility of luck egalitarianism adopting an institutional focus. It is also, more basically, fueled by the tendency of treating the luck/choice principle, meant as a justificatory or grounding principle of distributive equality, as a substantive principle of distributive equality. As mentioned earlier, luck egalitarianism is specifically a response to the question "Why does distributive equality matter?" Its luck/choice principle is meant to motivate and ground the commitment to distributive equality and is not offered as a complete expression of what that commitment entails. What substantive principle of distributive justice the luck/choice principle does ground will be distinct from the grounding principle itself but has to be developed from the luck/choice principle, and this can take different forms depending on how the luck/choice divide is defined as well as how different egalitarians interpret the various desiderata of equality. Luck egalitarians such as Dworkin, Cohen, and Arneson have offered different attempts at developing a substantive theory of distributive justice from the luck/choice principle. Whatever the independent merits of each of these attempts, they do each propose a systematic regulation of the distributional institutions of society, as is rightly expected of any theory of distributive justice.

It is hardly surprising that the luck/choice principle on its own seems woefully incomplete if it is wrongly expected to provide a substantive principle of distribution when it is not meant to do so.

It is worth noting that the ideal of democratic reciprocity too does not spell out who is to own what, what the proper terms of ownership and rightful transfers should be, or other matters of background justice. All the ideal of democratic reciprocity tells us is that inequalities in society must be regulated so as to be reasonably acceptable to members of a democratic order and why this matters. Like luck egalitarians, democratic egalitarians must derive their substantive distributive principle from their ideal of reciprocity. Rawls's difference principle is only one proposed derivation from the ideal of reciprocity. Anderson, on the other hand, proposes a different substantive distributive ideal calling for "equalities across a wide range of capabilities."[38] Since the difference principle is a substantive principle, and the luck/choice principle a grounding principle, it is a category mistake to compare the two.[39] The appropriate comparison would be between the luck/choice principle and the ideal of democratic reciprocity, and here luck egalitarianism is no more incomplete than democratic equality. If luck egalitarianism is incomplete on this count, then so too is democratic equality.

III

According to the second line of criticism, luck egalitarians fail to appreciate the social aspect of equality and so have "lost touch with the reasons why equality matters to us."[40] Luck egalitarians are allegedly fixated on the notion of the equal moral worth of persons, failing thus to see that equality has to do crucially with the "structure and character" of personal relationships.[41] Yet the "purging of the influence of brute luck from human relations," Scheffler argues, is not the motivating point of distributive equality.[42] The point of equality is to ensure that relations among persons are of the sort that ought to be expressed in a society of equals. Similarly, Anderson argues that democratic equality is a "relational theory of equality: it views equality as a social relationship."[43] Unlike luck egalitarianism, Anderson points out, democratic equality has the objective of ensuring that relations between persons are nonhierarchical and nonoppressive.

But luck egalitarianism is not blind to the inherently social and relational quality of equality. On the contrary, it recognizes that the motivation of distributive justice is to secure the relationship among persons that best reflects their equal status vis-à-vis each other. Its luck/choice principle is not meant as an (asocial) alternative to the social account of equality but is rather an alternative interpretation of what social equality demands. Luck egalitarianism holds that to relate to each other as equals is to, among other things, hold one another accountable for our choices but not for our luck in matters of distributive justice. It is precisely because of the importance of maintaining a relationship of social equality among persons that luck egalitarians hold that a distributive arrangement should not be affected by luck. Indeed, if luck egalitarianism takes the institutional form I am recommending, and its task is acknowledged to be that of regulating the background social conditions of ownership, it cannot but have a social dimension.

Accordingly, we can see why the related criticism, that luck egalitarianism is unable to address pressing issues of social justice having to do with race, gender, and ethnicity because of its asocial character, is baseless.[44] First, in as far as luck egalitarianism (as I have suggested) is also primarily concerned with the basic institutions of society—the norms and background rules of society—it will have something to say about race, gender, and ethnicity in situations where the institutions of society discriminate against or privilege members of particular racial or ethnic groups or gender in the distribution of social and economic goods. Luck egalitarianism as an account of distributive justice surely can have something directly to say about such arbitrary advantaging or disadvantaging through institutional design of persons on account of their race, gender, or ethnicity. So in as far as oppressive social relationships are supported by norms of the basic structure of society that distribute goods and resources on the basis of arbitrary factors, luck egalitarians can directly criticize such oppressive relationships.

Second, luck egalitarianism as an account of distributive justice does not deny that issues of race, gender, and ethnicity can raise important questions of political justice, distinct from the impact of such political injustices on the justness of economic distribution. Luck egalitarians focus on distributive equality not because they think "equality is inherently a distributive notion," contra Scheffler,[45] or that distributive equality exhausts the entire domain of equality and nothing else matters, but because social equality has an inherent distributive dimension that has to be addressed. Indeed, it is this specific dimension of equality that luck egalitarianism is designed to address. As mentioned, luck egalitarianism is best seen as a claim about the grounds of distributive justice, not about the whole of justice (which includes political justice). Luck egalitarians, on my account, can agree with its critics, like Scheffler and Anderson, that "the basic reason it [equality] matters to us is because we believe that there is something valuable about human relationships that are, in certain crucial respects at least, unstructured by differences of rank, power, or status."[46] What luck egalitarianism, as I understand it, offers is an interpretation of what such a relationship ought to consist in with respect to economic or distributive justice. That its luck/choice principle is designed to deal mainly with issues of distributive justice does not mean, though, that luck egalitarians must treat political justice as secondary or unimportant.

There is a sense, however, in which democratic equality is social where luck egalitarianism is not. A democratic society is understood as a fair system of social cooperation between free and equal members, and for democratic egalitarians it is in this context of fair social cooperation that the ideal of democratic reciprocity applies and where distributive egalitarian considerations can take hold.[47] Only persons engaged in fair social cooperation are in the position rightly to demand from one another certain classes of commitments, including the commitment of distributive equality. That is, only persons thus reciprocally related can ask that inequalities between themselves be those that all can reasonably accept, and that a distributive principle be collectively endorsed to regulate inequalities in light of this criterion. Thus, for democratic egalitarians, the value of distributive equality applies only among persons who see themselves as participants in a fair system of social cooperation, which is how a democratic society is to be conceived. Luck egalitarians, on the other hand, disengage the value of distributive equality from that of social cooperation in that they do not take social cooperation to be a necessary condition of distributive justice commitments. On my institutional approach, the existence of social engagement via institutions, when these institutions have the effect of transforming natural facts about persons into social advantages or disadvantages, is sufficient to trigger distributive egalitarian commitments. That these are not institutions based on social cooperation is beside the point.

What is important to note is that this denial that distributive equality matters only in the context of social cooperation is not a denial that distributive equality is a social ideal. Certainly it does not mean that distributive justice cannot have as its end that of regulating social relations between persons through the institutional structures of a social order against which they interact. It does not even mean that social cooperation is insignificant for luck egalitarians, for they can very well accept that fair social cooperation is a necessary means of realizing the ends of distributive equality, and demand that cooperative social institutions be established for this sake. Social cooperation is only one form of social engagement, and luck egalitarians deny that distributive equality is of value only among persons already participating in fair social cooperation. Rather than suggesting a mistakenly asocial conception of equality, this rejection of social cooperation as a necessary precondition of distributive justice shows that luck egalitarians have a more inclusive view of the "social" to which distributive justice commitments apply.

That luck egalitarianism takes distributive equality to be of value independently of the practice of fair social cooperation is not by itself a mark against it, for this is the very point of the debate: Why does equality matter, and in what social context does it matter? Does it matter only among persons engaged in fair social cooperation, or does it matter independently of the fact of social cooperation? Of course, I have not settled this issue here; my aim is only to preserve luck egalitarianism as a serious contender in this ongoing and important debate on the value of distributive equality.

IV

The luck egalitarian position I have outlined, even though it departs in some respects from well-known extant accounts, is still significantly a luck egalitarian position and distinct from democratic equality. First, even though it is limited to the domain of distributive justice, within that specific domain it takes the luck/choice principle to be fundamental. Second, even though it takes the subject matter of distributive justice to be social institutions rather than natural facts, it is still a luck egalitarian position in that it holds that institutions ought not to turn natural contingencies into social advantages or disadvantages. Third, it offers a different grounding for distributive equality from democratic equality, and hence specifies the conditions under which distributive equality matters quite differently. For convenience, I will label my account institutional luck egalitarianism.

The elementary difference between democratic equality and luck egalitarianism is preserved on my institutional account. As mentioned, democratic equality takes distributive equality to matter only when democratic reciprocity also matters. Institutional luck egalitarianism, in contrast, takes distributive equality to matter whenever there are common institutional arrangements that confer differential advantages to persons on account of arbitrary facts about them. That is, distributive egalitarian commitments are activated, on the institutional luck egalitarian view, when there are affective institutions that convert natural facts about persons into disadvantages for them. It is immaterial whether or not these are institutions based on democratic ideals.

A consequence of this difference lies in how each position understands the scope or reach of distributive equality. For democratic egalitarians, distributive equality is by definition confined to the social setting where the ideal of democratic reciprocity applies. Thus, while distributive equality clearly matters within the borders of a democratic society, it is not immediately the case that it also matters beyond these borders. For the luck egalitarian, distributive equality has potentially wider application in that it is not confined to the context of a democratic order but can take hold wherever there are effective institutional arrangements in place.

One obvious arena where this difference over scope has potentially important normative implications is in international relations. For democratic egalitarians, the case for global distributive equality, if it can be made at all, is going to be indirect. It will depend on a successful demonstration that the ideal of democratic reciprocity applies globally among persons across state boundaries even in the absence of a democratic global political society. It is not coincidental that in the current debate on global justice, many democratic egalitarians tend to be skeptical of the ideal of global distributive justice.[48]

Luck egalitarians, on the other hand, can argue for global distributive equality more directly. If matters of luck such as a person's place of birth and the distribution of the world's natural resources result in differential life chances for persons, then there ought to be some global distributive commitment to offset the effects of such arbitrary factors. Conversely, it is not surprising that many defenders of global distributive equality subscribe to some luck egalitarian premises.[49] To be exact, on my institutional account, the luck egalitarian will have to refer not just to natural facts about the world and its inhabitants as such, but also point out how global institutions have pervasively turned these facts into actual advantages for some and disadvantages for most. But the case for global distributive equality is still direct, even on the institutional view, in this sense: there is no need to justify global distributive equality by appealing to another value such as the ideal of democratic reciprocity. It is enough to show that there is a global institutional order that impacts persons' lives profoundly and pervasively, specifically by translating natural arbitrary conditions of the world into highly differential life chances for individuals.

How we understand why equality matters has important real world normative ramifications (and the reference to global justice is just one, though very poignant, example). Luck egalitarianism, if it is a correct account of why equality matters, will provide a very powerful case for global distributive equality. Some critics of global distributive equality have proceeded by exposing the luck egalitarian premises in some prominent arguments for global egalitarianism.[50] But if luck egalitarianism is a plausible account of why equality matters, as I have aimed to show here, and is therefore worthy of further philosophical examination and engagement, then its potential as a grounding for global distributive equality should also be further explored and developed and not be too quickly dismissed.

Notes

1. Richard J. Arneson, "Equality and Equal Opportunity for Welfare," *Philosophical Studies* 56 (1989): 77–93, and "Luck Egalitarianism and Prioritarianism," *Ethics* 110, 2 (2000): 339–349; G. A. Cohen, "On the Currency of Egalitarian Justice," *Ethics* 99 (1989): 906–944; Ronald Dworkin, *Sovereign Virtue* (Cambridge, MA: Harvard University Press, 2000), and "Equality, Luck, and Hierarchy," *Philosophy and Public Affairs* 31, 2 (2003): 190–206. See also Philippe Van Parijs, *Real Freedom for All* (New York: Oxford University Press, 1995); and Will Kymlicka, "Liberal Equality," in *Contemporary Political Philosophy*, edited by Will Kymlicka (New York: Oxford University Press, 1990), 50–94.

2. G. A. Cohen, *If You're an Egalitarian, How Come You're So Rich?* (Cambridge, MA: Harvard University Press, 2000), 130.

3. Elizabeth Anderson, "What Is the Point of Equality?," *Ethics* 109, 2 (1999): 287–337; Samuel Scheffler, "What Is Egalitarianism?," *Philosophy and Public Affairs* 31, 1 (2003): 5–39, and "Choice, Circumstances, and the Value of Equality," *Politics, Philosophy, and Economics* 4, 1 (2005): 5–28; Samuel Freeman, "Rawls and Luck Egalitarianism," in his *Justice and the Social Contract* (New York: Oxford University Press, 2007), 111–142. See also John Rawls, *Justice as Fairness: A Restatement*, edited by Erin Kelly (Cambridge, MA: Harvard University Press, 2001), for example, 130–133.

Anderson explicitly refers to her alternative to luck egalitarianism as "democratic equality" (see Chapter 2 of this book). Scheffler calls his account the "social and political ideal of equality," which treats distributive equality as grounded on the more fundamental concern for the equal status of democratic citizens ("What Is Egalitarianism?," 22–23, and "Choice, Circumstances, and the Value of Equality," 8). For Rawls, "democratic equality properly understood requires something like the difference principle" (*Justice as Fairness*, 49). I thus use the term "democratic equality" broadly to refer to these accounts of the point of equality. Rawls is sometimes perceived as a luck egalitarian (see, for example, Susan Hurley, *Justice, Luck, and Knowledge* [New York: Cambridge University Press, 2003]), but for discussions why Rawls is not a luck egalitarian, see Freeman, "Rawls and Luck Egalitarianism"; and Scheffler, "What Is Egalitarianism?," 24–31.

4. As Rawls puts it, one reason for "being concerned with inequality in domestic society" is to ensure that the gap between rich and poor "not be wider than the criterion of reciprocity allows" (John Rawls, *The Law of Peoples* [Cambridge, MA: Harvard University Press, 1998], 114; see also *Justice as Fairness*, 49, 124).

5. Rawls, *Justice as Fairness*, 55, 130; John Rawls, *A Theory of Justice*, rev. ed. (Cambridge, MA: Harvard University Press, 1999), 63.

6. This observation about Rawls has also been made by Andrea Sangiovanni, "Global Justice, Reciprocity, and the State," *Philosophy and Public Affairs* 35, 1 (2007): 3–39, at 26–28.

7. Anderson, "What Is the Point of Equality?," 296. Scheffler calls luck egalitarianism "morally implausible"—see "What Is Egalitarianism?," 17ff, and "Choice, Circumstances, and the Value of Equality," 14–16.

8. Anderson, "What Is the Point of Equality?," 313–314; Scheffler, "What Is Egalitarianism?," 21–22; and Freeman, "Rawls and Luck Egalitarianism," 132–135.

9. See, for example, the debate between Cohen, "On the Currency of Egalitarian Justice," and Dworkin, *Sovereign Virtue*, chap. 7, on where to draw "the cut" between luck and choice, and (hence) what the appropriate metric of equality ought to be. See also Arneson, "Equality and Equal Opportunity for Welfare"; Michael Otsuka, "Luck, Insurance, and Equality," *Ethics* 113 (2002): 40–54; Kasper Lippert-Rasmussen, "Equality, Option Luck, and Responsibility," *Ethics* 111 (2001): 548–579; Peter Vallentyne, "Equality, Brute Luck, and Initial Opportunities," *Ethics* 112 (2002): 529–557; and Martin Sandbu, "On Dworkin's Brute-Luck–Option-Luck Distinction and the Consistency of Brute-Luck Egalitarianism," *Politics, Philosophy, and Economics* 3, 3 (2004): 283–312. See Thomas Nagel, "Moral Luck," in his *Mortal Questions* (New York: Cambridge University Press, 1995), 24–38, for a nuanced discussion of the problem of luck in moral philosophy as a whole.

10. One could argue that duties of humanitarianism are duties of justice of sorts, or even duties of distributive justice given that some distribution of goods is involved in humanitarian cases. But I may leave aside this interesting conceptual question about the expansiveness of justice. For my present purpose, we need accept only that the duty to assist someone out of humanitarian concern has different objectives and imposes substantially different demands on agents compared with the duty to regulate inequalities between persons. Call these classes of duties what we want; my claim here is that the luck/choice principle is a principle intended for the latter category of duty. I am grateful to G. A. Cohen for helpful questions on this point.

11. For example, Rawls points out that his account of social justice presupposes some prior principle of basic needs, "at least insofar as their [basic needs] being met is necessary for citizens to understand and to be able to fruitfully exercise those rights and liberties"—*Political Liberalism* (New York: Columbia University Press, 1993), 7. See also Rawls, *The Law of Peoples*, 35, 38, 65.

12. Rawls, *The Law of Peoples*, 38, 65, 113–115. And recall that Rawls holds that some basic-needs principle is lexically prior to his two principles of justice, as noted above.

13. Thomas Nagel, "The Problem of Global Justice," *Philosophy and Public Affairs* 33, 2 (2005): 113–147, at 118. More generally, see Thomas Nagel, "The Fragmentation of Value," in *Mortal Questions*, 128–141.

14. John Rawls, "Kantian Constructivism in Moral Theory," in *Collected Papers*, edited by Samuel Freeman (Cambridge, MA: Harvard University Press, 1999), 303–358, at 337.

15. Some luck egalitarians reject the special institutional focus. See Cohen, *If You're an Egalitarian, How Come You're So Rich?* But Cohen's rejection of the institutional approach is not due uniquely to luck egalitarian considerations but to a more general skepticism of the view that personal choice within the rules of just institutions is not a direct concern of justice. I discuss Cohen's position in "Justice and Personal Pursuits," *Journal of Philosophy* 101, 7 (July 2004): 331–361.

16. Perhaps one could make the argument that to the extent that all human social institutions are set up on some presumptive notion of normal human functioning or capability, then persons who unluckily deviate from the ideal of normalcy are, in most cases, inevitably disadvantaged by institutions designed for the average person. For example, our society takes stairs rather than ramps to be the operative norm, thereby disadvantaging persons in wheelchairs if no alternative arrangements are also put in place. Given that disabled persons also have a share in our public space, when the majority puts in place an arrangement that limits their mobility, there is an institutional injustice against the disabled. I suspect that many kinds of natural ailments affecting persons can be shown to have an institutionally derived disadvantage in this way, and hence can move luck egalitarians to action. But what about natural disadvantages that are not institutionally influenced but still present a handicap to the unlucky person? I will comment on this in section II.B.

17. Amartya Sen, "Equality of What?" in his *Inequality Reexamined* (Cambridge, MA: Harvard University Press, 1992), 12–30.

18. Anderson's discussion in "What Is the Point of Equality?," 331–334, seems to me to be a critique of luck egalitarianism via a critique of equality of welfare. For example, Anderson writes that luck egalitarianism, or "equality of fortune," has to rely controversially on "subjective measures of welfare or the worth of personal assets" (333) and that luck egalitarians would want to compensate deaf people for their "less happy" lives (332–333). Anderson's target luck egalitarian here is Arneson.

19. Thus, see the debate among luck egalitarians such as Dworkin, Cohen, and Arneson, and also Sen, concerning what Cohen calls the "currency of egalitarian justice." My point is not that there is no right answer to the "Equality of what?" question within the luck egalitarian perspective, but that the starting premise of luck egalitarianism in itself does not directly furnish an answer.

20. Scheffler, "Choice, Circumstance, and the Value of Equality," 15. See also Anderson, "What Is the Point of Equality?," 303–307.

21. It is plausible that a person's basic needs entitlement could be overridden by other considerations under conditions of abject scarcity where trade-offs have to be made. A society may be compelled to provide the absolutely scarce resource to one who has suffered bad luck rather than to another who is equally devastated but is so because of a poor decision freely made. But contra hard-line luck egalitarians, to justify this particular allocation we do not need to say that the person who has made a bad choice has forfeited all claims to social assistance. We can say that this person is still entitled to basic assistance as a matter of principle but that under this pressing circumstance that entitlement cannot be met (but is not in-

validated). On my limited-domain account, the maker of a bad choice retains her principled claim to basic needs even if this principled claim cannot always be satisfied. So it is possible to allow choice to play some role when basic needs trade-offs must be made, but we do not need to adopt the "hard-line" view that the person who has chosen unwisely forfeits as a matter of principle all claims to social assistance. I presume here Dworkin's well-known point that principles can be overridden without being invalidated—see his *Taking Rights Seriously* (Cambridge, MA: Harvard University Press, 1976), 25–27.

22. See, for example, Eric Rakowski, *Equal Justice* (New York: Oxford University Press, 1991), 153.

23. Anderson, "What Is the Point of Equality?," 298.

24. Ronald Dworkin, "Equality, Luck, and Hierarchy," 192.

25. Dworkin, *Sovereign Virtue*, 88–98, 345.

26. In a recent paper, Shlomi Segall defends luck egalitarianism against Scheffler-type objections by presenting the luck/choice principle as a defeasible principle, that is, as a principle that can be overridden by other moral principles—"In Solidarity with the Imprudent," *Social Theory and Practice* 33, 2 (2007): 177–198. On Segall's account there is no need to limit the luck/choice principle to the domain of distributive justice; it can still apply across the board to cases of basic needs as well as distributive justice so long as it can be overridden also across the board. But this approach rescues luck egalitarianism by weakening its status throughout, and so is a Pyrrhic victory. The significance and distinctiveness of luck egalitarianism as an account of equality are eliminated, if even in the domain of distributive justice, the luck/choice principle is defeasible. Indeed one can imagine the trumping principle being that of democratic reciprocity, in which case Segall's defeasible luck egalitarianism simply collapses into democratic equality. My approach, contrarily and advantageously, maintains the primacy of the luck/choice principle within the domain of distributive justice.

27. Anderson, "What Is the Point of Equality?," 335.

28. Thus though I am partial to resource egalitarianism, my defense of luck egalitarianism in this essay is ultimately agnostic on the currency of equality.

29. Arneson, "Luck Egalitarianism and Prioritarianism," 346, my emphases.

30. Ibid.

31. One might object that the failing here is the failure of institutions not rectifying or responding to a natural calamity, rather than that of institutions turning a natural event into a disadvantage, and so is not institutional in the way I am proposing. In reply, I would say that the injustice in this case is the injustice of institutions not responding adequately, and this is an institutional injustice because members of a society have the legitimate expectation that the state will respond adequately within reason to such events. To fail to do so in a particular case is to allow a natural bad luck, the hurricane in this example, to affect people's lives adversely through an institutional neglect contrary to expectation, and this is an institutional injustice because we hold that institutions should not fail persons in society in this arbitrary way. I thank G. A. Cohen for raising this challenge.

32. The following is due to a question posed by Cohen. The eyeglasses example below is his.

33. The transinstitutional luck egalitarian might say that ugliness need not be a social disadvantage at all, unlike myopia, and so need not be a concern of distributive justice, thus avoiding the alleged absurdity. But it seems to me that we cannot properly understand how a condition is a social advantage or disadvantage without reference to how institutions handle these conditions, in the same way that we do not know what persons' natural talents are worth without reference to existing economic institutions that determine the "economic rent" of particular natural talents.

34. Anderson, "What Is the Point of Equality?," 302–307. See also Jonathan Wolff, "Fairness, Respect, and the Egalitarian Ethos," *Philosophy and Public Affairs* 27, 2 (1998): 97–122, at 109–112.

35. Freeman, "Rawls and Luck Egalitarianism," 135 and see 132–135. See also Freeman, *Justice and the Social Contract*, 305–308.

36. Rawls, *Justice as Fairness*, 10; Freeman, "Rawls and Luck Egalitarianism," 131.

37. Freeman, "Rawls and Luck Egalitarianism," 135.

38. Anderson, "What Is the Point of Equality?," 377.

39. Freeman offers this comparison in "Rawls and Luck Egalitarianism," 131.

40. Scheffler, "What Is Egalitarianism?," 23.

41. Ibid., 33.

42. Ibid.

43. Anderson, "What Is the Point of Equality?," 313.

44. See Scheffler, "What Is Egalitarianism?," 38; and Anderson, "What Is the Point of Equality?," 312–313.

45. Scheffler, "What Is Egalitarianism?," 28n26.

46. Scheffler, "Choice, Circumstances, and the Value of Equality," 17.

47. For discussion on the idea of a democratic society regarded as a fair system of social cooperation and how fair social cooperation grounds distributive commitments, see Freeman, *Justice and the Social Contract*, 319–320; Scheffler, "Choice, Circumstances, and the Value of Equality," 18; and Rawls, *Justice as Fairness*, 133, also 6.

48. See, for example, Rawls, *The Law of Peoples*; Nagel, "The Problem of Global Justice"; Freeman, "Distributive Justice and the Law of Peoples," in *Justice and the Social Contract*; Joseph Heath, "Rawls on Global Distributive Justice: A Defense," *Canadian Journal of Philosophy*, supplementary volume 31 (2005): 193–226; and Sangiovanni, "Global Justice, Reciprocity, and the State." For an attempt to defend global distributive equality on democratic egalitarian terms, see Charles Beitz, "Does Global Inequality Matter?," *Metaphilosophy* 32, 1–2 (2001): 95–112. I also consider this possibility in "The Boundary of Justice and the Justice of Boundaries," *Canadian Journal of Law and Jurisprudence* 19, 2 (2006): 319–344.

49. For two key examples, see Charles Beitz, *Political Theory and International Relations*, 2nd ed. (Princeton, NJ: Princeton University Press, 1999), part III; and Thomas Pogge, *Realizing Rawls* (Ithaca, NY: Cornell University Press, 1989), part III.

50. See, for example, Freeman, *Justice and the Social Contract*, 287, 309; Heath, "Rawls on Global Distributive Justice," 205–207; and Sangiovanni, "Global Justice, Reciprocity, and the State," 22–25.

Discussion Questions: Equality

1. Should all inequalities be redressed, whether due to luck or choice? Is the distinction between the two clear?
2. Is equality only among those who are members of the same society an appropriate ideal?
3. What does Tan mean by an institutional view of egalitarianism?

Part II

JUSTICE

Rawls famously declared that justice is the "first virtue" of social institutions. By this assertion he meant that an unjust institution should be rejected, no matter how successful it may be in other respects. Even if we accept Rawls's claim, questions remain about the nature of justice.

G. A. Cohen is a sharp critic of Rawls's conception of justice. He finds fault with both Rawls's methodology and his idea that principles of justice should apply only to the basic institutions of society. Holding that principles of justice should *not* be understood as the outcome of a rational decision in the original position, he argues that principles of justice should be understood to apply to society as such, not simply to its basic institutions. Cohen argues that justice calls for a socialist society based on a robust conception of equality. David Miller similarly examines the idea that the requirements of justice primarily apply to social institutions rather than to relations among people as such. Miller argues that the requirements of justice apply to persons who share the relevant social institutions and relationships. Amartya Sen challenges the prevailing idea that principles of justice should be concerned with the way in which *resources* are distributed in society. Arguing against both Rawls and Dworkin, Sen holds that justice should be focused on the distribution of basic human *capabilities*.

READING

4

Rescuing Justice from Constructivism and Equality from the Basic Structure Restriction

G. A. COHEN

This essay concatenates excerpts from my book called *Rescuing Justice and Equality*.[1] The first two sections of the essay correspond to the distinct rescues indicated by that book title. Section 1 pursues the rescue of justice from constructivism. It is about the *identity* of justice. Section 2 pursues the rescue of equality from the basic structure restriction. It is about the *scope* of justice. The identity question is at issue in an argument that I present against the Rawlsian identification of justice with the principles that constructivist selectors select. The scope question is at issue in an argument that I present against the Rawlsian restriction of the application of principles of distributive justice to the basic structure of society. The two Rawlsian positions (on identity and on scope) here under criticism are, as I shall explain, mainly in a very brief section 3, substantially independent of each other, and so, too, as will be seen, are my arguments against them.

1. Rescuing Justice from Constructivism

In its most general description, constructivism is the view that a principle gains its normative credentials through being the product of a sound selection procedure. But I am not concerned in this essay with constructivism in its entirely general form. I am concerned with, precisely, the constructivist approach to social justice in particular, which is constructivism understood as characterized in general terms above, but with two differentiating features. First, social justice constructivism is applied to the identification of, in particular, fundamental (or "first") principles of social justice, fundamental principles being ones that are not derived from other principles.[2] Second, it proceeds by putting and answering the question "What rules of governance are to be adopted for our common social life?" Unless otherwise indicated, I shall mean all that by "constructivism" here.

A leading example of the constructivist procedure, so understood, is John Rawls's use of the original position to determine the nature of justice, and that is the constructivism that I shall have centrally in view. But the broad outline of my critique of Rawlsian constructivism also applies, mutatis mutandis, to Scanlonian contractarianism, to Gauthier's contractarianism, and to Ideal Observer theory, where each is recommended as a procedure for identifying what justice, in particular, is.

I argue in what follows that the constructivist approach to social justice mischaracterizes justice *both* because it treats justice as sensitive to *certain sorts of facts* *and* because it fails to distinguish between justice and other virtues. The two errors reflect the single disfigurement by that constructivism from which I seek to rescue justice, and that is constructivism's identification of principles of justice with the optimal set of principles to live by, all things considered. My objection to that identification is that, simply because they *are* the *all*-things-considered best principles to live by, optimal all-things-considered principles are not necessarily the best principles considered from the point of view of justice alone. I argue that the constructivist approach to social justice is, for that particular, and transparently simple, reason, misguided.

Social justice constructivism's misidentification of principles of justice with optimal principles of regulation is dictated by the question that it puts to its privileged selectors of principles. *They* are not asked to say what *justice* is: it is we who ask that question, and the constructivist doctrine is that the answer to *our* question is the answer to the different question that is put to constructivism's specially designed selectors, which is, What rules of social regulation would you choose? My generative criticism of constructivism is that the answer to that question need not, and could not, be the same as the answer to the question "What is justice?"

I should acknowledge here a distinction among constructivisms that is of the first importance philosophically but that is not engaged within my proceedings. In one form of constructivist view, what it *is* for a principle to be valid is that it is the product of some favored constructivist procedure. In a contrasting but still constructivist view, the favored constructivist procedure merely (in some or other way) *makes* the principles it selects valid, but the view does not say that its-having-been-produced-by-the-favored-procedure is what it *is* for a principle to be valid.[3] The stated distinction is at the pinnacle of metaethics, a pinnacle that my discussion does not reach. My question is whether its being the product of a favored procedure for choosing the general rules for social existence establishes that a principle is one of justice, whether or not those who think so think it because they *also* think that they are describing what is, in a principle, the very property of validity itself when they lay out what their favored procedure is.

Finally, let me point out, before I proceed, that the question of the primacy of the basic structure as a site of justice is not to the fore in the present critique of constructivism. My critique is of *how* constructivism selects principles of justice, and not, here, of what I conceive to be, and what I shall later argue is, an independent and unjustified restriction on the *scope* of principles of justice that Rawls and the Rawlsians enforce. If constructivists were to allow that the principles of justice that their procedure generates apply to government and citizens alike, if they imposed no restriction to the basic structure of the *scope* of social justice, then they would remain constructivists, and they would remain open to the challenge that I raise in section 1 of this essay.

My critique of constructivism rests upon two distinctions. The first is the exclusive but not exhaustive distinction between (a) fundamental normative principles, that is, normative principles that are not derived from *other* normative principles, and (b) principles of regulation or, as I have preferred to say, *rules* of regulation, whether they be those rules that obtain by order of the state or those that emerge within the milder order of social norm formation: income tax rules are state rules of regulation, and rules about what we owe to each other beyond the realm of state force, such as the rules that govern (or misgovern) the battle of the sexes, are nonstate rules of regulation.[4] (The distinction is not exhaustive because there exist derivative normative principles that are not rules of regulation.)[5] We *create*, we *adopt*, rules of regulation to order our affairs: we adopt them in the light of what we expect the effect of adopting them to be. But we do not in the same sense of "adopt" adopt our fundamental principles any more than we adopt our beliefs about matters of fact. (Or, indeed, our sentiments: my denial that we adopt our normative principles does not require a cognitivist view of ethics.)

Our fundamental principles represent our convictions. They are not things that we *decide* to have and that we consequently work to install or instill and sustain; we do not proceed with them as we do with rules of regulation. We do not decide what to believe, whether about fact or about value and principle, in the light of what we expect the effect of believing it to be. The adoption of rules of regulation is a practical task; the formation of conviction and attitude is not. It is our principled convictions that justify what we do, and that includes the doing that is adopting rules of regulation.

The question "What are the rules of regulation that govern society?" is a sociological question, whereas the question "What rules of regulation ought to govern society?" is a philosophical question, or, if you prefer, a question in political theory, because the answer to that second question depends strongly on general social facts. The question "What is justice?" is a philosophical question, and there is no coherent question of the form "What ought justice, or the principles of justice, to be?" The incoherence of that question reflects the status of justice as something that transcends rules of regulation.[6]

In further illustration of the confusion of levels that is to be avoided between fundamental principles and rules of regulation, consider an analogous, and, indeed, closely connected, possible confusion regarding rights. Some doctors who are educated at state expense take their services abroad. We may deplore that, but on grounds of freedom we may be loath to restrict their ability to do so. And we may grant that freedom consistently with thinking that the doctors behave unfairly and unjustly when they do what we believe they should be granted the freedom to do. But, and this is my key point here, we need not think that the doctors we educate should be free to go abroad *because* they have a *right* to go abroad. What we rather think is that they *should* have a right to go abroad *because* they should be free to go abroad. But the rights that doctors, or anybody else, *should have* are, transparently, not (necessarily) rights that they (just) have. The first are legal rights, the second not. The example shows that we cannot determine what rights people have, in the fundamental nonlegal sense, on the basis of what legal rights they *should* have. Deriving the content of justice from that of the optimal rules of regulation is, similarly, traveling in the wrong direction.

Let me now add to the distinction between fundamental principles and rules of regulation a simpler distinction: between justice and other values and therefore between (c) principles that express or serve the value of justice and (d) principles that express or serve other values, such as human welfare or human self-realization or the promotion of knowledge. (In the senses that I intend here of the forthcoming emphasized words, fundamental principles *express* values and rules of regulation *serve* them by serving the principles that express them.)

Now, Rawlsians believe that the correct answer to the question "What is justice?" is identical to the answer that specially designed choosers, the denizens of the Rawlsian original position, would give to the question "What general rules of regulation for society would you choose in your particular condition of knowledge and ignorance?" Their answer to *that* question is supposed to give us the fundamental principles of justice. But in thus identifying justice with rules of regulation, Rawlsians breach *both* of the distinctions that were drawn above.

The present charge is not a criticism of the particular device, that is, the original position, that Rawls employs to *answer* the question, namely, "What rules should we choose?," that the denizens of the original position answer. Mine is not a criticism of the original position device *as* a device for answering *that* question. Instead, I protest against the identification of the answer to *that* question with the answer to the question "What is justice?" The said identification represents a double conflation, of fundamental principles with rules of regulation and of principles of justice whether they be fundamental ones that express justice, or rules of regulation that serve to realize justice (as much as is possible and reasonable), with principles, whether, again, they be fundamental ones or rules of regulation, that respectively express or serve other values. The upshot is a misidentification of fundamental principles of justice with optimal principles of regulation quite generally.

The two criticisms that I make of the Rawlsian procedure can be presented within a simple two-by-two matrix (see Table 4.1):

TABLE 4.1 Conflation of Fundamental with Optimal Principles of Justice

	(a) Fundamental principles	(b) Rules of regulation
(c) Justice	(1) Fundamental principles of justice	(2) that serve justice in particular
(d) Values in general	(3) Fundamental principles generally	(4) that serve fundamental principles generally

The effect of the original position procedure is to identify (1) and (4), and thereby to locate justice both in the wrong column and in the wrong row.[7]

I argued in an article of 2003 called "Facts and Principles" that fundamental principles, principles, that is, that are not derived from other principles, do not rest on factual grounds. But I have not appealed to that premise in the foregoing presentation. The charge that justice cannot be identified with optimal rules of regulation does not require the claim that justice is wholly fact-insensitive: justice might, for all that the stated charge is sound, still depend (as I elsewhere argue that it does not) on the character of basic facts of human nature. So I have not here asked you to agree with my strong view, demonstrable though it is, that no facts control fundamental principles, but only with the weaker and overwhelmingly intuitive claim that the sorts of facts about practicality and feasibility that control the content of sound rules of regulation do not affect the content of justice itself. The point will be illustrated later with respect to a property tax example.

Let me now summarize the foregoing critique of constructivism.

On the constructivist view of justice, fundamental principles of justice are the outcome of an idealized legislative procedure whose task is to elect principles that will regulate our common life. In Rawls's version of constructivism, the legislators, the denizens of the original position, are prospective real-world citizens who are ignorant of how they in particular would fare under various candidate principles. In a Scanlonian version of constructivism about justice, the legislators are motivated to live by principles that no one could reasonably reject. But however the different versions of constructivist theories of social justice differ, whether in the nature of the selection procedure that they mandate or in the principles that are the output of that procedure, they all assign to principles of justice the same *role.* That role is determined by the fact that constructivism's legislators are asked to elect *principles that will regulate their common life*: the principles they arrive at are said to qualify as principles of *justice* because of the special conditions of motivation and information under which principles that are to serve the role of regulating their common life are adopted.

But, and here I restate the general ground of my disagreement with the constructivist metatheory, in any enterprise whose purpose is to select the principles that I have called "rules of regulation," *attention must be paid, either expressly or in effect, to considerations that do not affect the content of justice itself*, while justice (whatever it may be: the present point holds independently of who is right in disagreements about the *content* of justice) must of course influence the selection of regulating principles, factual contingencies that determine how justice is to be applied or that make justice infeasible, *and* values and principles that call for a compromise with justice, also have a role to play in generating the principles that regulate social life, and legislators, whether flesh-and-blood or hypothetical, will go astray unless they are influenced, one way or another (that is directly, or by virtue of the structure of the constructivist device), by those further considerations.[8] It follows that any procedure that generates the right set of principles to regulate society fails thereby to identify a set of fundamental principles of justice, by virtue of its very success in the former, distinct, exercise. The influence of other values means that the principles in the output of the procedure are not principles of *justice*, and the influence of the factual contingencies means that they are not *fundamental* principles of anything.

The relevant nonjustice considerations do indeed affect the outcome of typically favored constructivist procedures. My complaint is not at all that constructivism fails to take them into account, but precisely that it *does* take them into account inappropriately when purporting to identify what justice is. For the influence of alien factors on the output of the constructivist procedure means that what it produces is not fundamental justice, and is, sometimes, not justice at all. Given its aspiration to produce fundamental principles of justice, constructivism sets its legislators the wrong task, although the precise character, and the size, of the discrepancy between fundamental justice and the output of a constructivist procedure will, of course, vary across constructivism's variants. That it sets its idealized legislators the wrong task is my principal—and generative—complaint against constructivism as a metatheory of fundamental justice.

If I am right that constructivists miscast fundamental principles of justice in the role of principles of social regulation, what, I may be asked, *is* the (contrasting and) proper role of fundamental principles of justice? The answer is that they have no proprietary role, apart from the obvious role of spelling out what justice is. Not everything in this world, not even every kind of principle, has the character that it does because of some role that it fulfills.[9]

Let me now make a point about placing justice in the wrong row of Table 4.1. If an institution is capable of more than one virtue, then you may properly have regard to each of the virtues of which it is capable in designing it. But the answer to the question "What is the right design of the institution?" could not, therefore, by itself, tell you the content in general of any one of the virtues, or even the particular distinctive contribution that that virtue makes to the design. You have to understand the content of any given virtue independently of knowing what the rules of the design are in order to identify the subset of rules that reflect *that* particular virtue.[10] And the point holds for the virtue of justice even if justice is, as I personally do not think it is, the first virtue of social institutions in the sense that Rawls said that it is.[11] For that would not mean that justice is the *only* virtue that would be manifest in an acceptable design. Whether or not justice is the first virtue of institutions, they have, or lack, other virtues, too, and constructivist devices, whether or not they are capable of getting right all the principles that all the virtues of institutions require, cannot tell us which principles are ones of justice and which not. To discriminate principles of justice within the set of constructively selected principles, we need a contentful conception of justice that isn't constructed.[12]

Let me now illustrate the distinction between fundamental principles of justice and rules of regulation. "Council tax," a British local property tax, works like this. Properties are divided into seven bands, according to their estimated market value. The tax rate varies from municipality to municipality, but in any municipality there are seven levels of tax, corresponding to the seven market-value bands.

Council tax bands illustrate the proper influence of the nonjustice considerations of feasibility and Pareto optimality on rules of regulation. The bands are justified by a principle of justice that says that the broadest backs should bear the greatest burdens: so the more valuable your dwelling is, the more tax you should pay. But the bands ensure that same-band people whose properties are of different value pay the same tax, and so the very principle of justice that inspires the banding scheme *also* condemns it of an injustice, because, for example, across a £90,000–99,999 band, the £90,000 person pays the same tax as the £99,999 person. Yet, although that is a flaw in the scheme from the point of view of the very principle of justice that inspires it, that flaw, from the point of view of justice, does not condemn the scheme *as* a rule of regulation. If Mr. 90,000 were to complain about the injustice of his paying as much as Mr. 99,999, the right thing to say to him would be that the only way to eliminate the injustice would be by designing a more fine-grained scheme, which would impose so much extra administrative cost that everyone, including Mr. 90,000, would lose.[13]

I say that it is the very *concept* of justice that tells us that justice is not fully realized by a rule that embodies a step function of the sort that the council tax employs. You don't have to accept the principle that the broadest backs should bear the greatest burden to see that a step-functional rule of regulation like the council tax rule could not fully realize a principle of justice.

Someone has objected that in those claims about property taxation, I am contentiously supposing that justice is a precisely specifiable relation (between, in this case, tax and wealth), whereas it is in fact only a rough relation.

According to the objector, justice says that tax should correspond merely *roughly* to wealth; within an extreme form of the objection, it might be said to suffice for justice that tax be merely weakly monotonic with respect to wealth (which is to say that there is no injustice as long as wealthier folk don't pay less than *less* wealthy folk). The objector claims that justice *itself* can say no more than that about this sort of taxation; the rest is a matter of practical detail. Inspired by justice, we decide to adopt *some* such scheme, but we leave the domain of justice behind, and therefore institute no injustice when we work out the practical details.

I have three responses to this objection. First, that while we can maybe just about tolerate the thought that it is not unjust, from the "broadest back" point of view, that Mr. 90,000 pays the *same* as Mr. 99,999, it is much harder to accept that such justice smiles on the circumstance that Mr. 90,000 pays significantly more than Mr. 89,999 does. More generally, the strongest objection to the property taxation scheme from the point of view of the justice that it is intended to deliver is not to the spread within the band, a spread that such justice might well be thought to permit, but to the step-functional character of workable bands.

Second, consider how the proposed supposedly "postjustice" purely practical discussion of exactly what divisions we should have would go. Suppose someone says that there should be twenty-five bands. The reply will be "That would be impracticable." But suppose someone says, "Let's have two." The objection could not now be that *that* would be impracticable: two bands are more practicable than any larger number of bands. So the objection to the two-bands proposal would be . . . what? What conceivably other than that two bands would be *too* unjust? So the idea that justice, being rough, is left behind when we discuss how *many* rungs we should have is false.

Third, suppose, perhaps impossibly, that a supercomputer could calculate cheaply all property values with precision (within the limits of the conceptual barrier that was explained in note 13). The function from dwelling price to property tax would then approximate to a straight line. Who could deny that the distribution of tax burden would then be *more* just than the distribution that we are actually able to achieve?

I conclude that, as I said, the example shows that rules of regulation can run counter to the very principle of justice by which they are inspired, because of the legitimate influence on the formation of rules of regulation of considerations other than justice, such as, in the present case, efficiency.

2. Rescuing Equality from the Basic Structure Objection

I said earlier that my case against constructivism is neutral with respect to the question of whether the basic structure of society is the sole site at which justice applies. Whether or not that restriction on the *scope* of principles of justice is sound, their *derivation* by constructivist means is flawed for the two reasons that I have labored. Let us now pass from the question of what justice is to the question of its *scope*: Is Rawls right to restrict its purview to the basic structure of society?

The basic structure restriction is pressed against a train of argument that I develop in challenge to the Rawlsian claim that the difference principle justifies unequalizing incentive payments to productive people, since the surplus production that those incentives induce is necessary to render the worst off as well off as they can be made to be. My objection to that justificatory claim does not challenge the difference principle itself (objections to which compose Chapter 4 of *Rescuing Justice and Equality*), but, rather, the credentials of the incentives argument *as* an application of the difference principle. I claim that, properly understood, the difference principle does not justify unequalizing incentives.

My challenge to that supposed application of the principle asks *why* the inequality in question should be thought *necessary* to benefit the worst off. And the answer has to be that if the inequality is indeed necessary, then it's necessary because and only because productive people would be unwilling to be as productive as they are if they did not prosper better than others do. That's pretty obvious, but it has two important consequences.

The first thing that follows is that the inequality isn't *really* or strictly necessary to make the worst off better off. It is not necessary independently of human will. It is necessary only because and insofar as the productive are unwilling to act otherwise: it is *their choices* that *make* the inequality necessary. But how could *the better off* justify the inequality by saying that it is *necessary* when they themselves *make* it necessary? If I make it necessary for you to pay the toll to go through the gate, and there is good reason for you to go through the gate, and you ask me to justify the toll, can I say, "Well, the toll is necessary for you to be able to go through the gate"? My reply presents an offer that you would be unwise to refuse, but it does not justify the demand that I was asked to justify.

And the second thing that follows from the fact that the inequality is necessary only because productive people would be unwilling to be as productive as they are without it is that the productive people act as they do only because they *themselves* reject the principle that an inequality is justified only if it benefits the worst off. They couldn't act as they do if they *themselves* accepted the difference principle, and acted in conformity with the conception of justice that it states. So the incentive justification of inequality works only in a society that by Rawlsian criteria is unjust because not everybody in it observes the right principle of justice. How, then, could the result be justice?

It follows from my case against the Rawlsian endorsement of incentives that a full implementation of the difference principle requires it to be observed not only by the state but also by citizens at large: potential high earners must forbear from seizing the advantages that their bargaining power puts within their reach and that the state cannot efficiently prevent them from seizing. It follows, in a word, that a full implementation of the difference principle requires the presence across society of an *ethos* of egalitarian justice, a set of attitudes and dispositions whose effect is to assign a certain priority to the interests of the worst-off people in society. I'll explain why I say (only) a *certain* priority a little later.

Now, the basic structure objection to my position on incentives says that principles of justice apply to the basic structure of society alone, and not to the choices of citizens *within that structure*. Because they endorse the difference principle, conscientious citizens comply with the rules of the structure, but, so the objection to my position runs, they are not only free as a matter of fact but also *morally* free, and free as far as justice is concerned, to choose as they wish within those rules. It is only public decisions, the decisions of the state and of institutions allied to it, that are up for assessment at the bar of justice, and not the decisions, within the law, of agents acting in their private capacity.

I do not claim, in response, on absolutely general grounds, that people *must* have the same obligations as states, and that the difference principle must *therefore* apply to individual choice. I do not say, with Liam Murphy, that "all fundamental normative principles that apply to the design of institutions apply also to the conduct of people."[14] I eschew that Murphyan premise because there are plenty of cases where the point of a set of rules should *not* be directly pursued by those who operate within them, even when they themselves endorse the rules *because* of that point. As I have said elsewhere, it is not "*in general* true that the point of the rules [that govern] an activity must be aimed at when agents pursue that activity in good faith. Every competitive sport represents a counter-example to that generalization."[15] And even if Murphy's position is too sophisticated to be falsified by that simple counterexample, the example nevertheless suffices to show that one cannot require that citizens apply the difference principle in their daily lives on absolutely *general* grounds.

Without, then, embracing Murphy, who is a hedgehog, I simply ask, in my contrastingly foxlike way, *why* the difference principle should *not* apply to individuals, and I argue against three reasons that are given in answer to that question, which we can call the impact reason, the moral division of labor reason, and the publicity reason.[16]

The chief reason for the basic structure restriction that is offered in Rawls's *A Theory of Justice* is that the impact of the basic structure on our lives is profound and present from the start. But that is a feeble argument for restricting the purview of justice to the basic structure, because it is certainly not in *general* true that coercive structure has more impact than social ethos on how much inequality there will be. Ethos has a huge impact, on, for example, how *progressive* taxation can safely be without becoming counterproductive.

Suppose that a country called "Swedeland" once had a strong welfare state that greatly benefited the worst off, but that the Swedeland state taxed its financially more successful people at rates against which the upper and middle classes in time rebelled, through various forms of literal and "internal" emigration, to the detriment, of, principally, the worst off, as tax revenue, and therefore, the welfare state sagged. Some think that that story is true of Swed*en*, but I say "Swede*land*" to cater to possible dissidence on that score. Whether or not the story is true of some actual state, it is not only coherent but also credible, and its credibility suffices to demonstrate the extreme importance of the presence or the absence of the ethos for which I contend.

A second reason that may be derived from *A Theory of Justice* for resisting the extension of the difference principle into the personal domain pleads the propriety of a moral division of labor, under which the state sees to justice, and the individual, having herself willingly seen to justice insofar as the state requires her to do so, sees, then, to the imperatives and values of her own personal life. That moral division of labor is justified, so it is thought, by the presence in morality of two standpoints: an impersonal standpoint on the one hand, to which the state responds, and a personal standpoint, on the other, to which the individual, other than in her capacity as a law-abiding citizen, may rightly be dedicated. Those who in this fashion criticize my extension of the reach of distributive justice into personal choice might be disposed to cite on behalf of their view the pregnant observation by Thomas Nagel that "institutions," such as the state, "unlike individuals, don't have their own lives to lead."[17]

I accept both the thesis of the duality of standpoints, personal and impersonal, that animates this objection, and also Nagel's point that the state contrasts with individuals in not having its own life to lead. But I reject the conclusion that impersonal justice is a matter for the state only, a conclusion that neither Nagel himself nor Rawls actually draws.

Chapters 6 and 9 of Nagel's *Equality and Partiality* articulate a more nuanced view of the matter under inspection than the one described above, but it is not relevant, here, to go into the Nagel details. What matters here is that the view described above is not that of Rawls: so much is evident from Rawls's assignment to individuals of a set of "natural duties," duties, that is, that lie on individuals rather than on the state and that include the duties to respect others, to uphold and foster just institutions, to do a great good when the cost of doing so is not excessive, and so forth. These Rawlsian duties respond to utterances of the impersonal standpoint, but they apply at the heart of personal life: they are, expressly, principles for individuals rather than for institutions. So Rawls can affirm at most a *reduced* version of the moral division of labor thesis, one that restricts it to the domain of distributive justice, and in *this* domain Rawls *indeed* divides the task of the state, which is to set the just framework, from the nontask of the individual, which is to do as she pleases within that framework. The real opposition between Rawls and me on the present issue is not, therefore, whether the impersonal standpoint reaches personal decision but whether the demands of distributive justice in particular do so. And while it is quite consistent for Rawls to think both that *they* do not and that other deliverances of the impersonal standpoint do, the Rawlsian position about distributive justice cannot be *based* on a general bar to impersonal justice entering individual decision: it diminishes the plausibility of the division of labor thesis with respect to distributive justice in particular that it cannot be said to reflect something more general.

The profound truth that there exist Nagel's two standpoints, and the further truth that the state, unlike individuals, has no life of its own to lead, do not justify a moral division of labor between a justice-seeking state and justice-indifferent (save insofar as they are willingly obedient citizens) individuals. The Nagelian premises provide no warrant for the asserted division of labor or, therefore, for extruding the demands of impersonal justice from personal choice.

We can, in fact, distinguish three possible views, with respect to who must see to distributive justice in particular, that are consistent with the Nagelian premises of the argument, each of which contradicts the view, often misattributed to me, that the individual must be as dedicated to such justice as the state is. There is, first, the Rawlsian view that distributive justice is a task for the state alone. A second view would say that the individual must show some regard to what the state is fully dedicated to in this domain. Finally, there is my own view, which is that both the state, with no life of its own, and the individual, who is indeed thus endowed, must, in appropriately different fashions, show regard in economic matters both to impersonal justice and to the legitimate demands of the individual.

To elaborate: there are many forms of motivation along the continuum between unrestrained market maximizing at one end and full self-sacrificing restraint in favor of the worst off on the other. The first extreme is permitted by Rawls (and I regard that as absurd), but the second extreme isn't required by me. Requiring the second extreme is, in my view, excluded by a legitimate personal prerogative. The prerogative grants each person the right to be something other than an engine for the welfare of other people: we are not nothing but slaves to social justice. But the individual who affirms the difference principle must have some regard to it in her economic choices, whatever regard, that is, that starts where her personal prerogative stops.

The final argument for exempting individual choice from the writ of distributive justice to be reviewed today is due to the Welsh philosopher Andrew Williams. According to Williams, principles of social justice are principles that we fulfill collectively: a given individual person is not obliged to observe them unless others are doing so, too. Accordingly, the individual cannot be expected to observe them, she cannot be *obliged* to observe them, unless she can be *assured* that others, too, are observing them. But she cannot be assured of that unless she can *tell* whether others are observing them, and she cannot tell whether others are appropriately observant unless the principle in question issues precise and unambiguous instructions. But the egalitarian ethos, properly tempered by a personal prerogative, is, as I would amply concede, vague and general in its directive, and not at all precise. It requires people to have appropriate regard to the worst off in their economic decisions, but within the limits of a reasonable personal prerogative. And that prescription, Williams urges, is too vague to count as a demand of justice. The implications of the difference principle for personal choice are too vague, partly because it is vague where the line is to be drawn that acknowledges our personal prerogative, and partly because it is unclear what we should do, in the service of the difference principle, beyond that line.

The Williams argument has four premises:

1. Obligations of social justice are collective.
2. You are obliged to fulfill a collective obligation only if you can be assured that others, too, will comply with it.
3. You can be assured that others are complying with an obligation only if you know precisely what it means to comply with that obligation so that you can check whether others are indeed complying with it.
4. You cannot know precisely what would fulfill the obligations of an egalitarian ethos.
5. ∴ The egalitarian ethos is not required by justice.

I argue against each of Williams's four premises in Chapter 7 of *Rescuing Justice and Equality*, but I shall restrict myself here to some remarks about the third premise of the argument.

Contrary to that third premise, we *can* know that good-faith effort on behalf of a principle obtains, broadly, in a society even when people's obligations under that principle are *not* precisely defined. During the Second World War in Britain, a social ethos induced people to sacrifice personal interests for the sake of the war effort, and everyone was expected, as a matter of justice, to "do his bit," to shoulder his just share. But no one could have stated precisely what amount of sacrifice that injunction required, and it is true, therefore, that, with respect to many people, one couldn't tell, and, with respect to some, they couldn't even themselves tell, whether they were sacrificing on the required scale. There are too many details in each person's life that affect what the required sacrifice should be: Max has a bad back, Sally has a difficult child, George has just inherited £20,000, etc. "Yes, Jack goes out only once a week, not, like most of us, twice, on guard duty, but then Jack has to take care of his mother." But "the extent to which individuals conform[ed] to" the requirements of sacrifice could certainly be known in rough-and-ready terms.[18] The sacrifice ethos *was* amenable to sufficient sub-Williamsian rough-and-ready public checkability for social assurance, and "do your bit," despite its vagueness, was understood and applied as a principle of justice. It would have been crazy to have asked for it to be carefully defined, but it would also be crazy to deny that "do your bit" performed a task of social regulation in the interest of justice. And all of that can be said, mutatis mutandis, about the egalitarian ethos that I claim to be required for justice.

I would add that Williams's views of this matter are demonstrably at variance with those of Rawls himself. For Rawls lays duties on individuals whose characterization is vague in the extreme. So, for example, the Rawlsian "duty of justice" "requires us to support and to comply with just institutions that exist and apply to us. It also constrains us to further just arrangements not yet established, at least when this can be done *without too much cost to ourselves*."[19] Rawls does not say how much cost is too much, and Aristotle and I don't think he has to. But Williams, who purports to be Rawls's champion, must tell us why the duty of justice, with its reference to the vague "without too much cost to ourselves," is not, despite its vagueness, defeated by a publicity constraint, when a duty to forgo economic benefit "without too much cost to ourselves" is, according to Williams, defeated by that same constraint.

Or consider the "natural duty to bring about a great good." Although we are under that duty if we can discharge it "relatively easily, we are released from [it] when *the cost to ourselves is considerable*."[20] But what constitutes a "considerable" cost, and how can we know how considerable the cost is that someone would have to incur to discharge the duty? The Williams questions apply as much here as they do to the egalitarian ethos. And I say that they have no bite in either case. Speaking of the natural duties in general, Rawls allows that "their definition and systematic arrangement are untidy," but he does not therefore set them aside.[21] I propose the same conceptually and epistemically relaxed attitude to the claims of egalitarian duty in everyday life.

3. Rescuing Justice and Rescuing Equality

My attempt to rescue equality from the basic structure restriction is part of a wider campaign in defense of the claim that, very roughly speaking, equality constitutes distributive justice. I want to indicate, in closing, how my case against constructivism's mismanagement of the concept of justice helps to sustain that egalitarian campaign. It does so because each of the two errors in the Rawlsian identification of principles of justice with optimal rules of regulation induces us to disidentify justice and equality. The first error, the placing of justice in the wrong column of the matrix (see Table 4.1), induces that disidentification because difficulties of obtaining relevant information and other practical problems make equality an infeasible policy goal: one can only approach it, but that is not a reason for someone of an initially egalitarian persuasion to identify justice with whatever workable rule comes closest to equality, as opposed to with what she is trying to approach, that is, equality itself. And the second error, the placing of justice in the wrong row, introduces principles other than that of justice that may rightly compete with equality in various contexts. Accordingly, the rescue of the *concept* of justice serves the end of rescuing an egalitarian view of the *content* of distributive justice.

Although the two rescues are in that way connected, it remains true that, as I have already said, the constructivism issue and the basic structure restriction issue are substantially independent of each other. You can be a constructivist without imposing the basic structure restriction on the scope of principles of justice, and you can impose that restriction without being a constructivist. Constructivism divorces justice from equality by conflating justice with other values, but that conflation supports no basic structure restriction on the scope of justice. Constructivism also divorces justice from equality by conflating questions about justice with questions about what sorts of rules can and cannot be implemented. That second antiegalitarian element in constructivism would support a basic structure restriction only if the difficulties of obtaining relevant information, of the sort that rules of regulation might be thought to demand, disqualify egalitarian rules from consideration, because, for example, those rules are too *vague* to be implemented. But my reply to Williams shows that vagueness is no bar to implementation. So constructivism doesn't support the basic structure restriction in that way, and perhaps also not in any other way, and in my view, or conjecture, they are indeed independent threats to equality.

Afterword One

In the wake of the recent financial ructions in the United States, two sets of agents were criticized. Government was criticized for having deregulated, and bankers were criticized for having behaved greedily and riskily in the new, deregulated environment. And there is, among the various ways of specifying those criticisms, an inverse relationship between how strongly the government is to be criticized and how strongly the bankers are to be criticized. For the government is criticized in two styles: (a) the deregulation was foolish, because *any* normally self-seeking marketer would act in the way the bankers did once it had been introduced, and (b) the deregulation was foolish, not because (a) is true, but because it *enabled* the greedy and selfish action on the part of at least some bankers that ensued, and government should have realized that some bankers would be bastards. My "inverse relationship" claim is that the more severe the criticism of the bankers—it is more severe in (b)—the less severe is the criticism of government.

Clearly, in one way or another, both what the government did and what the bankers did substantially produced the result, including the injustice in the result.

You might think that not too much must be made of this, in support of my aim of breaking the barrier between the basic structure and individual choice, since the context was not a Rawlsian one in which government had legislated optimally. But it is not realistic to expect that government could find rules that are so well honed that greed could not pervert their intent. So whatever is optimal in practice requires an ethos for principle to be properly served. Rawls supposes that the basic structure can be rendered optimal, with respect, for example, to fulfilling the difference principle, but that would probably require intolerably directive directives. Absent same, you *have* to rely on private virtue.

Contrast Rawls's early attitude to people and institutions:

> There is also the temptation to blame objective institutions for the evil in the world. It was an 18th-century idea that bad institutions were one of the great barriers to a fully good mankind. Individuals cannot, however, be separated from institutions. Institutions are merely the objective rules and methods which men set up to deal with social problems. Bad institutions are a sure sign of sinful men. There would be no oppressive institutions were there not greed and malice to reinforce them.[22]

Afterword Two

It has been suggested that the principles that the original position is designed to produce are not rules of regulation but principles for judging rules of regulation. I need not disagree. For any such principles, if defensible, must have regard both to values other than justice and to practical constraints. Accordingly, such principles cannot be ones of justice, nor can they be ones for the assessment of the *justice* of rules of regulation.

Notes

1. Roughly two-thirds of this essay consist of such excerpts, which were seamlessly incorporated. In order of their appearance in this essay, the excerpts are from 274–277, 277–279, 282–284, 286, 313–315, 375–376, 8–10, 353, 357–358, and 279 of G. A. Cohen, *Rescuing Justice and Equality* (Cambridge, MA: Harvard University Press, 2008).—Ed.

2. That is John Rawls's word for them.

3. Thomas Scanlon draws the stated distinction at 391n21 of his *What We Owe to Each Other* (Cambridge, MA: Harvard University Press, 1998) and classifies his own theory as one that says "what it *is* for an act to be wrong" (emphasis added).

4. See sections 13, 19, and 20 of Chapter 6 of Cohen, *Rescuing Justice and Equality.*

5. Some are fact-insensitive and some not.

6. Its incoherence also explains why I consider Andrew Williams's concepts of "constraints on" and "desiderata of" justice to be incoherent. See section 7 of Chapter 8 of Cohen, *Rescuing Justice and Equality.*

7. As Cohen explained in a draft of the material that constitutes this chapter, his questions (i)–(iii) relate as follows to the distinctions among (a), (b), (c), and (d) drawn in Table 4.1: the (a)/(b) distinction generalizes the (i) part of the (i)/(iii) distinction and provides an instantiation of the (iii) part of the (i)/(ii) distinction, (a) generalizes (i) beyond mere justice to

all fundamental principles, and (b) instantiates the (iii) question, which is what social states of affairs ought to be brought about—rules of regulation are instances of social states of affairs. And the (c)/(d) distinction is related to the original distinctions in that among the reasons that the (i) question is different from the (ii) and (iii) questions is that justice is not the only value to consider when we confront the (ii) and (iii) questions.—Ed.

8. The denizens of Rawls's original position do not, of course, expressly distinguish between considerations of justice and other considerations. They simply choose whatever principle that, given their particular combination of knowledge and ignorance, they see (not as serving justice but) as serving their interests. But in order that they choose principles of regulation well, their choice must in *some* manner reflect both justice and nonjustice considerations.

In partly parallel fashion, the rules of criminal justice, which govern judgments of innocence and guilt, must take into account considerations other than what innocence and guilt *are* and therefore cannot tell us what innocence and guilt are. They are, on the contrary, fashioned against the background of an antecedent understanding of what guilt and innocence are. See, further, the discussion of loyalty in section 7 of Chapter 8 of Cohen, *Rescuing Justice and Equality.*

9. See, further, 267 of Chapter 6, ibid.

10. Note, further, that no particular subset need reflect exclusively any particular virtue, as opposed to the resultant of balancing several competing virtues.

11. See section 4 of Chapter 7 of Cohen, *Rescuing Justice and Equality.*

12. Rawls *in effect* recognizes the truth of what I say here when he writes as follows:

A conception of social justice, then, is to be regarded as providing in the first instance a standard whereby the distributive aspects of the basic structure of society are to be assessed. This standard, however, is not to be confused with the principles defining the other virtues, for the basic structure, and social arrangements generally, may be efficient or inefficient, liberal or illiberal, and many other things as well as just or unjust. A complete conception defining principles for all the virtues of the basic structure, together with their respective weights when they conflict, is more than a conception of justice; it is a social ideal. The principles of justice are but a part, though perhaps the most important part, of such a conception. (*A Theory of Justice*, rev. ed. [Cambridge, MA: Harvard University Press, 1999], 8–9).

Rawls fails to see that justice cannot be *both* one virtue among several of institutions *and* the answer to the question the denizens of the original position answer, which is "How should institutions be organized?" So, for example, those denizens are unquestionably moved by considerations of efficiency, but efficiency is contrasted with justice in the above passage. (It is independently curious that the value of being liberal is contrasted here with justice, since the first principle of justice seems to confer what liberals require.)

13. The very concept of the *precise* value of a piece of property is, moreover, obscure, unlike the concept of what it will *actually* command on the market, which is not quite the same thing. And that complicates the practical problem of identifying it. (By itself, without the practicality point, the conceptual point cuts no ice with respect to contrasting fundamental principles and rules of regulation. But it does so indirectly by enriching the practicality problem.)

14. Liam Murphy, "Institutions and the Demands of Justice," *Philosophy and Public Affairs* 27, 4 (1999): 251.

15. G. A. Cohen, *If You're an Egalitarian, How Come You're So Rich?* (Cambridge, MA: Harvard University Press, 2000), 12.

16. Cf. Isaiah Berlin, *The Hedgehog and the Fox* (London: Weidenfeld and Nicolson, 1953).

17. Thomas Nagel, *Equality and Partiality* (New York: Oxford University Press, 1991), 59. Typical of many, A. J. Julius, "Basic Structure and the Value of Equality," *Philosophy and Public Affairs* 31 (2003): 327, describes the stated position as the "Rawls/Nagel ideal of a division of labor."

18. This is a quotation from Andrew Williams, "Incentives, Inequality, and Publicity," *Philosophy and Public Affairs* 27 (1998): 233.—Ed.

19. John Rawls, *A Theory of Justice* (Cambridge, MA: Harvard University Press, 1971), 115 (rev. ed., 99), emphases added.

20. Ibid., 117 (rev. ed., 100), emphases added.

21. Ibid., 339 (rev. ed., 298).

22. John Rawls, *A Brief Inquiry into the Meaning of Sin and Faith*, edited by Thomas Nagel (Cambridge, MA: Harvard University Press, 2009), 190.

READING

5

Justice and Boundaries

DAVID MILLER

Let me begin with a much-cited quotation from Michael Walzer's book *Spheres of Justice*: "The idea of distributive justice presupposes a bounded world within which distributions take place: a group of people committed to dividing, exchanging and sharing goods, first of all among themselves."[1] I believe that what Walzer says here is true: distributive justice is always justice within a group, and that implies the existence of a boundary between those who are members of the group and those who are not. But neither the meaning nor the truth of this proposition is self-evident. There are in fact two questions that we need to explore. First, should boundaries matter in the way that Walzer assumes, or should the scope of distributive justice be universal, that is, should all human beings fall within its range (I will not consider here the issue of creatures other than human beings)? Second, if Walzer is right about the bounded nature of distributive justice, which boundaries should count? What must be true of a group of human beings in order for us to say that they form the kind of group within which principles of distributive justice apply?

Walzer's answer to this second question is not as clear as it might be. The passage I quoted above goes on as follows: "That world, as I have already argued, is the political community, whose members distribute power to one another and avoid, if they possibly can, sharing it with anyone else. When we think about distributive justice, we think about independent cities or countries capable of arranging their own patterns of division and exchange, justly or unjustly."[2]

Walzer does not tease out the various different senses that might be given to the idea of "political community." Is a political community simply a group of people subject to a common sovereign power, or does community here suggest something more than this—that the group's political arrangements reflect a social bond among the group's members that is independent of those arrangements? In addition, if we speak of countries as sites of distributive justice, what does "country" actually mean? Does it refer to a geographical territory, a nation, a state, or all of these at once? Walzer's emphasis in the passage I have quoted seems to fall on the capacity of the political community to determine a pattern of distribution, in other words on its *power* to create and enforce a scheme of distributive justice without outside interference. But as readers of *Spheres of Justice* will know, in other places in that work he attaches great weight to the idea that principles of distributive justice depend upon the goods being distributed having *shared social meanings.* Shared social meanings, however, require more than just the existence of a power that can create and enforce a distributive pattern. They presuppose a community with a common language in which the meanings can be expressed, interaction over time between the members of the community, and so forth.

I do not intend to try to excavate Walzer's thought any further here; I point to his ambiguities in order to suggest that the issue of justice and boundaries is not straightforward. It does in fact raise several distinct questions. At the most general level, it raises the question of whether principles of justice are universal in nature (the same principles apply in all circumstances) or whether they are contextually specific, with different principles applying in different situations. I have defended the second position (contextualism) in earlier work and do not intend to revisit the issue here.[3] It also raises the distinct question of whether principles of justice must necessarily be universal in *scope* such that when they apply, they must apply to all human beings regardless of whether they belong to some smaller subdivision of humanity, however defined.[4] It further raises the question of whether, if some version of particularism is true (justice is not, as a matter of conceptual necessity, universal in scope), the political community in any of its senses is the right kind of subdivision to bring principles of justice into play. That is, one might be a particularist about the scope of justice, but reject Walzer's claim that the important boundary lies between those who form part of the political community and those who do not.

In order to assess that claim, we need to discover what features a political community might possess that would make it appropriate to treat it as a distinct "world" when we apply principles of justice to its members. What is supposed to connect membership in such a community with having special claims of justice against other members that one does not have against human beings at large? As we shall see, there are competing answers to this question, and we need to explore the plausibility of each of these before we can decide whether there is reason to restrict the scope of justice in the way that particularists recommend. So after considering and rejecting arguments to the effect that the scope of justice *must* be universal, I shall explore critically three different ways of setting the boundaries of justice, before returning to see why political communities might be regarded as privileged sites of justice.

Let us be clear to begin with, however, that the argument is specifically about *distributive* justice. Those like Walzer who want to defend some version of particularism need not deny that there can be forms of justice that apply universally, between human beings considered simply as such and regardless of any kind of group membership. This idea is implicit in *Spheres of Justice* and spelt out more fully in later works such as *Thick and Thin*, where Walzer contrasts distributive justice as a "maximalist" morality with a "minimalist" concept of justice that comprises injunctions against murder, torture, oppression, and so forth.[5] We might equally well capture these universal principles of justice using the language of basic human rights: human rights identify the claims people can make on each other regardless of boundaries and memberships.[6] Justice in this minimal sense can be distinguished from distributive justice in several ways. It is concerned with the allocation of goods only insofar as these goods are necessary means to fulfil basic rights, so it has nothing to say about the distribution of the many other kinds of goods (wealth, honours, rewards, status, and so forth) that principles of distributive justice are meant to regulate. Moreover, principles of distributive justice are mainly comparative in form (they concern the share of goods received by each person measured against the shares received by relevant others), whereas minimal justice is noncomparative. It is not about how one person is being treated relative to others, but about how they are being treated, period—about whether their situation is such that they are able to enjoy minimally adequate amounts of liberty, security, nutrition, medical aid, and so forth.

With this distinction in place, we can now begin to consider the arguments of those who deny the relevance to justice of boundaries of any kind—who believe that distributive justice, too, must be universal in scope. These arguments fall into two classes, negative and positive. The negative arguments take the following form. The scope of distributive justice must be global because there are, in fact, no morally relevant boundaries between people. If there were such boundaries, the scope of distributive justice might perhaps be restricted. But as things now are, in the light of all those processes that go under the names of "globalization," "multiculturalism," and so forth, there is no way of dividing up people into groups such that restricted principles of justice apply to them. Certain boundaries do of course exist (state boundaries and administrative boundaries of other kinds), but these are not relevant from the point of view of justice. The relationships that exist between people inside these conventional borders are not qualitatively different from the relationships that increasingly exist across them. For example, people no longer identify exclusively or primarily with the other members of their ethnic group or their nation, say, but are just as likely to have, instead or in addition, alternative identities that cut across these narrower ones.

That is the negative argument for justice having universal scope—its principles must apply globally because belonging to the human species is the only kind of membership that is robust enough to carry the necessary weight. The problem with this argument is that it depends very heavily on some broad empirical theses about the contemporary world that may prove on closer inspection to be quite challengeable. Every claim to the effect that political identities are becoming transnational or even global, for instance, is liable to be met with a counterclaim that points to the resurgence of substate nationalism in many places. Claims about economic globalization are challenged by the observation that widely varying rates of economic development in different societies appear to be explicable mainly by domestic factors such as the nature of the political regime. So the negative argument for universal justice rests on a fragile empirical basis. It is vulnerable, too, because as standardly advanced, it fails to specify *which* boundaries are the ones whose irrelevance it sets out to demonstrate. In other words, it does not take into account the possible range of particularist arguments that may be advanced. As I suggested above, particularism about justice can potentially take a number of different forms, depending on which aspect of group membership is supposed to ground the claim that principles of distributive justice apply only among those who belong to the group. Negative arguments for universal justice try to undermine particularism about justice in whatever form it is advanced. In this vein, the universalist says to the particularist, "Whatever boundaries between people you think are relevant to determining the scope of distributive justice, I know in advance that those boundaries are not going to do what is required of them." This is a bold thing to say, it seems to me. Should not the universalist wait to see which specific boundaries the particularist thinks are relevant, and then produce evidence that the world is such that those boundaries do not exist or do not have the properties they would need to have to support a claim about the restricted scope of distributive justice?

So it seems that claims about the bounded nature of (more than minimal) justice cannot be defeated by the negative argument alone, where that consists simply in marshalling some rather general facts about the contemporary world order. What about the positive arguments, which are normative in character and aim to show that justice by its very nature must be universal in scope? I shall consider two of these, neither of which appears to be successful.

The first positive argument starts with a widely held moral intuition, namely, that every human being is of equal worth, and as such is entitled to equal respect. By drawing boundaries in such a way that we apply our principles of justice to some people, but not to others (or at least apply different principles to those falling inside and outside the boundary), we fail to treat those outside with equal respect, so it is claimed. But in fact this is far from obvious. The problem is that very little follows concretely from the ideas of equal human worth or equal respect taken by themselves. Perhaps we can say that there are ways of treating human beings (degrading them or torturing them, for instance) that are ruled out by these ideas. It would also violate equal respect if we were simply to ignore the effects of our actions on some people when deciding what to do to, for example, if a government when deciding on its energy policy paid no attention at all to the fact that one of the means of generating energy being considered would have harmful effects on a group of noncitizens, say by creating acid rain or nuclear fallout. This would be tantamount to saying that the affected group counts for nothing, and that is inconsistent with the idea of equal moral worth. But it is a big step from this premise to the conclusion that we are bound to treat the claims of people everywhere as counting equally when we establish our practices of distributive justice. Assuming there are morally relevant reasons for limiting the scope of distributive justice, why must it show disrespect for those outside the boundaries when we act on those reasons?[7]

Another popular argument in this area is that boundary drawing is always morally arbitrary. The argument usually proceeds roughly as follows. Within the boundary we apply a certain principle—for instance, equality of opportunity or distribution according to need. What someone gets as a matter of justice will depend on his or her personal features, such as academic potential if we are distributing scarce educational places or medical condition if we are allocating health care. The feature serves as the ground of the distribution. But now consider someone outside the boundary who exhibits the same academic potential or the same medical need. Surely it is arbitrary, in an objectionable sense, to deny that person an equivalent educational place or access to health care. They also have the feature that grounds just distribution within the boundary, so why should they be treated differently?

The problem with this argument is that it begs the crucial question. It simply assumes that the scope of a principle of justice is determined by the distributive criterion it embodies—so if that criterion is need, then all needs must count equally. But this is what has to be shown. Alternatively, it has to be shown that there can be no good reasons for restricting the scope of a principle. But this is far from obvious. Why should not the fact that somebody belongs to a particular group or participates in a particular practice be a relevant fact when determining whether a principle of justice applies to that person or not? It is not self-evidently arbitrary to restrict the universe of distribution on this basis, as it would be, say, to restrict it to people whose third finger is longer than their first.

Since the arbitrariness argument has proved to be popular in recent debates about global justice, it is worth pausing for a moment to pinpoint exactly where it goes astray.[8] What does it mean to say that someone has a feature that is "morally arbitrary"—their ethnicity or nationality, for instance? It may mean one of two different things. It may mean, first, that the feature is not one that the person in question can claim moral credit for having. No one, for example, is responsible for having been born into a particular nation (if they are French rather than German, it is because their parents were French and raised them as French citizens), so they have done nothing to earn their membership. This seems obviously true in the case of most forms of group membership that particularists appeal to when they argue for the restricted scope of distributive justice. So that is the first sense of moral arbitrariness: a personal feature is morally arbitrary when the person who has it is not morally responsible for having it—has not, for example, chosen to have it or earned it in some way.

But "morally arbitrary" may also mean something different—it may mean that a feature is such that it should not count when deciding how a person should be treated. When we say that it is morally arbitrary whether a person has blue eyes or brown eyes, what we mean is that eye colour is morally irrelevant, for almost all practical purposes. Here, moral arbitrariness is being used as the conclusion of a moral argument, not as the premise. We believe that eye colour should not count when deciding how people should be treated, so we say that having blue eyes rather than brown is a morally arbitrary personal feature.

I think that arguments for the universal scope of distributive justice often trade on this ambiguity. They suppose that because group membership is normally a morally arbitrary feature in the first sense (people are not in general morally responsible for belonging to particular groups, certainly not ethnic groups or nations), it must also be morally arbitrary in the second sense, that is, it should not count for practical purposes. But this by no means follows. As a counterexample, consider special needs. If a child is born handicapped, this is morally arbitrary in the first sense—the child is not morally responsible for having the disabilities that she now has. But it is certainly not morally arbitrary in the second sense. We think that having special needs is a valid reason for receiving treatment that others do not receive, to compensate for the disability. So if group membership should not count when deciding what people are owed as a matter of justice, it cannot merely be on the grounds that membership is arbitrary in sense one. There must be something more specific about group membership that disqualifies it from counting when distributive justice is at issue. But to show that, we need to have a substantive argument—we cannot get there simply by talking about moral arbitrariness.

So far, I have been looking at, and rejecting, the arguments of those who think that the scope of distributive justice must be universal. But I have not yet tried to offer any positive reasons in support of the opposite view. In reality, clearly, bounded justice is the norm, both in terms of what happens by way of distributive practice and in terms of how people think. Principles of social justice are applied within state boundaries by institutions that are powerful enough to ensure that rights, opportunities, and resources are distributed according to relevant principles such as equality, desert, and need. Distributive justice is also practised at a much more local level, in families, workplaces, and universities, for example. When people think about whether they are being fairly treated, they worry much more about small inequalities of treatment among those who are close to them (classmates, work colleagues, and so forth) than about very much larger inequalities between these groups and others. At the national level, citizens become very agitated about what in Britain we call the "postcode lottery," where place of residence determines whether you have access to particular schools or the speed at which you can be treated at your local hospital, even though these differences are very minor when compared with the huge inequalities in education or health care that exist across national borders, especially when these comparisons involve both developed and developing countries. But, of course, this does not settle the matter. It might just be a case of myopia or warped human psychology. To show that bounded justice is legitimate, we have to explain why falling within a certain boundary should count when deciding what someone is owed as a matter of justice.

The argument for bounded justice has the following general form: principles of distributive justice apply to people who have a certain relationship to one another. It is by virtue of being so related that they can advance particular claims of justice against one another, invoking distributive principles such as various principles of equality. Once we understand the relationship, it is claimed, we will see why those particular principles apply. This leaves open, however, which kind of relationship is relevant. As I have already noted, social justice is for us the most prominent form of distributive justice. But to what, more precisely, does the "social" in social justice refer? Societies are complex entities: they are made up of a large number of separate practices, they are governed by political institutions, they have common cultures as well as being to a greater or lesser extent multicultural, and so forth. Which of these features, if any, is relevant to setting the boundaries of distributive justice? Is it one feature in particular, or it is a combination of several? We are back to the questions that I raised at the outset in relation to Walzer's appeal to the political community as the arena of distributive justice.

I want to proceed by considering three answers to the boundaries question that have featured prominently in recent debates about social justice—answers given by those who want to endorse particularism about distributive justice. I shall suggest, to anticipate, that none of the three answers taken by itself is adequate but that taken together they can be used to explain what is special about the idea of social justice. I shall label the three positions to be examined the *cooperative practice* view, the *political coercion* view, and the *common identity* view.[9] The claim to be considered, in each case, is that the designated feature provides a necessary and sufficient condition for principles of distributive justice to apply. So, to illustrate in the case of the first of the three views, the relevant claim is that principles of distributive justice apply to a group of people if, and only if, they are related to one another as fellow participants in a cooperative practice; similarly for the second and third views.

Let us begin, then, with the cooperative practice view. This is most famously associated with John Rawls, who at the very beginning of *A Theory of Justice* announces that principles of social justice are to apply to a society conceived of as a rule-governed association of persons—"a system of cooperation designed to advance the good of those taking part in it." He continues:

> Then, although a society is a cooperative venture for mutual advantage, it is typically marked by a conflict as well as by an identity of interest. There is an identity of interests since social cooperation makes possible a better life for all than any would have if each were to live solely by his own efforts. There is a conflict of interests since persons are not indifferent as to how the greater benefits produced by their collaboration are distributed, for in order to pursue their ends they each prefer a larger to a lesser share.[10]

Now Rawls's complete view of the form of human association to which principles of justice apply is more complex than this opening quotation suggests, but let us for the moment examine the simple idea of a cooperative practice as outlined above. What are its main features? First, it is a *system* of cooperation in the sense that the practice continues over time with the same (or largely the same) set of participants involved in it—it is not a one-off event. Second, it is rule governed, meaning that people coordinate their efforts on the basis of a commonly agreed set of rules of conduct. Third, the participants engage in the practice for mutual advantage: they understand that they can each do better by participating than they could by going it alone. Fourth, it is an open question how the surplus generated by the practice should be shared among the participants: there are no prior entitlements that already determine the answer. It is these four features taken together, Rawls implies, that make it necessary for the practice to be regulated by principles of (distributive) justice. Here there is a contrast with, in particular, a simple exchange between two individuals, or two groups of individuals, where although there may be mutual advantage (both parties expect to benefit from the exchange), the issue is one of reaching agreement from an established baseline and where the only issues of justice raised by the transaction may be procedural ones (no force, fraud, and so on).[11]

It is fairly easy to see how a cooperative practice as described above requires principles of distributive justice to regulate it. For, first, the practice is rule governed, but the rules themselves stand in need of justification, since different sets of rules are likely to produce outcomes that relatively advantage or disadvantage different people. Second, participation is voluntary, so participants will only remain committed to the practice if they can see that it treats each of them fairly. Third, the cooperative surplus has to be allocated somehow, given that there are no preexisting entitlements that already settle this question. So, insofar as the surplus takes the form of divisible benefits, some distributive principle (for instance, equality or a desert-based principle such as contribution) is needed to allocate it. This suggests that the existence of a cooperative practice is sufficient for principles of distributive justice to apply among those who participate in it. But is it also a necessary condition?

There are good reasons to believe that it is not necessary. One is that principles of distributive justice can apply to individual decisions that do not form part of ongoing practices. Aristotle famously used the example of allocating flutes among would-be flautists to illustrate the concept.[12] Of course, this is not social justice. But, first, it is nonetheless distributive justice, so more has to be said about why we need to draw a sharp distinction between justice within cooperative practices and justice in particular acts of distribution, as Rawls apparently wants to do. Second, it seems that the substance of the principles may often be the same in both cases: *contribution* and *need* may be relevant criteria for distributing resources both within ongoing practices and in making individual decisions. In an attempt to avoid this assimilation, Rawls contrasts social justice with allocative justice, and suggests that the latter tends to collapse into utilitarianism.[13] But although considerations of utility may indeed be used to guide particular distributive decisions (we may give the flutes to those we think likely to produce the best music), there is no reason that this must always be so. We may be guided by past contribution, by considerations of equality, and so forth. There may be good reasons to treat social justice as special (I shall argue for this later on), but the cooperative practice view, taken by itself, does not sufficiently explain why we should.

A second reason for doubting that the boundaries of distributive justice must be aligned with the boundaries of cooperative practices is that principles of distributive justice seem also to apply to those who are included in such practices without themselves contributing to the cooperative surplus. Indeed, it has often been argued against Rawls that there is at least a dissonance, if not an outright contradiction, between the way that he frames the problem of social justice, as applying within "a cooperative venture for mutual advantage," and the substantive principles that he proposes by way of solution (why would people setting up a cooperative practice from which each participant must gain commit themselves to maximizing the position of the worst-off group?).[14] Thus we would surely want to include within the scope of social justice people who for one reason or another (lack of opportunity, disability, and so on) were unable to contribute to the cooperative surplus. Such people are owed, for example, various forms of equal treatment as a matter of justice. Rawls, however, makes it clear that his theory of justice applies to citizens regarded as "normally cooperating members of society over a complete life," so although it can accommodate those who, as a result of illness or accident, are unable to contribute in one particular time period, it excludes those who make no net contribution overall, such as the severely disabled.[15] As he concedes, "We must see whether justice as fairness can be extended to provide guidelines for these cases; and if not, whether it must be rejected rather than supplemented by some other conception."[16] But it seems wrong to treat such cases as peripheral from the point of view of social justice, as the metaphor of "extension" implies.

I have argued that the cooperative practice view, which regards cooperation for mutual advantage as not only sufficient, but also necessary, for principles of distributive justice to apply, is too demanding as a way of setting the boundaries of justice. But we should equally reject, as not demanding enough, the idea that such principles apply whenever people interact economically, as some of the arguments against bounded justice seem to assume. That is, the mere fact that something A does with resources she holds has an impact on the economic position of B and others does not by itself seem to bring principles of distributive justice into play. A might destroy one of her holdings, thereby increasing the value of B's, because of scarcity. But this does not mean that B, as a matter of justice, must redistribute some part of his gain to A. Of course, if resource holdings are already subject to some principle of justice such as equality, B's windfall gain may bring the principle into play. But my point is that the fact of interaction does not by itself entail that such a principle must apply. Equally, if A worsens B's position, for instance, by producing something whose effect is to make one of B's holdings less valuable, this by itself does not impose any requirement of distributive justice. Some ways of worsening other people's position do certainly produce legitimate claims for compensation, but this is justice of a different kind: rectificatory, not distributive. Furthermore, other ways of worsening B's position (for instance, through fair competition) appear, on their own, to generate no justice claims at all.

So while the suggestion that principles of distributive justice apply *only* among people who are related to one another by virtue of common participation in a cooperative practice seems too stringent, the claim that they apply whenever the activities of one agent make some impact on the material position of others is too lax. Let me turn then to the second of the three views that I want to consider: the political coercion view defended, for instance, by Ronald Dworkin in his book *Sovereign Virtue*, and in later articles by Michael Blake and Thomas Nagel.[17] The claim here is that questions of distributive justice arise among people who are subject to a coercively imposed set of laws and policies, which in the standard case means that they are citizens of the same state. The boundaries of social justice, then, are the boundaries of systems of political coercion. Why should we think this? The key argument here is not that coercively enforced laws are necessary in order to implement principles of distributive justice effectively. That might well be so, but such an instrumental account of the link between political coercion and justice is not what the authors in question have in mind. Their argument is rather that if someone is made subject to coercive laws that restrict her freedom in a number of ways, and that may impose punitive costs if she is found to be in breach of them, then she is owed a justification for those laws, and the justification that succeeds is one that shows that the system as a whole is distributively just.[18] In other words, the argument ties together distributive justice and legitimacy: systems of coercion can be legitimate if, and only if, they comply with principles of distributive justice, in which case those unavoidably subject to them have no complaint if they are coerced. One popular way of spelling out the argument is via the notion of hypothetical consent: if the system as a whole is fair, then all those involved in it would have given their consent to it if asked in advance, in which case they have no justified complaint when they are now made to comply with its rules.[19]

As with the cooperative practice view, the political coercion view clearly contains something of relevance to the boundaries issue we are addressing. How we think about social justice is properly shaped by the fact that its requirements are primarily delivered by a legal and political system that is also coercive. But is the link quite as tight as this view suggests? If we accept it, then we seem to be committed to drawing a sharp line between human relationships that involve coercion and those that do not.[20] Yet questions of distributive justice appear to arise in both settings: they arise, for instance, in workplaces, clubs, churches, universities, and so forth. One answer might be that this is a different kind of distributive justice. But once again, it is by no means obvious that the principles that apply in these noncoercive settings are categorically different from those that arise at the state level. For example, certain principles of equality (such as equal rights to stand for office) seem to apply in both cases.

The proposed tight link between distributive justice and political legitimacy is also open to question. Political legitimacy is to a considerable degree a matter of procedures. That is, a system of coercive laws may be legitimate if it has been authorized in a certain way, say, through a democratic procedure such as majority voting, even if it fails fully to meet standards of social justice. To someone who asks, "Why should I be subject to this coercive law that I personally find objectionable?," it may be enough to say, for example, "The law was enacted by a procedure that was fair—it gave everyone equal rights to vote for their representative." It would be wrong to suggest, however, that political legitimacy can be understood entirely in terms of procedures. A radically unjust law (such as one that imposes severe burdens on a minority) may be illegitimate even though authorized by an otherwise fair procedure such as democratic voting. Thus the political coercion view is not wholly off the mark in seeing some connection between distributive justice and legitimacy. But by overlooking the predominantly procedural character of political legitimacy, it exaggerates the significance of that connection.

So although questions of distributive justice may become especially pressing between people whose relationships to one another involve routinely applied coercion, it seems that such relationships are neither strictly necessary nor sufficient to bring principles of distributive justice into play. The political coercion view, taken by itself, does not provide an answer to the boundaries question. What about the third candidate for this role, the common identity view? This holds that to understand the boundaries of justice, we need to begin with people who form a community of some kind, who identify with each other and therefore feel a sense of solidarity among themselves. Why is this said to be a necessary condition for distributive justice? There are two complementary arguments to consider here.

One has to do with the need for agreement—agreement both about the nature of the goods whose distribution will be subject to the relevant principles and about the principles themselves. Before we can talk about the fair distribution of education or health care, say, we have to understand what these goods are—what counts as an instance of being educated or given medical aid. These common understandings arise only in communities whose members interact with each other, speak a common language, and so forth.[21] Of course, such understandings may overlap to a considerable extent across different communities. Nevertheless, broad agreement is not enough to make distributive justice possible—the level of agreement has to be sufficiently high, and that, so it is claimed, will obtain only within groups of people united by a common culture, by language, and so forth. Equally, there must be agreement on the criteria of distribution. If principles of justice are couched in terms of *desert* or *need*, for example, this presupposes some consensus on the qualities that should count as the basis of desert or on the components of a decent human life that enable us to distinguish genuine needs from mere wants or demands. Where no real community exists, it is argued, appeals to desert or to need become merely self-serving demands by particular groups for an increased share of social resources.[22]

The second argument in support of the common identity view is an argument about motivation. The argument runs roughly as follows. In order for people to be willing to abide by principles of distributive justice, particularly in circumstances in which they might be able to do better for themselves by departing from these principles, they have to feel the need to justify themselves to those who would bear the impact of their decision. But such a need for justification arises only among those who identify with each other, in a way that is more powerful than the identification that we might have with other human beings considered merely as such. Distributive justice, in other words, presupposes solidarity. When we feel a sense of community with others, we want to live with them on terms that all can accept—in other words, terms of justice. This argument applies not only to individuals contemplating whether to keep or break the social rules laid down in the name of justice, but also to citizens having to decide which rules to support—do I vote for whatever is most in my material interest or for the law or policy that I regard as fair? The argument is further reinforced by the observation that willingness to abide by principles of justice, in either of the ways just distinguished, depends on a belief that others will reciprocate. But this belief is also powerfully affected by people's sense of identity, by whom they see as members of their community and whom they regard as outsiders.

So the common identity view is supported by two strands of argument, one concerning agreement on principles of justice and the goods to which they apply and the other concerning the motivation to apply and conform to such principles. Do either of these arguments, or both together, yield necessary and sufficient conditions for distributive justice, to ask the question already asked of the cooperative practice and political coercion views?

Contrary to the common identity view, it seems that principles of distributive justice can apply among people who are engaged in common practices or common enterprises whether or not they also identify with one another other than as fellow participants, or feel a sense of solidarity. It may be enough that they agree about the general purpose of the practice or enterprise. Thus, suppose that a group of people is brought together for purposes of economic production. They may be able to agree on principles for distributing the fruits of their labours simply because they agree on what counts as contribution (number of hours worked, say) and what counts as reward (money, say). There need be no deeper level of agreement about, for example, how money is to be valued relative to other goods. Of course, this group does not have a complete conception of distributive justice, and it may be that in order to have such a conception, they would need to enjoy a higher degree of cultural unity. But if the question is simply what level of agreement is necessary for *any* principle of distributive justice to apply, then the common identity view gives too demanding an answer.

A similar point can be made about the motivational argument. It is not clear why distributive justice in a group such as the one just described cannot be sustained by enlightened self-interest. That is, we can imagine the members of such a group choosing to introduce, and comply with, a rule such as distribution of rewards according to the number of hours each person works, because each calculates that such a rule will protect his or her interests most effectively. Each might like simply to grab as much of the product as he can, but he also wants to protect himself against the grabbing proclivities of others. On the other hand, a rule of equal distribution regardless of contribution would suit those who are inclined to free ride on the efforts of others, but expose everyone to the same risk of exploitation. What this shows, I believe, is that the motivational argument applies, at best, to a subset of distributive principles—essentially those whereby it is easy to see in advance who will gain and who will lose by their application, so the prospective losers will be willing to accept them only if they are motivated by the wish to live on terms of justice with the prospective gainers.

If common identity fails as a necessary condition for distributive justice, it fails too as a sufficient condition, since it has long been argued that communities in which shared identity and solidarity are very strong may be able to move "beyond justice," allocating their resources in a way that takes no account of considerations of justice as these are normally understood, such as personal responsibility for outcomes. Drawing upon David Hume's claim that if human benevolence and generosity were extensive enough, "justice and injustice would be equally unknown among mankind,"[23] Michael Sandel has suggested that we should see justice as a remedial virtue, one that is required only because our attachments to one another are not strong enough for us "to govern by the common good alone."[24] Whether any real human community could achieve a level of solidarity high enough to allow it to dispense with justice altogether is uncertain, but the relevant point is that community by itself is not sufficient to bring principles of justice into play.

It seems, therefore, that the common identity view cannot by itself solve the problem of boundaries and justice. It has to be taken in conjunction with the other two views that I canvassed. If we look back to the cooperative practice view, then, as I suggested earlier, if a group of people are participating in a cooperative venture for mutual advantage, they may appropriately apply certain principles of distributive justice within that group whether or not the cooperators share a common identity; even if their association is purely instrumental (each looks on the others just as useful contributors to the project and nothing more), questions of fairness naturally arise when the benefits of cooperation are being allocated. A similar point can be made about those who are subject to a system of political coercion, but neither cooperate economically nor share an identity beyond the fact of their common subjection.

So none of the three positions I have considered (cooperative practice, political coercion, or common identity) seems to yield necessary and sufficient conditions for bounded distributive justice. Each seems to fit some cases, but to leave out others in which, intuitively at least, distributive principles apply. If that conclusion is correct, there are two main corollaries that I want to draw.

The first is this: it is a common observation, among supporters and critics alike, that the nation-state has been and still is the favoured vehicle of social justice. Social justice as understood, and above all as practised, is justice within the boundaries of independent states whose members have a common national identity. Consider an ideal-typical nation-state: one that exercises sovereignty over a well-defined territory, all of whose inhabitants share the national identity in question. Few if any states in the world match this ideal type (they are often multinational to a greater or lesser degree, and include populations whose identities may involve allegiance to more than one homeland), but let us set these qualifications aside for the moment in order to explore the link between the nation-state and social justice. What is interesting about the ideal-typical nation-state is that it *combines* the three features discussed above: it applies coercive laws to all its members; those members identify with one another as compatriots; and although it is not fully self-contained from an economic point of view, its economy and accompanying set of social services can be regarded as a large-scale cooperative practice, since most production, exchange, and distribution occur within the borders of the state. So when John Rawls, for instance, said that his principles of social justice applied to a well-ordered society that was "a self-sufficient association of human beings" and "a closed system; there are no significant relations to other societies, and no one enters from without, for all are born into it to lead a complete life," he was idealizing a bit, but not to a ludicrous extent.[25] But because nation-states combine the three features in question, it is harder to see which of them is playing the crucial role in setting the boundaries of social justice: is it the economic and social cooperation or the political coercion or the shared sense of identity among compatriots?

In consequence, although it is correct to say that nation-states remain privileged sites of distributive justice, it is also important to acknowledge that this claim rests ultimately on a contingent fact, namely that political communities of this kind combine at least three different modes of human relationship, each of them relevant to distributive justice. I believe that fact also explains why social justice is a complex idea—why no single principle, such as equality, can adequately capture all of its requirements.[26] But the main point I want to make is that the existence of the nation-state has made life easier for those of us on the particularist side of the fence than it ought to be: we have been able to tie nation-states and distributive justice together without having to specify precisely by virtue of what that tie is supposed to hold. Walzer's idea of the political community, which I cited at the beginning of this essay, illustrates this well: by implication, the political community is a cooperative unit (its members divide, exchange, and share goods); it is able to exercise coercive power (it can control the distribution of these goods); and yet it remains a community in the true sense of the word (its members are committed to each other and attach shared meanings to the goods they distribute). Given the degree of overlap that has existed in many developed societies over the past century or so (the age of social justice) between economic and social cooperation, subjection to a common set of coercive laws, and national identities, we have largely been able to avoid the task of specifying *which* forms of justice apply within *which* boundaries.

The second corollary has to do with the implications of that overlap beginning to break down, as many now claim is happening in the world today. Systematic coercion may remain very largely the prerogative of the state, but economic cooperation takes place increasingly in networks that run across state boundaries, and identities appear to be shifting both upwards and downwards—to transnational collectives and to cultural groups below the national level. If this is indeed happening, what are the implications for distributive justice? Can we any longer think in terms of a single subject of social justice in Rawls's sense, or will we have to talk about multiple justices, corresponding to the different boundaries that may be relevant in each case?

This is by no means intended as an argument in favour of justice without boundaries. Those who speak of "global social justice" or who interpret global justice in such a way that it has the same content as social justice used to have (equality, the Rawlsian difference principle, and so on) are tacitly presupposing that "the globe" has, or could have, those features that support distributive justice at the national level. But this is very implausible. The absence of political institutions able to wield coercive force is the condition most often highlighted, but equally important, in my view, is the lack of a common identity among people who, if they are not still primarily attached to their ethnic groups or nations, may align themselves in religious terms, say, rather than as "citizens of the world." I am therefore arguing for a middle position between those who defend global principles of distributive justice and those who, like Nagel, maintain that "the idea of global justice without a world government is a chimera."[27] For Nagel, only humanitarian duties between people can exist in the absence of a sovereign able to wield coercive power. He reaches this conclusion because he holds the political coercion view of just boundaries. But this view, I have argued, is too simple. Cooperative practices and common identity matter too. So where we find forms of economic cooperation arising at the transnational level or where people begin to acquire new identities, say, of a regional kind, then the scope of distributive justice will also enlarge even in the absence of coercive political institutions.

The idea of distributive justice will, then, continue to presuppose "a bounded world within which distributions take place," and social justice within nation-states will be its strongest form. To deny that boundaries are relevant to distributive justice, or to underestimate the significance of political units that can bring boundaries of different kinds into closer alignment with each other, would be a serious error. But we should also expect to see new boundaries becoming salient, and with them new kinds of distributive claim. Alongside "thin" global justice, cashed out primarily in terms of human rights, there will also be "thicker" forms of international justice, prescribing, for instance, how to share the benefits of international trade or how to allocate the costs of environmental protection.[28] Philosophers wedded to simple, monistic principles of justice may find this conclusion unsatisfying. But having started with Walzer, I want to end with Rawls, who, even in his earlier thinking when problems of global justice did not yet loom large, remarked that "the correct regulative principle for anything depends on the nature of that thing."[29] Once we grasp the force of that remark, we can more readily grant that boundaries matter for distributive justice, and different boundaries matter in different ways.

Notes

1. Michael Walzer, *Spheres of Justice: A Defence of Pluralism and Equality* (Oxford: Martin Robertson, 1983), 31.

2. Ibid.

3. See David Miller, "Two Ways to Think About Justice," *Politics, Philosophy, and Economics* 1 (2002): 5–28.

4. It is important to insist that these two questions are distinct. One may believe that principles of justice are universal in content in the sense of being context independent, while at the same time believing that they are limited in scope. For example, one might think that justice is always best understood in terms of a principle such as equality of resources, while holding that such a principle is to be applied within separate political communities: the equality that justice requires is equality between the members of such communities, not between human beings as such. I refer later to Ronald Dworkin as someone who appears to hold such a view. Nevertheless, I think that there is a looser connection between the questions, such that contextualists about justice are also likely to support restrictions on its scope: Walzer illustrates this case well.

5. Michael Walzer, *Thick and Thin: Moral Argument at Home and Abroad* (Notre Dame, IN: University of Notre Dame Press, 1994), chaps. 1–2.

6. Rewriting Walzer's conception using the language of human rights does also involve expanding the content of minimal justice somewhat if we include among the basic rights

various rights to provision, such as rights to subsistence and medical care. The injunctions of minimal justice are then no longer purely negative in character, but include positive duties of aid. For further discussion, see David Miller, *National Responsibility and Global Justice* (Oxford: Oxford University Press, 2007), chap. 7, section 3.

7. See also here the acute discussion in Samuel Scheffler, "Conceptions of Cosmopolitanism," in his *Boundaries and Allegiances: Problems of Justice and Responsibility in Liberal Thought* (Oxford: Oxford University Press, 2001).

8. I draw here on my discussion in Miller, *National Responsibility and Global Justice*, chap. 2, section 3.

9. I do not claim that this list exhausts all possible ways of explaining the boundaries of justice. Hume made the interesting suggestion that the boundaries were set by how essential rules of justice were to safeguarding basic human interests. This, he thought, explained why rules that were treated as obligatory within societies, such as promise-keeping, were taken more lightly in international relations: "Tho' the intercourse of different states be advantageous, and even sometimes necessary, yet it is not so necessary nor advantageous as that among individuals, without which 'tis utterly impossible for human nature ever to subsist." See David Hume, *A Treatise of Human Nature*, edited by L. A. Selby-Bigge, revised by P. H. Nidditch (Oxford: Clarendon Press, 1978), book III, section 11.

Another possibility, canvassed in the course of a critical discussion by Philippe Van Parijs, is that distributive justice presupposes a democratic regime, and its boundaries are therefore coextensive with existing democracies. See Philippe Van Parijs, "Global Distributive Justice," in *A Companion to Contemporary Political Philosophy*, edited by Robert Goodin, Philip Pettit, and Thomas Pogge, 2nd ed. (Oxford: Blackwell, 2007). I believe, however, that it may be better to treat democracy as playing a role within some versions of the political coercion view, such as Nagel's discussed below.

10. John Rawls, *A Theory of Justice* (Cambridge, MA: Harvard University Press, 1971), 4.

11. See also here Brian Barry, "Humanity and Justice in Global Perspective," in his *Democracy, Power, and Justice: Essays in Political Theory* (Oxford: Clarendon Press, 1989), section 2.

12. Aristotle, *The Politics*, translated by T. A. Sinclair (Harmondsworth, UK: Penguin, 1962), 128.

13. See Rawls, *A Theory of Justice*, 88–89; and John Rawls, *Justice as Fairness: A Restatement* (Cambridge, MA: Harvard University Press, 2001), 51–52.

14. Rawls, *A Theory of Justice*, 4. See, especially, Brian Barry, *Theories of Justice* (Hemel Hempstead, UK: Harvester Wheatsheaf, 1989), chap. 6.

15. John Rawls, *Collected Papers*, edited by Samuel Freeman (Cambridge, MA: Harvard University Press, 1999), 317.

16. See Rawls, *Justice as Fairness*, 171–176, at 176n.

17. Ronald Dworkin, "Introduction," in his *Sovereign Virtue* (Cambridge, MA: Harvard University Press, 2000); Michael Blake, "Distributive Justice, State Coercion, and Autonomy," *Philosophy and Public Affairs* 30 (2001): 257–296; Thomas Nagel, "The Problem of Global Justice," *Philosophy and Public Affairs* 33 (2005): 113–147. By considering these three authors together, I do not mean to imply that they spell the political coercion view out in the same way—they do not. But I believe that what I say in the following applies to that view generally.

18. Nagel adds the further claim that by virtue of their (nonvoluntary) membership, citizens become responsible for the content of the law. As he puts it, the will of each citizen is "actively engaged" in the making and sustaining of coercively enforced rules, which adds

extra weight to the requirement that the rules must be justified to (all of) those who are subject to them. See Nagel, "The Problem of Global Justice," section 5.

This seems to imply that the political coercion view applies only within democratic states. However, Nagel resists this implication, claiming in a footnote (on 129) that even societies governed by colonial or occupying powers may fulfil the conditions for distributive justice. As he admits, this "requires a broad interpretation of what it is for a society to be governed in the name of its members." In my view, such an interpretation is implausibly broad. Nagel would have been better advised to confine his argument to democratic states and authoritarian regimes that, nonetheless, can reasonably claim to be ruling with the support of the people and in conformity with their values. Under these circumstances, subjects can be held collectively responsible for what the regime does, as I have argued in Miller, *National Responsibility and Global Justice*, chap. 5.

19. Blake deploys this line of argument in Blake, "Distributive Justice, State Coercion, and Autonomy."

20. For a fuller critique of Nagel, in particular, that argues that state-based coercive relationships are only one among several types of relationship that can give rise to duties of justice, see J. Cohen and C. Sabel, "Extra Rempublicam Nulla Justitia?," *Philosophy and Public Affairs* 34 (2006): 147–175.

21. I have expanded upon this claim in David Miller, "Against Global Egalitarianism," *Journal of Ethics* 9 (2005): 55–79; and in Miller, *National Responsibility and Global Justice*, chap. 3.

22. These arguments can, of course, be turned around so as to claim that the scale and diversity of modern societies mean that they are no longer suitable sites of distributive justice. Alasdair MacIntyre famously made this claim (with particular reference to desert) in Alasdair MacIntyre, *After Virtue* (London: Duckworth, 1981). See also Chandran Kukathas, "The Mirage of Global Justice," *Social Philosophy and Policy* 23 (2006): 1–28, esp. sections II–III.

23. Hume, *A Treatise of Human Nature*, 495.

24. Michael Sandel, *Liberalism and the Limits of Justice* (Cambridge: Cambridge University Press, 1982), 183. It is possible to argue, against Sandel, that the effect of strong communal attachments is not to displace justice by rendering it unnecessary, but rather to alter its content, for example, by substituting principles of need for Humean principles of property rights or for principles of desert. Sandel's description of the ideal family governed by mutual affection wavers between saying that in these circumstances members will not wish to insist on their individual *rights* and saying that they will not claim their fair shares in a more general sense (33). Perhaps we should distinguish here between what strong community implies under conditions of scarcity (need-based justice) and what it might imply under conditions of plenty, such as those described by Hume.

25. John Rawls, "Kantian Constructivism in Moral Theory," in *Collected Papers*, 323.

26. I have argued for this at greater length in David Miller, *Principles of Social Justice* (Cambridge, MA: Harvard University Press, 1999), esp. chap. 2.

27. Nagel, "The Problem of Global Justice," 115.

28. Thinking about these questions is still in its infancy. For political philosophers, it should now be a major task to explore these intermediate forms of justice, neither "social" nor "global" as these terms are usually understood.

29. Rawls, *A Theory of Justice*, 29.

READING

6

Capabilities and Resources

AMARTYA SEN

That income or wealth is an inadequate way of judging advantage was discussed with great clarity by Aristotle in *Nicomachean Ethics*: "Wealth is evidently not the good we are seeking; for it is merely useful and for the sake of something else."[1] Wealth is not something we value for its own sake. Nor is it invariably a good indicator of what kind of lives we can achieve on the basis of our wealth. A person with severe disability cannot be judged to be more advantaged merely because she has a larger income or wealth than her able-bodied neighbour. Indeed, a richer person with disability may be subject to many restraints that the poorer person without the physical disadvantage may not have. In judging the advantages that the different people have compared with each other, we have to look at the overall capabilities they manage to enjoy. This is certainly one important argument for using the capability approach over the resource-centred concentration on income and wealth as the basis of evaluation.

Since the idea of capability is linked with substantive freedom, it gives a central role to a person's *actual* ability to do the different things that she values doing. The capability approach focuses on human lives, and not just on the resources people have, in the form of owning—or having use of—objects of convenience that a person may possess. Income and wealth are often taken to be the main criteria of human success. By proposing a fundamental shift in the focus of attention from the *means* of living to the *actual opportunities* a person has, the capability approach aims at a fairly radical change in the standard evaluative approaches widely used in economics and social studies.

It also initiates a very substantial departure from the means orientation in some of the standard approaches in political philosophy, for example, John Rawls's focus on "primary goods" (incorporated in his "difference principle") in assessing distributional issues in his theory of justice. Primary goods are all-purpose means such as income and wealth, powers and prerogatives of office, the social bases of self-respect, and so on. They are not valuable in themselves, but they can, to varying extents, help the pursuit of what we really value. Nevertheless, even though primary goods are, at best, means to the valued ends of human life, they themselves have been seen as the primary indicator of judging distributional equity in the Rawlsian principles of justice. Through the explicit recognition that the *means* of satisfactory human living are not themselves the *ends* of good living (the point that Aristotle was making), the capability approach helps to bring about a significant extension of the reach of the evaluative exercise.[2]

Poverty as Capability Deprivation

One of the central issues in this context is the criterion of poverty. The identification of poverty with low income is well established, but there is, by now, quite a substantial literature on its inadequacies. Rawls's focus on primary goods is more inclusive than income (indeed, income is only one of its constituents), but the identification of primary goods is still guided, in Rawlsian analysis, by his search for general all-purpose means, of which income and wealth are particular—and particularly important—examples. However, different people can have quite different opportunities for converting income and other primary goods into characteristics of good living and into the kind of freedom valued in human life. Thus, the relationship between resources and poverty is both variable and deeply contingent on the characteristics of the respective people and the environment in which they live—both natural and social.[3]

There are, in fact, various types of contingencies that result in variations in the conversion of income into the kinds of lives that people can lead. There are at least four important sources of variation.

1. *Personal heterogeneities*: people have disparate physical characteristics in relation to age, gender, disability, proneness to illness, and so on, making their needs extremely diverse; for example, a disabled or an ill person may need more income to do the same elementary things that a less afflicted person can do with a given level of income. Indeed, some disadvantages, for example, severe disabilities, may not be entirely correctable even with huge expenditure on treatment or prosthesis.

2. *Diversities in the physical environment*: how far a given income will go will depend also on environmental conditions, including climatic circumstances, such as temperature ranges, or flooding. The environmental conditions need not be unalterable—they could be improved with communal efforts, or worsened by pollution or depletion. But an isolated individual may have to take much of the environmental conditions as given in converting incomes and personal resources into functionings and quality of life.

3. *Variations in social climate*: the conversion of personal resources into functionings is influenced also by social conditions, including public health care and epidemiology, public educational arrangements, and the prevalence or absence of crime and violence in the particular location. Aside from public facilities,

the nature of community relationships can be very important, as the recent literature on "social capital" has tended to emphasize.[4]

4. *Differences in relational perspectives*: established patterns of behaviour in a community may also substantially vary the need for income to achieve the same elementary functionings; for example, to be able to "appear in public without shame" may require higher standards of clothing and other visible consumption in a richer society than in a poorer one (as Adam Smith noted more than two centuries ago in the *Wealth of Nations*).[5] The same applies to the personal resources needed for taking part in the life of the community, and in many contexts, even to fulfil the elementary requirements of self-respect. This is primarily an intersocietal variation, but it influences the relative advantages of two persons located in different countries.[6]

There can also be some "coupling" of disadvantages between different sources of deprivation, and this can be a critically important consideration in understanding poverty and in making public policy to tackle it.[7] Handicaps, such as age or disability or illness, reduce one's ability to earn an income. But they also make it harder to convert income into capability, since an older or more disabled or more seriously ill person may need more income (for assistance, for prosthetics, for treatment) to achieve the same functionings (even if that achievement were, in fact, at all possible).[8] Thus real poverty (in terms of capability deprivation) can easily be much more intense than we can deduce from income data. This can be a crucial concern in assessing public action to assist the elderly and other groups with conversion difficulties in addition to their low income-earning ability.[9]

Distribution of facilities and opportunities within the family raises further complications for the income approach to poverty. Income accrues to the family through its earning members, and not to all the individuals within it irrespective of age, gender, and working ability. If the family income is disproportionately used to advance the interests of some family members and not others (for example, if there is a systematic preference for boys over girls in the family allocation of resources), then the extent of the deprivation of the neglected members (girls, in the example considered) may not be adequately reflected by the aggregate value of the family income.[10] This is a substantial issue in many contexts; sex bias does appear to be a major factor in the family allocation in many countries in Asia and North Africa. The deprivation of girls is more readily—and more reliably—assessed by looking at capability deprivation reflected, for example, in greater mortality, morbidity, undernourishment, or medical neglect, than can be found on the basis of comparing incomes of different families.[11]

Disability, Resources, and Capability

The relevance of disability in the understanding of deprivation in the world is often underestimated, and this can be one of the most important arguments for paying attention to the capability perspective. People with physical or mental disability are not only among the most deprived human beings in the world; they are also, frequently enough, the most neglected.

The magnitude of the global problem of disability in the world is truly gigantic. More than 600 million people—about one in ten of all human beings—live with some form of significant disability.[12] More than 400 million of them live in developing countries. Furthermore, in the developing world, the disabled are quite often the poorest of the poor in terms of income, but in addition their *need* for income is greater than that of able-bodied people, since they require money and assistance to try to live normal lives and to attempt to alleviate their handicaps. The impairment of income-earning ability, which can be called "the earning handicap," tends to be reinforced and much magnified in its effect by "the conversion handicap": the difficulty in converting incomes and resources into good living, precisely because of disability.

The importance of the conversion handicap from disability can be illustrated with some empirical results from a pioneering study of poverty in the United Kingdom undertaken by Wiebke Kuklys, in a remarkable thesis completed at Cambridge University shortly before her untimely death from cancer: the work was later published as a book.[13] Kuklys found that 17.9 percent of individuals lived in families with income below the poverty line. If attention is shifted to individuals in families with a disabled member, the percentage of such individuals living below the poverty line is 23.1. This gap of about 5 percentage points largely reflects the income handicap associated with disability and the care of the disabled. If the conversion handicap is now introduced, and note is taken of the need for more income to ameliorate the disadvantages of disability, the proportion of individuals in families with disabled members jumps up to 47.4 percent, a gap of nearly 20 percentage points over the share of individuals below the poverty line (17.9 percent) for the population as a whole. To look at the comparative picture in another way, of the 20 extra percentage points for poverty disadvantage for individuals living in families with a disabled member, about a quarter can be attributed to income handicap and three-quarters to conversion handicap (the central issue that distinguishes the capability perspective from the perspective of incomes and resources).

An understanding of the moral and political demands of disability is important not only because it is such a widespread and impairing feature of humanity, but also because many of the tragic consequences of disability can actually be substantially overcome with determined societal help and imaginative intervention. Policies to deal with disability can have a large domain, including the amelioration of the effects of handicap, on the one hand, and programmes to prevent the development of disabilities, on the other. It is extremely important to understand that many disabilities are preventable, and much can be done not only to diminish the *penalty* of disability but also to reduce its *incidence*.

Indeed, only a fairly moderate proportion of the 600 million people living with disabilities were doomed to these conditions at conception, or even at birth. For example, maternal malnutrition and childhood undernourishment can make children prone to illnesses and handicaps of health. Blindness can result from diseases linked to infection and lack of clean water. Other disabilities can originate through the effects of polio, measles, or AIDS, as well as road accidents and injuries at work. A further issue is that of landmines that are scattered across the troubled territories of the world, and maim as well as kill people, especially children. Social intervention against disability has to include prevention as well as management and alleviation. If the demands of justice have to give priority to the removal of manifest injustice (as I have been arguing throughout this work), rather than concentrating on the long-distance search for the perfectly just society, then the prevention and alleviation of disability cannot but be fairly central in the enterprise of advancing justice.

Given what can be achieved through intelligent and humane intervention, it is amazing how inactive and smug most societies are about the prevalence of the unshared burden of disability. In feeding this inaction, conceptual conservatism plays a significant role. In particular, the concentration on income distribution as the principal guide to distributional fairness prevents an understanding of the predicament of disability and its moral and political implications for social analysis. Even the constant use of income-based views of poverty (such as the repeated invoking of the numbers of people who live below $1 or $2 of income per day—a popular activity by international organizations) can distract attention from the full rigour of social deprivation, which combines conversion handicap with earning handicap. The 600 million handicapped people in the world are not plagued just by low income. Their freedom to lead a good life is blighted in many different ways, which act individually and together, to place these people in jeopardy.

Rawls's Use of Primary Goods

Given the importance of the distance between capabilities and resources, for reasons already discussed, it is hard not to be sceptical of John Rawls's difference principle, which concentrates entirely on primary goods in judging distributional issues in his "principles of justice" for the institutional basis of society. This divergence, important as it is, does not of course reflect Rawls's lack of concern about the importance of substantive freedom—a point I have already made earlier on in this work. Even though Rawls's principles of justice concentrate on primary goods, he pays attention elsewhere to the need for correcting this resource focus in order to have a better grip on people's real freedom. Rawls's pervasive sympathy for the disadvantaged is plentifully reflected in his writings.

In fact, Rawls does recommend special correctives for "special needs," such as disability and handicap, even though this is not a part of his principles of justice. These corrections come not in setting up "the basic institutional structure" of the society at the "constitutional stage," but as something that should emerge later on in the *use* of the institutions thus set up, particularly in the "legislative stage." This makes the reach of Rawls's motivation clear enough, and the question to be asked is whether this is adequate as a way of rectifying the partial blindness of the perspective of resources and primary goods in Rawlsian principles of justice.

In the exalted place that Rawls gives to the metric of primary goods, there is some general downplaying of the fact that different people, for reasons of personal characteristics, the influences of physical and social environments, or relative deprivation (when a person's absolute advantages depend on her relative standing compared with others), can have widely varying opportunities to convert general resources (like income and wealth) into capabilities—what they can or cannot actually do. The variations in conversion opportunities are not just matters of what can be seen as special needs, but reflect pervasive variations—large, small, and medium—in the human condition and in relevant social circumstances.

Rawls does indeed talk about the eventual emergence of special provisions for special needs (for example, for the blind or for those who are otherwise clearly disabled), at a later phase in the unfolding of his multistage story of justice. The move indicates Rawls's deep concern about disadvantage, but the way he deals with this pervasive problem has quite a limited reach. First, these corrections occur, to the extent they do, only after the basic institutional structure has been set up through the Rawlsian principles of justice—the nature of these basic institutions are not at all influenced by such special needs (primary goods such as incomes and wealth rule supreme in setting up the institutional base dealing with distributional issues, through the role of the difference principle).

Second, even at a later stage, when particular note is taken of special needs, there is no attempt to come to terms with the ubiquitous variations in conversion opportunities between different people. The prominent and easily identifiable handicaps (such as blindness) are, of course, important to pay attention to, but the variations in many different ways (linked, for example, with greater proneness to illness, more adverse epidemiological surroundings, various levels and types of physical and mental disabilities, etc.) make the informational focus on functionings and capabilities essential for thinking about social arrangements and social realizations, both in setting up the institutional structure and in making sure that they function well and with adequate use of humane and sympathetic reasoning.

I believe Rawls is also motivated by his concern for fairness in the distribution of freedom and capabilities, but by founding his principles of justice on the informational perspective of primary goods in the difference principle, he leaves the determination of "just institutions" for distributional fairness exclusively on the slender shoulders of primary goods to provide the basic institutional guidance. This does not give his underlying concern for capabilities enough room for influence at the institutional phase with which his principles of justice are directly concerned.

Departures from Rawlsian Theory

Unlike in Rawls's focus on transcendental institutionalism, the approach to justice explored in this work does not pursue a sequential and prioritized scenario of the unfolding of a perfectly just society. In focusing on the enhancement of justice through institutional and other changes, the approach here does not, therefore, relegate the issue of conversion and capabilities into something of second-category status, to be brought up and considered later. Understanding the nature and sources of capability deprivation and inequity is indeed central to removing manifest injustices that can be identified by public reasoning, with a good deal of partial accord.[14]

The Rawlsian approach has also had extensive influences outside its own domain as specified by Rawls, since it has been such a dominant mode of reasoning on justice in contemporary moral and political philosophy. For example, those who have tried to retain the Rawlsian contractarian foundation in a new—and more ambitious—theory of justice encompassing the whole world (such a "cosmopolitan theory of justice" has a much larger domain than Rawls's country-by-country approach) have continued to look for a complete ordering for distributional judgements, needed for transcendental institutional justice for the entire globe.[15] Not surprisingly, these theorists are not placated by the partially incomplete ordering based on capabilities, and as Thomas Pogge puts it, there is a demand for much more than "merely a partial ordinal ranking" needed to work out "how an institutional order ought to be designed."[16] I would like to wish good luck to the builders of a transcendentally just set of institutions for the whole world, but for those who are ready to concentrate, at least for the moment, on reducing manifest injustices that so severely plague the world, the relevance of a "merely" partial ranking for a theory of justice can actually be rather momentous.[17]

The central issue, I would submit, is not whether a certain approach has a total reach in being able to compare any two alternatives, but whether the comparisons it can make are appropriately directed and reasoned. Comparisons of freedoms and capabilities place us in the right territory, and we should not be moved to relocate ourselves to a different territory through being tempted by the attractions of a complete ordering (seen independently of *what* it completely orders).

The advantage of the capability perspective over the resource perspective lies in its relevance and substantive importance, and not in any promise of yielding a total ordering. Indeed, as Elizabeth Anderson has persuasively discussed, the capability metric is "superior to a resource metric because it focuses on ends rather than on means, can better handle discrimination against the disabled, is properly sensitive to individual variations in functioning that have democratic import, and is well suited to guide the just delivery of public services, especially in health and education."[18]

Dworkin's Equality of Resources

While Rawls uses the perspective of resources in his principles of justice through the index of primary goods, effectively ignoring the conversion variations between resources and capabilities, Ronald Dworkin's use of the resource perspective is to make room explicitly for taking note of these variations through artful market-oriented thinking, in particular by the use of an imagined primordial market for insurance against conversion handicaps. In this thought-experiment it is assumed that people, under a Rawls-like veil of ignorance of an original position, enter this hypothetical market, which sells insurance against having these respective handicaps. While no one, in this imagined situation, knows who is going to have which handicap, if any, they all buy this insurance against possible adversities, and ("later on," as it were) the ones who actually end up having the handicaps can claim their compensation as determined by the insurance markets, thereby obtaining more resources of other kinds in compensation. That is, argues Dworkin, as fair as you can get, based on what he sees as effective "equality of resources."

This is certainly an interesting and highly ingenious proposal (having taught a class jointly with Ronald Dworkin for ten years at Oxford and knowing the astonishing reach of his mind, I could not, of course, have expected anything less). But after that brilliantly imagined contribution about a possible hypothetical market, Dworkin seems to go straight into something of a "Beat that!" programme, addressed particularly to those afflicted by the capability-based approach.[19] He claims *either* that equality of capability amounts really to equality of welfare, in which case (Dworkin argues) it is a mistaken view of equity, *or* that it amounts actually to the same solution as his own equality of resources, in which case there is no real difference between us (and no advantage in pursuing the capability approach).

Despite my immense admiration for Ronald Dworkin's work, I have to say I am somewhat at a loss in deciding where to begin in analysing what is wrong with this argument against a capability-based approach. First (to begin with a very minor point, only to get it out of the way), even if equality of capability were to amount to equality of the capability for welfare, that would not be the same thing as equality of welfare.[20] However, more importantly, it should have been clear from what I had said about the capability perspective from its first presentation that I am arguing neither for equality of welfare nor for equality of capability to achieve welfare.[21]

Second, if equality of resources were no different from equality of capability and substantive freedom, why is it more interesting normatively to think about the former rather than the latter, since resources are only instrumentally important as means to other ends? Since resources are "merely useful and for the sake of something else" (as Aristotle put it), and since the case for equality of resources rests ultimately on that something else, why not put equality of resources in its place as a way of getting to equality of the capability to achieve—if the congruence between the two does actually hold?

There is, of course, no great mathematical difficulty in thinking of one object that can be seen as an end (such as utility or capability) in terms of "equivalent" amounts of something else (such as income or resource) that serves as a means to achieve the corresponding end, so long as the latter is instrumentally powerful enough to allow us to get to any particular level of the former. This analytical technique has been much used in economic theory, dealing particularly with utility analysis, in thinking of utility not directly but in terms of equivalent incomes (often called "indirect utility"). Capability equality and Dworkinian resource equality, which can be seen in this sense as "indirect capability," could be congruent if and only if insurance markets were to work in such a way that under Dworkin's formula for equality of resources everyone would have much the same capability. But then why thrill merely at the instrumental achievement ("all have the same resources—hurrah!"), rather than about what really matters (all have the same substantive freedom or capability)?

Third, the congruence may not actually hold, since insurance markets can deal more easily with some objects than with others. Some of the sources of capability disadvantage arise not from personal features (like disability), but from relational and environmental features (like being relatively deprived, originally discussed by Adam Smith in the *Wealth of Nations*). It is easily checked why the market for insurance against such nonpersonal characteristics is much harder to accommodate in insurance markets with individual clients.[22]

Another reason for the possibility of noncongruence is that whereas the assessment of interpersonal differences in deprivation is the subject matter of public reasoning in my approach, that assessment is left to the atomistic operators in Dworkin's insurance markets. In Dworkin's system, it is the interplay of the different individuals' respective assessments that determines the market prices and compensation levels of different types of insurance. The market in the Dworkin system is charged to do the valuation exercise, which may actually demand engaging public reasoning and interactive discussion.

Fourth, Dworkin's focus, in common with other transcendental institutionalist approaches, is on getting to perfectly just institutions (in one step). But in dealing with the task of advancing justice through the removal of radical cases of injustice, even when there is no hope of achieving perfectly just institutions (or even any agreement on what they would be like), we can have much use for what has been dismissively called "merely a partial order ranking."

The *as if* market for insurance against disability in the Dworkinian form does not even claim to take us to ways and means of identifying advancements of justice, because of its exclusive concentration on the make-believe exercise of transcendental justice.

Fifth, Dworkin takes the existence, uniqueness, and efficiency of perfectly competitive market equilibria, which he needs for his institutional story, to be entirely unproblematic. And this is all assumed, without much defence, despite what we know about the huge difficulties that exist in these presumptions, as shown by half a century of economic research on "general equilibrium" theory. Indeed, many of the problematic features, related to informational limitations (especially asymmetric information), the role of public goods, economies of scale, and other impediments, apply particularly strongly to the markets for insurance.[23]

There is, I am afraid, some institutional fundamentalism in Dworkin's approach, and some innocence in his presumption that once we have agreed on some rules for insurance-based resource redistribution, we would be able to forget about the actual outcomes and the actual capabilities that different people enjoy. It is assumed that the actual freedoms and outcomes can be left in the secure hands of institutional choice through *as if* markets, without ever having to second-guess the correspondence between what people expected and what actually happened. The insurance markets are supposed to work as one-shot affairs—with no surprises, no repeats, and no discussions about what was hoped for and what actually emerged.

If there is usefulness in Dworkin's ingenious device of imagined insurance markets, that use lies elsewhere than in its claim as a new and viable theory of distributional justice. Resource equality in Dworkin's way is hardly a substitute for the capability approach, but it can serve as one way—one of several ways[24]—of understanding how compensation for handicaps can be thought of in terms of income transfers. In this difficult field, we can do with any help that thought-experiments can provide, so long as they do not pretend to have imperial powers as institution-based arbitrators.

Advancement of justice and the removal of injustice demand joint engagement with institutional choice (dealing, among other things, with private incomes and public goods), behavioural adjustment, and procedures for the correction of social arrangements based on public discussion of what is promised, how the institutions actually work out, and how things can be improved.[25] There is no leave to shut off interactive public reasoning, resting on the promised virtue of a once-and-for-all market-based institutional choice. The social role of institutions, including imaginary ones, is more complex than that.

Notes

1. Aristotle, *Nicomachean Ethics*, translated by D. Ross, rev. ed. (Oxford: Oxford University Press, 1980), book I, section 5, 7.

2. I have presented arguments for this change of focus in "Well-Being, Agency, and Freedom: The Dewey Lectures 1984," *Journal of Philosophy* 82 (April 1985), and "Justice: Means Versus Freedoms," *Philosophy and Public Affairs* 19 (Spring 1990).

3. In an early contribution in 1901, Rowntree noted an aspect of the problem by referring to "secondary poverty," in contrast with "primary poverty," defined in terms of low income (B. Seebohm Rowntree, *Poverty: A Study of Town Life* [London: Macmillan, 1901]). In pursuing the phenomenon of secondary poverty, Rowntree focused specifically on influences of habits and behaviour patterns that affect the commodity composition of a family's consumption. That issue remains important even today, but the distance between low income and actual deprivation can arise for other reasons as well.

4. See, among other writings on this important subject, Robert Putnam, *Bowling Alone: Collapse and Revival of American Community* (New York: Simon and Schuster, 2000).

5. See Adam Smith, *An Inquiry into the Nature and Causes of the Wealth of Nations*, edited by R. H. Campbell and A. S. Skinner (1776; repr. Oxford: Clarendon Press, 1976), 351–352. On the relation between relative disadvantage and poverty, see the more recent works of W. G. Runciman, *Relative Deprivation and Social Justice: A Study of Attitudes to Social Inequality in Twentieth-Century England* (London: Routledge, 1966); and Peter Townsend, *Poverty in the United Kingdom* (Harmondsworth, UK: Penguin, 1979).

6. In fact, relative deprivation in terms of incomes can yield absolute deprivation in terms of capabilities. Being relatively poor in a rich country can be a great capability handicap, even when one's absolute income is high by world standards. In a generally opulent country, more income is needed to buy enough commodities to achieve the same social functioning. On this, see my "Poor, Relatively Speaking," *Oxford Economic Papers* 35 (1983), reprinted in my *Resources, Values, and Development* (Cambridge, MA: Harvard University Press, 1984).

7. On this, see ibid. See also Dorothy Wedderburn, *The Aged in the Welfare State* (London: Bell, 1961); and J. Palmer, T. Smeeding, and B. Torrey, *The Vulnerable: America's Young and Old in the Industrial World* (Washington, DC: Urban Institute Press, 1988).

8. There is also a problem of coupling in (1) undernutrition generated by income poverty, and (2) income poverty resulting from work deprivation due to undernutrition. On these connections, see Partha Dasgupta and Debraj Ray, "Inequality as a Determinant of Malnutrition and Unemployment: Theory," *Economic Journal* 96 (1986), and "Inequality as a Determinant of Malnutrition and Unemployment: Policy," *Economic Journal* 97 (1987).

9. The contribution of such handicaps to the prevalence of income poverty in Britain was brought out sharply by a pioneering empirical study by A. B. Atkinson, *Poverty in Britain and the Reform of Social Security* (Cambridge: Cambridge University Press, 1969). In his later works, Atkinson has further pursued the connection between income handicap and deprivation of other kinds. See his "On the Measurement of Poverty," *Econometrica* 55 (1987), and *Poverty and Social Security* (New York: Harvester Wheatsheaf, 1989). For a powerful examination of the general idea of disadvantage and its far-reaching relevance both for social evaluation and for public policy, see Jonathan Wolff, with Avner De-Shalit, *Disadvantage* (Oxford: Oxford University Press, 2007).

10. On this, see my *Development as Freedom* (New York: Knopf, 1999), chaps. 8, 9, and the literature cited there. Two of the pioneering contributions in this area are Pranab Bardhan, "On Life and Death Questions," *Economic and Political Weekly* 9 (1974); and Lincoln Chen, E. Huq, and S. D'Souza, "Sex Bias in the Family Allocation of Food and Health Care in Rural Bangladesh," *Population and Development Review* 7 (1981). See also my joint paper with Jocelyn Kynch, "Indian Women: Well-Being and Survival," *Cambridge Journal of*

Economics 7 (1983); and jointly with Jean Drèze, *India: Economic Development and Social Opportunity* (New Delhi and Oxford: Oxford University Press, 1995), and *India: Development and Participation* (New Delhi and Oxford: Oxford University Press, 2002).

11. Gender bias is clearly not as central a concern in assessing inequality and poverty in Europe or North America, but the presumption—often implicitly made—that the issue of gender inequality does not apply to "Western" countries can be quite misleading. For example, Italy had one of the highest ratios of "unrecognized" labour by women (mostly unglamorous family work) among all the countries of the world included in the standard national accounts in the mid-1990s, according to UNDP's *Human Development Report 1995* (New York: United Nations, 1995). The accounting of effort and time expended, and its implications for the personal freedom of women, has some bearing for Europe and North America as well. There is also in many cases considerable gender bias in the richest countries in terms of opportunities for advanced education, or for the prospects of being selected for top levels of employment.

12. These estimates come from the World Bank.

13. Wiebke Kuklys, *Amartya Sen's Capability Approach: Theoretical Insights and Empirical Applications* (New York: Springer-Verlag, 2005).

14. In investigating the limitations of focusing on the index of primary goods in the formulation of the principles of justice in the Rawlsian general approach, I do not, of course, intend to suggest that all would be well in his transcendental institutionalist approach if concentration on primary goods were to be replaced by direct engagement with capabilities. The serious difficulties arising from Rawls's transcendental rather than comparative orientation and from the purely institutional focus of his principles of justice, discussed earlier, would remain no matter what informational focus is used to assess distributional concerns. I am arguing here that in addition to the general problems of relying on a transcendental institutionalist approach, the Rawlsian theory is *further* impaired by its concentration on primary goods to deal with distributional issues in its principles of justice.

15. Thomas Pogge has made important contributions on this line. See, particularly, his *World Poverty and Human Rights: Cosmopolitan Responsibilities and Reforms*, 2nd ed. (Cambridge: Polity Press, 2008).

16. Thomas Pogge, "A Critique of the Capability Approach," in *Measuring Justice: Primary Goods and Capabilities*, edited by Harry Brighouse and Ingrid Robeyns (Cambridge: Cambridge University Press, 2010), 51.

17. This issue was discussed in the Introduction and in Chapters 1–4 of my *The Idea of Justice* (Cambridge, MA: Harvard University Press, 2009).

18. Elizabeth Anderson, "Justifying the Capabilities Approach to Justice," in *Measuring Justice*, 81. On related issues, see also her "What Is the Point of Equality?," *Ethics* 109 (1999).

19. I suppose I should feel honoured to be taken seriously enough to be identified as the main protagonist of what he sees as the less than satisfactory approach of capabilities. See Ronald Dworkin, *Sovereign Virtue: The Theory and Practice of Equality* (Cambridge, MA: Harvard University Press, 2000), 65–119. See also his "Sovereign Virtue Revisited," *Ethics* 113 (2002).

20. For example, the *actual* pursuit of expensive modes of living by some, which Dworkin does not want to subsidize, should not be confused with the *capability* to indulge in expensive modes—a capacity that many people may share without actually using it. (The distinction between capability and achievement is discussed in my *The Idea of Justice*.)

21. My 1979 Tanner Lecture on the use of capability, which was published as "Equality of What?," in *Tanner Lectures on Human Values*, edited by S. McMurrin (Cambridge: Cam-

bridge University Press, 1980), vol. 1, presented the capability perspective not merely as a contrast with the Rawlsian focus on primary goods but also as a rival to—and critique of—any welfare-based approach. Dworkin does not comment on it in his first paper on equality of resources: "What Is Equality?: Part 1: Equality of Welfare," and "What Is Equality? Part 2: Equality of Resources," *Philosophy and Public Affairs* 10 (1981), and the attribution first occurs, as far as I can see (unless I have missed something), in Dworkin, *Sovereign Virtue*.

22. Some of the reasons for the divergence of resource equality and capability equality have been analysed by, among others, Andrew Williams, "Dworkin on Capability," *Ethics* 113 (2002); and Roland Pierik and Ingrid Robeyns, "Resources Versus Capabilities: Social Endowments in Egalitarian Theory," *Political Studies* 55 (2007).

23. See Kenneth Arrow and Frank Hahn, *General Competitive Analysis* (San Francisco: Holden-Day, 1971; Amsterdam, the Netherlands: North-Holland, 1979); George Akerlof, "The Market for 'Lemons': Quality Uncertainty and the Market Mechanism," *Quarterly Journal of Economics* 84 (1970); and Joseph Stiglitz and M. E. Rothschild, "Equilibrium in Competitive Insurance Markets," *Quarterly Journal of Economics* 90 (1976), among many other important contributions in this area.

24. An important alternative to giving extra private income to the handicapped is, of course, the much-used practice of providing free or subsidized social services—a procedure that is central to the "welfare state" of Europe. That is how, for example, a national health service runs, rather than giving ill people more income to pay for their medical needs.

25. See Sen, *The Idea of Justice*, esp. chap. 3.

Discussion Questions: Justice

1. Is the "basic structure of society" the only site of justice?
2. Do individuals owe justice to strangers living in distant lands?
3. Does justice require that individuals be given the opportunity to develop their preferred capabilities?

Part III

LIBERTY

A longstanding debate in the history of philosophy concerns the nature of liberty. Many hold that individuals are free just insofar as no one is able to prevent them from doing what they want to do. Other philosophers hold that freedom consists in being one's own master. On the first view, known as the *negative* conception of liberty, the prisoner is a paradigmatic case of a person who lacks freedom; on the latter view, known as the *positive* conception of liberty, the addict who struggles against his internal impulses is the paragon of unfreedom.

Philip Pettit rejects both the negative and positive conceptions of liberty, opting instead for his own conception, which holds that liberty is nondomination. According to Pettit, freedom consists neither in the absence of interference nor in the presence of self-mastery, but rather in the absence of the mastery by others. He argues that compelling considerations proposed in favor of negative liberty actually support his own nondomination conception. John Christman shares Pettit's view that negative liberty is insufficient, but he defends a conception of liberty according to which freedom consists in authentic and reflective self-control. Ian Carter defends the negative conception of liberty against a standard objection according to which negative liberty is too thin (or "formal") to capture what is valuable about freedom.

READING

7

The Instability of Freedom as Noninterference: The Case of Isaiah Berlin

PHILIP PETTIT

Introduction

Most theories of what makes people free in relation to the external world treat the obstacles that derive from the ill will of others as the primary restrictions on freedom; in other words, they equate external freedom with social freedom.[1] Natural limitations reduce the range over which you can enjoy your freedom from the will of others and may even be instrumental in making you vulnerable to that will—and on those grounds they will call for remedy. But according to these theories, such limitations do not in themselves take away from your freedom; they do not make you unfree in the way that other agents can do so. Immanuel Kant gives expression to an assumption these theories might unite in endorsing: "Find himself in what condition he will, the human being is dependent on many external things. . . . But what is harder and more unnatural than this yoke of necessity is the subjection of one human being under the will of another. No misfortune can be more terrifying to one who is accustomed to freedom."[2]

But notwithstanding the common assumption that freedom primarily requires nonsubjection to the will of others, these theories of external freedom divide sharply on what such nonsubjection means. In terms explained later, some theories claim that freedom is reduced when others frustrate you, some when others interfere with you, some when others dominate you. In maintaining this line, they may focus on the freedom of a particular choice or on the freedom of a person, where people's freedom as persons is usually identified with their freedom over a common range of important choices on a common social and legal basis. The issue among these different theories is of immense importance in political theory, since the institutional requirements for promoting freedom as nonfrustration across a society are weaker than the requirements for promoting freedom as noninterference, and they in turn are weaker than the requirements for promoting freedom as nondomination.[3]

The best-known adherent of the middle conception, freedom as noninterference, is Isaiah Berlin, and I develop an argument for the stronger conception of freedom as nondomination by way of interrogating his work, in particular, his 1958 lecture "Two Concepts of Liberty" and some of his later commentary.[4] I claim that while Berlin introduced persuasive considerations against freedom as nonfrustration, these ought to have led him—and ought to lead us—not to rest content with freedom as noninterference, but rather to go the full distance and embrace a notion of freedom as nondomination. The position he took up is an unstable halfway house between the other two positions.

Although much has been written on Berlin's conception of freedom as noninterference, few commentaries foreground his critique of the weaker conception of freedom as nonfrustration. This weaker conception is endorsed most clearly by Thomas Hobbes, though Berlin does not seem to have recognized him as an antagonist.[5] I present the Hobbesian view in the first section of the essay and look at the way in which Berlin breaks with it. Then, in the second section, I consider Berlin's argument for rejecting that view and adopting freedom as noninterference. In the third section, I show how that argument suggests a case for the more radical conception of freedom as nondomination and demonstrate that the notion of freedom as noninterference is unstable. And in the fourth section, I bolster the instability claim by showing that the more radical conception also fits better with Berlin's views on what is required for the freedom of the person. In a final, short conclusion, I speculate on why Berlin might have failed to endorse the idea of freedom as nondomination.

The conception of freedom as nondomination counts as republican in the classical, neo-Roman sense of the term, according to many recent accounts.[6] Hobbes spent much of his work trying to displace that view of freedom, of course, which he cast as an unfortunate legacy of classical thought.[7] Once we see the grounds of Berlin's opposition to Hobbes's central contentions, we can recognize in Berlin someone who ought to have been deeply sympathetic to the republican tradition that Hobbes repudiated.

I. Berlin's Break with Hobbes

Freedom as Nonfrustration in Hobbes

The Hobbesian view of freedom—corporal freedom, to be exact[8]—is summed up in the famous definition of a freeman in *Leviathan*: "A free-man is he that in those things which by his strength and wit he is able to do is not hindered to do what he has a will to."[9] Putting aside the issue of how Hobbes understands hindrance, on which I comment later, there are two surprising claims built into this definition.[10] The first is that being externally hindered in the choice of a given option takes from your freedom only if you have "a will to" do it, only if you prefer that option. And the second is that to be a "freeman"—to deserve to be accorded this status—is to escape all external hindrance in the options you prefer to take.

The first claim is surprising because it makes it too easy to be free in a given choice: you are not made unfree by having an option removed or replaced if you happen not to want to enact it. The second claim is surprising because, going to the other extreme, it makes it impossibly hard to count as a freeman or free person: you must be lucky enough, or perhaps powerful enough, for none of your choices to be frustrated; it is not enough, for example, to escape frustration in a designated range of choices.

While Berlin breaks with Hobbes on both of these claims, as we shall see, I focus on his rejection of the first in this section. That first claim is not just an implication of the definition that may have escaped Hobbes's attention. It is also a thesis that he emphasizes elsewhere. He does so most strikingly in a debate with Bishop Bramhall about the preconditions for having a free choice between playing tennis or not.

Bramhall suggests that if you are considering whether or not to play tennis—we may assume a willing partner—and in the end you decide against doing so, you may still have been wrong to think that you had a free choice. After all, unbeknownst to you, someone may have shut the door of the ("real") tennis court against you. Hobbes is undaunted by the claim, asserting that for anyone in your position, "it is no impediment to him that the door is shut till he have a will to play."[11] We may all agree that you freely decided against playing tennis and that you might therefore be held responsible for this decision.[12] But this is just to say that you made a decision on the false assumption that you had a free choice, not that you actually had a free choice. Hobbes, however, differs. He thinks that your freedom of choice requires only that the option you prefer, and not necessarily any other option, is available to you.

The Hobbesian view equates freedom with the nonfrustration of your preference and your choice. You will not be frustrated if an option you do not actually prefer—in this case, playing tennis—is blocked; you will be frustrated only if the option you prefer is obstructed. And according to Hobbes, you will enjoy freedom in any choice in which you avoid such frustration.

Berlin's Alternative

Berlin agrees with Hobbes that freedom of choice requires the absence of external hindrance, focusing—unlike Hobbes—on "the deliberate interference of other human beings."[13] They both hold that the freedom with which they are concerned—in Hobbes's explicit reference, the freedom required for being a freeman—is jeopardized by such intervention. But the issue for Berlin is whether Hobbes is right that intervening to obstruct a nonpreferred option is irrelevant to an agent's freedom of choice. Suppose I am disposed to interfere, not with the option you choose, but with an option that you might have chosen to take and didn't; suppose I am not disposed to frustrate your preference but only to block an option you don't actually prefer. Does this take from the freedom of your choice or not?

In the opening part of his 1958 lecture, Berlin appears to go along with the Hobbesian answer that no, it doesn't. Thus, he explicitly endorses Hobbes's definition, though without commenting on this implication.[14] He suggests that on "the 'negative' definition of liberty in its classical form," interference is "bad as such" because "it frustrates human desires."[15] And in later commentary, he describes his initial take on freedom in that lecture—"the formulation with which I began"—as mistaking freedom for the absence of such frustration.[16]

But though his initial formulation of the notion of liberty may have been Hobbesian in this way, Berlin insists in this commentary that the main arguments of the original lecture were not affected by this "genuine error." And that is certainly so, for he explicitly argues in the course of the lecture that your negative liberty is not ensured by being positioned to do what you actually want to do; you must be positioned to do whatever you might happen to want or try to do among the relevant alternatives.[17] Freedom is not "the absence of obstacles to the fulfillment of a man's desires," as he later puts it, but "the absence of obstacles to possible choices and activities."[18]

In the later commentary, Berlin gives telling expression to his non-Hobbesian point of view. The options in a choice are like doors you can push on, he says. How extensive the choice is depends on how many doors there are. How significant the choice is depends on what the doors lead to. And, crucially, how free the exercise of choice is depends on whether and how far the doors are open. "The extent of a man's negative freedom is, as it were, a function of what doors, and how many are open to him; upon what prospects they are open; and how open they are."[19]

The important point in this metaphor is that the freedom of a choice turns, not just on whether the door you push on is open, but also on whether all the doors are open, including those you might have pushed on but didn't. Interference may be the enemy of freedom, but it is not just frustrating interference, as in Hobbes's picture, that matters, not just interference with the actual option preferred. The fact that you would have suffered interference in the choice of another option, even though you don't suffer interference in the option you adopt, will equally take from your freedom of choice. Freedom as noninterference, as we can put his claim, requires more than freedom as nonfrustration.

When Hobbes speaks of the external hindrance that affects freedom, even that which originates in human beings, he only has in mind the preventive sort of obstacle that removes one or more of the agent's options.[20] When Berlin speaks of interference, he has a wider category of intervention in mind, as have most philosophers who write about social freedom. It includes not just removing an option but replacing it by a penalized alternative, as in a coercive threat; and it may include not just intervening in the options available but also undermining the informed, deliberative character of the choice by deception or manipulation.[21]

These different approaches suggest different readings of the open-doors metaphor. On the Hobbesian story, a door will be open just in case it is unlocked. On the story that Berlin proposes, a door may be unlocked without strictly being open: to suggest analogues of nonpreventive interference, it may be jammed, for example, or concealed from view or misrepresented in a play of mirrors. We won't have much reason to return to this divergence but, for the record, I shall have the wider conception of interference in mind when arguing later about the radical implications of Berlin's line of argument.

II. Berlin's Argument

No Freedom by Adaptation

Berlin does not rely on just the appeal of the open-doors metaphor for undermining the view of freedom as nonfrustration. Nor does he merely observe that on this view you may enjoy freedom in a choice where you are left only one option, provided that is the option you prefer. He offers an imaginative argument against that conception.[22] This argument is of general interest and may represent Berlin's most lasting contribution to our thinking about freedom.

In full, perhaps pedantic dress, the argument goes like this:

1. Suppose with Hobbes that you enjoy freedom in a choice between A and B just in case you avoid interference in the option that you actually choose; you avoid frustration.
2. By supposition, you do not enjoy freedom of choice in the case where A attracts my interference, B does not, and you choose A.
3. But, by supposition, you would enjoy freedom of choice in that case were you to choose B.
4. If you know the situation, it therefore appears that you can ensure your freedom of choice without constraining my interference by adapting your preferences and choosing B.
5. But this is absurd. You cannot make yourself free just by accommodating yourself to my disposition to interfere.
6. Thus, the original supposition that nonfrustration is enough for freedom must be false.

The thrust of the argument is easily illustrated. Imagine that I am a prisoner who, being forcibly imprisoned, does not have freedom of choice as between staying behind bars and living in the outside world. Do I lack freedom, as the conception of freedom as nonfrustration implies, just because the option I prefer is living outside prison? If so, then I can make myself free—I can give myself freedom in the choice between living in prison or outside—just by adapting my preferences and coming to want to stay in prison. As Berlin expresses the thought in the original lecture, "I need only contract or extinguish my wishes and I am made free."[23] Or, as he expands on this later, "if to be free—negatively—is simply not to be prevented by other persons from doing whatever one wishes, then one of the ways of attaining such freedom is by extinguishing one's wishes."[24]

In the prison example, as in any examples that might be used to illustrate Berlin's lesson, the choice between living in prison and living outside is taken as given, and the crucial observation is that adapting preferences in the face of obstruction to one or another option cannot give you freedom in that choice. But it is worth noting that there is a related context in which adaptation is not objectionable. Suppose you want to spend time with me on the weekends but do not share my preference for hiking. You might reasonably work at getting yourself to like hiking in order to make yourself into an acceptable weekend companion. And having won me around, your preference-adaptation would then have given you a choice on one or another weekend between going hiking with me or staying at home. This sort of adaptation is designed to give you more options and more choices by making me into a willing partner in certain joint activities. It is not designed, like the adaptation Berlin addresses, to make you free in a choice between given options.

Freedom and Preference-Satisfaction

The counterintuitive consequence that undermines the Hobbesian view is avoidable under the open-doors claim that every option in a free choice must escape interference. And that becomes Berlin's main argument for the claim. The significance of the claim shows up in the fact, emphasized in the work of Amartya Sen, that the ideal of freedom is distinct from that of preference-satisfaction—that is, the satisfaction of unadapted preferences.[25] The ideal of preference-satisfaction requires only that actual interference and actual frustration of preference be avoided. The ideal of freedom of choice requires the avoidance of counterfactual interference, too. Berlin marks the contrast between the ideals nicely: "To teach a man that, if he cannot get what he wants, he must learn to want only what he can get may contribute to his happiness or his security; but it will not increase his civil or political freedom."[26]

Berlin's open-doors view implies that freedom has a modal character. You are free in a choice not just in virtue of enjoying noninterference in the actual world where you choose A but in virtue also of enjoying it in a range of possible worlds: presumptively, the nearest possible world or worlds in which you choose B.[27] You are free in the actual world not just in virtue of its being a world without interference but also in virtue of its being a world where certain features mean that you would not suffer interference even if you chose other than you actually did.

Berlin's argument shows quite effectively that freedom of choice is a distinct goal from actual preference-satisfaction and, if we assume it is desirable, a distinct ideal. He makes the a priori assumption—an assumption expressive of how we conceptualize freedom—that you cannot make yourself free by accommodating yourself to restrictive constraints, only by challenging them. And then he shows that if we are to be faithful to this assumption in looking after your freedom, we must try to ensure that the doors associated with your different options are all open. We cannot settle for the more parsimonious strategy of worrying about keeping an option open only to the extent that it is likely you will choose it. That would be to worry about promoting your preference-satisfaction, not strictly your freedom of choice.[28]

There are some situations, of course, where we should settle for the more parsimonious ideal. It may be that we cannot protect your access to both options A and B—at least not at a reasonable cost—and so that we cannot ensure your freedom of choice as between those options. In that situation, it would certainly make sense to invest our resources in protection of each option in a measure that corresponds to the likelihood of your choosing it. In other words, it would make sense, given the infeasibility of ensuring freedom of choice, to settle for promoting expected preference-satisfaction.[29] But the fact that second-best circumstances might force this strategy on us does not mean that there is reason in general to prioritize preference-satisfaction over freedom of choice or to treat the two goals as equivalent. Berlin's message remains in place.

III. Building on Berlin's Argument

No Freedom by Ingratiation

Berlin argues that it is necessary for the freedom of a choice, say, between options A and B, that each option should remain accessible, each door open. But is this sufficient for the freedom of the choice? That is the question that I want to raise in this section. I try to show that an argument that parallels Berlin's own argument against Hobbes suggests that it is not sufficient. As he argues for freedom as noninterference over freedom as nonfrustration, so it is possible in parallel to argue for freedom as nondomination over freedom as noninterference.

Berlin's argument starts from the assumption that you cannot make yourself free by adapting your preferences to the constraints of another's interference and uses this in a reductio ad absurdum of the Hobbesian theory of freedom. The argument is that if the Hobbesian theory were true, then it follows, absurdly, that you can make yourself free by a suitable form of preference-adaptation. It turns out, however, that there is a similar sort of absurdity that follows if Berlin's own theory were true so that his position is exposed to a parallel reductio.

This is how the argument goes:

1. Suppose with Berlin that you enjoy freedom in a choice between A and B just in case both options are open; you avoid interference in each option, not just interference in the option preferred.
2. By supposition, you do not enjoy freedom of choice in the case where I have a power of interference and, being ill willed, am disposed to interfere with one or the other option.
3. But, by supposition, you would enjoy freedom of choice in that case if I were disposed, notwithstanding my power, to interfere with neither.
4. If you know the situation, then, it appears that you can make yourself free, without reducing my power of interference, just by ingratiating yourself with me and getting me to let you have your way.
5. But this is absurd. You cannot make yourself free just by accommodating yourself to my power of interference.
6. Thus, the original supposition that noninterference is enough for freedom must be false.

Berlin's argument against Hobbes turns on the intuition that adapting your preferences so as to choose things that are accessible cannot make you free, even if it can increase your comfort or contentment. This argument against Berlin turns on the intuition that, equally, adapting your attitudes so as to ingratiate yourself with me—or with any power in your life—cannot make you free, even if, again, it can make life more comfortable. You cannot make yourself free, so the idea goes, by cozying up to the powerful and keeping them sweet. That sort of deference—that sort of toadying, fawning, or kowtowing, to use some established terms of derogation—testifies to the unfreedom of your situation; it is not a strategy whereby you might overcome it. As freedom cannot be won by adaptation, so it cannot be won by ingratiation.

The Anti-ingratiation Assumption

Berlin's theory of freedom as noninterference entails that ingratiation is a possible means of liberation in the same way that Hobbes's theory of freedom as nonfrustration entails that adaptation is a possible means of liberation. And this entailment argues against the Berlinian theory, as the corresponding entailment argues against the Hobbesian. Let the antiadaptation assumption be granted and Hobbes's theory must fail; let the anti-ingratiation assumption be granted and Berlin's must fail. The problem is not that adaptation or ingratiation in the relevant contexts is intuitively objectionable, as it surely is, or even that it will occur very often, which it may not do. The problem, rather, is that neither adaptation nor ingratiation counts as a possible means of liberation, and any theory that entails that either can serve a liberating role has to be inadequate.

Where the antiadaptation assumption is that all the options in a free choice must be open, the anti-ingratiation claim is that not any old way of opening them will do. You may be free in a choice between A and B insofar as the accessibility of those options derives from natural obstacles to my interference—or anyone else's—or from other agencies that protect you from my interference or from your power of retaliating against my interference or from the fact that such interference will have various social or even psychological costs. But the anti-ingratiation assumption is that you will certainly not be free if it remains just a matter of will or taste or favor, as it will remain in the wake of the most successful ingratiation, that I leave the options open and up to you.[30]

The point is not that it would be a solecism to say that you were free to take either option in such a case—in suitable contexts, it would be perfectly good English to say this—but rather that the sort of latitude enjoyed does not rule out subjection to my will and does not live up to the more demanding connotations of freedom. In particular, it does not live up to the connotation whereby you are free in a given choice only to the extent that you are not subject to the will of another as to how you should choose. According to Berlin, you will be subject to my will in a choice between A and B just in the event of my deliberately interfering—presumably without your license—with the option you actually choose, A, or with the option you might have chosen, B. But you will also be subject to my will if it is a mere artifact of taste or inclination, not the product of any constraint, that I am happy for you to choose as you wish between A and B. When I grant you the favor of choosing as you wish, it remains the case that should my will change, then I will interfere with one or the other option. You depend on my will remaining the favorable way it is, therefore, for having the choice between A and B. You have an open choice between those options only because it is my will that you should have that choice.

In discussing adaptation, I mentioned that while it is not a possible means of liberation in a choice between given options, there is a related sort of context where it may serve a useful role. In the illustration given, you might work on your preferences in order to induce an attachment to hiking and make yourself into an acceptable weekend companion of mine. And you might thereby give yourself a choice on one or another weekend between going hiking with me or staying at home. As this is true for adaptation, so it is clearly true for ingratiation; you might also make yourself into an acceptable weekend companion by using your charms and wiles to win me over. Adaptation and ingratiation may be sensible ways of making me or any other person willing to participate in some joint activity, and they can serve in this role to give you more options and more choices. But that is entirely consistent with the claim that in a choice between given options, neither initiative counts as a possible means of liberation: a way of giving yourself freedom in that very choice.

Freedom as Nondomination

The upshot of this discussion is that insofar as I have the resources to interfere without cost in a choice of yours—insofar as I have the power and knowledge required—your ability to make the choice is dependent on my will as to what you should do, and you are in that sense subject to my will. To the extent that I have a power of interfering without cost in your choice, I count as dominating you; I am in a position associated iconically with a master or dominus.[31] And so the endorsement of the anti-ingratiation assumption, and of the argument in which it figures, leads to replacing the conception of freedom as noninterference with the conception of freedom as nondomination. The price that has to be paid for denying that ingratiation is a possible means of liberation is to take freedom to require nondomination.[32]

Domination is a pervasive phenomenon, and to hold that freedom rules it out is to make freedom into quite a demanding ideal. The domination whereby I take away your freedom in a choice between A and B may not manifest itself in my frustrating that choice or even in my interfering in the choice without frustrating it: that is, in interfering with a nonpreferred option. It may just consist in my having the power to interfere more or less without cost should my will incline that way.[33] And it may consist in the possession of such power even when domination is the last thing I seek. If the power of interference is one that I cannot abjure or contain—if I enjoy it, for example, by grace of the superior legal standing that husbands used to have over wives, masters over servants—then I cannot unmake the fact that whether or not you are to suffer my interference depends on the state of my will. It is the existence of my power of relatively costless interference, not its exercise—not even its exercise against a nonpreferred option—that makes you unfree. The ideal of freedom as nondomination would argue, then, for quite dramatic limitations on the power that one person or group of persons may have of imposing their will on another.

This ideal has deep roots in the history of thought. There is a long tradition of thinking that if the options in a choice are open only by virtue of the goodwill of the powerful, then the agent is not free in making that choice. The tradition goes back to at least the Roman republican way of thinking about freedom, and it survived through the Renaissance and the English republic—Hobbes notwithstanding—to become a centerpiece of political thought in the eighteenth century. You are not free in any choice, to quote the eighteenth-century republican Richard Price, if your access to the options depends on an "indulgence" on my part or an "accidental mildness."[34] Freedom, as Algernon Sidney had put it in the 1680s, is "independency upon the will of another."[35] In the words of *Cato's Letters*, a popular tract of the eighteenth century, "Liberty is, to live upon one's own terms; slavery is, to live at the mere mercy of another."[36]

Modeling and Illustrating This Freedom

The republican idea is made vivid in the traditional image of the free horse. Does the horse that is given free or loose rein enjoy freedom of choice in virtue of the implied permission to go in this direction or that? It may do so if freedom requires merely that the relevant options be open; after all, the horse can go in any direction it likes. But it will not enjoy freedom of choice if the accessibility of the options cannot depend on the will of another. For whether the horse can go in one direction or another depends on the will of the rider. As republicans see it, the horse will be unfree just in virtue of having someone in the saddle; free rein is not enough for free choice.

But the republican idea can also be expressed with the help of the open-doors metaphor on which Berlin relies. Are you free just insofar as both doors are open in the choice between A and B? Not necessarily. What freedom ideally requires in the republican book is not just that the doors be open but also that there be no doorkeeper who can close a door—or jam it or conceal it—more or less without cost; there is no doorkeeper on whose goodwill you depend for one or another of the doors remaining open. If I am in the position of such a doorkeeper, therefore, your access to the A and B options is not supported in the manner that freedom of choice strictly requires.

As the plausibility of the antiadaptation assumption argues that all the doors in a free choice must be open, so the plausibility of the anti-ingratiation assumption argues that there must be no dependence on the good graces of a doorkeeper. When you ingratiate yourself with me and I let you go by a door that I would otherwise have closed, you do not cease to be subject to my will. You have not escaped the constraint that made you unfree in the first place, or done anything to reduce the effectiveness of the constraint, say, by raising the assured or expected costs, physical or psychological, of my acting against you. While continuing to operate under the yoke of my will, you have merely adjusted so as to make your life more comfortable. You have done exactly the sort of thing that the prisoner does in adjusting to life behind bars.

Where the image of the prisoner illustrates the illusion of freedom by adaptation, there are many images available to illustrate the illusion of freedom by ingratiation. One of the most vivid is presented in Mary Wollstonecraft's description of the subjection of women in her time.[37] The woman who lives under the will of a husband may rely on mincing steps and beguiling smiles to keep her husband sweet and to get her way in a variety of choice. But she doesn't succeed thereby in getting out from under his will, escaping the constraint that it represents. She may delude herself that she is free in those choices, as the adaptive prisoner may delude himself about his freedom, but no one should be deceived. Certainly, Wollstonecraft is quite clear: however kindly or gullible, however much he is a pushover, the husband remains a master. And to live under the will or power of a master—to live *in potestate domini*—is not to be free.

IV. Freedom of the Person

Berlin's View of the Free Person

For all that has been said so far, Berlin might go along with the spirit of Hobbes's view on what it is to be a "freeman" or free person. He might say that you are a free person only if you enjoy freedom in all your choices: among the things that you have the ability to do—perhaps on your own, perhaps in the presence of willing partners—you do not suffer the interference of others. Or he might go along with a modified version of that ideal according to which you are a free person to the extent that you are not interfered with; you enjoy such freedom in greater measure, the greater the range of choices in which you are free.

Berlin does neither of these things, however. Without commenting explicitly on the relationship between the ideal of having a free choice and the ideal of being a free person, he makes absolutely clear that on this matter too his view is very different from the Hobbesian one. In later commentary on his 1958 lecture, he says that to be free—in effect, to be a free person—is "to be accorded an area . . . in which one is one's own master"; it is to enjoy a domain where one "is not obliged to account for his activities to any man so far as this is compatible with the existence of organized society."[38] As he put it in the lecture itself, it is to have access to "a certain minimum area of personal freedom which must on no account be violated."[39]

A Republican View

It is no accident that Hobbes made it so hard for someone to count as a freeman, taking it to require the enjoyment of freedom across the full gamut of choice, and that he thereby marginalized the ideal. He would have relished that marginalization, since the republican way of thinking made the freedom of the person or citizen central to political thought. In Roman thinking, to be a free person just was to be a citizen incorporated in the matrix of protection for certain basic choices afforded to each—in theory, afforded equally to each—by the rule of law. Under this approach, as one commentator puts it, "full *libertas* is coterminous with *civitas*";[40] being a free person means nothing more or less than being a citizen. By making the category of the freeman or *liber* impossible of realization, Hobbes challenged a foundational concept in the ideology of his main opposition. He struck out against those in Parliament and elsewhere who took the freedom of the freeman to be a status that all citizens ought to be able to enjoy.[41]

Without connecting with the debate between Hobbes and the parliamentarians, Berlin shows that on this issue he is clearly on the republican side. He is with that tradition in recognizing that it is legal conventions, not metaphysical rights, that determine the range of choices in which people are to be equally protected; the "area of men's free action must be limited by law," he says, and has to be "artificially carved out, if need be."[42] And he is also on the republican side in holding that not any old way of demarcating the area is satisfactory. The "field of free choice"—the range of choices or liberties that are to be protected[43]—should be available equally to each, and it should be as large as possible consistently with "the existence of organized society."[44] Society should provide for each "a maximum degree of noninterference compatible with the minimum demands of social life."[45]

While the field of free choice envisaged by Berlin clearly includes the traditional liberties in the domain of thought, speech, association, location, occupation, ownership, and the like, these comments show that he thinks of them as liberties established and variously interpreted in the conventions and laws of particular societies. As in the republican tradition, he sees them as institutional artifacts, the legacy of a cultural and legal heritage, not as god-given, natural rights. They are the product of what he sees as "rules so long and widely accepted that their observance has entered into the very conception of what it is to be a normal human being."[46]

Berlin associates the ideal of living in a society that enables you to be your own master, and that extends this possibility to everyone, with "the fathers of liberalism—Mill and Constant," but it clearly conforms closely to earlier republican thinking.[47] The guiding insight is that "to be free to choose, and not to be chosen for, is an inalienable ingredient in what makes human beings human."[48] That insight attracted special emphasis and accrued novel connotations in the liberal writers to whom Berlin refers, but it is already present in the republican image of the agents who live, as Sidney put it, "in independency upon the will of another": the citizens, in the phrase from Roman law, who live sui juris, on their own terms.

A View That Requires Nondomination

But not only does Berlin rejoin the older tradition in his particular ideal of freedom in the person. What I now wish to point out is that he also cannot really secure this ideal while holding that the freedom it requires in designated choices is freedom as noninterference. Were the free person to be provided only with freedom as noninterference in the "field of free choice," then that provision would not ensure that it is an area "in which one is one's own master." If I am to be free in this sense, as Berlin puts it at one point, there must be "room within which I am legally accountable to no one for my movements."[49] But I will certainly be accountable to others if I have to depend on their goodwill for the capacity to make a choice in favor of one option or another within the designated domain. I may not be legally or morally obliged to those others, but I will be obliged in the more basic currency of prudence; I will be obliged to stay in the good books of those others, on pain of a setback to my interests. Enjoying freedom as noninterference in that domain is consistent, as we know, with such dependence. And so the freedom required in Berlin's ideal of the free person has to be more demanding: it has to amount to something close to freedom as nondomination.

How might a society seek to promote freedom as noninterference among its members without giving them freedom as nondomination? A legal regime that gave the relatively powerful rewards for not interfering with the relatively powerless—perhaps rewards artificially created by the law, perhaps rewards available via the gratitude of beneficiaries—might fit the bill. It might do better by maximizing noninterference overall—in particular, noninterference in the domain of basic choice—than a regime that established defenses or deterrents for the protection of the weak. And so, for all that freedom as noninterference requires, such a regime would be a more attractive prospect.

Another regime that might do quite well by the maximization of freedom as noninterference, yet jeopardize freedom as nondomination, is the benevolent dictatorship. This would give supreme, unchallengeable power to one wholly virtuous individual or body. Being benevolent, that dictator would not perpetrate any undue interference against the citizens of the society. And being benevolent, the dictator would at the same time prevent citizens from interfering with one another. This dictatorship too might do much better by way of promoting noninterference than any system of democratically established defenses and deterrents.[50]

Berlin would have found both of these regimes objectionable and repugnant on grounds of freedom alone. For under either regime, it would clearly be the case that many people were obliged and accountable to others, being dependent on their continuing goodwill for the enjoyment of noninterference, even noninterference in the supposedly entrenched field of free choice. We saw earlier that his argument against freedom as nonfrustration and in favor of freedom as noninterference suggests grounds for going further still and thinking of freedom of choice as requiring nondomination. We now see that his ideal of the free person points in the same direction. That ideal requires this more radical form of freedom in the choices that are socially privileged—the basic liberties—and not merely freedom as noninterference.

Conclusion

Why does Berlin miss the republican direction in which many of his insights ought to have led him? The question becomes particularly telling in view of the fact that by 1969 he had begun to articulate his image of the free person in terms that have republican connotations. "Freedom, at least in its political sense, is coterminous," he says, "with the absence of bullying or domination."[51]

The answer to the question, I think, is that his history of freedom let him down. The negative conception of freedom as noninterference, though not always distinguished from nonfrustration, was the familiar ideal of classical liberal and utilitarian thought; Jeremy Bentham, who took himself to be its inventor, described it as the "cornerstone" of his system.[52] Berlin identified with this tradition of thought, even as his anti-Hobbesian argument should have pushed him away. And he did so, I suspect, because of thinking that the only alternative was the positive conception of freedom, institutionally interpreted. Under this conception, your social or political freedom does not just rely on law—and perhaps, as republicanism would require, a democratic, nondominating law[53]—for its realization. It also consists in being the enfranchised member of a self-determining collectivity such that its will is a will in which you partake. Where the negative conception looked like the modern way of thinking about freedom, this was cast as the unique premodern alternative: the ancient conception of freedom, as Benjamin Constant had described it in 1819.[54]

Far from being the only premodern alternative, this positive conception was the form that the republican conception took in the wake of Jean-Jacques Rousseau's reconstrual of republican ideas.[55] Rousseau himself adopted the conception of freedom as nondomination—nondependency on the will of another—in line with the Italian-Atlantic tradition of republican thought: the tradition that originated in Rome, matured in Renaissance Italy, and became popularized in the eighteenth-century English-speaking world.[56] But he rejected the traditional republican belief that only a mixed, contestatory constitution could further the cause of such freedom. Instead, he followed Jean Bodin and Hobbes in arguing that the state had to be ruled by a unified sovereign and so, in the republic, by a unified assembly of citizens. Thus, he generated a new form of republicanism in which the citizens are lawmakers, and their freedom or nondomination is guaranteed by the fact that they live under laws of their own, collective making: they live under the shared general will. As this new republicanism took root, it gave rise to the idea that not only is freedom guaranteed by incorporation in collective self-government; that is what freedom means.

What Berlin missed was that while freedom is to be considered as a negative ideal, requiring the absence of some evil, there are a number of different evils in whose absence it might be taken to consist. According to the Hobbesian story, the evil that has to be absent is frustration. According to Berlin's own story, it is interference, actual or counterfactual. And according to the republican story, it is any form of subjection to the will of another—any form of domination—whether this is imposed by interference or not. If the argument of this essay is correct, then Berlin's concerns about the Hobbesian view of freedom ought to have led him toward this republican conception, as should his own ideal of the free person. If he failed to embrace the republican view, that is because he just didn't recognize that it was a genuine alternative to the positive conception that he, quite reasonably, rejected. He thought that the only alternative—or at least, given his arguments against freedom as nonfrustration, the only appealing alternative—was the conception of freedom as noninterference.

In conclusion, let me offer a caution: while I think that Berlin ought to have been moved in the direction of republican theory by his argument against the Hobbesian view, and by his attachment to the ideal of a free person, I do not say that he would have been willing to embrace all the implications of such a position. My own view is that when the republican ideal of the free person is universalized to all citizens, it supports a broadly egalitarian program of domestic policy making, a contestatory image of democracy, and an ideal of undominated, well-ordered peoples in the sphere of international relations.[57] I do not know whether Berlin could have lived with such implications. He had reason to endorse premises on the basis of which I think they can be supported, but he might have taken those implications to show that the premises require revision. My *modus ponens* might have been his *modus tollens.*

Notes

1. Pace, e.g., Philippe Van Parijs, *Real Freedom for All* (Oxford: Oxford University Press, 1995).

2. Immanuel Kant, *Notes and Fragments*, edited by Paul Guyer (Cambridge: Cambridge University Press, 2005), 11.

3. Philip Pettit, *Republicanism: A Theory of Freedom and Government* (Oxford: Oxford University Press, 1997).

4. Isaiah Berlin, *Four Essays on Liberty* (Oxford: Oxford University Press, 1969). This contains Berlin's 1958 lecture "Two Concepts of Liberty" but also, especially in the long introduction, a good deal of later commentary. In the text, I often distinguish between references to the lecture itself and references to the commentary.

5. The thinker in whom Berlin finds the view he rejects is not Hobbes but John Stuart Mill (ibid., 139). This is strange, as Hobbes quite clearly endorsed the view, while Mill was guilty, at most, of using a formulation that may seem to give it support: a formulation that refers to being in a position to do what you actually want rather than to do whatever you might come to want.

6. Pettit, *Republicanism*; Quentin Skinner, *Liberty Before Liberalism* (Cambridge: Cambridge University Press, 1998); Maurizio Viroli, *Republicanism* (New York: Hill and Wang, 2002); John Maynor, *Republicanism in the Modern World* (Cambridge: Polity Press, 2003).

7. Quentin Skinner, "Freedom as the Absence of Arbitrary Power," in *Republicanism and Political Theory*, edited by C. Laborde and J. Maynor (Oxford: Blackwell, 2008), 83–102.

8. Philip Pettit, *Made with Words: Hobbes on Language, Mind, and Politics* (Princeton, NJ: Princeton University Press, 2008), chap. 8.

9. Thomas Hobbes, *Leviathan*, edited by E. Curley (Indianapolis: Hackett, 1994), chap. 21.2.

10. I ignore questions raised by Hobbes's assumption that freedom presupposes the ability to take the options over which you are free: they must be within your "strength and wit." For the record, Berlin denies that freedom presupposes ability in this way, insisting that you may be free to vote even when you are too ill to go to the polls: "Mere incapacity to attain a goal is not lack of political liberty" (*Four Essays on Liberty*, 122). In fairness to Berlin, he argues that in order to make liberty truly valuable, it might be necessary to institute welfare measures for giving people abilities to match their political liberties. "What is freedom to those who cannot make use of it? Without adequate conditions for the use of freedom, what is the value of freedom?" (124; see also lii). He is followed in this view of what is required for the value as distinct from the nature of freedom by John Rawls, *A Theory of Justice* (Oxford: Oxford University Press, 1971).

11. Thomas Hobbes and John Bramhall, *Hobbes and Bramhall on Freedom and Necessity*, edited by Vere Chappell (Cambridge: Cambridge University Press, 1999), 91.

12. Harry Frankfurt, "Alternate Possibilities and Moral Responsibility," *Journal of Philosophy* 66 (1969): 829–839.

13. Berlin, *Four Essays on Liberty*, 122. Given that Hobbes thought that any form of external hindrance takes from your freedom, he did not belong to the school of thought described in the introduction. Casting him as a foil to Berlin, however, I concentrate only on the hindrance imposed by other human beings; I treat him as if he did belong to that school. Berlin defends his focus on the hindering effects of human action, quoting Rousseau's claim that "the nature of things does not madden us, only ill will does" (122). The reference to ill will strongly suggests the need for intention—as other passages also do—but Berlin goes on, confusingly, to say that when other human beings restrict us, this action oppresses us, whether it is performed "with or without the intention of doing so." I take this to be just a slip.

14. Ibid., 123.

15. Ibid., 128.

16. Ibid., xxxviii.

17. Ibid., 139. Strictly, there is a problem in saying that to be free in the choice of A, it must be the case that you could have chosen the alternative B, had you wanted to—had you preferred that option. This condition might be incapable of fulfillment because you are the sort of person who would only want to do B if it were not available; the possibility will be salient from Groucho Marx's quip that he would only want to join a club that would not accept him as a member. The problem can be overcome if what is required is that you could have chosen B had you tried to do so, where it is not required in that eventuality that you actually prefer B. For expressive convenience, I ignore this complication in the text. I am grateful to Lara Buchak for drawing the problem to my attention.

18. Ibid., xxxix.

19. Ibid., xlviii; see also xxxix. In the original lecture, he comes close to endorsing the open-doors metaphor, despite his endorsement of Hobbes, when he denounces those who would "block every door but one," albeit a door that opens on a "noble prospect" (127).

20. This approach is adopted by Hillel Steiner, *An Essay on Rights* (Oxford: Blackwell, 1994); Ian Carter, *A Measure of Freedom* (Oxford: Oxford University Press, 1999); and Matthew H. Kramer, *The Quality of Freedom* (Oxford: Oxford University Press, 2003).

21. Berlin, *Four Essays on Liberty*, 155. Although I shall speak in what follows of interference without qualification, it might be more appropriate and even more faithful to Berlin's point of view—though not, as it happens, his precise formulations—to take him to have only unlicensed interference in mind. Licensed or nonarbitrary interference, as I think of it, materializes on terms laid down by the interferee, as in the example of how his sailors treat Ulysses. See Philip Pettit, "Republican Liberty: Three Axioms, Four Theorems," in *Republicanism and Political Theory.*

22. Berlin, *Four Essays on Liberty*, xxxix.

23. Ibid., 139.

24. Ibid., xxxviii. But see Carter, *A Measure of Freedom*; and Kramer, *The Quality of Freedom.* They will argue that where adaptation is required for being able to take a particular option—and also, to anticipate, where ingratiation is required for that result—the agent loses out in overall freedom, not being in a position to choose the option-without-adaptation or the option-without-ingratiation. The observation may soften the difficulty of living with the conclusion of Berlin's argument—that one can make oneself free in a given choice by adaptation or ingratiation—but it does not remove it; the intuition remains that one cannot achieve freedom in that given choice just by adapting preferences or just by ingratiating yourself with an obstructive agent. For a general comment on the limitations of this overall-freedom line, see Pettit, "Republican Liberty."

25. See Philip Pettit, "Capability and Freedom: A Defence of Sen," *Economics and Philosophy* 17 (2001): 1–20.

26. Berlin, *Four Essays on Liberty*, xxxix.

27. It may be enough, according to Berlin, that you enjoy noninterference in the nearest possible world or worlds in which you choose the other option, B. Or it may be required that there is a larger range of possible Y-worlds where noninterference is absent. These might be defined in a context-sensitive way but certainly cannot include all possible worlds in which you choose B. The fact that you would attract interference in the remote possible world where B would bring about the end of all sentient life, e.g., hardly shows that you are actually unfree in choosing between A and B. I abstract from this issue here, as I abstract from the related issue of whether it is necessary, not just that you are actually not interfered with in choosing A, but also that you would not be interfered with in a range of other possible A-worlds: worlds that differ in intuitively irrelevant ways from the actual world. On issues about the relation between noninterference and freedom and about how robust noninterference must be in order to constitute freedom, see Pettit, "Capability and Freedom"; and Christian List, "The Impossibility of a Paretian Republican? Some Comments on Pettit and Sen," *Economics and Philosophy* 20 (2004): 1–23, and "Republican Freedom and the Rule of Law," *Politics, Philosophy, and Economics* 5 (2006): 201–220. These issues are parallel to issues in epistemology about the relation between true belief and knowledge. See, e.g., Timothy Williamson, *Knowledge and Its Limits* (Oxford: Oxford University Press, 2000).

28. That the ideals are distinct does not rule out the possibility, however, that interference-with-frustration is worse, worse even in freedom terms, than interference-without-frustration.

29. Jeremy Waldron, "Pettit's Molecule," in *Common Minds: Themes from the Philosophy of Philip Pettit*, edited by G. Brennan, R. E. Goodin, F. Jackson, and M. Smith (Oxford: Oxford University Press, 2007), 143–160. But see also the previous footnote.

30. What if you were close to certain that I would not be put off by any line you took in the choice between A and B, or in any other choice of that kind? What if you were so sure of my favorable attitude toward you that you had no fear of alienating me and triggering in-

terference? Would there still be a sense in which your choice was subject to my will? The right response to this query is that you could not think of me as such a mechanically predetermined entity—and certainly could not manifest that view—while continuing to see and treat me as an agent. Suppose that you are disposed to hold me responsible as an agent for whatever I turn out to do in a given choice that affects your interests so that you will feel gratitude or resentment at the decision I take. You must then think of me, before the decision is made, as being in a position to take one or another course depending on my will. And that attitude rules out the sort of certainty envisaged here. For such a viewpoint, see the work of a contemporary and colleague of Berlin's: Peter Strawson, *Freedom and Resentment and Other Essays* (London: Methuen, 1962).

31. Pettit, *Republicanism*, chap. 2.

32. Inevitably, this presentation of freedom as nondomination is not as cautious as it might be. Two points of caution, in particular, should be registered. One is that you do not depend on the will of another in the relevant sense just in virtue of your options being dependent on what they, perhaps in ignorance of your existence, choose to do; in that case, you do not depend on their will as to what you should do: they may have no wishes about what you should do. And another is that you do not depend on the will of others just in virtue of the fact that a majority in your society might coalesce and take against you; short of coalescing or incorporating, they do not constitute an existent agency that dominates you, and the possibility of such a development testifies only to possible, not actual, domination.

33. Indeed, the varieties of domination are even richer than this suggests. I may interfere with you, as explained earlier, by removing or replacing an option, by denying you information about the options, or by undermining your capacity to reason properly about them. But this means that I may have the power to interfere with you in a given choice should my will incline that way—i.e., I may dominate you—not just in virtue of superior resources, intuitively understood, but even in virtue of your believing that I have such resources. If you do believe that I have those resources, then I will have the power to deceive you in the choice: say, by making a bluff threat to stop you doing one or another option. All of this illustrates Hobbes's remark that "reputation of power is power." See Hobbes, *Leviathan*, chap. 10.5.

34. Richard Price, *Political Writings* (Cambridge: Cambridge University Press, 1991), 26.

35. Algernon Sidney, *Discourses Concerning Government* (Indianapolis: Liberty Classics, 1990), 17.

36. John Trenchard and Thomas Gordon, *Cato's Letters* (New York: Da Capo Press, 1971), 2:249–250.

37. Mary Wollstonecraft, *A Vindication of the Rights of Woman* (New York: Whitston, 1982).

38. Berlin, *Four Essays on Liberty*, lx.

39. Ibid., 123.

40. Ch. Wirszubski, *Libertas as a Political Ideal at Rome During the Late Republic and Early Principate* (Oxford: Oxford University Press, 1968), 3.

41. Quentin Skinner, *Hobbes and Republican Liberty* (Cambridge: Cambridge University Press, 2008).

42. Berlin, *Four Essays on Liberty*, 123, lx.

43. Philip Pettit, "The Basic Liberties," in *Essays on H. L. A. Hart*, edited by M. Kramer (Oxford: Oxford University Press, 2008), 201–224.

44. Berlin, *Four Essays on Liberty*, lxi.

45. Ibid., 161; see also lxii.

46. Ibid., 165.

47. Ibid., 161.

48. Ibid., lx.

49. Ibid., 155.

50. Perhaps this is what Berlin himself registers in saying that the "connection between democracy and individual liberty is a good deal more tenuous than it *has* seemed to many advocates of both" (ibid., 130–131; emphasis added).

51. Ibid., lvi.

52. Douglas C. Long, *Bentham on Liberty* (Toronto: University of Toronto Press, 1977), 54.

53. Philip Pettit, "Law and Liberty," in *Law and Republicanism*, edited by S. Besson and J. L. Marti (Oxford: Oxford University Press, 2009), 39–59.

54. Benjamin Constant, *Constant: Political Writings* (Cambridge: Cambridge University Press, 1988).

55. Jean-Jacques Rousseau, *The Social Contract and Discourses* (London: Dent, 1973). See also Philip Pettit, "Two Republican Traditions," in *Republican Democracy: Liberty, Law, and Politics*, edited by A. Niederberger and P. Schink (Edinburgh: Edinburgh University Press, forthcoming).

56. Jean-Fabien Spitz, *La Liberté Politique* (Paris: Presses Universitaires de France, 1995).

57. Frank Lovett and Philip Pettit, "Neo-Republicanism: A Normative and Institutional Research Program," *Annual Review of Political Science* 12 (2009): 11–29; Philip Pettit, "A Republican Law of Peoples," in "Republicanism and International Relations," edited by Duncan Bell, special issue, *European Journal of Political Theory* 9 (2010): 70–94.

READING

8

Can Positive Freedom Be Saved?

JOHN CHRISTMAN

The supposed conceptual distinction between negative and positive freedom was a great preoccupation of philosophers and political theorists for several decades after Isaiah Berlin directed renewed attention to it.[1] That preoccupation seemed to reach an apex as writers remarked on the obvious plasticity of the notion of freedom (or liberty) and the numerous ways in which elements of that notion could be conceptualized. Also noted was the clear fact that freedom was an "essentially contested concept" that could not be neutrally unpacked in order to decide other questions of value or justice. Conceptions of liberty *embodied* answers to such questions.[2]

However, those who want to cling to a positive conception of freedom of some sort insist that liberty should be seen as not merely an absence of constraints, whether those are considered as internal or external to the agent, the product of human action or accident, and so on. Such theorists want to place the focus of our concern for liberty on the *quality of agency* and not merely the opportunity to act. Defenders of such an understanding of freedom insist that merely establishing *opportunities* to act upon one's current desires (or whatever defines the motives of rational action) fails to secure the conditions of self-governing agency that make freedom meaningful as an ideal. Seeing freedom as a quality of agency is different conceptually from seeing it as an absence of something, no matter how robust one's conception of that "something" turns out to be.

Now it is true that various attempts to construct a purely negative counterpart to positive notions such as this have been made in the recent literature.[3] Some of these views are motivated by the suspicion that positive freedom represents or ushers in problematic value commitments. But that normative position is different from the view that such an idea is not *conceptually* distinct from its negative counterparts at all. In order to clarify this point, and hopefully locate some of the most poignant issues that motivate those who call for the promotion and protection of a kind of freedom that goes beyond simply leaving people alone, I will examine in some detail an attempt to reduce positive notions of liberty to, essentially, variants on a negative concept. Before turning to that, however, I will briefly (and rather superficially) lay out the contours of this debate. In my critical discussion of the attempt to reduce positive conceptions of freedom to negative forms, I hope to locate the specific *normative* disagreements that have divided thinkers in the field, disagreements that mark some of the deepest fault lines in modern political thought.

I. Liberties

Undertaking a thorough overview of the various conceptions of freedom or liberty that have been developed over the past decades (and centuries!) is beyond our present scope. However, the general distinction between (more or less) positive conceptions of freedom and negative ones concerns whether the conditions of liberty refer only or chiefly to *constraints* on the agent or to the nature of *agency* itself, or as Charles Taylor put it, the difference between an "opportunity concept" and an "exercise concept."[4] Of course, Gerald MacCallum claimed famously that both categories of notions can fit into a schema with three variables, signifying a *person X* who is free or not free from some *Y* to do or be *Z*.[5] But even if this matrix is adopted—and I would claim that MacCallum focused overmuch on the distinction between freedom *to* and freedom *from* as the mark of the positive-negative contrast—we still are left with the question of how those variables are to be filled out to capture the key notion. Negative theorists attempt to focus all attention on the "Y" variable, the constraints that prevent action, arguing that further conditions concerning agency or action are irrelevant to freedom. These variables, they suggest, regard other factors such as the status of the agent, her abilities, and the actions and values she pursues. Freedom, they claim, should be seen only as a function of the barriers that stand in front of her, so to speak.

Conceptions of positive freedom can be motivated by various considerations. Among such is the view that freedom concerns not only the absence of intrusion (by others or by natural circumstance) but also one's *effectiveness as an agent*. Some have stressed, for example, that effective agency is manifested not only in one's internal or psychological capacities to govern oneself but also in one's positive ability to carry out one's wishes through action in the world. A person who faces no restrictions on action that can be called an "intrusion" or "constraint" (at least as that has been typically understood) may still be palpably unable to act in any meaningful way. She may, for example, lack basic resources that are readily available to most others. Leftist critics of liberalism, especially those influenced by Marx, have seized upon this thought to insist that resources that enable effective action increase freedom (and so radical inequalities of resources amount to unequal freedom).[6]

While this push to link freedom with material condition raises powerful issues, it is not actually the focus here, though it brings up issues similar to ones that will be. For instance, defenders of this approach argue that the rhetorical power of claiming a society (or group or person) is *free* is denuded when it is pointed out how the freedom in question is merely the condition of being left alone to fend for oneself in a state of impoverishment, powerlessness, or incapacity. To be free, it is claimed, is more than merely to enjoy open spaces; it is to be able to act effectively within those spaces to pursue goals worthy (to the agent) of pursuit.[7]

This last sentence raises the issue of the relation between agency and *values* in that it expresses (albeit loosely) the idea that freedom is meaningful only if it is understood as a condition within which valuable aims can be pursued.[8] This is the thought that has caused such philosophical and political consternation. In his complex critical analysis, for example, Isaiah Berlin argued along various lines that the reemergence of a positive conception of liberty in the modern period carried with it certain dangers concerning the possibility of unpalatable exercise of state (and social) power to impose values on individuals in the name of freedom itself. He worried that seeing freedom as fundamentally an answer to the question "How should I be governed?" rather than "What is the area within which I can act?" opens up the possibility that freedom can be increased by (paradoxically) expunging desires rather than increasing opportunity and, more problematically, allowed states or social majorities to impose their will on us in the name of our own self-government.[9]

It is true that many who have developed notions of positive freedom have construed that idea in overtly normative terms, commingling the idea of being free with the idea of leading a flourishing or good life.[10] Such "moralized" conceptions of freedom (positive or negative) run up against the liberal view that values are plural, and the ineliminable plurality of values and conceptions of the good life must be held paramount in our understanding of modern social conditions, what John Rawls called the permanent fact of reasonable pluralism, or what others call the politics of difference.[11] Berlin's trepidations about the ideal of positive liberty turned on this very tenet of liberal principle, namely, the rejection of value monism and the wholehearted embrace of pluralism.[12]

I will return to this issue in section III below. What must be considered now is whether positive freedom is conceptually distinct from its negative cousin in the first place. The idea of a "restriction" central to negative freedom has traditionally been understood as an external, physical barrier to movement, and so a material restriction on action. Many theorists, however, have attempted to broaden this idea to include internal restrictions on the consideration of options or on thinking in general so as to capture the intuitive idea that our ability to act intentionally can be thwarted in these ways just as readily as with external constraints.[13] Indeed, some have insisted that a sensitive enough understanding of the ways that restrictions can act internally as well as externally can broaden the notion of negative freedom to such an extent that it swallows up the idea of positive liberty altogether.

Let us consider an attempt along these lines in detail. This sustained critical analysis of such an effort to conceptually eliminate the very *idea* of positive freedom will show, I will suggest, that the controversy is not really about concepts after all but about values, bringing us back to the clash of positions central to liberal (and leftist) political thought: namely, whether we can understand and promote freedom as a kind of effective agency without thereby opening the gates for oppressive imposition of contestable values.

II. Reducing Positive to Negative Liberty

Eric Nelson has argued that, despite attempts by Quentin Skinner and others to resurrect a distinctively positive conception of liberty, that concept can always be understood in a negative fashion, with disagreements over its meaning amounting really to disputes over the meaning of "constraint." Historical figures who have famously been designated as "positive theorists," he argues, can all be understood as promoting a conception of negative freedom, albeit one that includes "internal" constraints—constraints that operate to prevent the true, authentic self from emerging. Such thinkers—from ancient writers such as Plato and the Stoics, to classical and civic republicans such as Machiavelli and Rousseau, to Hegel and the neo-Hegelians—all tout the notion that the free "man" is one who embodies a form of self-realization, independent self-rule, or some related state of being reflective of the most rational or virtuous life. But for Nelson this state turns out to be nothing more than the *absence* of barriers to such realization and hence to a negative conception of freedom after all.[14]

I want to suggest, however, that this reductionist conceptual argument fails on its own terms and also serves to disguise a more straightforwardly normative position that freedom *ought not* to be construed in any manner other than a negative one. Nelson's treatment of this controversy fails to take sufficiently seriously the way in which positive freedom can be *conceptually* distinguished from its negative counterpart whether or not such a positive notion is morally or politically palatable in the end.

Nelson's discussion revolves around conceptions of positive liberty that focus on internal achievements of the self. Positive freedom in this sense was indeed the brunt of Isaiah Berlin's famous analysis in that Berlin drew critical attention to those traditions that saw freedom as the operation of the "higher" more "rational" self, as some sort of self-realization. But it is important to note that in addition to the "historical" and "analytical" claims that Berlin made in his famous essay, he also advanced a straightforwardly *normative* argument that construing freedom in a positive sense dangerously masked a contentious ideal of the good life behind the veneer of liberty. For a liberal like Berlin, liberty was the fundamental requirement of a society that sees questions of fundamental value, including the ideals of the best life, as open and as subject to ongoing debate and contestation. To label as "freedom" the mastery of the "lower" desires by the "higher" capacities of morality and virtue, not to mention mastery by the supposedly superior wisdom of a general will, marked a treacherous tilt toward the justification of centralized power under the guise of moral superiority. Berlin was keen to alert us to the tendency that could be found in writers such as Kant, Hegel, Rousseau, and neo-Hegelians such as T. H. Green to construe freedom in ways that enacted this masquerade.

This is more than merely a historical or an analytical claim as Nelson suggests; it is very much a political one. Berlin mounted what we could call a pluralist, antiperfectionist argument against construing freedom in a positive manner. For Berlin, skepticism about positive liberty was inextricably linked to worries about the dominance of narrow and parochial horizons of value.

Nevertheless, Berlin's ruminations sparked a sustained conceptual debate about the subtle and variable differences among concepts of freedom. As I mentioned, the locus classicus for the schematic organization of conceptual elements of the idea of freedom is MacCallum's "Negative and Positive Freedom," where he claimed that all conceptions of freedom were composed of the same (variable) elements related in a single schematic way.[15] According to Nelson, MacCallum "dissolved" the distinction between negative and positive notions. But I'd prefer to say that this schema does not actually dissolve the distinction; it merely locates it in a different place. Rather than thinking there are two (or more) fundamentally different *concepts* of freedom, MacCallum's analysis shows that we should think about freedom as one overarching conceptual schema allowing for several different *conceptions*. Positive understandings of freedom denote one set of interpretations of the variables in the schema and negative notions, another.

The main focus of Nelson's comments is Quentin Skinner's attempt to revitalize a positive understanding of liberty as "self-realization" and the claim for a historical imprimatur for it in the work of, among others, neo-Hegelians such as Green and Bernard Bosanquet. Nelson replies by looking more closely at the manner in which such thinkers articulated their conceptions. According to Nelson, Green did see freedom as self-realization, since it amounts to the absence of "wants and impulses which interfere with the fulfillment's of one's possibilities." But Nelson adds that it is also true that for Green, "once such encumbrances are disposed of, man will indeed 'find his object' (what else could he do?)" (161–162). This shows that the key element of freedom for Green is the absence of obstacles after all and not the establishment of some positive state.

But this last parenthetical statement by Nelson ("what else could he do?") reveals the difficulty. For I would insist that finding oneself *is* freedom for Green, and removing encumbrances is but the necessary means to achieve that state; it is not sufficient (conceptually) for freedom itself. And it is true, as

Nelson claims, that Green said that this "shares a 'community of meaning' with freedom as the absences of physical interference," but *sharing a community* of meaning is different from meaning the same thing.

Nelson considers an objection that comes close to representing the view I just stated (62). The objection resists. The objector claims that Nelson's move (that positive liberty is merely disguised negative liberty because all claims that freedom is a positive state can be reanalyzed into the idea that freedom is nothing more than the removal of all obstacles to that state) confuses "removing the obstacles to *x*" with "*x*." Nelson replies that Green and Bosanquet both reverted to the "language of constraint" when called upon to defend their idea that freedom is actually self-realization. Nelson's reply misses the point, however. Green and Bosanquet may well have tried to motivate their alternative conceptualization of freedom by showing that it shares a "community of meaning" with negative notions, in that self-realization involves (*but cannot be reduced to*) removal of internal obstacles to the functioning of my true self. But this is merely to motivate our understanding of why freedom is *more than* the absences of obstacles, for unless we see the final outcome of that absence in positive terms, we have not fully understood the meaning of freedom.

Similarly with Kant: freedom as self-imposition of the moral law is possible only when I can act independently of pathological impulses; it is a mistake to equate the former with the latter. Independence, the negative component of freedom, simply *makes possible* the positive element. As Thomas Hill puts it, for Kant "to conceive a person as having positive freedom is to think of the person as having (1) in addition to negative freedom, (2) a deep rational commitment to some principle(s) of conduct as (rationally) binding but (3) not adopted for the sake of satisfying desires, (4) not just prescribing means to rationally contingent ends, and yet (5) in some sense necessarily imposed on oneself by oneself as a rational agent."[16] To think that this can be reduced to the removal of barriers to the operation of the will is to misunderstand the profound (and controversial) contribution Kant is making here to our understanding of free agency. (I say this acknowledging, as Nelson does in note 41, that there is interesting scholarly debate about whether, or how, Kant may be committed to equating free action with applying the moral law to oneself.)

Nelson goes on to say that the objection involves a "fundamental error" in that it confuses debates about concepts of freedom with disputes over the specificity with which the behavior of the free person can be described. This gets to the heart of the matter but not quite in the way Nelson claims. For it is true that critics of the use of freedom in a positive sense are concerned that equating freedom with a narrow range of life pursuits, say, those coming under the banner of "self-realization," is to give an overly narrow account of the possibilities of a valuable (free) life. That point may well be right, or at least its cautionary intent is well taken, but it is a normative claim about whether we or a society ought to design institutions that promote "freedom" in this way or not. It is not a claim, not a plausible one at least, about what freedom must *mean*.

Nelson does point to an important insight here, though. Even so-called value-neutral negative conceptions of freedom fail to escape the charge of linking freedom to ideals of the good life. Defining a "constraint" necessarily involves specifying (if only implicitly) the range of human actions and pursuits that such constraints make impossible. Fences only one foot high cannot be counted as a constraint for normal adults, unless, that is, such adults feel obligated to participate in a religious ritual that involves shuffling along without lifting their feet and such fences are in the way. The very meaning of constraint presupposes a range of normal (and perhaps morally valued) action types that humans are thought to pursue. Attempts to fashion value-neutral accounts of freedom, either negative or positive, merely aim to allow the widest possible range of such pursuits in the conceptual architecture of these ideas.[17]

A parallel point can be made concerning Nelson's discussion of Taylor's attempt to locate the positive understanding of freedom. For Nelson, Taylor's insistence that positive freedom is an *exercise concept* shows it to be "incompatible" with negative liberty. But first, this is a slight misconstrual: defenders of freedom in this positive sense do not argue that such an ideal is *incompatible* with negative freedom but only that it *goes beyond* that goal or that the securing of simply negative freedom is incoherent or incomplete as a social aim. Taylor and others argue that there is no conception of freedom as simply the absence of constraints that does not rest on the more robust (positive) conception of freedom as a quality of agency, for what *counts* as a constraint is only specified by presuppositions of what final state such interference makes impossible. As Taylor argues, it is not possible to "count" constraints unless one clearly understands what effective agency amounts to. How many "constraints" am I laboring under right now? Who knows, unless I understand what authentic agency amounts to, which such constraints constrain.

There is indeed a parallel here with what Michael Sandel argued concerning Rawls's use of the original position in justifying principles of justice.[18] The contrast between "voluntarist" and "cognitivist" models of justification is parallel to the contrast between negative and positive freedom in the following way: A voluntarist claims that what justifies an outcome is simply that it was *chosen*, while a cognitivist insists that what justifies it is that it was *the right choice*. Similarly, a positive theorist denies that an action is free simply because it occurred (and so was not prevented by obstacles). It must be the *right sort* of action (expressive of the person's authentic self, for example). But this shows that defending positive freedom as a value promotes a *conceptually distinct* state of affairs concerning human action and development, one that engages different machinery in the justification of that action.

An example may make this clearer. A person who faces neither internal nor external constraints to action may well simply fail to act, or she may act randomly or inauthentically. Imagine a person who acts on every impulse that occurs to her, willy-nilly and without any coherent plan. A defender of a positive conception of freedom would say that she lacked something that is over and above the absence of constraints to her thought and action—namely, some quality of her action (and here fill in the blank with the particular theorist's model of positive freedom).

Any positive view of freedom can be understood as an identity statement to the effect that one is free if and only if one is or does X (where X specifies the particular positive conception in question, such as self-realization or self-mastery). Nelson unpacks this identity statement, but the syntax he utilizes in so doing is problematic. For we might say that "freedom" means "being or doing X" (where X can stand for some quality of agency), and therefore this should be uncoupled as "if people are free, they are X, and if people are X, they are free." But this is not how Nelson explicates that claim. He disaggregates the biconditional as "if people are free, they *will do or be* X" and "if people do or are X, they *will be* free." The use of the future tense here shifts the question to the contingent one of what will allow a person to be free. This plays into the hand of a reductionist-negative theorist such as Nelson since it focuses on what will lead to or allow the touted state of being (or doing). But this is to alter the conceptual thrust of the positive view, which is not to fix the meaning of freedom in terms of what will lead to it or allow it to flourish. Using the present tense retains the *logical* connection meant here, that freedom *is* X (and not the conditions that allow it).

Nelson claims, however, that using the copulative "is" begs the question, since it assumes an identity that negative theorists deny. That's right, but what is labeled an analytical claim here is really a normative one. For it is not that there is no separable *concept* of freedom (as self-realization); rather it is that there is not (according to Nelson) an acceptable *value* (self-realization) that we should pursue in the way we pursue or protect freedom. When Nelson claims, then, that the argument is really over what counts as a constraint and not over what freedom means, he mistakenly construes a moral and political dispute as a conceptual one. Those such as Skinner and Taylor (and, I would argue, their historical predecessors such as Kant, Hegel, and Rousseau) claim that a just society must protect or promote freedom construed in this positive way and see as an ideal the ability of citizens to act as authentic, self-governing agents—that is, be self-realized. This is different from saying that obstacles should be removed (internal or external), for it is specifying forthrightly the goal to be achieved independently of removing the obstacles a person might face in reaching that or any other goal.

When Nelson considers, for example, the Protestant ideal that being in the service of God is "perfect freedom" or Hannah Arendt's claim that participation in politics constitutes (in part) freedom, he again twists the claim into an instrumental one about the contingent relation between certain ways of life and the presence of constraints on action. But such theorists are not focusing on what constrains these ideals—that would be a conceptually (and for Arendt a politically) separate matter. They are focusing on what way of life is *truly* a free one.

One could go on with virtually every claim about major thinkers in the "positive" tradition Nelson discusses: Hegel is paraphrased (accurately enough) as claiming that we "can only be liberated from our passions and sense impressions once we have been made to realize that we ourselves will the 'universal' . . . through the practice of citizenship in a Hegelian state." And Rousseau is glossed as purporting that "people are governed by their 'higher,' 'rational' selves (and, hence, free from internal constraint) only when they are guided by a general Will" (70). But this is followed by a summary statement that misses the point altogether: "For both theorists, constraints are stripped away through the actual experience of citizenship rightly practiced" (70). Yes, *but* it is not the stripping away of constraints that makes for freedom for either of these writers; it is the achievement of a certain mode of political life, one manifesting agency of a certain idealized sort. One is hard-pressed, for example, to find in Rousseau's *Social Contract* any attention to the barriers to action and self-development that make for the free citizen. What he focuses on are the social relations and internal self-government that manifest civic freedom (and ideally moral freedom) itself.

Finally, I should add that I wholly agree with what Nelson says about Philip Pettit's recent attempt to fashion a unique conception of freedom as nondomination, which he (Pettit) has claimed captures much of the civic republican tradition of political writing on the subject.[19] I have argued elsewhere that Pettit's notion is, in the end, a negative conception but one that adds a robust normative component that requires that procedural justice be operative for the constraints that an agent faces not to amount to limitations on his or her freedom.[20] That is, domination occurs when the processes by which a certain de facto constraint comes into being have not met the requirement of respect and citizen input (or representation of that input) demanded by justice. This implies that justice is fundamental in consideration of the acceptability of citizens' conditions and that freedom is only derivatively so (in that one is free to the extent that one lives under just conditions).

My intentions in this discussion of Nelson are more than to make a narrowly conceptual point. The suggestion that positive conceptions of liberty can all be reduced to negative notions threatens to seriously misunderstand efforts to include idealized models of agency in our broadest understandings of social freedom. Seeing freedom as more than a set of opportunities created by removing constraints from the path of thought and action—even "constraints" defined in a robust and nuanced manner—is to set out a view of human agency as a set of powers and abilities regarding the development and expression of authentic and effective self-government. Certain political institutions and policies may well remove or minimize constraints faced by an agent but do nothing to establish or protect those powers. The injustice that many claim this involves fails to get a foothold in a conceptual terrain that disallows (or misunderstands) the core concepts of that injustice.

What emerges from this discussion, however, is that what appears to be a dispute over the concepts of negative and positive freedom is really a normative dispute: namely, whether we want to accept that freedom construed as effective agency (or self-realization, and so on) is a fundamental political value. Various thinkers in the liberal tradition have answered negatively, many inspired by Berlin's suspicion that the promotion of freedom in this sense conflicts with a robust value pluralism that all liberals should accept (as should others committed to toleration of "difference"). This bring us back to questions of the relation between freedom and value and whether anything but a negative notion protects us from this overly restrictive social perspective. Let me close, then, with a brief discussion of that issue.

III. Positive Freedom and Value(s)

One critic of positive conceptions of freedom who worries about the value implications of such an ideal is Ian Carter. Carter rejects positive understandings of liberty but is also generally critical of any "value-based" account of freedom. Value-based accounts see the measure of freedom as dependent, in part, on the value of the actions one is free to do (when one is free). This approach has been defended most famously by Taylor, which Carter understands to be freedom as self-mastery.[21] Such a view distinguishes preferences that manifest our positive freedom from those that, while just as motivating, are better classified as compulsions and as such stifle such freedom. This contrast cannot be captured by understanding freedom as simply the opportunity to act. Moreover, the mark of this distinction, for Taylor, is that pursuits that express our positive freedom, unlike compulsions and the like, are grounded in our "strong valuations," things we value independently of mere desire. Carter argues that such a view fails as the basis of a measure of *overall freedom* since there is no plausible way of distinguishing, weighing, and comparing such valuations. Moreover, such valuations would commit us to the kind of normative inflexibility—value monism—that Berlin warned so forcefully against.[22]

In a parallel manner, Carter argues against Amartya Sen's view that what he calls "agency freedom"—which is a positive notion—has intrinsic value. Sen supports this idea with examples such as contrasting fasting with starving: both involve not eating, but the first is a terrible imposition, while the second is a (perhaps heroic) expression of agency. But Carter argues that such examples show not that agency freedom has value as such but rather that it has value as a necessary condition of the activities that are themselves valuable. But attaching the value of freedom to the value of activities has implications that run against the broad value neutrality of liberal political theory (to which Sen and others are on record as being committed).[23]

What is required, then, is indeed an argument for the value of positive liberty that is not so overly specific as to collapse into other concepts that make liberty eliminable or attach to specific pursuits the value of which is reasonably contestable. This last worry is, of course, the source of the alarms sounded by Berlin. But many have attempted to work out a conception of the value of freedom (as effective agency) that does not run afoul of the commitment to diversity, tolerance, and value neutrality characteristic of liberal polities. My own approach, which is inspired by Rousseau but echoes Rawls's political liberalism in many ways, ties the value of autonomous agency to the value of democratic culture, where the latter is understood as what is necessary for persons to see themselves as a part of a set of processes that form social structures within which they pursue their lives, and either see their interests represented fairly in such processes and/or see themselves as a direct part of the collective decisions that form their core. For Rawls, the possibility of an overlapping consensus regarding the central principles of justice among citizens with divergent but reasonable comprehensive conceptions of morality and the good is intertwined with the values of rational autonomous agency that operates in the generation of that consensus, all of which can be accepted in reflective equilibrium.[24]

This is highly controversial and much discussed, but it is not by any means obviously implausible. Reference to such projects of justifying positive freedom without connecting it to specific (contestable) values is made here merely to show the contours of such a project, though not, of course, to fully defend it.

More directly, the strategy in play here is the attempt to adopt a conception of positive liberty that is value *neutral*, or at least is value invariant relative to a wide array of norms, ideals, and conceptions of the good. That is, one could adopt a *procedural* conception of authentic values relative to which one has the capacity for freedom in the positive sense. I (and others) have attempted to defend such a notion of "autonomy," which for present purposes amounts to a positive conception of freedom (as self-government).[25]

Carter, in fact, discusses my attempt to develop such an account.[26] His general objection regards what, in other contexts, has been called the "regress" problem with notions of autonomy: namely, that insofar as autonomy requires second-order reflection on one's motivational states, then the authenticity of those higher order states must be tested; this merely moves the question back a step (or up one level) requiring further iterations of the test for authenticity. Carter puts his version of this difficulty this way: to identify authentic values procedurally (historically), one must be able to apply a counterfactual test to the effect that *were* one to have avoided the effects of whatever authenticity-impairing factors undermined authenticity (in the development of one's desire), one would have desired this or that. But that presupposes that desiring this or that (in the counterfactual condition) would have been authentic. But how is this established without positing still further reflexive tests for authenticity?[27]

The reply to this objection is to require that the acts of authenticity-establishing reflection in fact "speak for the agent" and do not require ever-further acts of reflective endorsement. Harry Frankfurt's attempt to do this involves reference to one's "deepest cares," which do not need further authentication because this just *is* the agent's motivational voice, so to speak.[28] And as we saw, Taylor's version of this attempt is to posit strong valuations (or "foundational commitments"), but a value-neutral conception of freedom would want to avoid this reference if such valuations were viewed in any nonsubjective manner. My own attempt is to require that the reflection in question be invariant over a number of conditions and reflect one's diachronic practical identity, and that, additionally, one's reflective capacity itself is not undermined by various debilitating factors.[29]

Such a view may itself meet any number of objections,[30] but it is at least a prima facie plausible candidate for a conception of freedom that goes beyond minimal negative ideas but does not run afoul of worries about value pluralism. I mention it here only to suggest that the debate over whether positive freedom is a social ideal worth promoting is not settled merely by noting that many attempts to articulate that notion tied it too closely to controversial conceptions of value.

As this brief discussion indicates, the idea of individual autonomy should be put alongside the idea of positive freedom as a concept that attempts to capture the ideal of effective agency that negative notions of liberty occlude. Adopting such a value as a central political ideal connects freedom to various other social conditions, including the distribution of basic resources. To see freedom as nothing more than the removal of certain interferences blinds us to the need for such resources, as well as their precise character, and so blinds us to the demands of that aspect of just institutions. Therefore, including central reference to positive freedom (or autonomy) is far from using "too many" concepts. Rather, it is a crucial component of the articulation of principles of justice and the resistance to certain forms of oppression. And while a defense of this last claim must be mounted elsewhere—all I have attempted here is to clear conceptual space for it—it is, I think, a claim worth debating fully on its merits.

Notes

1. Isaiah Berlin, "Two Concepts of Liberty," in *Four Essays on Liberty* (Oxford: Oxford University Press, 1969), 118–712. For discussion, see, e.g., the essays in David Miller, ed., *Liberty* (Oxford: Oxford University Press, 1993). For my own attempt to explicate the concept, see *The Myth of Property* (New York: Oxford University Press, 1994), chap. 4.

2. For general discussion, see, e.g., Richard Flathman, *The Philosophy and Politics of Freedom* (Chicago: University of Chicago Press, 1987); George Brenkert, *Political Freedom* (London: Routledge and Kegan Paul, 1991), chap. 1; and Ian Carter, "Positive and Negative

Liberty" in *The Stanford Encyclopedia of Philosophy* (http://plato.stanford.edu/entries/liberty-positive-negative/), 2007.

3. Recent attempts to defend a conception of negative liberty include Matthew Kramer, *The Quality of Freedom* (Oxford: Oxford University Press, 2003); and Ian Carter, *A Measure of Freedom* (Oxford: Oxford University Press, 2004).

4. Charles Taylor, "What Is Wrong with Negative Liberty?," in his *Philosophy and the Human Sciences: Philosophical Papers, II* (Cambridge: Cambridge University Press, 1985), 211–219.

5. Gerald MacCallum, "Negative and Positive Freedom," *Philosophical Review* 76 (1967): 3112–3134.

6. For an example of this sort of view, see Lawrence Crocker, *Positive Liberty* (The Hague, Netherlands: Martinus Nijhoff, 1980). See also Andrew Levine, *Arguing for Socialism* (London: Verso Press, 1988).

7. See, e.g., Taylor, "What Is Wrong with Negative Liberty?".

8. See, e.g., Will Kylmicka's specification of the fundamental tenet of liberalism, to wit: "Liberals aren't saying that we should have the freedom to select our projects for its own sake. . . . [Rather,] . . . it is our projects and tasks that are the most fundamental important things in our lives" (*Liberalism, Community, and Culture* [Oxford: Oxford University Press, 1989], 48).

9. Berlin, "Two Concepts of Liberty," 121–122. I should note that I think this anti-Stoical line of argument, which is widely followed in the literature, is overdrawn—namely, many argue that any view of freedom that implies that freedom is increased by expunging desires is problematic. (See, e.g., Richard Arneson, "Freedom and Desire," *Canadian Journal of Philosophy* 15, 3 (1985): 425–448.) On my view, it entirely depends on the manner in which desires change, and if the process of "expunging" desires is of the right sort, concluding (via a concept of freedom) that our freedom is increased as a result is an acceptable implication. See my "Liberalism and Individual Positive Freedom," *Ethics* 101, 2 (1991): 343–359.

10. See Quentin Skinner, *Liberty Before Liberalism* (Cambridge: Cambridge University Press, 1998), though Skinner insists that the republican notion of freedom he is defending is a negative one. For critical analysis, see Kramer, *The Quality of Freedom*, chap. 2.

11. See John Rawls, *Political Liberalism* (New York: Columbia University Press, 1993). On the "politics of difference," see Iris Marion Young, *Justice and the Politics of Difference* (Princeton, NJ: Princeton University Press, 1991).

12. Berlin, "Two Concepts of Liberty." For a recent discussion that highlights this point, see Thomas R. V. Nys, "Re-sourcing the Self? Isaiah Berlin and Charles Taylor: The Tensions Between Freedom and Authenticity," *Ethical Perspectives* 11, 4 (2004): 215–227.

13. See, e.g., Joel Feinberg, *Social Philosophy* (Englewood Cliffs, NJ: Prentice Hall, 1973), chap. 1.

14. Eric Nelson, "Liberty: One Concept Too Many?," *Political Theory* 33, 1 (February 2005): 58–78. Unmarked page numbers in the text refer to this article.

15. MacCallum, "Negative and Positive Freedom."

16. Thomas Hill, "The Kantian Conception of Autonomy" in *The Inner Citadel: Essays on Individual Autonomy*, edited by John Christman (New York: Oxford University Press, 1989), 91–105, 99.

17. As I mentioned, two recent attempts to work out a negative, value-neutral conception of freedom can be found in Carter, *A Measure of Freedom*; and Kramer, *The Quality of Freedom*. For discussion of this issue, see also Hillel Steiner, "How Free: Computing Personal

Liberty" in *Of Liberty*, edited by A. Phillips-Griffiths (Cambridge: Cambridge University Press, 1983), 73–83.

18. This is a point discussed by Nelson (68–69), but as my discussion will show, I interpret the controversy slightly differently from the way he does.

19. Philip Pettit, *Republicanism: A Theory of Freedom and Government* (New York: Oxford University Press, 1997).

20. John Christman, "Review of Republicanism," *Ethics* 109, 2 (1998): 202–206, reprinted in *The Good Society* 9, 3 (2000): 47–49.

21. Carter, *A Measure of Freedom*, chap. 6; Taylor, "What Is Wrong with Negative Liberty?".

22. Carter, *A Measure of Freedom.*

23. Amartya Sen, "Well-Being, Agency, and Freedom," *Journal of Philosophy* 82 (1985): 169–221; Carter, *A Measure of Freedom*, 56–58.

24. Rawls, *Political Liberalism.* My own view is developed in *The Politics of Persons: Individual Autonomy and Socio-historical Selves* (Cambridge: Cambridge University Press, 2009), chap. 7.

25. Christman, *The Politics of Persons.*

26. Carter's target is an earlier paper of mine discussing positive liberty ("Liberalism and Individual Positive Freedom"). The view I allude to in the text and that I would now defend concerns the idea of autonomy, a notion that for our purposes can double as a kind of positive freedom.

27. Carter, *A Measure of Freedom*, 155–156.

28. Harry Frankfurt, "The Faintest Passion," *Proceedings and Addresses of the Aristotelian Society* 49 (1992): 113–145.

29. Christman, *The Politics of Persons*, chap 7.

30. For example, several writers have claimed that purely procedural views of this sort must, in the end, include at least "weakly substantive" conditions. See Catriona Mackenzie, "Relational Autonomy, Normative Authority, and Perfectionism," *Journal of Social Philosophy* 39, 4 (Winter 2008): 512–533.

READING

9

The Myth of "Merely Formal Freedom"

IAN CARTER

Ever since Marx, it has been common for socialist and egalitarian political theorists to criticize classical liberals or libertarians (hereinafter, laissez-faire liberals) for their exclusive concern with "formal" freedom and their consequent neglect of "substantive" or "effective" or "real" freedom. Roughly speaking, formal freedom is said to be achieved through the rule of law and the safeguarding of people's rights of property and contract; by contrast, substantive or effective or real freedom is said to exist only when people possess the material means necessary to realize their plans.[1] Thus, I am formally free to take a trip from Britain to China if there is no law forbidding me to do so; I am substantively free to take that trip if, as well as enjoying the legal permission to do so, I also have the resources and the ability actually to reach China. My formal freedom to swim across a lake depends on the owner of the lake granting me the permission to do so; my substantive freedom to do so depends not only on that permission but also (among other things) on the fact that "my lungs or my limbs would not give in before reaching the other side."[2] Laissez-faire liberals tend to advocate merely formal freedom for all; socialists or egalitarians, by contrast, favour substantive freedom for all.[3] Or so we are told.

I believe that the supposed contrast between substantive freedom and merely formal freedom is mistaken, and that it is misleading to characterize the difference between laissez-faire liberals and egalitarians as a difference between advocates of merely formal freedom and advocates of substantive freedom. One reason for the persistence of the distinction in the literature is that the notion of formal freedom is itself not very clear. It is easy enough to see that formal freedom must depend in some way on certain norms. But when we come to explicate the concept more precisely, we find that the exact role of those norms is open to interpretation. In the first section of this essay, I discuss three possible interpretations of the notion of formal freedom. On any one of these interpretations, either formal freedom turns out not to be the kind of freedom endorsed by laissez-faire liberals, or else the contrast between substantive freedom and merely formal freedom breaks down. In the second section, I try to provide a diagnosis of our inability to make clear sense of the notion of "merely formal freedom," drawing on two more coherent distinctions commonly made in the literature on freedom. According to my diagnosis, the notion of merely formal freedom involves slippage between these two distinctions, as well as among the different interpretations of formal freedom set out in the first section.

None of this is to deny that the notion of formal freedom can be meaningful in itself. The problem lies in its supposed contrast with substantive freedom, and the supposed relevance of this contrast to the ideological divide between egalitarianism and laissez-faire liberalism.

I. Three Interpretations of Formal Freedom

A first attempt to make sense of the notion of formal freedom might consist in saying that formal freedom is purely normative freedom. Normative freedom, as opposed to material or physical freedom, consists in the absence of deontic constraints—that is, the absence of prohibitions and/or the presence of permissions (for simplicity's sake, I leave aside here the distinction between weak and strong permissions[4]). Thus, for example, I can have the normative freedom (i.e., the permission) to leave the room I am currently occupying, even though someone or something might be physically preventing me from leaving, so rendering me materially unfree to leave. Conversely, I might be materially free to leave, because nothing is physically preventing me from leaving, even though I lack the permission, and hence the normative freedom, to do so.[5] Presumably, the kind of normative freedom with which laissez-faire liberals are concerned is the absence of legal prohibitions—in Hohfeldian terms, the presence of legal liberty-rights.

Hohfeldian liberty-rights can be classified as either "naked" or "vested."[6] If *A* has a naked liberty-right to do *x*, *A* has the permission to do *x*, but *A* might still be permissibly prevented from doing *x* because some other person, *B*, has a liberty-right to do *y*, and B's doing *y* precludes A's doing *x*. If, on the other hand, *A* has a vested liberty-right to do *x*, *A* has the permission to do *x*, and that permission is protected by a structure of claim-rights on the part of *A* that others act or refrain from acting in various ways. I shall assume that the kind of formal freedom that concerns us here cannot consist in the mere presence of naked liberty-rights. "Merely formal freedom" must therefore include claim-rights as well as liberty-rights. For the laissez-faire liberal, these claim-rights will consist in claims to noninterference.

Here, then, is a first possible interpretation of formal freedom: agent *A* is formally free to perform action *x* if *A* is legally permitted to do *x* and others are legally prohibited from preventing *A* from doing *x*; by contrast, *A* is substantively free to do *x*—*is* "really" free to do x—only if, in addition to having this normative freedom, *A* is materially able to do *x*.[7]

This is certainly one plausible way of characterizing formal freedom. However, purely normative freedom cannot be what egalitarians are referring to when they say that laissez-faire liberals are exclusively concerned with formal freedom. Imagine that the structure of legal rights in *A*'s society is such that *A* is legally permitted to do *x* and all other people are legally prohibited from preventing her from doing *x*. Next, imagine that someone nevertheless does, as a matter of fact, physically prevent *A* from doing *x*. (To make this point particularly clear, imagine that the preventing agent is a policeman who is acting illegally.) Although *A* is not suffering any *normative* unfreedom in this example, no liberal would deny that the act of physical prevention renders *A* unfree. So, if the distinction between formal freedom and substantive freedom is identical to the distinction between purely normative freedom and material freedom, the dispute between laissez-faire liberals and egalitarians is not about formal freedom versus substantive freedom.

In order to avoid this shortcoming in the first interpretation, one might suggest a second interpretation: formal freedom consists in the presence of legal claim-rights not to be prevented from exercising certain liberty-rights, plus the fact that those legal claim-rights are actually respected. On this second interpretation, formal freedom is material as well as normative: it is freedom from any material constraints that would constitute violations of one's legal rights not to be prevented from pursuing one's legally permitted aims. One is formally free to the extent that the legal claim-rights protecting one's legal liberty-rights are respected by others, and one is formally unfree to the extent that those legal claim-rights are violated by others. One is substantively free, on the other hand, to the extent that one possesses the material means to exercise one's legal liberty-rights.

Again, it is difficult to think of any laissez-faire liberal who would endorse a merely formal conception of freedom in this second sense. Imagine a society in which it has recently become legal to shoot one's neighbour on sight (natural law theorists may want to deny that such a change could properly be called "legal"; they should pass straight on to the third interpretation supplied below). Imagine, further, that a great many members of the society decide to take advantage of this new opportunity, as a result of which almost no one is able to leave their home without being physically wounded or killed. No liberal would deny that the members of this society have become drastically less free as a result of the legalization of the act of shooting one's neighbour (together with the consequent increase in the probability of being wounded or killed), even though, in purely formal terms (on this second interpretation of formal freedom), the shootings do not create any "formal unfreedoms." At the time of the shootings no one possesses the legal claim-right not to be shot. Therefore, the shootings do not violate anyone's legal claim-rights to noninterference; their only effect is that of limiting the means with which people are able to exercise their legal liberty-rights. The legal change imagined in this example does, of course, *remove* certain legal claim-rights. But to remove legal claim-rights is not to restrict formal freedom on our second interpretation of the notion, according to which one has formal freedom to the extent that the legal claim-rights *that one has* (to noninterference) are actually respected.

As the above example makes clear, there are many material constraints on freedom that are recognized as such by laissez-faire liberals and yet are not captured by our second interpretation of formal freedom. Something therefore needs to be said about the legal claim-rights that one *ought* to have—that is, about the *content* of the claim-rights that one must have in order for their observance to be sufficient to guarantee the merely formal freedom supposedly favoured by laissez-faire liberals.

Consider then a third interpretation: formal freedom consists in the legal recognition of all *morally just* claim-rights not to be prevented from exercising *morally just* liberty-rights, plus the fact that those morally just claim-rights are actually respected.[8] For the laissez-faire liberal, the relevant claim-rights are determined by morally just property rights. Thus, one is free to the extent that no one else is preventing one from exercising one's morally just property rights, and one is unfree to the extent that others are preventing one from doing so. In a society characterized by economic inequality and a perfect enforcement of people's morally just private-property rights (specified on the basis of a classical liberal conception of justice), the laissez-faire liberal will see the rich and the poor as equally free (because both groups enjoy full formal freedom), whereas the egalitarian will see the rich as freer than the poor (because the former enjoy a greater degree of substantive freedom).[9]

On this third interpretation, formal freedom amounts to what some theorists have called "moralized" or "justice-based" freedom.[10] Now it is true that such a conception of freedom *has* been assumed, at least implicitly, by a number of contemporary laissez-faire liberals—including, arguably, Robert Nozick and Murray Rothbard.[11] However, the objection that some critics have, with good reason, moved against moralized conceptions of freedom is not that they fail to capture the idea of substantive or effective or real freedom. Rather, the objection is that, on such conceptions, freedom loses its status as one of the fundamental moral values grounding a liberal theory of justice. Because freedom gets defined in terms of rights, we can no longer appeal to freedom as one of our reasons for favouring a certain structure of rights. Once one endorses such a conception, freedom falls out of the picture, and the burden of justification rests instead on the moral values in terms of which freedom is defined.[12] If, by contrast, we adopt a morally neutral conception of freedom (according to which a person is free to do *x* if that person is materially unconstrained from doing *x regardless* of the moral acceptability of doing *x* or of being prevented from doing *x*), then freedom can be considered an independent value the promotion or preservation of which can supply a reason for supporting a particular structure of rights. Only if the liberal adopts a nonmoralized conception of freedom can she accord freedom this fundamental justificatory role.

There is no conceptual reason for associating moralized or justice-based conceptions of freedom with laissez-faire liberalism or for dissociating them from egalitarianism. After all, some prominent egalitarians have similarly endorsed such a conception of freedom—on the assumption that "justice" means *egalitarian* justice. For example, Ronald Dworkin has defined freedom, at least implicitly, as the power to act in ways that are permitted by the norms of an ideally egalitarian society.[13] If formal freedom is justice-based freedom, then Dworkin's conception of freedom is no less formal than those of Nozick and Rothbard. Yet, because the conception of justice appealed to by Dworkin is an egalitarian conception, each and every person's morally just claim-rights (on that conception) already include the claim to be accorded a fair share of the material means necessary to realize a life plan. If formal freedom is justice-based freedom, and justice requires substantive freedom for all, then formal freedom qualifies as substantive freedom. At this point, the contrast between formal and substantive freedom appears to have broken down.

Moreover, the fact that formal freedom can be egalitarian and, in this sense, substantive is a conclusion that applies not only where formal freedom is conceived in terms of moral norms (as in the third interpretation), but also where it is conceived in terms of legal norms (as in the second interpretation). For the third interpretation of formal freedom is simply the moralized counterpart of the second interpretation: where formal freedom is conceived in terms of moral norms, formal freedom can qualify as substantive freedom because it is possible for the relevant moral norms to be norms that prescribe material equality; where formal freedom is conceived in terms of legal norms, formal freedom can qualify as substantive freedom because it is possible for positive law to prescribe material equality.

The following difference remains: Dworkin defines freedom in terms of the power to act, whereas on our third interpretation, more in line with the conceptions of freedom favoured by laissez-faire liberals, formal freedom was defined in terms of noninterference. Still, there is no good reason for considering the latter conception to be "formal" in a way in which the former conception is not. On the latter conception, freedom is the absence (and unfreedom the presence) of formally prohibited material interference with a person's exercise of her capacities; on the former conception, freedom is the absence (and unfreedom the presence) of formally prohibited material limitations of those capacities themselves.

II. "Merely" Formal Freedom

In order to see what has gone wrong, it will be useful to draw on two distinctions commonly made in the literature on freedom. These distinctions reflect two separate debates about the nature of freedom.

The first distinction is between *normatively loaded* and *normatively neutral* conceptions of freedom.[14] If the second or third interpretation of formal freedom is correct, then to object to a formal conception of freedom is to favour a normatively neutral conception of freedom—one that does not involve defining freedom in terms of moral or legal norms and instead allows us to base a liberal theory of justice on (among other things) the fundamental value of freedom.

The second distinction is between *interpersonal* or (alternatively put) *social* conceptions of freedom, on the one hand, and *freedom-as-ability*, on the other—that is to say, between freedom as the absence of material constraints *created by other agents*, and freedom as the absence of material constraints *of all kinds* (where constraints are classified according to whether they have their origin in the actions of other agents, in the actions of the agent herself, or in the workings of nature).[15] When egalitarians argue in favour of substantive or effective or real freedom, what they really have in mind is the importance, not of normatively neutral freedom, but of freedom-as-ability, the opposite of which is not normatively loaded freedom, but interpersonal or social freedom.

These two distinctions are logically independent of each other. One can endorse a *normatively neutral*, *interpersonal* conception of freedom. Such is the case, for example, of Hillel Steiner, according to whom *A* is unfree to do *x* if and only if some other agent physically prevents *A* from doing *x*, regardless of the justice or injustice of *A's* doing *x* or of A's being prevented from doing *x*.[16] Conversely, one can endorse a *normatively loaded* conception of *freedom-as-ability*, according to which freedom is the absence of constraints of all kinds on actions that conform to the rules of egalitarian justice. Such a conception represents a plausible interpretation of Ronald Dworkin's justice-based conception of freedom. Combining the two distinctions, we obtain a classification of four different families of conceptions of freedom, each of which is exemplified by a particular author in Table 9.1.

In light of the above analysis, it is curious that so many egalitarians have accused laissez-faire liberals of advocating *merely* formal freedom. The use of merely in the expression "merely formal freedom" is suggestive of a subset relation—as if formal freedom were all well and good as far as it goes, and that freedom for the egalitarian meant "formal freedom and more besides." If the second or third interpretation of formal freedom is correct, however, the view that freedom, properly conceived, *includes* formal freedom—that it is formal *among other things*—ought at most to be shared only by that minority of egalitarian thinkers who, despite the plausibility of the fundamental objection to normatively loaded conceptions of freedom, follow Dworkin in endorsing just such a conception. The view ought not to be shared by any egalitarian (or, for that matter, by any nonegalitarian) who, more in line with the liberal tradition broadly conceived, rejects normatively loaded conceptions of freedom and instead accords freedom the status of a fundamental value. As Table 9.1 shows, such a view is indeed not shared by the egalitarian Cohen or by the left-libertarian

TABLE 9.1

	freedom as an interpersonal relation	freedom-as-ability
freedom as normatively loaded	Robert Nozick	Ronald Dworkin
freedom as normatively neutral	Hillel Steiner	G. A. Cohen*

*I place Cohen in the bottom right-hand corner of the table because, although he devotes much space to demonstrating that a person lacks interpersonal freedom whenever that person lacks economic means, he is interested in interpersonal freedom merely for the sake of argument and maintains, in addition, that inability is a sufficient condition for unfreedom. See G. A. Cohen, "Freedom and Money," *Contemporary Debates in Social Philosophy*, edited by L. Thomas (Oxford: Blackwell, 2008), 19–42, at 20–21, 38n10. (According to my analysis, Cohen's subversive antilibertarian argument that the poor lack interpersonal freedom is indeed best formulated as an argument from *interpersonal* freedom, and not as an argument from *formal* freedom. Swift, *Political Philosophy*, 57–58, appears to hold otherwise, on the assumption that formal freedom means the absence of legal restrictions backed up by effective sanctions. On this assumption, which differs from all three of the interpretations of formal freedom discussed above, presumably the optimal social arrangement in terms of merely formal freedom would be one of anarchy.)

Steiner. Both of these authors reject outright the idea of defining freedom in a norm-dependent way, as a result of which neither of them thinks that freedom, when properly conceived of as a fundamental political value, is formal and more besides. Exactly because they think of freedom as a fundamental value, their conceptions of freedom are not in *any* way formal. (Neither does their rejection of the formal dimension of freedom automatically imply an interest on their part in freedom-as-ability, as the example of Steiner indicates.)

If substantive freedom means freedom-as-ability, why have so many theorists contrasted it with merely formal freedom? Two factors may help to explain this tendency.

The first factor is that of conceptual slippage between the two distinctions just discussed: the words "merely" and "formal" in the expression "merely formal freedom" are themselves used with implicit reference to two different issues. The use of the word "merely" in that expression is meant to imply the inadequacy of concentrating on interpersonal or social freedom rather than on the broader phenomenon of freedom-as-ability. The set of obstacles generally recognized as constraining material freedom on the interpersonal conception is indeed a *subset* of the set of obstacles generally recognized as constraining material freedom-as-ability, so it makes sense to talk of the mere absence of constraints of the first kind. However, the word "formal" in the expression "merely formal freedom" is (at the best of times) meant to imply not the fact of material freedom being interpersonal freedom, but the fact of it being normatively loaded freedom.

The second factor consists in the correct perception that the idea of merely formal freedom *can* be made sense of if we adopt the *first* interpretation of formal freedom, according to which formal freedom is purely normative and therefore nonmaterial. In other words, the persistence of the contrast between substantive freedom and merely formal freedom may well be traceable not only to slippage between interpersonal freedom and normatively loaded freedom, but also to slippage among the different interpretations of formal freedom set out in the previous section. On the first interpretation, we can make sense of the notion of merely formal freedom by saying that it is the mere absence of certain deontic constraints, whereas freedom properly conceived is the absence both of those deontic constraints and of their material counterparts, thus implying that the set of possible constraints on formal freedom is a subset of the set of possible constraints on freedom properly conceived. But, as we have seen, the distinction between deontic and material constraints has little direct bearing on the differences between laissez-faire liberals and egalitarians.

Whichever of the three interpretations one endorses, it is incorrect to characterize the laissez-faire liberal's refusal to identify freedom with ability as depending on an exclusive attachment to something called formal freedom. The issue of whether and when freedom should be conceived in a formal or a nonformal way is no doubt an important one, but it transcends the divide between egalitarianism and laissez-faire liberalism, and it is obscured by attempts to draw a relevant distinction between formal freedom and substantive freedom.

Notes

1. The distinction occurs in numerous places in political debates over the last century, but here are three influential contemporary sources. First, Philippe Van Parijs, *Real Freedom for All: What (if Anything) Can Justify Capitalism?* (Oxford: Oxford University Press, 1995), 20–24, contrasts "real freedom" with "formal freedom," where real freedom consists in "security, self-ownership, and [material] opportunity," and formal freedom consists only in the first two of these conditions—i.e., security and self-ownership (see note 10, below). Second, Amartya Sen, *Development as Freedom* (Oxford: Oxford University Press, 1999), 17–19, 25–30, contrasts "substantive freedom" (or "real opportunity") with "procedural liberty" (as well as with "procedures for liberty"), where the latter appears to correspond more or less to formal freedom on the third of the interpretations presented in this essay. Third, Adam Swift, *Political Philosophy: A Beginner's Guide for Students and Politicians* (Cambridge: Polity Press, 2001), 55–59, distinguishes between "effective freedom" and "formal freedom," where effective freedom means "the power or capacity to act" and formal freedom means "the mere absence of interference" in a "narrow legalistic sense." Swift rightly emphasizes that the distinction is less clear-cut than is often supposed, but he suggests that it can still do useful normative work. Sen uses the term "effective freedom" in a rather special way, which I shall not discuss here. For an account of formal freedom versus real freedom in Marx, see Jon Elster, *Making Sense of Marx* (Cambridge: Cambridge University Press, 1985), 204–211 (see also note 9, below).

2. Van Parijs, *Real Freedom for All*, 23.

3. John Rawls, *A Theory of Justice* (Cambridge, MA: Harvard University Press, 1971), section 32, is often seen as having one foot in each of these camps, given his distinction between "liberty" and "the worth of liberty." Rawls is seen as siding with the laissez-faire liberals inasmuch as his conception of liberty is a merely formal one, even though his commitment to

promoting the worth of liberty for the least well-off nevertheless commits him to egalitarian redistribution: "without a social minimum, the basic liberties are merely formal protections and are worth little to people who are impoverished and without the means to take advantage of their liberties" (Samuel Freeman, "Introduction," *The Cambridge Companion to Rawls*, edited by Samuel Freeman [Cambridge: Cambridge University Press, 2003], 1–61, at 9). See also Frank I. Michelman, "Rawls on Constitutionalism and Constitutional Law," *The Cambridge Companion to Rawls*, 394–425, at 414–415.

4. An action is permitted in the weak sense if its performance is not prohibited. It is permitted in the strong sense if there is a norm explicitly stating this to be the case. G. H. von Wright, *Norm and Action* (London: Routledge and Kegan Paul, 1963), 86.

5. Matthew H. Kramer, *The Quality of Freedom* (Oxford: Oxford University Press, 2003), 60–65. As Kramer notes, normative freedom is necessarily bivalent (for any given action, *j*, one is either free or unfree to *j*), whereas physical freedom can be interpreted as either bivalent or trivalent (one can be free to *j*, unfree to *j*, or neither free nor unfree to *j*). In this essay I shall assume bivalence throughout. Relaxing this assumption complicates matters without significantly affecting my central claims.

6. See H. L. A. Hart, *Essays on Bentham: Jurisprudence and Political Theory* (Oxford: Clarendon Press, 1982), 172; and Hillel Steiner, *An Essay on Rights* (Oxford: Blackwell, 1994), 75–76.

7. On a more precise account, formal freedom would be characterized as including naked liberties *as well as* vested ones. For example, exercising the liberty to make a contract with Smith is dependent on Smith's agreement, even though the making of the contract is normatively protected by duties of third parties not to prevent its occurrence in certain ways. For simplicity's sake, I confine my attention to vested liberties.

8. Given the reference to content in the final sentence of the previous paragraph, this third interpretation of formal freedom is diametrically opposed to the idea that we can usefully distinguish between formal and substantive freedom in terms of the distinction between *form* and *content*—i.e., the idea that substantive freedom, unlike formal freedom, is contentful. The latter view might have appealed to Marx, for whom real freedom meant positive freedom in the sense in which Isaiah Berlin uses the term (self-mastery or self-realization). Marxian real freedom has a content in the sense that it consists in the actual performance of certain courses of action (those that realize one's "true" interests). But this way of distinguishing between real freedom and formal freedom is a nonstarter for most contemporary advocates of real or substantive or effective freedom, given their rejection of the conception of freedom as self-realization in favour of the conception of freedom as the power to act.

9. Van Parijs, *Real Freedom for All*, 20–24, uses the term "formal freedom" to denote a hybrid of my second and third interpretations: a system (any coherent system) of enforced legal rights (what he calls security), together with the specification that those rights include self-ownership rights. The first of these two conditions (security) is identical to formal freedom on my second interpretation, while the second condition (self-ownership) specifies the content of some of the security rights and therefore represents one possible (if rather restricted) version of formal freedom on my third interpretation. Van Parijs's interpretation of formal freedom fares only slightly better than my second interpretation in capturing what laissez-faire liberals mean by freedom. To see this, one need only substitute the permission to shoot one's neighbour, in the counterexample to my second interpretation, with the permission to perform some non-self-ownership-violating but clearly freedom-restricting action, such as burning down one's neighbour's house when he or she is not at home.

10. G. A. Cohen, *History, Labour, and Freedom: Themes from Marx* (Oxford: Clarendon Press, 1988), 12, and *Self-Ownership, Freedom, and Equality* (Cambridge: Cambridge University Press, 1995), chap. 2; Cheyney C. Ryan, "Yours, Mine, and Ours: Property Rights and Individual Liberty," in *Reading Nozick: Essays on Anarchy, State, and Utopia*, edited by J. Paul (Oxford: Blackwell, 1982), 323–343; Peter Jones, "Freedom and the Redistribution of Resources," *Journal of Social Policy* 2 (1982): 217–238; Serena Olsaretti, "Freedom, Force, and Choice: Against the Rights-Based Definition of Voluntariness," *Journal of Political Philosophy* 6 (1998): 53–78; Ian Carter, *A Measure of Freedom* (Oxford: Oxford University Press, 1999), 68–74.

11. Robert Nozick, *Anarchy, State, and Utopia* (New York: Basic Books, 1974), 262; Murray N. Rothbard, *The Ethics of Liberty* (Atlantic Highlands, NJ: Humanities Press, 1982), part IV. See also, for example, Bruno Leoni, *Freedom and the Law* (Los Angeles: Nash, 1961), chap. 2.

12. Cohen, *History, Labour, and Freedom*, 296; Jones, "Freedom and the Redistribution of Resources," 222; Carter, *A Measure of Freedom*, 71.

13. See, for example, Ronald Dworkin, "Do Liberty and Equality Conflict?" in *Living as Equals*, edited by P. Barker (Oxford: Oxford University Press, 1996), 39–57, *Sovereign Virtue: The Theory and Practice of Equality* (Cambridge, MA: Harvard University Press, 2000), and "Do Liberal Values Conflict?," in *The Legacy of Isaiah Berlin*, edited by M. Lilla, R. Dworkin, and R. B. Silvers (New York: New York Review of Books, 2001), 73–90, at 84–85, 88–89.

14. I use the term "normatively loaded," rather than the more common term "moralized," so as to allow that the norms in question may be legal (in line with the second interpretation of formal freedom) rather than moral.

15. The notion of interpersonal or social freedom is discussed in detail by, among others, Felix E. Oppenheim, *Political Concepts: A Reconstruction* (Oxford: Blackwell, 1981); and Kristján Kristjánsson, *Social Freedom: The Responsibility View* (Cambridge: Cambridge University Press, 1996). The term "negative" is sometimes used in lieu of "social" or "interpersonal," but "negative freedom" is an ambiguous and contested term, and its use in this context misleadingly suggests that freedom-as-ability amounts to positive freedom in Isaiah Berlin's sense of the term.

16. Steiner, *An Essay on Rights*, chap. 2.

Discussion Questions: Liberty

1. Is someone who wishes to stay in a locked room acting freely?
2. What does Pettit mean by his claim that freedom consists in the absence of domination?
3. Is freedom ever increased by forcing people to do what they do not want to do?

Part IV

DEMOCRACY

Like equality, justice, and liberty, democracy is widely regarded as a fundamental political value. Indeed, the claim is often made that in the absence of a democratic political framework, none of the other values can be realized. One may wonder, though, what precisely democracy is and in what the goodness of democracy consists.

Richard Arneson argues that the value of democracy lies solely in its ability to produce reliable results that accord with what justice demands. Democracy, he says, is not intrinsically good, but only instrumentally so. Thomas Christiano disagrees and argues that democracy is intrinsically valuable in that it is a constitutive element in the kind of equality that legitimate government should recognize and protect. Joshua Cohen is concerned mainly with the question of the nature of democracy. As one of the most prominent defenders of the conception of democracy known as "deliberative democracy," Cohen contrasts it with competing conceptions of democracy, then argues in favor of the deliberative model.

READING

10

Democracy Is Not Intrinsically Just

RICHARD ARNESON

In Bertolt Brecht's glorious Communist propaganda play *The Caucasian Chalk Circle*, a character who is a mouthpiece for the author declares that "things belong to people who are good for them."[1] In other words, you are entitled to ownership of some item only if your exercise of ownership promotes the common good. This should be understood to be a maximizing doctrine. If one person's ownership of land prevents another person from using the land more productively, the first is wasting resources.[2] At this point in the play what is at issue is rights to use land, but later the same point is applied to politics. The wily judge Azdak displays Solomonic wisdom and demonstrates that it is a grave misfortune for the country that his political rule is coming to an end. Political power rightfully belongs to those people who are good for it.

I am an egalitarian liberal and a democrat, not a communist, but I accept the principle of political legitimacy that Brecht espouses. Systems of governance should be assessed by their consequences; any individual has a moral right to exercise political power just to the extent that the granting of this right is productive of best consequences overall. No one has an ascriptive right to a share of political power. Assigning political power to a hereditary aristocracy on the ground that the nobles deserve power by birth is wrong, but so too it is wrong to hold that each member of a modern society just by being born has a right to an equal say in political power and influence, to equal rights of political citizenship and democratic political institutions. The choice between autocracy and democracy should be decided according to the standard of best results.[3] Which political system best promotes the common good over the long run? Many types of evidence support the conclusion that constitutional democracies produce morally best results on the whole and over the long run, but this judgement is contingent, is somewhat uncertain, and should be held tentatively rather than dogmatically. In some possible worlds, probably some past states of the actual world, and possibly in some future actual scenarios, autocracy wins by the best results test and should be installed. Democracy is extrinsically not intrinsically just.[4]

Many contemporary political philosophers addressing the issue of the justification of democracy reject the purely instrumental approach this essay defends.[5] The alternative view is that democracy is a uniquely fair process for reaching political decisions. Democratic political procedures may be valued for their tendency to produce morally superior laws and policies than would tend to emerge from other procedures, and democracy may also be valued for other good effects that it generates. But even if the results overall of having a nondemocratic political regime would be better than the results of having democracy, given that democracy itself qua fair procedure is a substantial intrinsic component of justice, it might well be that opting for democracy would still be morally preferred all things considered.

Formulating the issue as a dispute between those who assert and those who deny that democracy is intrinsically just can be misleading. The former do not hold that a democratic system of government is unconditionally morally valuable in virtue of its nonrelational properties. Most would say democracy is conditionally valuable. It is valuable only given mass literacy and the presence of other cultural background conditions, according to its advocates. The idea rather is that democracy is not merely instrumentally valuable but also qualifies as a worthwhile moral goal and also that democracy is one of the requirements of justice so that, other things being equal, the more democratic the society, the more just it is.

Some philosophical accounts of political democracy take a more radical position. They hold that what constitutes justice for a given society is in principle indeterminable apart from consulting the outcome of proper democratic procedures.[6]

A related view holds that although we cannot ever know what is just, we can reliably distinguish fair from unfair procedures for determining how to cope with persistent disagreement about what we owe to each other. Democracy is a fair political procedure, and moral knowledge extends only to judgements about fair procedures.[7] From this standpoint the idea that we should judge democracy—the intrinsically fair procedure—to be morally required, optional, or prohibited depending entirely on the degree to which it contributes to some supposed substantive standard of "justice" is a nonstarter.

Refuting the radical positions just described is not the aim of this essay. My position is that democracy, when it is just, is so entirely in virtue of the tendency of democratic institutions and practices to produce outcomes that are just according to standards that are conceptually independent of the standards that define the democratic ideal. Democracy, in other words, should be regarded as a tool or instrument that is to be valued not for its own sake but entirely for what results from having it. I take it to be obvious that we have a lot of knowledge about the substance of justice—that slavery is unjust, for example, or that it is unjust if some people avoidably face horrible life prospects through no fault or choice of their own. Moreover, our grounds for holding these beliefs are independent of any convoluted account one might give to the effect that these positions would win a majority rule vote under procedurally ideal conditions.

My focus in this essay is on the moderate and seemingly reasonable position that political institutions and constitutions should be assessed both according to the extent to which they promote substantively just outcomes and according to the extent that they conform to standards of intrinsic fairness for political procedures. This essay argues against moderation.[8] I also target a view that lies between the moderate and radical positions as just described. This view holds that even if, as a matter of moral metaphysics, there are truths about substantive justice, they are epistemically unavailable when what is at issue is the justification of democracy, because the need for politics stems from the fact that deep and intractable disagreement about what justice requires persists in modern times even among reasonable people.[9]

The purely instrumental approach to democracy can sound more extreme than it needs to be. The instrumentalist holds that democracy is to be assessed by the consequences of its adoption and operation compared with alternatives. Some might hear this as implying that "we" now have infallible knowledge of the correct moral standards, the principles of justice. This is not so. The instrumentalist as I conceive her is a realist about morality but can and should be a fallibilist about our present moral knowledge. There is moral truth, but our current epistemic access to it is uncertain, shaky. Hence one crucial standard for judging a society's institutions and practices is the extent to which they are efficiently arranged to increase the likelihood that as time goes on our epistemic access to moral truth will improve. All of this is perfectly compatible with pure instrumentalism. Analogy: we are searching for genuine treasure, and our practices should be assessed instrumentally, by the degree to which they enable us to gain treasure. Our current maps guiding us to treasure are flawed, and our current ideas about what "treasure" is are somewhat crude, and we have reason to believe there are better maps to be located and better conceptions of "treasure" to be elaborated. So our practices should be judged by the degree to which they enable us to attain genuine treasure, and the extent to which our practices improve our understanding of the nature of treasure and help us locate better maps is an important aspect of their instrumental efficacy.

The Idea of Democracy

The question whether or not it is intrinsically just that society be governed democratically cannot be addressed without some specification of the idea of democracy. As is well known, the idea is complex. In a society governed democratically, elections determine what laws will be enforced and who will occupy posts that involve political rule. In these elections, all adult members of society have a vote, and all votes are weighed equally. All adult members are eligible to run for political office in these elections, or can become eligible by some nononerous process such as establishing residency in a particular state or federal division. Majority rule determines the outcome of elections. Political freedoms, including freedom of association and freedom of speech, are protected in the society, so the group or faction that currently holds power cannot rig election results by banning or restricting the expression of opposing views.

A democratic society may operate in indirect rather than direct fashion. That is, rather than its being the case that all citizens together vote on proposed laws, citizens might vote for the members of a representative assembly, whose members enact laws. But indirectness does lessen the degree to which a society qualifies as democratic. This becomes clear if one imagines indirectness iterated many times—voters vote for an assembly that votes for an assembly that votes for another assembly that votes for a political group that votes for laws and votes in officials to administer them. Indirectness diminishes the democratic character of a regime because it lessens the extent to which the present will of a majority of voters controls political outcomes. The contrast between direct and indirect democracy is connected to another, between immediate and mediate accountability of elected rulers to majority rule of citizen voters. In a political system that allows for immediate recall of officials by citizen initiative, the accountability is more immediate, other things being equal, than it would be if recall by this means were not permitted. If some part of the lawmaking power is exercised by a judicial branch of government, top members of which are appointed by some process that is more rather than less indirect, the political process is to that extent less democratic. If political officials in any branch of government, legislative, executive, or judicial, may not be removed from office once they are validly appointed, this factor also lessens the extent to which the society qualifies as democratic.

Another dimension on which a political system can register as more or less democratic concerns the scope of the authority of the majority will of the citizen voters. If there is a substantial set of restrictions, for example, a list of individual or group rights, that are constitutionally specified as the supreme law of the land, and that may not validly be altered or extinguished by majority will vote, the greater the extent of these limits on majority rule, the lesser the extent to which the political system qualifies as democratic. A provision here is that there are some individual rights that are themselves conceptually required by democracy itself, and the insulation of these rights from majority will does not render a society less democratic.

Finally, a political system qualifies as more democratic insofar as all citizens have equal opportunity for political influence. This norm admits of various construals. Let us say that citizens have equal opportunity for political influence when all citizens with the same ambition to influence politics and the same political talents will have equal prospects of influencing political outcomes. The idea is roughly that if such factors as one's wealth or family connections affect the impact one could have on the political process if one worked to achieve an impact, then opportunities are unequal and the society to that extent is less democratic. If only ambition and political talent, which includes administrative and entrepreneurial skill and the ability to persuade others and build coalitions, affect the chances that one could influence the outcomes of the political process if one tried, then opportunities in the relevant sense are equal and the society to that extent is more democratic.

The statement of equal opportunity given above takes individuals as they are, with the political talents they happen to possess at a particular time, as setting the standard of equal opportunity. One might view this statement as inadequate in view of the following sort of example. Society might give access to the opportunities for training and developing political talent only to a restricted social group. If some individuals lack the opportunity to become politically talented, then one might hold equal opportunity does not prevail even though the equally ambitious and talented enjoy equal opportunities. One might then, in a Rawlsian spirit, hold that citizens have equal opportunity for political influence only when all citizens with the same native potential for political talent and the same ambition to develop and exercise it have equal prospects for affecting the outcomes of the political process. This version of equal opportunity for political influence might seem better as a theoretical formulation than the one stated in the previous paragraph, but in practical terms it has the defect that it may be hard in many situations to tell whether it is being fulfilled, given that the idea of potential for political talent is a vague notion.

Democracy is, then, a complex ideal. The judgement as to how democratic the political process of a given society is combines several dimensions of assessment, each of which varies by degree.

Against the Right to a Democratic Say

Consider the proposition that each member of society has a basic moral right to an equal say in the political process that determines the laws that the government enforces and also that people shall be political rulers or top public officials. One has an equal say when one could, if one chose, have the same chance of influencing the outcomes of the political process as any other member of society with equal political skills and equal willingness to devote one's resources to participation in politics. Saying the right to an equal say is a basic moral right includes denying that one has the right merely derivatively, on instrumental grounds. Call this right the "right to a democratic say."

The right to a democratic say so understood is a right to political power—a right to set coercive rules that significantly limit how other people will live their lives. With this right secured, one has power over the lives of other people—a small bit of power, to be sure, but power nonetheless. My position is that there is no such basic moral right, because one does not have a basic moral right to exercise significant power over the lives of other people, to direct how they shall live their lives. Rights to power over the lives of others always involve an element of stewardship. If one has such a moral right, this will be so only because one's having the right is more conducive to the flourishing of all affected parties than any feasible alternative.[10]

Parents standardly have extensive power to control the lives of their children who have not yet attained adult age. My position is that there is no basic moral right to have such power. The system of parental control is justified just in case it is maximally conducive to the flourishing of those affected. In just the same way, no one has a basic moral right to be the chief warden of a prison or the director of an insane asylum.

This position has attracted the objection that any substantive moral right involves power over the lives of other people. If you have full private property in some object, you have the right to determine what shall be done with it and to forbid other people from interacting with it. Since all rights involve power to direct the lives of others to some degree, nothing yet has been said to single out the right to a democratic say as specially problematic and not an appropriate candidate for inclusion in the class of basic moral rights.[11]

In response: everything is like everything else, I suppose, in some way or to some degree. Still, a rough line can be drawn between rights that confer on the right-holder the power to direct how another shall live and rights that do not confer such power. Consider the moral right not to be "bashed"—severely injured by unprovoked nonconsensual violent physical attack. If this right is enforced, the right-holder has power over the lives of others to an extent, since she can give or withhold consent to attack and thus determine by fiat whether any other person may attack. But a right that constrains other people from engaging in a certain type of conduct toward the right-holder differs from a right to set rules that might specify what others shall do across a broad range of important types of conduct. I concede this is a difference in degree, but when the difference in degree is large, the difference is large and in my view morally significant.[12]

A second response is that perhaps we should acknowledge that many ordinary rights, such as rights to private ownership, do often involve significant power over others. These rights, then, on my view are not appropriate candidates for the status of basic moral rights. Consider the owner of a factory, the sole employer in a region, who is also the owner of a company town. Here, private ownership definitely gives the right-holder significant power over others. Perhaps, strictly speaking, only rights to capabilities (real freedom to achieve important human functionings) or rights to opportunities to genuine well-being or the like should count as appropriate candidates for the status of basic moral rights. Even if, in particular circumstances, one's right to capability is secured by control over resources that give one power over others, what one is strictly morally entitled to on an approach that takes capabilities to be basic will never be the power over others but the freedom to achieve and enjoy in the ways central to human flourishing, where these core freedoms could always in principle be secured in some alternative way without the control and the power.

These two responses have some force, but to the advocate of the right to a democratic say they might seem close to question-begging. After all, what rules it out that the freedom to participate on equal terms with others in collective decision-making is a core human capability, on a par with the capabilities to attain knowledge, friendship and love, and achievement? Saying no one has a basic moral right to power over others invites the counterassertion that the examples of parental rights and democratic rights show that people do indeed have such moral rights. To make further progress, we need to investigate the positive arguments for the right to a democratic say. The case for instrumentalism would be strengthened if the search were to turn up empty pockets. The rest of this essay follows this roundabout strategy.

What Free and Equal Rational Persons Can Accept

We are looking for the strongest and most plausible arguments for the right to a democratic say, regarded as tantamount to the claim that democracy is an intrinsic component of justice. My search strategy is to elaborate simple considerations, raise objections, then attempt to refine the argument to see if it becomes more compelling.

Start with the idea that each person is owed equal concern and respect. Each person's interests should be given equal consideration in the design of political institutions. But any system that violates the right to a democratic say, assigning or allowing some people greater rights to participate than others, manifestly violates the basic right to equal concern and respect. This argument might be put in a contractualist formulation: free and equal rational persons would not agree to principles that give some greater basic political rights than others. Any such principle would be reasonably rejectable.

The instrumentalist will maintain that principles of equal concern and respect are best satisfied by choice of political arrangements that maximize the fulfilment of basic human rights (other than the disputed right to an equal democratic say). We show concern and respect for people by showing concern and respect for the fulfilment of their rights. It would be question-begging to say in reply that one can only show equal concern and respect by showing respect for all basic moral rights including the right to a democratic say. This argument is supposed to establish, not presuppose, the existence of such a right.

Much the same applies to the contractualist formulation. The instrumentalist need not reject the contractualist idea that what is morally required is what free and equal rational persons would agree to as morally required. But if the choices of ideal moral reasoners determine what is moral, it should be noted that these ideal reasoners are choosing principles for a world in which human agents are not perfectly rational. There is nothing prima facie puzzling in the thought of ideal reasoners choosing moral principles that require that some actual persons less than fully rational be denied equal rights to political power if that is necessary to produce morally best results.

Persons are not equally free and equal in ways that matter for the question, whether democracy or autocracy is morally superior as a form of governance for people under modern conditions. People vary significantly in the degree to which they are motivated to discover what is just and conform to its requirements. They vary significantly in their capacity to figure out what the requirements of justice are, either in general or in particular circumstances. They vary significantly in their capacity to figure out what ways of life and conceptions of the good are choiceworthy. They also differ significantly in the extent to which they are motivated to exercise whatever practical reasoning abilities they have in order to bring it about that they end up affirming more rather than less reasonable conceptions of what is valuable and worthy of human pursuit. Moreover, all of these significant inequalities bear directly on the issue of who should have political power. These differences in competence render it the case that it could be that under some types of circumstances some autocratic constitution of society would predictably and reliably bring about morally superior outcomes to the outcomes that any feasible form of democracy would reach. In such circumstances (which may not be the actual circumstances of our world), autocracy would be the morally superior form of governance. Given all of this, persons who are free and equal in the threshold sense specified above may reasonably accept an undemocratic political constitution for their governance.

Recall that the question at issue is not whether autocracy is morally required all things considered, but rather whether autocracies (nondemocratic political arrangements) are intrinsically unjust, other things being equal.[13]

Must Competence Tests Be Objectionably Controversial?

Perhaps we can make headway toward understanding the claimed intrinsic justice of democracy by noting that substantive claims regarding the shape and content of people's basic moral rights are controversial in modern diverse democracies. Reasonable members of society do not converge to agreement. Nor is there a long-term tendency toward agreement.

In the face of such disagreement, any assertion that this particular group of persons is more competent than others at determining what rights people have and designing laws and policies to implement rights is bound to be intractably controversial. Why this particular group and not some other? Any proposal of a set of qualifications that determines who is more competent and should rule will run up against the objection that it is morally arbitrary to favour this particular proposal over many alternatives that might have been advanced. The claim that the specially competent should rule thus conceals a naked preference for some conceptions of justice and against others with just as much rational backing.

David Estlund urges a similar argument against what he calls the doctrine of Epistocracy—rule by competent knowers. Estlund asserts that "no knower will be so knowable as to be known by all reasonable persons."[14] Disagreeing about justice, reasonable people will also disagree about proposed criteria of competence and about who is more qualified than others to rule. He combines this assertion with a contractualist premise and concludes that political rule by a knowledgeable elite could never be morally legitimate. The contractualist premise is that it is wrong to act in ways that affect people except on the basis of principles they could not reasonably reject. The conclusion is that any version of Epistocracy is reasonably rejectable, hence morally illegitimate.

This line of thought collapses when one asks what counts as a "reasonable" person. If a reasonable person makes no cognitive errors and deliberates with perfect rationality, then reasonable people will agree in selecting the conceptions of justice and rights that are best or tied for best. There are other conceptions of justice that attract the allegiance of less than fully reasonable persons, but these can be set aside. The notion of competence that figures in the idea of a competent political agent can then be calibrated in terms of the best conceptions of justice. This notion of competence will not be controversial among reasonable people. So if a "reasonable person" is identified with the idea of a maximally reasonable person, a notion of competence can be nonarbitrarily selected.

Suppose instead that we use the idea of a satisficing threshold to identify the reasonable person. A reasonable person is reasonable enough. The lower the satisficing threshold level is set, the more plausible becomes Estlund's conjecture that "no knower [or knowledge standard] will be so knowable as to be known by all reasonable persons." The question then arises, Why set the threshold at any particular less than maximal point? Estlund's set of reasonable persons might be unable to agree on a competence standard for political rule because some of them are adding two plus two and getting five or making some comparable subtler mistake of reasoning. Given that the political rulers will be charged with the task of designing and administering laws and policies that will maximize fulfilment of human rights, it is incorrect to accept any satisficing standard (unless in context the maximizing strategy calls for satisficing). Only the best is good enough.

One might attempt to defend a satisficing standard for identifying the reasonable person by appeal to a requirement of respect. If a person has sufficient rational agency capacity to be able to recognize and formulate reasons and debate about principles, then it is wrongfully disrespectful to act toward him in ways that dismiss or slight this rational agency capacity, as though he were a mere tool to be manipulated for the common good. The requirement that the principles on the basis of which we interact with people, including the principles that determine the proper mode of political governance for our society, should be able to elicit their assent at least if they qualify as reasonable expresses a fundamental norm of respect for persons.

The reply is that appropriate respect for an agent's rational agency capacity is shown by recognizing it for what it is. It shows no wrongful disrespect to me to notice that I am imperfectly rational and to take efficient steps to prevent my proclivity to mistakes from wrongfully harming others or for that matter myself. This is true in face-to-face personal interaction, and it is just as true in a context where what is at issue is identifying institutional procedures and norms for collective decision-making. Respect for rational agency should not be interpreted as requiring us to pretend that anyone has more capacity than she has or to pretend that variation in capacity does not matter when it does. Respect for rational agency in persons requires treating them according to the moral principles that fully rational persons would choose, the principles best supported by moral reasons. Supposing there is a divergence between the principles that threshold reasonable people would unanimously accept and the principles that ideally reasonable people would accept, I submit that the latter not the former are the norms, acting on which manifests respect for persons (beings with rational agency capacity). The point I am trying to make in this paragraph was stated clearly by John Stuart Mill long ago: "Every one has a right to feel insulted by being made a nobody, and stamped as of no account at all. No one but a fool, and only a fool of a peculiar description, feels offended by the acknowledgement that there are others whose opinion, and even whose wish, is entitled to a greater amount of consideration than his."[15]

In passing I observe that those who deny that standards of political competence that in some circumstances might justify nondemocratic forms of governance can be nonarbitrarily and rationally identified seem to have no trouble with the idea that minimal competence standards can be nonarbitrarily formulated.[16] But if we say correctly that insane and feebleminded persons lack rational agency capacity and are in virtue of these facts rightly deemed incompetent in certain contexts for certain purposes, we are pointing to traits that vary by degree above whatever threshold level is singled out as "good enough."

Of course, nothing guarantees that fully reasonable persons will be able to select a single uniquely best conception of justice, which can serve as the reference point for defining a nonarbitrary standard of political competence. Suppose ten conceptions are tied for best, given the best moral theorizing and reasons assessment that are presently ideally available. In that case, it would not be unreasonable to implement a political system geared to achieving any of the ten. From the possibility of reasonable disagreement one gets a loose disjunctive standard of moral acceptability, not an argument for the unique fairness of democracy. Note that the fact that several conceptions of justice are equally acceptable for all we can know is fully compatible with there being a plethora of popular and decisively unreasonable views concerning the requirements of justice, any of which might command a majority vote in a democracy.

In the face of disagreement about what justice requires, one might flatly deny that the opinion of any member of society can be dismissed as unreasonable. In that case one is abandoning the moderate position about justice and democracy that is my main target in this essay and is instead dismissing the possibility that a standard of justice can be available to provide an independent standard for assessing the political outcomes produced by the democratic process. The moderate, as I imagine her, agrees that we can have knowledge about justice but insists that democracy is an intrinsically just and fair procedure independently of its tendency to produce good results. Perhaps moderation, when pressed, slides toward radicalism.

Some readers will suspect that my position involves an illicit sleight of hand. What we observe is the members of society disagreeing about justice. From their different standpoints they will affirm opposed standards of political competence. Even if one grants that metaphysically there are right answers to questions about the substance of justice, one cannot in this context invoke these right answers to justify some elite form of political rule, because our agreed circumstances preclude any claim that any of us has epistemic access to the truth about justice. If we disagree, then we disagree. Jeremy Waldron expresses the sense that the instrumentalist is playing an illogical trick when he writes that "any theory that makes authority depend on the goodness of political outcomes is self-defeating, for it is precisely because people *disagree* about the goodness of outcomes that they need to set up and recognize an authority." Or again: "Rights-instrumentalism seems to face the difficulty that it presupposes our possession of the truth about rights in designing an authoritative procedure whose point is to settle that very issue."[17]

These are sensible concerns.[18] There are sensible ways to address them. Consider a simple example with epistemic uncertainty. A violent altercation is under way in the street. Many people observe some of it. It is not certain who has done what to whom, with what justification or lack of justification. Among onlookers, some have a better vantage point to see what is happening, some make better use of the observational data they get, and some have a better, some a worse grip on the moral principles of self-defence, provocation, and proportionality that determine who of those involved in the altercation have right on their side. There is no consensus among reasonable spectators as to what is taking place or what should be done. Any proposal as to what intervention is justified meets with reasonable suspicion from some person's standpoint. Still, none of this excludes the possibility that you in fact perceive correctly what has happened and judge correctly what ought to be done and are rationally confident that your opinions on these matters are correct. If you happen to have the power to implement this correct assessment, you should do so, despite the fact that your assessment will not attract the unanimous assent of those affected. As Elizabeth Anscombe observes, "Just as an individual will constantly think himself in the right, whatever he does, and yet there is still such a thing as being in the right, so nations will constantly think themselves to be in the right—and yet there is still such a thing as their being in the right."[19] Paraphrasing this to highlight its relevance to our topic, we should say that just as people think they are acting justly, whether they are or not, yet there is such a thing as acting justly, so also people will think their preferred standards of competence and criteria for eligibility for political office are correct, yet there is such a thing as there being correct standards of political competence and correct inferences from these standards to judgements as to what form of political governance in given actual circumstances is just.

The resourceful Waldron has another arrow in his quiver.[20] He argues that to suppose that an individual possesses moral rights is already to suppose that the individual has the competence to exercise them. A being who lacks rational agency capacity is not the sort of being who can be regarded as a right-bearer. Hence, there is tension and perhaps incoherence in arguing that to achieve the overall fulfilment of the rights of all members of society, we must deny some the right to participate as equals in the political governance process on grounds that they are incompetent. If they are incompetent, how can they be right-bearers at all?

The tension Waldron sees eases when we look more closely. Competence is not all-or-nothing. An individual might be fully competent for many tasks but less competent at some. I may have rational agency capacity that a snake or even a gorilla lacks, and so I may be a candidate for ascription of moral rights that they could not sensibly be thought to possess, yet lack political competence at the level needed to contribute in a positive way to the determination of what laws and policies should be passed in order best to protect human rights. Also, the ground for ascribing some rights to people need not include strong claims about their competence to exercise the rights. I may believe that each individual has the right to live her own life as she chooses within wide moral limits. I may believe that each person has this right of autonomy without for a moment doubting that some persons have marginal or problematic competence to make good life plans and execute them. (Notice that one might believe there is a presumption in favour of each person being free to live her own life without believing that there is any presumption that everybody has an equal right to participate on equal terms in the governance of everybody's life.) The particular nature of the putative right to a democratic say is such that competence requirements apply with special force to it.

Publicity

Some theorists who claim that democratic governance is intrinsically just point to the requirement of publicity. It is not enough that justice is done; it should be manifest that justice is done. Moreover, this requirement that justice be visible at least to a reasonable and careful observer is itself a further requirement of justice.

In a narrow sense, a society satisfies publicity when all members of society can check for themselves that the practices and institutions of the society as they actually function fully satisfy the norms and rules to which it is committed.[21] In a broader sense, publicity requires in addition that all members of society if they engage in reflective deliberation can see that the rules and norms to which the society is committed are themselves morally justifiable.[22]

This asserted requirement of publicity is parlayed into an argument for the intrinsic justice of democracy. The idea is that in a world rife with reasonable disagreement about morality and the good, it can be difficult to discern whether or not a government's policies conform closely to elementary requirements of justice. Consider the fundamental norm that each person should be treated with equal consideration and respect. All persons are of fundamentally equal worth; no one's life is inherently worth more than anyone else's.

The fact that a society is autocratic thereby fuels a suspicion that some people's lives are being counted as more valuable than other people's. A society that is substantively democratic, that brings it about that all its citizens enjoy equal opportunity to influence political outcomes, goes further toward manifesting a commitment to the principle of equal consideration. The society with democratic governance, other things being equal, satisfies publicity to a greater degree than it would if it were undemocratic, and since publicity is a component of justice, this democratic society simply in virtue of being democratic is more just.

In reply: neither the wide nor the narrow ideal of publicity qualifies as an element in the set of basic moral rights definitive of justice. That it is manifest that the rules a society claims to enforce are actually fully implemented likely tends to elicit people's allegiance and in this way contribute to the long-run stability of the system. If the rules manifestly conform to principles that almost all citizens accept, this tendency is likely reinforced. If these speculative hunches are empirically corroborated, publicity promotes justice and should be valued in this purely instrumental way.

None of this provides any support at all for the quite different claim that there is a basic moral right to publicity, that publicity is intrinsically just. Consider cases in which the aim of achieving publicity and the aim of achieving justice (aside from publicity) conflict. Let us say we must choose between a policy that over the long run secretly prevents more murders or an alternative policy that prevents fewer murders but does so in a way that satisfies publicity. Once we get the issue clearly in focus, and set aside the here irrelevant likely instrumental benefits of publicity (that it possibly might prevent more murders overall in the long run), I submit that publicity should have no weight at all in conflict with other justice values.

I deny that publicity is an intrinsic component of justice. But I also deny that autocracy inherently is incompatible with publicity. If instrumental or best-results justifications of democracy in a particular setting do not succeed, and autocracy would in that setting produce morally superior results—let's say, more just results—then autocracy can satisfy publicity.

In the argument from publicity to the claim that democracy is intrinsically just, the fact that society is democratic evidently conveys a message to members of society. Democratic governance procedures are used to signal the commitment of society to the principle of equal consideration. But messages can be communicated in various ways. Why suppose that the only effective way to convey a commitment to justice is through instituting and maintaining democracy?

If autocracy is chosen on the ground that it leads to morally superior results, and this surmise is correct, then over time autocracy will produce justice, or at least more justice than would be obtainable under any other type of political regime. What could manifest a commitment to doing justice more obviously and credibly than actually doing justice over time? We are not talking here about private acts performed in people's bedrooms; we are talking about the public policies pursued by a government and the changes over time in its institutions, social norms, and practices.

The claim is made that in a diverse society whose members fan out to embrace a wide array of conflicting views of morality and value, there will inevitably be a degree of uncertainty and a lack of precision in people's estimation about the extent to which their government over time brings about basic social justice. So publicity cannot be satisfied merely by aiming at morally better policies. More is needed. The symbolism of democracy—everyone counts for one, nobody for more than one—has an important role to play in securing that it is manifest that justice is done, or approximated to a good enough degree.

If the fact that the government over the long haul enacts policies that bring it about that social justice requirements are fulfilled across the society does not suffice to satisfy publicity, because people of diverse standpoints disagree about justice, I do not see why the fact that the society is democratically run must succeed in conveying the message to all that the society is committed to justice. Some may see democracy as catering to the lowest common denominator of public opinion.

The thought might be that the very existence of an autocratic system, a clique of persons who wield power and are not accountable to those over whom power is wielded, must fuel suspicion. But an autocracy need not select the members of the ruling group by a hidden process. The process by which membership in the ruling group is set may be open for public inspection, and conform to the norm of careers open to talents or a stronger meritocratic principle such as the Rawlsian norm of equality of fair opportunity.

For concreteness, imagine an egalitarian social justice party that overthrows a clearly unjust regime and institutes autocratic rule. Any adult member of society is eligible to apply for party membership, and the criteria for membership are a matter of public record. Applications are assessed on their merits, and those deemed most qualified are admitted to the ruling group. Moreover, education and other forms of societal assistance to child-rearing practices are set so that any individuals with the same ambition to participate in political rule by joining the ruling party and the same native (potential for) political talent have identical prospects of success in gaining party admission. In other words, the political process satisfies norms of formal equality of opportunity and also substantive equality of opportunity (Rawlsian equality of fair opportunity). Here, then, is a further response to the demand for publicity. The imagined autocratic society makes manifest its commitment to social justice, especially to the fundamental norm that all are entitled to equal consideration and respect, by bringing it about that its policies and practices achieve justice and also by regulating access to membership in the group that exercises political power according to meritocratic norms. So if publicity were itself an intrinsic component of justice, this would not tend to show that democracy is intrinsically just, because some versions of autocracy can satisfy publicity.

Fans of publicity and democracy have a riposte to the argument made to this point. The idea is that the meritocratic ideal that political rule should be exercised by the competent, not by all citizens, unravels and reveals itself as inherently unfair as we try to specify it. There are no neutral criteria of competence. The criteria of political competence will inevitably be calibrated in terms of some controversial moral ideal, which the ruling autocrats label "justice." But this gambit takes us back to the claim—already discussed and rejected in this essay—that standards of political competence invoked to support some type of nondemocratic regime must be morally arbitrary and capricious.

Conclusion

This essay has searched without any success for sound arguments for the claim that there is a noninstrumental moral right to a democratic say. This is good news for the purely instrumental approach that I favour. The victory for instrumentalism is nonetheless incomplete pending a full account of human rights that enables us to see why the justifications for the fundamental human rights do not include a justification of a fundamental intrinsic right to a democratic say. This is a story for another day.

Notes

1. Bertolt Brecht, *The Caucasian Chalk Circle*, translated by Eric Bentley (New York: Grove Press, 1947). Why call this a "propaganda" play? At the time of its writing, Brecht aims to cast in a favourable light Stalinist political regimes, the horrific nature of which is reasonably described in Jonathan Glover, *Humanity: A Moral History of the Twentieth Century* (New Haven, CT: Yale University Press, 1999), chap. 5. Why then call the play

"glorious"? In my judgement, it has considerable aesthetic merit and addresses significant issues in intellectually interesting ways.

2. Locke asserts a version of this idea in the form of a "no waste" condition on justified appropriation of land. He writes, "Nothing was made by God for man to spoil or destroy." He does not interpret the no waste condition as requiring maximally productive use, however. See John Locke, *Second Treatise of Government*, edited by C. B. Macpherson (Indianapolis: Hackett, 1980), chap. 5.

3. In this essay I leave it an open question of what the moral standard is for assessing results that determines which ones are best. Some of my formulations suggest that the best results standard is consequentialist, or more specifically a consequentialism of rights. But nonconsequentialist moral views could embrace a best-results standard for assessing forms of governance. For example, a version of a Lockean natural rights view might hold that a state is morally more acceptable the more it promotes the fulfilment of natural rights (without itself violating any). Locke, *Second Treatise on Government*, suggests such a view, though he does not fully commit to it.

4. John Stuart Mill, "Considerations on Representative Government in John Stuart Mill," in *Collected Works*, edited by J. M. Robson, vol. 19 (Toronto: University of Toronto Press, 1977), chap. 8, defends this position. See also Ronald Dworkin, *Taking Rights Seriously* (Cambridge, MA: Harvard University Press, 1977), chap. 5; and Richard J. Arneson, "Democratic Rights at National and Workplace Levels," in *The Idea of Democracy*, edited by David Copp, Jean Hampton, and John E. Roemer (Cambridge: Cambridge University Press, 1993), 118–148.

5. Theorists who hold that democracy is intrinsically just include Charles Beitz, *Political Equality: An Essay in Democratic Theory* (Princeton, NJ: Princeton University Press, 1989); Thomas Christiano, *The Rule of the Many* (Boulder, CO: Westview Press, 1996), and "Knowledge and Power in the Justification of Democracy," *Australasian Journal of Philosophy* 79 (2001): 197–215; David Estlund, "Making Truth Safe for Democracy," in *The Idea of Democracy*, 71–100, and "Beyond Fairness and Deliberation: The Epistemic Dimension of Democratic Authority," in *Deliberative Democracy: Essays in Reason and Politics*, edited by James Bohman and William Rehg (Cambridge, MA: MIT Press, 1997), 173–204; Harry Brighouse, "Egalitarianism and Equal Availability of Political Influence," *Journal of Political Philosophy* 4 (1996): 118–141; Joshua Cohen, "Procedure and Substance in Deliberative Democracy," in *Deliberative Democracy*, 407–438, and "For a Democratic Society," in *The Cambridge Companion to Rawls*, edited by Samuel Freeman (Cambridge: Cambridge University Press, 2003), 86–138; Jeremy Waldron, *Law and Disagreement* (Oxford: Oxford University Press, 1999); John Rawls, *Political Liberalism* (New York: Columbia University Press, 1993), and *Political Liberalism: With a New Introduction and "Reply to Habermas"* (New York: Columbia University Press, 1999); William Nelson, *On Justifying Democracy* (London: Routledge and Kegan Paul, 1980); Robert Dahl, *Democracy and Its Critics* (New Haven, CT: Yale University Press, 1989); and Allen Buchanan, "Political Legitimacy and Democracy," *Ethics* 112, 4 (2002): 689–719, who asserts that "where democratic authorization of the exercise of political power is possible, only a democratic government can be legitimate" (689). But as he develops this claim, he leaves it open that the choice of democratic governance is only morally required when democracy "can produce laws that satisfy the requirement of equal regard for all persons' basic interests" (712). If "can produce laws" means "actually produces laws," then Buchanan is only committed to the claim that a moral preference for democracy is a tiebreaker to be employed when democratic and nondemocratic governance procedures would equally satisfy the relevant best-results standard.

6. Dahl, *Democracy and Its Critics*, endorses something in the neighbourhood of this position.

7. See Stuart Hampshire, *Justice Is Conflict* (Princeton, NJ: Princeton University Press, 2000), for a subtle discussion that finds insistence on fair procedures more sensible than insistence on any conception of substantive fairness of outcomes. Hampshire does not endorse the radical affirmation of the intrinsic fairness of democratic procedures as I characterize it in the text of this paragraph.

8. "Moderation" as conceived here includes a wide array of possible views. At one extreme, the moderate might hold that the right to a democratic say is just a tie-breaker that favours a democratic over a nondemocratic regime if the results of each would be equally good. At the other extreme, one might hold that the right to a democratic say is the right of rights in the sense that it trumps all others combined, and one should always prefer the more democratic over the less democratic regime, allowing the justice of the results of the operation of the system only to act as a tie-breaker among equally democratic regimes. Of course, there are indefinitely many intermediate views.

9. Christiano, *The Rule of the Many*, and "Knowledge and Power"; and Waldron, *Law and Disagreement*, develop versions of this position. For Christiano, the intrinsic fairness of democratic procedures follows as a uniquely uncontroversial inference from a conception of substantive justice whose other significant implications are controversial.

10. "Flourishing" here is just a placeholder referring to whatever the correct best-results standard turns out to be. That standard might be a consequentialism of rights position along the lines developed by Amartya Sen, "Rights and Agency," *Philosophy and Public Affairs* 11 (1982): 3–39. For some doubts about Sen's position, see Richard J. Arneson, "Against Rights," *Philosophical Issues* 11, *Social, Political, and Legal Philosophy,* supp. to *Nous* (2001): 172–201.

11. Christiano, "Knowledge and Power," makes a criticism close to this one. Griffin (2003) develops this and other criticisms of the purely instrumental view of democracy. See Richard J. Arneson, "Defending the Purely Instrumental Account of Democracy," *Journal of Political Philosophy* 11 (2003): 122–132, for a reply. Robert Sugden, "Justified to Whom?," in *The Idea of Democracy*, 149–154, first developed the criticism.

12. The claim in the text that rights vary in the extent to which they confer power over the lives of other people and that rights that involve significant power over the lives of others require a best-results justification might be challenged. The challenge repeats the point that any moral right involves power over others. Consider many people's exercise of their private ownership rights over small resource holdings. In the aggregate, these exercises of a very small degree of power might very significantly restrict other people's life options. Millions of people might exercise their rights in ways that leave some individuals with just a single employment option or access to just one person who is willing to sell them food needed to live. How does this differ from the way that many people's exercises of the franchise might aggregate to issue in coercive rules that specify how others shall live their lives?

In reply: I don't deny that any moral right you might care to name might in some circumstances confer power over the lives of others. I deny this must be so. Consider a world in which small groups of voluntarily associating adults live at great distance from each other. The members of each group may have many moral rights that do not, in isolation or in the aggregate, involve significant power over the lives of others. Moreover, in the case just imagined, where many people exercise rights over small bits of property that in the aggregate significantly begin to restrict the lives of others, I would say the "intrinsic moral right" gives way and a best-results standard becomes operative.

Here I intend to contrast moral rights that confer lots of power over the individual's own life and moral rights that involve significant power to direct the lives of others. One might hold that moral rights that confer significant control over the direction of one's own life are justified by a principle of autonomy or personal sovereignty. Hence your right to act as you choose so long as you do not harm others in certain specified ways might be thought not to require a best-results justification. Your right stems from a right of personal sovereignty, not from the fact that you are more competent to run your own life than others are to run it for you.

13. Why do the proautocracy considerations adduced here not suffice to establish at least a strong presumption in favour of the claim that autocracy is morally superior to democracy all things considered? Four countervailing concerns are pertinent. One is "*Quis custodiet custodes*?" Concentrating political power in the hands of an elite can produce horrible consequences if the elite becomes corrupt or incompetent. In choosing forms of governance, we should give special weight to preventing moral catastrophes. (A system of Madisonian checks and balances might mitigate this problem.) A second consideration is that political science has not devised a feasible reliable procedure for distinguishing competent from less competent agents and installing only the former as rulers. A third consideration, prominent in democratic theorists such as Mill, is that aside from a possible tendency to produce better legislation and policies and better implementation of these laws and policies, democracy tends to produce other indirect morally valuable results, such as social solidarity and the moral and intellectual development of the democratic citizens. A fourth consideration is that if people are somewhat disposed to use whatever power they have to advance their interests, it is better (though not good), other things being equal, that laws and policies cater to the interests of majorities than to the interests of smaller groups.

14. Estlund, "Making Truth Safe for Democracy," 88. It should be noted that Estlund himself is trying to defeat the claim that authoritarianism in the form of rule by moral experts is morally required. I am treating his argument as though he were making a positive argument for the right to a democratic say. For commentary on Estlund, see David Copp, "Could Truth Be a Hazard for Democracy?," in *The Idea of Democracy*, 101–117.

15. Mill, "Considerations on Representative Government," 474. Mill's statement occurs in the course of an argument for a plural votes scheme, in which more-educated citizens, and those who pass a political competence examination, are allotted extra votes beyond the single vote that every adult citizen gets.

16. Christiano, "Knowledge and Power," 207–208, accepts a minimal competence qualification for the right to a democratic say.

17. Waldron, *Law and Disagreement*, 253. For criticism of Waldron, see David Estlund, "Waldron on Law and Disagreement," *Philosophical Studies* 99 (2000): 111–128.

18. However, Waldron overreaches in stating that the point of political procedures is to settle the truth about what rights we have. A vote can fix the content of legal rights in some political jurisdiction, but this does not settle the issues (1) whether it is morally right that these legal rights are instituted and enforced and (2) whether these legal rights coincide with the moral rights that people have in this setting.

19. G. E. M. Anscombe, "War and Murder," in her *Ethics, Religion, and Politics: Collected Papers*, vol. 3 (Minneapolis: University of Minnesota Press, 1981), 52.

20. Waldron, *Law and Disagreement*, 250–251.

21. Christiano, "Knowledge and Power," deploys a narrow publicity requirement in his argument.

22. On wide publicity, see Rawls, *Political Liberalism: With a New Introduction*, chap. 3. For an interesting deployment of this publicity requirement in a controversy concerning what distributive justice requires, see Melissa Williams, *Voice, Trust, and Memory* (Princeton, NJ: Princeton University Press, 1998).

READING

11

The Authority of Democracy

THOMAS CHRISTIANO

Democratic decision-making has two very different evaluative aspects that sometimes collide and usually complement each other to some degree. On the one hand, we judge democratic decisions from the point of view of the quality of the outcomes. We concern ourselves with whether the outcomes are just or whether they are efficient or whether they protect liberty and promote the common good. This is sometimes called the substantive or outcome dimension of assessment of democratic procedures. On the other hand, we evaluate the decisions from the point of view of how they are made or the quality of the procedure. We are concerned to make the decision in a way that includes everyone who by right ought to be included and that is fair to all the participants. Here we may think that the method by which the decisions are made should be intrinsically fair.

In my view these two dimensions of assessment are irreducible. But this is not the way everyone sees it. Some, whom I shall call monists, think that there is only one form of assessment and that other assessments are reducible to it. For example, instrumentalists or best-results theorists like Philippe Van Parijs think that the way in which democratic decisions ought to be made is entirely a matter of what will produce the best outcomes.[1] On their view, the only question to be asked in evaluating democratic procedures regards the quality of the outcomes of these procedures. Pure proceduralists, on the other hand, see outcomes as essentially evaluable solely in terms of the procedure that brought them about.

There are two versions of this kind of view. One version of the view is attributed to some American legal theorists who wish to justify a rather strong form of judicial restraint with regard to the decisions of the American Congress. They argue that the Supreme Court of the United States ought to defer to virtually all the decisions that Congress makes except in the most obvious cases of violation of the literal words or specific intentions of the framers of the

Constitution.[2] Some theorists of deliberative democracy, for quite different reasons, appear to hold to a kind of pure procedural view as well. They think that if a process is one that is genuinely deliberative and democratic, then it justifies the outcome, or the fact that the outcome results from the procedure constitutes its justice.[3]

I wish to defend a form of evaluative dualism with regard to the assessment of democratic institutions. It is dualistic because it regards democratic institutions as evaluable from two distinct and irreducible points of view that may sometimes conflict. Evaluative dualism raises the question of whether and when democratic decisions have authority. If the results of democratic decision-making are unjust, we might ask, what reason do we have for going along with the decision? And if there is a reason to go along with democratic decisions, how are we to balance that reason with the reason associated with the injustice of actions required by the democratic assembly? A conception of democratic authority must show that while decisions can be evaluated from an independent standpoint, the fact that the democratic assembly has made the decision gives each person a preemptive and content-independent reason for complying.

In this essay, I set out to complete three tasks: in section I, I defend a particular kind of dualism. I will do this by defending an account of democracy that requires both dimensions. In section II, I argue that though there are two evaluative stances in the assessment of democracy, the procedural typically has authority when there is conflict with the substantive. And finally, I show that there are limits to the authority of the procedural over the substantive and these limits are founded on the same principle as that which grounds the authority of democracy. In brief, I want to defend the authority of democracy and define its limits.

I. A Dualistic Account of Democracy

There are two dimensions of evaluation for democracy. And the reasons associated with these dimensions can give conflicting recommendations. On the one hand, we clearly do think that political institutions are important because of the ends they serve. And citizens within the democratic process argue in favor or against proposals on the grounds that certain policies and laws are just or desirable and others are not. On the other hand, I argue that the democratic process has an intrinsic fairness.

A. Democracy and the Equal Advancement of Interests

Here, I lay out the basic conception of justice, which is the principle of the public realization of equal advancement of interests. Second, I articulate and defend principles of respect for judgment and publicity on the basis of this principle. Thus, justice demands the public realization of equal advancement of interests. Third, I argue that democracy is required by justice understood as the public realization of equal advancement of interests. These theses will permit us to answer the questions about the dual nature of the evaluation of democracy and about its authority and the limits of its authority pursued in section II.

The basic principle of justice from which my argument proceeds is the principle of equal advancement of interests. It has two parts. First, it is a welfarist principle. It states that justice is concerned with the advancement of the interests of persons. Interests are understood as parts of what is good overall for a person. Second, justice strikes an appropriate balance between the interests of individuals when they conflict. It gives each person a claim to his or her share in that appropriate balance of conflicting interests. The appropriate balance between these conflicting interests is given by the idea of equality. The interests of individuals are to be advanced equally by the society. This equality proceeds from the importance of interests as well as the separateness of persons. No one's good is more important than anyone else's. No one's interests matter more than anyone else's. Each person has a life to live, and the interests of each person are combined into a special unity within that life. Thus the principle of equal advancement of interests requires that the interests of individuals be equally advanced in terms of lifetime prospects. But I cannot provide further defense of this principle in this essay.

B. Social Justice as a Weakly Public Principle

Since social justice concerns the kinds of claims people can make against each other in determining the appropriate balance of well-being, justice is essentially a weakly public principle. It is not enough that justice is done; it must be seen to be done. So the principle that requires that the basic institutions of society equally advance the interests of the members of the society must do so in a way that is compatible with this inevitable requirement. It must be given an interpretation that satisfies publicity.

The weak notion of publicity demands that the principles of justice be ones that people can in principle see to be in effect or not. The notion of "in principle possibility" here is to be specified relative to facts about the limitations on human cognitive abilities. To be sure, publicity does not require that each person actually see that he or she is being treated justly. It requires only that each person can see that he or she is being treated justly given a reasonable effort on his or her part. So a principle that requires that we go beyond our ordinary cognitive limitations to determine whether it has been realized or not is not a public principle of justice. But a principle that a person can, given normal cognitive faculties, see to be realized if he makes a reasonable effort is a public principle even if the person does not in fact see it to be realized on account of not having made a reasonable effort. In this respect the principle of weak publicity is like the legal principle that law must be publicly promulgated.

An example may help to illustrate and lend plausibility to this idea. Imagine the case of a person who has borrowed money from another. When the agreed-upon due date arises, the other person asks for her money. The debtor then truthfully says that he has paid the creditor already. But the creditor has no recollection of this. Now the debtor explains that he has put the money somehow directly into the creditor's bank account. The creditor, let us say, cannot determine this because there are too many transactions going in and out of her account. She simply cannot verify the deposit. And the debtor was quite aware of this when he deposited the money. Contrast this case with one in which the debtor pays the creditor back by giving her the money personally. Here everything is out in the open. The first case is a case of justice done but not seen to be done, while the second case is one of justice being done and being seen to be done. What I want to say is that the first case is defective with regard to justice, while the second is not. The first payback is not worthless, nor is it completely unjust, but there is a defect in its justice compared to the second case.

Weak publicity requires only that the recipient be able to see that she is treated in accordance with what are in fact the correct principles of justice. This does not require that her views about justice are correct. In our example above, the creditor may, for some reason, believe that she is entitled to more than the agreed amount of money. So even if she is fully aware that the debtor paid his debt to her as their agreement specified, she may think that he has not acted justly because she has a (let us say) false conception of justice that requires debtors to pay back even more than what the agreement specified. In this case, the principle of weak publicity is still satisfied under the assumption that what the debtor did was in fact just and what he did was publicly accessible to the creditor.

C. The Arguments for the Principle of Publicity

There are two types of arguments for the principle of weak publicity: the formal argument and the substantive argument. First, social justice concerns the kinds of claims people can make against each other in determining the appropriate balance of benefits and burdens. That is, principles of justice must spell out ideals that people can appeal to in criticizing their relations with each other, and social justice must be able to provide, at least in principle, concrete guidance as to how to legitimate their relations. A principle that cannot be seen by individuals to be implemented or one that does not permit individuals to be able to see that it is not implemented is not able to provide the guidance justice provides. It is not enough that justice is done; it must be seen to be done.

Now I shall provide a substantive argument for publicity. I argue that each citizen has fundamental interests in being able to see that he is being treated as an equal in a society where there is significant disagreement about justice and wherein each citizen can acknowledge fallibility in their capacities for thinking about their interests and about justice.

The background conditions of these fundamental interests are the facts of pervasive disagreement and fallibility. The fallibility of moral judgment is pervasive, even when confined to the parameters set by a principle of equality. The principle of equality requires one to compare and weigh the interests of persons who are quite different from oneself and who have lived their lives in parts of the society that are quite different from one's own. The trouble is that one is likely to be quite often mistaken about what those interests are and how to compare them to one's own. Indeed, individuals are rarely able to give as much as rough sketches of their own interests in social life, and most often individuals find themselves in the process of continually adjusting their conceptions of what is good for themselves and others. Furthermore, the principles by which to bring together all these varied, complex, and obscure interests are quite often likely to be very difficult to discern and assess. Common sense and the ubiquity of controversy among intelligent persons on these matters are sufficient to underscore these points.

Against this background of universal fallibility and disagreement, citizens have fundamental interests in being able to see that they are being treated as equals. First, each citizen is aware that individuals' judgments are usually cognitively biased toward their interests in various ways, and as a consequence, controversy over principles often reflects conflict of interests. Individuals' judgments of what is just or unjust are in two main ways more sensitive to their own interests than to those of others. One, persons understand their own interests better than the interests of others. And so they tend quite reasonably to interpret the interests of others in the light of their understanding of their own interests. So each person's conception of the common good or of equality of interests will tend to be grounded in conceptions of other people's interests that assimilate them to their own, and assume that others' interests are qualitatively similar to their own. But this implies that conceptions of equality and the common good will reflect the interests of the persons who advance them. Since in complex societies individuals' interests are likely to be qualitatively quite diverse, failing to take account of a particular group's conception of the common good may well imply ignoring that group's qualitatively distinctive interests. Two, individuals are more sensitive to the harms they undergo than to those of others, so they may inadvertently unduly downplay harms to others. This holds especially when they do not fully understand those harms. The harms of others are assigned lesser weight. Both the tendency qualitatively to assimilate the interests of others to one's own and the tendency to assign a lesser weight to the clearly distinctive interests of others distort one's judgments about the proper distribution of benefits and burdens to the detriment of others. None of this is meant to suggest that individuals generally intentionally mold principles to their own advantage or use such principles as a mask for their own interests. Individuals simply have natural cognitive biases toward their own interests.

Given these natural biases, and given the prevalence of disagreement about justice, no citizen wants merely to be treated in accordance with someone else's conception of equality. Each has an interest in being treated as an equal, in at least some fundamental respects, in a way that he can agree that he is being treated as an equal. If all citizens have this perception, then there is at least to that extent a bulwark against the biases working against anyone's interests.

A second fundamental interest in publicity emerges when we see that individuals' judgments often reflect modes of life to which they are accustomed and in which they feel at home. To live in a world governed by the principles one adheres to as opposed to someone else's is often like living in one's own home furnished by one's own familiar things and not in someone else's or in a hotel.[4] To the extent that there are interests related to this sense of at-homeness, and their judgments about justice reflect this sense, individuals have interests in the world they live in conforming to their judgments. Each citizen has a fundamental interest in having a sense of being properly at home in the society in which he lives. To the extent that a person sees himself as being treated as an equal, he has that sense of being properly at home in an egalitarian world.

Third, each person has a fundamental interest in being treated as a person with equal moral standing among his fellow citizens. To be treated in a way that entirely ignores one's way of perceiving how one is treated constitutes a serious loss of status for a person in a society. A person whose judgment about that society is never taken seriously by others is treated in effect like a child or a madman. Such a person is denied recognition of his or her moral personality. Moreover, if the facts' cognitive bias, at-homeness, and standing are taken into account by citizens, it should be clear that those adult persons who are denied the right of being able to see that they are being treated as equals are being told that their interests are not worthy of equal or perhaps any consideration of justice. This is a disastrous loss of moral standing. Since there is a deep interest in having one's moral standing among one's fellows clearly recognized and affirmed, such a denial of the right to publicity must be a serious setback of interests.

Finally, it is clear that no society can fully publicly embody justice. This is because citizens are bound, as a consequence of the facts of disagreement, fallibility, and cognitive bias, to disagree about what justice requires in a society. Hence, the requirement of publicity will need to be modified to take into account the impossibility of full publicity. The only way it can do this is to publicly embody justice in a way that is compatible with a wide range of disagreements about what justice requires. This, in my view, is where democracy comes in.

D. Equality and Democracy

The institutions of the society must publicly embody the equal advancement of interests in a way that can be clear in principle to its members. Here I shall sketch an argument to the effect that democratic decision-making is uniquely suited for satisfying this principle.

The first premise is that equal advancement of interests provides a just solution to conflict of interests. When we consider that there are deep conflicts of interests in how we ought to organize our common world over the shared properties of society, we see that justice ought naturally to apply to these conflicts of interest. We have interests in shaping our common world, but since our interests are deeply intertwined and since they differ in many ways, they conflict. Hence, the principle of equality ought to apply to our common social world.

But we cannot divide up that world into pieces and then distribute them. Our common social world in many ways constitutes an indissoluble unity. We have to shape it in one way rather than another.

Now, of course, we could try to do this by trying to make everyone equally happy or in some other direct way. And given the principle of equality of advancement of interests, this is a legitimate aim to pursue. The trouble is that we have no clear ways to measure our own or others' happiness or how to compare them. Mostly this follows from the facts of disagreement, fallibility, and cognitive bias that I listed above. No effort at somehow equalizing well-being among participants with regard to these common features of society is publicly defensible even to those who accept equal advancement of interests. Hence, the only way publicly to realize equality at this level is to distribute resources and opportunities.

But we think of the common world as essentially a nondivisible good; we cannot divide it into resources and then distribute them. We can, however, distribute resources for participating in collective decision-making, such as votes, resources for bargaining and coalition building, as well as deliberation in reasonably clearly equal ways. This would be a democratic way of resolving the problem; is it justified?

I have spoken of conflicts of interests being resolved by democratic means. Democracy does not, however, directly constitute a solution to conflicts of interest. In a democracy, conflicts are resolved via processes of discussion, negotiation, and voting. And citizens carry out these activities on the bases of their judgments. Citizens advance their interests by talking and voting on the basis of what they judge to be their interests just as citizens advance the common good and justice by talking and voting on the basis of what they judge justice and the common good to be. The system of rights to property, rights of association, and rights to expression and privacy play a large role in defining our common world. But we would not say that disagreements about the contours of these rights are per se conflicts of interests. Do we have reason to offer a democratic solution to conflicts of interests and conflicts of judgment regarding what is right in matters that pertain to civil and economic justice?

The facts of diversity, fallibility, disagreement, cognitive bias, and the interests we have in publicity provide the key to the final stretch of argument for democracy. We have fundamental interests in being publicly treated as equals. But what is the best way to do this? Democratic decision-making on the issues in contention is the uniquely public way of realizing equality among citizens.

First, democracy is a publicly clear way of realizing a kind of equality. It involves equality in voting power, equality of opportunities to run for office, and, ideally, equality of opportunities to participate in the processes of negotiation and discussion that lead up to voting. And it is a form of equality that has most often been taken as a sine qua non of treating persons as equals. Historically, it has been, aside from basic civil rights, the main way in which members of society have recognized and affirmed the equality of their fellow citizens. Hence, we have good reason to think that it is a publicly clear way of recognizing and affirming the equality of citizens. And democracy realizes equality publicly in a way that is uniquely tailored to the problem of pervasive disagreement.

Second, the facts of diversity, disagreement, fallibilism, and cognitive bias and the interests in being able to correct for others' cognitive biases, in being at home in society, and in having one's equal moral standing publicly recognized and affirmed ground the principle of respect for the judgment of everyone in society. Moreover, each has an interest in learning about his interests as well as justice, which is best realized in a process of discussion with others wherein others take one's views seriously and respond to one's views about justice and interests.

Given these facts and interests, each person's judgment about how society ought to be organized must be taken seriously. If someone's judgment is not permitted a hearing in society, then the interests described above will be set back. Anyone who is excluded from participation in discussion and debate can see that his or her interests are not being taken seriously and may legitimately infer that his or her moral standing is being treated as less than that of others. So justice, which requires public equality, demands equal respect for the judgment of each.

This requirement of equal respect for judgment is only a principle for regulating the political institutions of society and must not be imposed on each citizen beyond that. Otherwise the principle would be inconsistent. One way in which we extend respect to each individual is by allowing each individual to formulate his or her own judgments about the worth of other people's judgments. People may choose for themselves whom to believe and whom to ally with or whose arguments are most reliable. What is essential for political institutions is that they give each person an equal right to participate in this process of debate and adjudication; this is how all citizens must respect each person's capacity for judgment.

The argument for the principle of respect for judgment points beyond the claim that each must have a right to participate in the process of discussion and adjudication. It shows in addition that each ought to have rights to participate in the process of decision. The reason for this is easy to see. When someone is excluded from the process of decision, the facts of diversity, disagreement, fallibility, and cognitive bias and the interests in being able to correct for others' cognitive biases and in being at home entail that one's interests are likely to be neglected in the process of decision. Moreover, the interest in having people respond to one's views is not likely to be well served if one does not have the power to affect the decision-making. Others are forced not to take one's views seriously when one has no power and so many others do have power and must be listened to. Finally, recognition of these facts and interests and the effect that lack of power has on the advancement of the interests makes it amply clear to those who are excluded that their interests are not treated as equally worthy of advancement. The excluded can see that they are being treated as if they have a lesser moral standing. Hence, all the facts and interests that are aligned in favor of the principle of publicity also favor equality in the rights to participate in the processes of discussion and decision. So when there is disagreement about justice and the common good, the uniquely best way to take everyone's judgment seriously, so that equality is publicly embodied, is to give each person an equal say in how the society ought to be organized. And this in turn is the way publicly to realize equal advancement of interests. Therefore the principle of the public realization of equality supports democracy as the uniquely best realization of equality under the circumstances of disagreement and fallibility.

This argument establishes the intrinsic justice of democratic decision-making even though some of the premises rely on the effects of differences of power on different persons. The intrinsic justice of democracy derives from the foundational concern with publicity and the idea that only democracy (and basic liberal rights, as we will see in the last section) can realize public equality in the light of the facts and interests described above.

Intuitively, if one dissents from an outcome that has been democratically chosen and one attempts to bring about another outcome by means of revolution or intrigue or manipulation of the system, one is acting in such a way that cannot be thought of by others as treating them as equals. One is putting one's judgment ahead of others', and in the light of the facts about judgment and the interests in respect for judgment, one is in effect expressing the superiority of one's interests over others.

II. Democracy and Authority

The main purpose of the state is to establish justice among persons within a limited jurisdiction. And justice is something we owe to one another on a constant basis. What does it mean to say that the state and its legal system establish justice? It means that the legal system of a reasonably just society determines how one is to treat others justly if one is to treat them justly at all. What the state does, if it is reasonably just, is settle what justice consists in by promulgating public rules for the guidance of individual behavior.

Why are public rules for the guidance of behavior so important to justice? First, justice underdetermines what system of rules we must adopt.[5] Many different systems of rules can realize the same principles of justice. To be sure, we may have a general sense that human beings have conditional rights to own property, but, in general, we do not know whether this person has a right to this particular property and what the particular implications are until we know what the rules for the society are. To act justly it is essential for us to be on the same page with others, to coordinate with them on the same rules. Otherwise, though two people may be perfectly conscientious and even believe in the same basic principles, they will end up violating each other's rights if they follow different sets of rules that implement the same principles. To suppose otherwise is to suppose that there are clear natural rights and duties accessible to all (or a set of highly salient conventional rules) concerning how we should act even in the most detailed circumstances. Since in order to treat others justly, we must be acting on the basis of the same rules, we need an authority for promulgating those rules in a publicly clear way, and we must expect individuals to comply with the rules the authority lays down.

Since the rules are likely to be quite complex, individuals must take the rule maker to be authoritative in order successfully to act on the basis of the same rules. Why are they likely to be complex? One reason is that the constraints we must abide by in dealing with other people justly are quite complex and subject to a number of different realizations. Rules defining property rights, such as when they are acquired, when a voluntary exchange occurs, when exchange is not exploitative, when one person's use of his property imposes too much of an externality on others, when a person loses his property as a result of lack of use, etc., are all very complex on their own and require that there be public rules. A second reason is that justice is at least in some significant part concerned with assuring the common good and certain kinds of distributions of power, opportunities, education, and income. Rules defining property and its limits, as well as taxation, are necessarily quite complex because they must satisfy both the concern that certain constraints be respected and that certain overall distributional properties be maintained in the society.

The complexity of these rules and the variety of possible rules that could realize the same principles of justice simply make it impossible for people to be able to have coordinated expectations of them without their accepting an authoritative rule maker. And it is necessary for people to have coordinated expectations with one another in order to treat each other justly.

Someone might reply that I have reason to obey the state in this situation, not because the state has ordered me to act, but because these actions are just.

But this will not do. The complexity of the rules and the variety of realizations of justice make it such that I cannot determine for myself what to do; I must comply with the rules because they are made by the public rule maker. Otherwise, I will often be mistaken about what a useful public rule will do, and I will also not be able to depend on my fellow citizens to treat me properly. These particular rules determine what are just interactions among persons only because there is an artificially created public set of rules that defines property, fair contribution to political society, and other matters in social life.

A second reason for having settled public rules that are made by an authoritative rule maker is that publicity is a basic value in considerations of justice, as I argued in a previous section. And to be treated in accordance with the rule of law and on the basis of equality under the law is a public way of treating a person as an equal. Without public rules and a common authoritative rule maker, the public realization of equality is impossible. Once again, the complexity of rules required for justice and the variety of ways in which justice can be realized make the likelihood of individuals being able to see that they are being treated justly by others nearly zero in many cases of detail. Once there are public rules made by an authoritative source, each person is at least guaranteed a treatment in accordance with commonly accepted rules.

Finally, I wish to enlist the arguments I gave in the first part of this essay for the idea that there must, morally speaking, be an authoritative rule maker. In the earlier half of the essay, I argued that people disagree quite a bit about justice. There I argued that the facts of disagreement and fallibility, together with the interests in respect for judgment, provide a powerful argument for democratic decision-making as the unique way of treating persons publicly as equals. Here we have in effect not only an argument for an authoritative rule maker; we also have an argument for a rule maker with features that imply the equal participation of citizens in the task of rule-making.

A. The Authority of Democracy

I have argued that a fair way of making decisions in the light of disagreement, which treats people's judgments and interests with respect without defeating the point of political society, is to give each a reasonably equal say in the process of deciding. This approach treats each publicly as an equal and respects each citizen's judgment without requiring that everyone agree to the outcome of the decision-making or be equally satisfied with the outcome. I also argued for the moral necessity of the state's establishment of justice. These two results set the stage for my defense of an account of the authority of democracy and its limits.

Here is the basic structure of the argument for democracy's authority:

1. If legislative institutions publicly realize justice, then they have legitimate legislative authority over those people within their jurisdiction.

1a. So if a democratic assembly publicly realizes justice, then it has legitimate legislative authority over those people within its jurisdiction.
2. If there is reasonable disagreement on the justice of legislation, then a democratic assembly will publicly realize justice in itself and only in itself. (Reasonable disagreement is disagreement on how to understand equality that remains after reasonable efforts have been made.)
*3. (from 1a and 2) Therefore, democratic assemblies have legitimate legislative authority if there is reasonable disagreement on the justice of the legislation at issue.
4. If and only if legislative institutions publicly realize justice in themselves, then they have genuine legitimacy, that is, they have a claim-right to rule and they are owed obedience.
4a. If legislative institutions realize justice only in their outcomes, then they have a weak legitimacy, that is, citizens do not owe them obedience, though they may usually be morally required to obey many of their laws.
*5. (from 2 and 4) Therefore, democratic assemblies have genuine legitimacy if there is reasonable disagreement on the justice of the legislation at issue.

I should explain some of the terms in use here. First of all, I refer only to legislative authority here. There are, of course, other kinds of authority in the state, such as judicial authority, executive authority, and administrative authority. All of these are essential in a large state, and my account does not discuss them.

I regard legislative authority as the most fundamental kind of authority in a democratic state, and I think that legislative authority is the authority that must be democratic, while the others may be held by people who are experts. That is why I limit my discussion to it.

In the argument, I distinguish among different types of legitimacy. One highly unusual form of legitimacy is where everyone can see that the substance of legislation is just. This is not a circumstance that arises in modern democratic states, or in any states for that matter, and so the argument takes no account of it. The second kind (described in premise 4a) is one in which the state acts justly but many do not know it. Many disagree with its actions. Here people have some duty to do what the state tells them to do, but they do not owe the duty to the state as if it had a right to rule; they simply act better if they accept its authority.

The third type of legitimacy establishes a genuine right to rule in the alleged authority and thereby imposes duties on citizens. This is the kind of authority democratic assemblies have.

The first premise of the argument was defended at length in my discussions of the normal justification thesis and of the moral necessity of the state. I argued against the normal justification thesis that some significant degree of justice in political society is a necessary condition of legitimate authority, and I argued against consent theory that some significant degree of justice in political society is sufficient for legitimate authority. The second premise I defended in section I: democratic decision-making is a publicly just and fair way of making collective decisions in the light of conflicts of interests and disagreements about shared aspects of social life. Citizens who skirt democratically made law act contrary to the equal right of all citizens to have a say in making laws when there is substantial and informed disagreement. Those who refuse to pay taxes or who refuse to respect property laws on the grounds that these are unjust are simply affirming a superior right to that of others in determining how the shared aspects of social life ought to be arranged. Thus, they act unjustly.

I defend the fourth premise by arguing that democratic equality has precedence over the other forms of equality that are in dispute in a political society (save the kind of liberal equality I shall describe in the last section of this essay). The reason for this is because of its public nature. And the reason that the publicity of this equality carries so much weight is because of the importance of the interests that are involved in publicity. The idea is that the interests involved in being publicly treated as an equal member of a society are the preeminent interests a person has in social life. The interests in public equality are preeminent for three main reasons. First, the interests have great intrinsic importance for each person. In other words, the interest in knowing that others treat one as a person whose interests matter and matter equally among persons is of great importance to every human being. The interests in being at home in one's society are also fundamental. Second, public equality satisfies these interests in a way that is compatible with equality. Third, these interests harmonize with the other fundamental interests a person has. These interests do not conflict with other fundamental interests. This is because one cannot feel at home in a society that treats one clearly as an inferior either in body or in mind. One cannot be treated as an equal member in a society where one's basic interests in liberty, security, and material well-being are fundamentally threatened. I shall argue this more in what follows on the limits of democratic authority. The last two points guarantee that these interests and the public equality that rests on them are not overridden by other moral concerns.

If these claims are right, then only by obeying the democratically made choices can citizens act justly. Democratic directives give content-independent reasons since one must accept a democratic decision as binding even when one disagrees with it. And the directives give preemptive reasons since they derive from a source that is meant to replace and exclude the reasons that apply directly to the situation at hand. But what is striking is that the democratic assembly has a right to rule (within limits to be defined shortly) since one treats its members unjustly if one ignores or skirts its decisions. Each citizen has a right to one's obedience, and therefore the assembly as a whole has a right to one's obedience.

B. The Limits to Democratic Authority

The question is, When do considerations of justice or injustice in the outcome override democratic rights? We have seen that in the normal case, the exercise of democratic rights has authority with respect to civil and economic rights. But it seems clear that democratic rights are problematic, at least in cases of gross injustice. How can we countenance a democratic choice to introduce slavery for those who are among the minority? Surely this violation must be serious enough to override or defeat the democratic right. My answer to this question is that the limits to democratic authority can be derived from the same principle that underlies democratic authority.

Here I shall set out the basic argument for the limits to democratic authority:

1. Democratic assemblies have legitimate authority only when they publicly realize justice in themselves or they are instrumentally just.
2. Disenfranchisement of part of the sane adult population is a public violation of equality.
3. Democratic assemblies publicly realize justice in themselves only when their decisions do not publicly violate justice.

*4. (from 2 and 3) Therefore, when a democratic assembly votes to disenfranchise some of the population, it does not publicly realize justice in itself.

*5. (from 1 and 4) Therefore, when a democratic assembly votes to disenfranchise some of its members, it does not have legitimate authority.

6. Just as disenfranchisement of part of the adult population publicly violates equality, so enslavement or suspension of the core of their basic liberal rights or some form of radical discrimination against a part of the sane adult population publicly violates equality.

*7. (from 4, 5, and 6) Therefore, when a democratic assembly votes to enslave or suspend the core of liberal rights or radically discriminate against a part of the sane adult population, it does not publicly realize justice and so does not have legitimate authority.

The key premises here are 2, 3, and 6. Disenfranchisement is a violation of public equality if the argument of the first part of this essay is correct. Premise 2 states that disenfranchisement is not merely a violation of public equality; it is in effect a public violation of equality. That is to say that given the facts of judgment and the interests in having one's judgment respected, disenfranchisement is a publicly clear violation of a person's status as an equal and of the equal advancement of that person's interests. Were the majority to strip some minority of its democratic rights, then this would be a publicly clear way in which it acted as if its interests were of superior worth to those of the minority. Everyone would be able to see that the members of the minority were being treated as inferiors.

Premise 3 is the lynchpin of the argument. A democratic assembly that disenfranchises parts of its population no longer publicly embodies equality. For the institutions that embody public equality are not mere sets of rules, but they are the organized and rule-governed behaviors of individuals who thereby express the equality of citizens in their participation. But if the institutional rules are used to perpetrate a public violation of equality, then the institution no longer expresses equality but rather its opposite. Here is the basic idea. If a majority in the democratic assembly uses the rules of the assembly to take away the voting rights of the minority in clear violation of public equality, then the majority must not think that the rights it is exercising are morally required because they embody public equality. They would in effect be rejecting public equality as a norm over their behavior. If they thought that their voting rights were required by public equality and they exercised them under this understanding, then they would be committed to maintaining the equal rights of all. By disenfranchising some, they indicate that they do not think that their use of these rights implies a commitment to public equality. The institutions have become mere tools in the service of treating some as inferiors. But if this is the predominant understanding, then the institutions no longer publicly embody equality.

Since democratic equality is inherently just to the extent that it publicly embodies equality, in cases of disenfranchisement the decision-making process of the democratic assembly is no longer just. And since the authority of democracy is grounded in its justice, democracy no longer has authority when it disenfranchises some of its people.

Premise 6 asserts that there is a fundamental parallelism between democratic rights and basic liberal rights. This parallelism is grounded on the fact that the foundations of liberal rights are the same as those of democratic rights. The idea is that, given the background facts of diversity, fallibility, disagreement, and cognitive bias, each person has fundamental interests in being able to conduct their lives by their own lights, at least in certain defined areas of human activity. I will limit myself to displaying the interests behind the freedoms of association and the freedom to choose one's own aims in life as well as the basic plan for achieving one's aims. The interest in being at home in the world is advanced when one has the right to associate with others one chooses to associate with and on terms one chooses. The interest in being able to avoid the consequences of being imposed upon by another's paternalistic judgment that is cognitively biased toward that other's interests is also advanced by the basic liberal rights.

The interests in being able to learn from others and to learn from one's mistakes are advanced by one's having the right to freedom of association and the right to choose and pursue one's own aims in life and the basic plans for achieving those aims. Furthermore, freedom of association furthers the interest in being recognized and affirmed as the individual person I am by others whom I respect.

These and other interests are so fundamental to the well-being of a person that no society that set them back for all or some substantial proportion of the population could be thought to advance the common good. And no society that set them back for a few could be thought to be giving the interests of each equal consideration. Those whose liberal rights were set back would have reason to think that their equal moral standing was not recognized and affirmed by others. Indeed, given the facts of cognitive bias and the interests in at-homeness and learning, those whose freedoms of association were limited would have reason to think that their interests were being subordinated to those of the others in society. This would be a disastrous setback to their interests in being recognized and affirmed as citizens with equal standing. Thus, any fundamental undermining of a person's basic liberal rights would be a publicly clear violation of equality of advancement of interests.

Now consider the case in which a majority decides to enslave the minority; this is a clear violation of the principle of the public realization of equal advancement of interests. Why is this? If another enslaves me, that person assumes the power to decide what I ought to do and reaps the benefits from this.

He thereby implies that my interests are not of equal significance to his. Or if he thinks that my interests do matter equally, he implies that my capacity for judgment is not worthy of respect. But for all the same reasons that I gave for the importance of respect for the judgment of persons in cases of political decision-making, the principle of public equality and the interests and facts on which it is based require that my judgment regarding how I am to conduct my life must be given equal respect and therefore must not be subordinated to that of others. Hence, enslavement is a violation of the principle of public equality.

Any radical suppression of basic liberal rights of members of the population would fall afoul of the basic requirements of public equality. People may disagree about what liberal rights are basic and what their boundaries are as well as what equality in these liberal rights consists in, but some kind of equality in basic liberal rights is necessary to the public realization of equality given the facts of judgment.

To conclude, this argument shows that democracy loses its authority by losing its intrinsic justice altogether. One simply does not have a moral right to violate the requirements of public equality. To the extent that democratic rights generally embody public equality, and basic liberal rights embody public equality, no one has a moral right to undermine democratic rights or the basic liberal rights of any of the citizens. The authority is lost because the right is lost altogether. These ideas not only provide the foundation for a conception of democratic authority; they also provide for the basis of constitutional limits on democratic power.

Notes

1. See Philippe Van Parijs, "Is Democracy Compatible with Justice?," *Journal of Political Philosophy* 4 (1996): 101–117, and, more recently, his "The Disenfranchisement of the Elderly," *Philosophy and Public Affairs* 27 (1998): 292–333.

2. The view is attributed to Robert Bork. See his "Neutral Principles and Some First Amendment Problems," *Indiana Law Journal* 47 (1971): 1–35.

3. This view seems to be expressed in Iris Young, *Justice and the Politics of Difference* (Princeton, NJ: Princeton University Press, 1990); and Benjamin Barber, *Strong Democracy* (Berkeley and Los Angeles: University of California Press, 1984). A prominent defender of deliberative democracy who attempts to bring both dimensions of assessment under one principle is Joshua Cohen, "Substance and Procedure in Democracy," in *Democracy and Difference*, edited by Seyla Benhabib (Princeton, NJ: Princeton University Press, 1996), 95–119.

4. See G. W. F. Hegel, *The Philosophy of Right*, translated by T. M. Knox (Oxford: Oxford University Press, 1952), 24. See Michael Hardimon, *Hegel's Social Philosophy: The Project of Reconciliation* (Cambridge: Cambridge University Press, 1994), for a full discussion of this idea.

5. Joseph Raz says morality underdetermines the law. See his "On the Authority and Interpretation of Constitutions," in *Constitutionalism: Philosophical Foundations*, edited by Larry Alexander (Cambridge: Cambridge University Press, 1998), 152–193.

READING

12

Reflections on Deliberative Democracy

JOSHUA COHEN

1. Introduction

For more than two decades, egalitarian-democrats have sought to describe a "postsocialist" political project. The socialist project, including its social democratic variant, comprised a set of political values and an institutional and political strategy for advancing those values. The values were egalitarian and participatory. The institutional models and the political strategy focused on the state.

Contemporary debate among egalitarian-democrats begins in the conviction that this approach is misguided and moves along two paths.

The first, growing out of appreciation of the state's limits as an economic manager is sometimes called "asset egalitarianism." The idea is to shift the distribution of income by changing the distribution of income-generating assets. It is an important idea, particularly with pressures from globalization on income security, but not my topic here.[1]

A second—and this will provide my focus—is more political. Building on what I will describe as "radical-democratic" ideas, it seeks to construct models of political decision in which "local" players can be involved more directly in regulation and in collective problem solving, with a center that coordinates local efforts, rather than dictating the terms of those efforts. Thus, local—or, more exactly, lower-level actors (nation-states or national peak organizations of various kinds; regions, provinces, or subnational associations within these; and so on down to whatever neighborhood is relevant to the problem at hand)—are given autonomy to experiment with their own solutions to broadly defined problems of public policy. In return they furnish higher-level units with rich information about the goals as well as the progress they are making toward achieving them. The periodic pooling of results reveals the defects of parochial solutions, and allows the elaboration of standards for comparing local achievements, exposing poor performers to criticism, and making good ones (temporary) models for emulation.

This radical-democratic project builds on two distinct strands of thought.[2] With Rousseau, radical democrats are committed to broader *participation* in public decision-making—though not, as Rousseau supposed, through regular meetings of a legislative assembly open to all citizens.[3] According to this first strand, citizens should have greater direct roles in public choices or, in a less demanding formulation, participate in politics on the basis of substantive political judgments and be assured that officials will be responsive and accountable to their concerns and judgments. Though more participatory democrats disagree on the precise locus of expanded participation, they all are troubled when democratic participation is largely confined to a choice between parties competing for control of government, and particularly when that choice is not founded on clearly articulated substantive programmatic-political differences between and among parties and pursued with the expectation that the parties will be held accountable to their announced programs. The underlying participatory idea is that citizens in a democracy are to engage with the substance of law and policy, and not simply delegate responsibility for such substantive engagement to representatives.

Along with participation, radical democrats emphasize *deliberation.* Instead of a politics of power and interest, radical democrats favor a deliberative democracy in which citizens address public problems by reasoning together about how best to solve them—in which, at the limit, no force is at work, as Jürgen Habermas said, "except that of the better argument."[4] According to the deliberative interpretation, democracy is a political arrangement that ties the exercise of collective power to reason-giving among those subject to collective decisions. Once more, we see substantial differences among different formulations of the deliberative-democratic ideal. Some see deliberative democracy as a matter of forming a public opinion through dispersed and open public discussion and translating such opinion into legitimate law; others, as a way to ensure that elections—or legislative debates or perhaps discussions within courts or agencies—are themselves infused with information and reasoning; others, as a way to bring reasoning by citizens directly to bear on addressing regulatory issues. But in all cases, the large aim of a deliberative democracy is to shift from bargaining, interest aggregation, and power to the common reason of equal citizens—democracy's public reason—as a guiding force in democratic life.[5]

In this essay, I will explore these two distinct strands of the radical-democratic project—participatory and deliberative—though I will focus on the deliberative because that is the topic here. My central point is that participation and deliberation are both important, but different and important for different reasons. Moreover, it is hard to achieve both, but the project of advancing both is coherent, attractive, and worth our attention. I begin by presenting an idea of deliberative democracy. Second, I sketch three attractions of deliberative democracy. Third, I discuss four lines of skeptical argument. Fourth, I sketch three tensions between deliberation and participation. Fifth, I consider two political and institutional strategies for blunting those tensions. I conclude by mentioning two large challenges.

2. Deliberation

Carl Schmitt said that deliberation belongs to the world of the parliament, where legislators reason together about how to address public problems. It does not belong to the world of mass democracy, where ethno-culturally homogeneous peoples find leaders who pick the people's friends and enemies. According to Schmitt, "The development of modern mass democracy has made argumentative public discussion an empty formality."[6] Rejecting Schmitt's view, as well as its more benign contemporary progeny, deliberative democrats explore possibilities of combining deliberation with mass democracy. And not just explore: we are hopeful about the possibilities of fostering a more deliberative democracy.

Deliberation, generically understood, is about weighing the reasons relevant to a decision with a view to making a decision on the basis of that weighing. So an individual can make decisions deliberatively, a jury has a responsibility to deliberate, and a committee of oligarchs can deliberate: deliberation, in short, is not intrinsically democratic. The "democracy" in "deliberative democracy" is not pleonastic.

Democracy is a way of making collective decisions that connects decisions to the interests and judgments of those whose conduct is to be regulated by the decisions. The essential idea is that those governed by the decisions are treated as equals by the processes of making the decisions. Democracy, as Tocqueville emphasized, is also a kind of society—a society of equals—but I will be confining myself as a general matter to the more specifically political understanding of democracy. Of course, even if we think of democracy politically, as a way to make binding collective decisions, constructing a more deliberative democracy is not a narrowly political project: deliberative democracy requires attention to encouraging deliberative capacities, which is, inter alia, a matter of education, information, and organization.[7] I will return briefly to this point near the end.

Deliberative democracy, then, combines these two elements, neither reducible to the other. It is about making collective decisions and exercising power in ways that trace in some way to the reasoning of the equals who are subject to the decisions: not only to their preferences, interests, and choices, but also to their reasoning. Essentially, the point of deliberative democracy is to subject the exercise of power to reason's discipline, to what Habermas famously described as "the force of the better argument," not the advantage of the better situated. Deliberative democracy does not aim to do away with power, an idea that makes no sense; nor simply to subject power to the discipline—such as it is—of talking, because talking is not the same as reasoning (consider verbal assaults, insults, racial slurs, lies, blowing smoke, exchanging pleasantries, exploring common experiences); nor is it simply to reason together, because reasoning together may be without effect on the exercise of power.

Moreover, the notion of reason's discipline is not nearly definite enough. Plato's philosopher-guardians subject power to reason's discipline—that, at any rate, is what they say they are doing. But deliberative democracy is a kind of democracy, so the reasoning must be in some recognizable way the reasoning of the equal persons who are subject to the decisions. And not just the process of reasoning, but the content of the reasons themselves must have a connection to the democratic conception of people as equals. Deliberative democracy is about reasoning together among equals, and that means not simply advancing considerations that one judges to be reasons, but also finding considerations that others can reasonably be expected to acknowledge as reasons. That's why deliberation focuses, as a constitutive matter, on considerations of the common good, and also why—or so I have argued elsewhere—basic personal liberties are essential elements of a deliberative democracy. Deliberative democracy is not majoritarian, and these substantive conditions—the common good and personal liberties—are essential to democratic deliberation, under conditions of reasonable pluralism. In short, the ideal of deliberative democracy is to discipline collective power through the common reason of a democratic public: through democracy's public reason.[8]

To be sure, discussion, even when it is founded on reasons, may not—and often does not—issue in consensus. No account of deliberative democracy has ever suggested otherwise. All complex practical problems—from trade and security to organizing schools and transportation, providing clean water and public safety, allocating health care, and ensuring fair compensation—implicate a range of distinct values, and reasonable people disagree about the precise content of and weights to be assigned to those values. In any allocative decision, for example, there are likely to be people who think that the worst-off person should have priority, others who think there should be equal chances, others who think the person who benefits most should get the good. In allocating medical resources, some will think that priority goes to the worst off and others, to those who would benefit most; others will think we should assist the largest number of people; others may hold that we should ensure that all people have fair chances at receiving help, regardless of the urgency of their situation and of expected benefits from treatment. So no matter how deliberative the democracy gets, collective decisions will always be made through voting, under some form of majority rule. Indeed, deliberation may work best when participants do not (as in a jury setting) feel the pressure to adjust their views for the sake of consensus—as if attention to reasons ensured convergence, and disagreement revealed bias or incapacity or some other failure.[9]

There may be some temptation to think that the prospect of majority rule defeats deliberation. Because collective decision-making concludes with a vote, participants—anticipating that final stage of resolution—will not have any incentive to deliberate in earlier stages, so will focus instead on counting heads rather than on weighing reasons: aggregation at the end of the day, then aggregation all day. But that temptation should be resisted. Even if everyone knows that, at the end of the day, heads may be counted, they may still accept the idea of arriving at a collective judgment based on considerations that others acknowledge as reasons. They may, for example, believe that reason-giving is an important expression of respect, or that it is the right way to acknowledge the collective nature of the decision. If they do, they will be willing to deliberate in the stages leading up to the vote, even when they know a vote is coming.

Deliberative democracy, thus understood, is a distinctive interpretation of democracy: democracy, no matter how fair, no matter how informed, no matter how participatory, is not deliberative unless reasoning is central to the process of collective decision-making. Nor is democracy deliberative simply because the process and its results are reasonable: capable of being given a rational defense, even a rational defense that would be recognized as such on reflection by those subject to the decisions. The concern for reasonableness must play a role in the process. Thus the contrast between deliberative and aggregative democracy. In an aggregative democracy, citizens aim to advance their individual and group interests. If the process is fair, the results may well be reasonable. But unless the reasonableness is aimed at by participants in the process, we do not have deliberation.

Of course, it might be argued that reasonable results must be aimed at to be achieved, and that democracy must therefore be deliberative to be reasonable. So, for example, if we have a hypothetical test for the rightness of decisions, where the hypothetical process involves reasoning under idealized conditions about what is best to do, then it might be said that the actual process must look something like the hypothetical to provide a basis for confidence in the rightness of results.[10] Still, it is best to see this connection between reasonableness and deliberation as a broadly empirical claim, and to keep deliberation as a way of deciding—a way that comprises both the nature of the process and the content of the reasons—distinct from reasonableness as a property of decisions.

Aggregative and deliberative democracy do not exhaust the space of interpretations of democracy. Consider a community of politically principled citizens, each of whom endorses a conception of justice. The conceptions they endorse differ, but each person accepts some conception as setting bounds on acceptable policy and decent institutions. Assume further that they do not see much point in arguing about what justice requires, though they discuss issues with an eye to generating information, and each conscientiously uses his or her own conception in reaching political decisions. No one in this political community thinks that politics is simply about advancing interests, much less a

Schmittian struggle between friends and enemies. But reasoning together plays a very restricted role in public political life: the members accept that they owe one another an exercise of conscientious judgment, but not that they owe a justification by references to reasons that others might reasonably be expected to accept. I will not develop this distinction further here. I mention it to underscore that the case for deliberative democracy needs to be made not simply in contrast with accounts of democracy that focus on interests and power but also in contrast with views that assume a conscientious exercise of moral-political judgment by individual citizens, although not deliberation.

This emphasis on subjecting power to reason's discipline is a thread that runs through much of the literature on deliberative democracy.[11] Thus, Amy Gutmann and Dennis Thompson say that "deliberative democracy's basic requirement is 'reason-giving.'"[12] Jon Elster also emphasizes that deliberation is about argument, in fact arguments addressed to people committed to rationality and impartiality.[13] John Dryzek says that a "defining feature of deliberative democracy is that individuals participating in democratic processes are amenable to changing their minds and their preferences as a result of the reflection induced by deliberation."[14] Elsewhere he emphasizes "communication that encourages reflection upon preferences without coercion."[15] But Dryzek's characterizations of deliberative democracy are not literally *defining*: they follow from the more fundamental characteristics of deliberative democracy. The *point* of deliberative democracy is not for people to reflect on their preferences, but to decide, in light of reasons, what to do. Deciding what to do in light of reasons requires, of course, a willingness to change your mind, since you might begin the deliberative task with a view about what to do that is not supported by good reasons. But the crucial point is that Dryzek emphasizes that deliberation is basically about reasoning—about rational argument—and that other kinds of communication need to be "held to rational standards."[16]

3. Reasons for Deliberative Democracy

Why is deliberative democracy a good thing? It is of course hard to deny that the exercise of collective power should be supported by appropriate reasons. But deliberative democracy is not simply the undisputed idea that the exercise of power should be rationally defensible, thus nonarbitrary. The question is why it is important to discipline the exercise of power by actually reasoning together. I will mention three considerations.

The first is about promoting justice. Thus suppose we think that requirements of justice are fixed by idealized reasoning under conditions of full information and equal standing. One argument for deliberative democracy is that actual deliberation is needed if collective decisions are to meet the standards of political right that would be accepted under idealized conditions of information and equality. So if justice is fixed by impartial reasoning in hypothetical conditions in which agents aim to justify principles to others, then, arguably, we will only achieve justice if we make collective decisions using reasoning of a similar kind. We cannot trust the achievement of justice to the pursuit of individual and group interests, even under fair conditions.

A second line of argument is that reason-giving is a distinctive form of communication, and that it may have desirable consequences, apart from promoting justice. Thus, the requirement that I defend my proposals with reasons that are capable of being acknowledged as such by others will—whatever my own preferences—impose some desirable constraint on the proposals I can advance and defend. Of course if every proposal can be rationalized in an acceptable way, then the requirement of defending proposals with acceptable reasons will not have much effect. But I am skeptical about this claim. Moreover, the need to give reasons acceptable to others might produce desirable consequences if reason-giving itself changes preferences, or at least saliences. So while I start preferring most what is best for me or my group, the practice of defending proposals with reasons may change my preferences, dampening the tension between my beliefs about what is right or politically legitimate and my preferences: not because that is the point of deliberation, but because that is its effect. In addition, deliberation may improve results by eliciting information: though there are certainly truth-telling equilibria for strategic actors, I assume that the informational effects of deliberation depend in part on a commitment to truthfulness or sincerity in communication, which may itself be reinforced through deliberation, although it is hard to construct from nothing. But that is true about the entire account of deliberation: though deliberation may reinforce a prior commitment to argue on terms that others can acknowledge as reasons, some such prior commitment must be in place if the enterprise of mutual reason-giving is to get off the ground and be sustained.

A third case for deliberative democracy, not about consequences, is that the deliberative view expresses the idea that relations among people within a pluralistic, democratic order are relations of equals. It requires that we offer considerations that others, despite fundamental differences of outlook, can reasonably be expected to accept, not simply that we count their interests, while keeping our fingers crossed that those interests are outweighed. The idea of collective authorization is reflected not only in the processes of decision-making, but also—as I said earlier—in the form and the content of democracy's public reason.

This point about the attractions of the deliberative interpretation of collective decisions can be stated in terms of an idea of self-government. In a deliberative democracy, laws and policies result from processes in which citizens defend solutions to common problems on the basis of what are generally acknowledged as relevant reasons. To be sure, citizens will, as I mentioned earlier, interpret the content of those considerations differently, and assign them different weights. The reasons relevant to particular domains are complex and often competing, and there often will be no clear, principled basis for ranking them: reasonable people may reasonably disagree on how they should be weighted, even after all the reasons have been aired. Nevertheless, they may accept the results of the deliberative process in part by virtue of the process having given due consideration to reasons that all reasonably accept.

When citizens take these political values seriously, political decisions are not simply a product of power and interest; even citizens whose views do not win out can see that the decisions are supported by good reasons. As a result, members can—despite disagreement—all regard their conduct as guided, in general terms, by their own reason. Establishing such political deliberation would realize an ideal of self-government or political autonomy under conditions of reasonable pluralism. It may be as close as we can get to the Rousseauian ideal of giving the law to ourselves.

4. Skepticism About Deliberation

I want now to consider four objections that have been raised against the deliberative conception of democracy. The interest of exploring the tensions between deliberation and participation will be greater if some of these concerns can be dispelled.

1. The first is about inequality. It begins with the observation that reasoning is an acquired capacity, and not equally distributed among all. So collective decision-making through reason-giving may not *neutralize* power, but may instead create a "logocracy," in which political power is effectively shifted to the rhetorically gifted (or at least to the verbally uninhibited), which may well compound existing social inequalities, and deliver political power to the educated or economically advantaged or men or those possessed of cultural capital and argumentative confidence.[17]

While the concern is important and understandable, the evidence, such as it is, suggests that this objection exaggerates the feared effect, in part by "depoliticizing" it—more precisely, by underestimating the capacity to recognize and alleviate it, should it arise. Democracy, to borrow a phrase from Jane Mansbridge, is always a work in process, and much can be done to address this concern. Thus Archon Fung finds that citizen participation in Chicago policing efforts is greater in poorer neighborhoods (not a very large surprise, given crime rates in different neighborhoods), and that the city, cognizant of obvious concerns about cultural and class bias, invested resources in training participants in policing and schooling efforts.[18] Studying the case of participatory budgeting in Porto Alegre, Rebecca Abers and Gianpaolo Baiocchi find high rates of involvement by poorer, less-educated citizens, and substantial rates of participation by women and Afro-Brazilians.[19] The thread running through these and related cases is that participation is not exogenously given. Deliberative bodies can undertake affirmative measures to address participatory biases. In particular, they can help to train participants in the issues decided by the body and in how to frame arguments about the relevant policies.

Now it might be argued that in the favorable cases just noted, the deliberative bodies aim to solve relatively concrete problems—to improve policy in relatively well-defined areas (say, pertaining to the provision of local public goods)—not to have an open-ended public debate. Inequalities of argumentative skills on broader matters may resist remedy.[20] But evidence from deliberative polling suggests otherwise: deliberative capacities seem reasonably widely shared, even when issues are more abstract and less locally focused. Critics of deliberation, it seems, were too quick to conclude that deliberative decision-making empowers the verbally agile.

2. A second objection is about effectiveness. Thus it might be said that a deliberative process does not mitigate the effects of power on outcomes of collective decisions. In addressing this issue, we face a large methodological problem. As a general matter, and when we put aside the issue of deliberative democracy, it is hard to make an empirically compelling case that process changes produce outcome changes, because changes in process and in result may well both be produced by some third factor: as, for example, when a party with a redistributive project empowers the less advantaged and promotes a shift in economic resources as well, thus suggesting (incorrectly) that the change in process produced the change in result.

A few studies, though not of deliberative democracy, have forcefully addressed these problems of spuriousness. Stephen Ansolabehere, Alan Gerber, and James Snyder have shown that court-ordered reapportionment in the 1960s shifted public goods spending in the states in the direction of previously underrepresented districts: a special case because reapportionment was a court-ordered exogenous shock.[21] Similarly, Raghabendra Chattopadhyay and Esther Duflo have made the case that reserved seats for women on Indian village councils have led to shifts in public goods spending, with greater spending on goods that are preferred by women when the head of the village council is a woman.[22] Here the problem of spuriousness is solved by randomness in the process that determines which village councils will be headed by women. We have no comparably compelling case that increased deliberativeness leads to changes in the content of the decisions.

Still, we have some suggestive evidence. Thus, participatory budgeting in Porto Alegre and in village councils in Kerala appear to have produced substantial shifts in the allocation of public resources to the poor: in Porto Alegre, for example, there is now full coverage of water and sewers, and a threefold increase in school attendance.[23] Similarly, Lucio Baccaro has argued that internal democratic reform in Italian unions produced large shifts in union policy in directions more favorable to the interests of outsiders (pensions, employment, and regional development issues).[24] To be sure, the results in these cases may come not from deliberation, but from broader participation or the dominance of a left party. But deliberation seems to be part of the story, both because deliberation shifts preferences and because it shifts collective decisions by making some proposals harder to defend: namely, proposals that cannot be defended in public on the basis of acceptable reasons. (Baccaro makes a good case that deliberation made the difference.)

3. A third concern is about deliberative pathologies. A social-psychological variant of this concern says that group discussion imposes normative pressure on group members: a variance-reducing pressure not to be less extreme than the group median, and a mean-shifting pressure not to be less extreme than the group mean. A cognitive story claims that group discussion in a relative homogeneous group is dominated by arguments embraced by the majority, so that when people update on a relatively homogeneous argument pool, they consolidate. In either case, it is bad for outsiders.[25]

These are very serious concerns, but at least in principle, the remedies seem straightforward, whatever the likelihood of their adoption. If deliberation under conditions of homogeneity drives polarization, then it is important to ensure that deliberative settings in some way reflect the wider diversity: in some deliberative settings, the competitive quality of the decision—when the issue at stake is the allocation of scarce resources—engenders such expression. In other settings, ensuring diversity of opinion may be a matter of institutional principle or the responsibility of a moderator. In settings of group discussion, this might mean ensuring that some time is devoted to expressing beliefs or judgments that are assumed not to be shared by others in the group: ensuring that this happens seems to be well within the reach of moderators or participants themselves.

Putting it more generally, the point is that studies of deliberative pathologies need to be treated with some care. Those pathologies may emerge from group decision-making conducted without efforts to avoid the pathological results. So such studies may often be interpretable as sources of cautionary notes and recommendations for improvement rather than as undermining the case for deliberation. That said, it is also true that the more fragile deliberation is, the more structure that needs to be in place to move from discussion to good deliberation, the less confidence we can reside in the project of building a more deliberative democracy. A naïve version of the deliberative ideal supposes that people are waiting to deliberate, and need only to get competitive political structures out of the way. Deliberation may be a more fragile accomplishment.

4. The final objection is about naïveté concerning power.[26] Because constraints on what counts as a reason are not well defined, the advantaged will find some way to defend self-serving proposals with considerations that are arguably reasons. For example, they may make appeals to ideas of the common advantage, but press a conception of the common advantage that assigns great weight to a deeply unequal status quo. Or if they fail in this, the advantaged will simply refuse to accept the discipline of deliberation.

If this objection is right, then proposals for deliberative democracy that are inattentive to background relations of power will waste the time of those who can least afford its loss: those now subordinate in power. The time and energy they spend in argument, laboring under the illusion that sweet reason will constrain the power that suppresses them, could have been spent in self-organization, instrumental efforts to increase their own power, or like efforts to impose costs on opponents.

The complaint that deliberative democracy is touchingly naïve about power betrays vertiginously boundless confusion.

First, the importance of background differences in power is not a criticism of the deliberative ideal per se, but a concern about its application. Deliberative democracy is a normative model of collective decision-making, not a universal political strategy. And commitment to the normative ideal does not require commitment to the belief that collective decision-making through mutual reason-giving is always possible. So it may indeed be the case that some rough background balance of power is required before parties will listen to reason. But observing that does not importantly lessen the attraction of the deliberative ideal; it simply states a condition of its reasonable pursuit.

Thus, in Habermas's account of the ideal speech situation, or in my own account of an ideal deliberative procedure, inequalities in power are stipulated away for the sake of presenting an idealized model of deliberation.[27] These idealizations are intended to characterize the nature of reasoned collective decision-making and in turn to provide models for actual arrangements of collective decision-making. But actual arrangements must provide some basis for confidence that joint reasoning will actually prevail in shaping the exercise of collective power, and gross inequalities of power surely undermine any such confidence. So discussion that expresses the deliberative ideal must, for example, operate against a background of free expression and association, thus providing minimal conditions for the availability of relevant information. Equally, if parties are not somehow constrained to accept the consequences of deliberation, if "exit options" are not foreclosed, it seems implausible that they will accept the discipline of joint reasoning, and in particular reasoning informed by the democratic idea of persons as equals. Firms retaining a more or less costless ability to move investment elsewhere are not, for example, likely to accept the discipline of reasoned deliberation about labor standards, with workers as their deliberative equals.

Saying, "If you don't listen to reason, you will pay a high price" is not a joke: it is sometimes necessary to resort to destabilization, threats, and open conflict as answers to people who won't reason in good faith. A sucker may be born every minute, but deliberative democracy is not a recommendation that we all join the club. But if the willingness to reason does depend on the background distribution of power, doesn't that defeat the point of deliberative democracy by reducing deliberation to bargaining under a balance of power? Not at all. Once people do listen to reason, the results may reflect not only the balance of power that defeated their previous imperviousness, but also their attentiveness to reasons that can be shared. If I need to drink some espresso to concentrate hard enough to prove a theorem, it does not reduce theorem-proving to a caffeine high. So, similarly, paying attention to power and threats to exercise it doesn't reduce deliberation to bargaining. To suppose otherwise is like thinking that if you need to trust your math teacher in order to learn how to do a proof, then there is nothing more to proof than trust. It confuses conditions that make an activity possible with that activity itself.

5. Some Tensions Between Participation and Deliberation

I started by noting two strands in the radical-democratic tradition: participatory and deliberative. But I have not said much at all about political participation: deliberative democracy is about political reasoning, not the breadth and depth of participation. To be very brief: participation is particularly important in connection with achieving fair political equality, because shifting the basis of political contestation from organized money to organized people is a promising alternative to the influence conferred by wealth. Similarly, expanding and deepening citizen participation may be the most promising strategy for challenging political inequalities associated with traditional social and political hierarchies. Moreover, it may be important in encouraging a sense of political responsibility.

But participation is one thing, and deliberation is another, and they may pull in different directions. Consider three sources of tension.[28]

1. Improving the quality of deliberation may come at a cost to public participation. Suppose, for example, that legislators, regulators, and judges were to embrace a deliberative form of decision-making. Instead of seeking to advance the interests of their constituents or single-mindedly maximizing their prospects of reelection, for example, legislators would engage in reasonable discussion and argument about policies. Judges would, in turn, reinforce the legislators by requiring explicit attention to reasons in legislative and administrative decision-making. But doing so might require insulation from public pressures.

2. Expanding participation—either the numbers of people, or the range of issues under direct popular control—may diminish the quality of deliberation. Initiatives and referenda, for example, allow voters to exercise more direct and precisely targeted influence over legislation, policy questions, and even elected officials. But far from improving deliberation, such measures—in part because they ultimately focus on a yes/no decision on a well-defined proposition—may discourage reasoned discussion in creating legislation. And even bringing people together to discuss specific laws and policies may—with a homogeneous collection of people, or a lack of commitment to addressing a common problem—

diminish deliberation, as discussion dissolves into posturing, recrimination, and manipulation.[29]

3. More fundamentally, social complexity and scale limit the extent to which modern polities can be both deliberative and participatory. Deliberation depends on participants with sufficient knowledge and interest about the substantive issues under consideration. But on any issue, the number of individuals with such knowledge and interest is bound to be relatively small, and so the quality of deliberation will decline with the scope of participation. Of course, knowledge and interest are not fixed, and deliberation may improve both. Still, time and resource constraints make it undesirable for any particular area of public governance to be both fully deliberative and inclusively participatory.

6. And So?

These three tensions notwithstanding, public decision-making in liberal democracies could become both more participatory and deliberative. The challenge is to devise practical projects that can incorporate both. Radical democrats have two broad strategies for achieving that aim, which I will sketch in very broad strokes.

The first aims to join deliberation with mass democracy by promoting citizen deliberation on political matters in what Habermas calls the "informal public sphere," constituted by networks of associations in civil society.[30] Because such informal discussion does not aim at a practical decision but—insofar as it has an aim—at informed opinion, it can pursue an unencumbered discussion about political values and public goals. Moreover, these dispersed discussions—one element of a political society's process of collective decision-making—are potentially very broadly participatory, for they take place through structures of numerous, open secondary associations and social movements. For this mix of mass democracy and deliberation, the essential ingredients, apart from ensuring basic liberties, are a diverse and independent media; vibrant, independent civil associations; and political parties that operate independently from concentrated wealth and help to focus public debate. All of this arguably helps to foster deliberative capacities—a point I mentioned earlier, and promised to return to. The marriage of open communication in the informal public sphere with a translation—through elections and legislative debate—of opinion formed there into law provides, on this view, the best hope for achieving a greater mix of participation and deliberation under conditions of mass democracy and a rule of law.

Much of the attractiveness of this view, then, hinges first upon the deliberativeness of discourse in the public sphere and then upon the strength of the links between such deliberation and the decisions of legislative bodies and administrative agencies. But because dispersed, informal public deliberation and public policy are only loosely linked, a more participatory and deliberative informal public sphere may have little impact on decisions by formal institutions.

Citizen participation in the informal public sphere, then, may be of limited political relevance, and the marriage of reason with mass democracy may proceed in splendid isolation from the exercise of power. To be clear: I am not here objecting to this first approach, only pointing to a concern and a possible limitation.

A second radical-democratic approach builds on the distinctive practical competence that citizens possess as users of public services, subjects of public policy and regulation, or as residents with contextual knowledge of their circumstances. The idea is to draw on these competencies by bringing ordinary citizens into relatively focused deliberations over public issues. Typically, such strategies create opportunities for limited numbers of citizens to deliberate with one another or with officials to improve the quality of some public decision, perhaps by injecting local knowledge, new perspectives, and excluded interests, or by enhancing public accountability.

One approach randomly selects small groups of citizens to deliberate on general political issues such as laws and public policies. Citizen juries in the United States and planning cells in Germany, for example, empanel small groups (12–40) of randomly selected citizens to discuss issues such as agriculture, health policy, and local development concerns.[31] James Fishkin and his colleagues have sponsored larger gatherings of 300–500 citizens—with randomization—to deliberate upon such issues as the adoption of the Euro in Denmark, public utility regulation in Texas, and U.S. foreign assistance.[32] On an ambitious *analytical* interpretation, postdeliberation polls provide insight into what *the people* think about a policy issue. Political impact is another matter. As with citizens' juries and planning cells, their political impact—to the extent that they have impact—comes from their capacity to serve in an advisory role, and to alter public opinion or change the minds of public officials.

Another strategy convenes groups of citizens to deliberate and develop solutions to particular problems of public concern. Such participatory-deliberative arrangements—characteristic in different ways of associative democracy and directly deliberative polyarchy—differ from political juries in two main ways. Whereas political juries usually consider *general* issues such as economic, health care, or crime policy, these deliberations aim to address more specific problems, such as the management of an ecosystem, the operation of a public school or school district, crime in a neighborhood, or a city's allocation of resources across projects and neighborhoods. Whereas political juries recruit impartial and disinterested citizens by randomly selecting them, participatory-deliberative arrangements recruit participants with strong interests in the problems under deliberation.

Because of the specificity of these arrangements, citizens may well enjoy advantages in knowledge and experience over officials. In Chicago, for example, residents deliberate regularly with police officers in each neighborhood to set priorities on addressing issues of public safety, using their background knowledge as a basis for deliberation. And in Porto Alegre citizens meet regularly at the neighborhood level to agree upon priorities for public investment (for example, street paving, sanitation, and housing); the capital portion of the city's budget is produced by aggregating the priorities that emerge from those deliberations.

Participatory-deliberative arrangements—in areas such as education, social services, ecosystems, community development, and health services—show promising contributions to political equality by increasing popular engagement in political decision-making. As I mentioned earlier, in Chicago's community policing program, for example, participation rates in low-income neighborhoods are much higher than those in wealthy neighborhoods. Similarly, poor people are substantially overrepresented in both the budgeting institutions of Porto Alegre and local development and planning initiatives in Kerala, India. Directly democratic arrangements that address problems of particular urgency to disadvantaged citizens can invert the usual participation bias in favor of wealth, education, and high status. They can also, however, create large potential political inequalities. If systematic and enduring differences—in deliberative capabilities, disposable resources, or demographic factors—separate those who participate from those who do not, decisions generated by participatory-deliberative arrangements will likely serve the interests of participants at the expense of others.

The proliferation of directly deliberative institutions fosters democratic self-government by subjecting the policies and actions of agencies such as these to a rule of common reason. But these contributions to self-government are, however, limited by the scope of these institutions. Most participatory-deliberative governance efforts aim to address local concerns and do not extend to broader issues of policy and public priorities. Moreover, there is the danger of administrative "capture": that by entering the circuit of regulatory problem-solving with its pragmatic concern about the effectiveness of policy, participating citizens and groups lose their capacity for independent action and their sense of the importance of open-ended reflection and morally motivated criticism and innovation.[33] They may become dependent on the state and its official recognition for power and resources, and their political horizon may come to be undesirably confined by attention to policy constraints. If this is right, then the alleged limitation of informal, society-wide deliberation—the fact that its impact is so indirect—is really its virtue. The precondition of the unconstrained discussion on which public deliberation depends requires distance between civil society's associative life and the state's decision-making routines.

Final Reflections

So achieving both participation and deliberation is complicated. But because of their more direct bearing on the exercise of power, participatory-deliberative arrangements have a particular promise as a strategy for achieving the ends of radical democracy. Two large challenges, however, lie on that path.

The first concerns the relationship between conventional institutions of political representation and participatory-deliberative arrangements.[34] Participatory-deliberative arrangements make it possible to address practical problems that seem recalcitrant to treatment by conventional political institutions. But those arrangements are not a wholesale replacement of conventional political institutions: they have limited scope and limited numbers of direct participants. To the extent that they are successful, however, participatory-deliberative arrangements and conventional political representation can be transformed and linked so that each strengthens the other. If such arrangements became a common form of local and administrative problem-solving, the role of legislatures and public agencies would shift from directly solving a range of social problems to supporting the efforts of many participatory deliberations, maintaining their democratic integrity, and ensuring their coordination. Conversely, those who participated directly in these new deliberative arrangements would form a highly informed, mobilized, and active base that would enhance the mandate and legitimacy of elected representatives and other officials.

The second challenge is to extend the scope of radical democracy. Can participatory deliberation help democratize large-scale decisions about public priorities—war and peace, health insurance, public pensions, and the distribution of wealth? One way to address these larger questions is to connect the disciplined, practical, participatory deliberations about solving particular problems, such as efforts to reduce asthma rates in a low-income community or to provide decent medical care in New Orleans or Los Angeles, to the wider public sphere of debate and opinion formation about the costs of health care, access to it, and the importance of health relative to other basic goods. Participants in direct deliberations are informed by the dispersed discussions in the informal public sphere, and those more focused deliberations in turn invest public discussion with a practicality it might otherwise lack. The ambitious hope is that citizens who participate in constructing solutions to concrete problems in local public life may in turn engage more deeply in informal deliberation in the wider public sphere and in formal political institutions as well.

In the end, then, radical democracy—understood as an effort to combine the values of both participation and deliberation—has promise to be a distinctive form of democracy in which the informal public sphere and conventional democratic institutions are reshaped by their connections with participatory-deliberative arrangements for solving problems. Whether it will deliver on that promise remains, of course, a very open question.

Notes

1. For representative ideas, see John Roemer, *Equal Shares: Making Market Socialism Work* (New York and London: Verso, 1996); Samuel Bowles and Herbert Gintis, *Recasting Egalitarianism: New Rules for Communities, States, and Markets* (New York and London: Verso,

1999); Stuart White, *The Civic Minimum* (Oxford: Oxford University Press, 2003); Bruce Ackerman and Anne Alstott, *The Stakeholder Society* (New Haven, CT: Yale University Press, 2000); and Richard Freeman, *The New Inequality* (Boston: Beacon Press, 1998).

2. I have written elsewhere on this radical-democratic project: with Joel Rogers (on associative democracy), Chuck Sabel (on deliberative polyarchy), and Archon Fung (on participation and deliberation). In writing this essay, I have drawn freely on this joint work, and I am very grateful to my coauthors for the collaborations that produced it. See Joshua Cohen and Joel Rogers, *Associations and Democracy* (London: Verso, 1995); Joshua Cohen and Charles Sabel, "Directly Deliberative Polyarchy," *European Law Journal* 3, 4 (December 1997): 313–342; Joshua Cohen and Joel Rogers, "Power and Reason," in *Deepening Democracy: Institutional Innovations in Empowered Participatory Governance*, edited by Archon Fung and Erik Olin Wright (New York and London: Verso, 2003); Joshua Cohen and Charles Sabel, "Global Democracy?," *New York University Journal of International Law and Policy* 37, 4 (2006): 763–797; and Joshua Cohen and Archon Fung, "Radical Democracy," *Swiss Journal of Political Science* 10, 4 (2004): 23–24.

3. Rousseau himself explored other forms of democratic participation, particularly in his *The Government of Poland*, translated by Willmoore Kendall (Indianapolis: Hackett, 1985), where considerations of size precluded direct citizen participation in lawmaking.

4. Jürgen Habermas, *Legitimation Crisis*, translated by Thomas McCarthy (Boston: Beacon Press, 1973), 108. In this passage, Habermas is not describing an idealized democracy, but a hypothetical situation suited to the justification of norms.

5. We now have many statements of the deliberative conception. For my own, which I draw on here, see Joshua Cohen, "Deliberation and Democratic Legitimacy," in *The Good Polity*, edited by Alan Hamlin and Phillip Pettit (Oxford: Blackwell, 1989), "Procedure and Substance in Deliberative Democracy," in *Democracy and Difference: Changing Boundaries of the Political*, edited by Seyla Benhabib (Princeton, NJ: Princeton University Press, 1996), "Democracy and Liberty," in *Deliberative Democracy*, edited by Jon Elster (Cambridge: Cambridge University Press, 1998), and "Privacy, Pluralism, and Democracy," in *Law and Social Justice*, edited by Joseph Keim Campbell, Michael O'Rourke, and David Shier (Cambridge, MA: MIT Press, 2005).

6. Carl Schmitt, *The Crisis of Parliamentary Democracy*, translated by Ellen Kennedy (Cambridge, MA: MIT Press, 1985), 6.

7. In *Is Democracy Possible Here?* (Cambridge, MA: Harvard University Press, 2006), Ronald Dworkin emphasizes the importance of education in a well-functioning, deliberative democracy, and asserts that "the most daunting but also most urgent requirement is to make a Contemporary Politics course part of every high school curriculum" (148). The idea of such a course is sensible enough, but it hardly seems the most urgent issue about the reform of our educational system, for the purposes of fostering the partnership in argument that is so central to democracy.

8. As Rawls observes, an idea of public reason is one of the "essential elements of deliberative democracy." See John Rawls, "The Idea of Public Reason Revisited," in *The Law of Peoples* (Cambridge, MA: Harvard University Press, 1999), 139.

9. On problems with deliberation under a unanimity rule, see David Austen-Smith and Timothy Feddersen, "Deliberation, Preference Uncertainty, and Voting Rules," *American Political Science Review* 100 (2006): 209–218.

10. See, for example, Jürgen Habermas, *Between Facts and Norms*, translated by William Rehg (Cambridge, MA: MIT Press, 1996), 296, 304.

11. The emphasis on deliberation as reason-giving is not captured in models of deliberation as cheap talk signaling, where the point is to convey some piece of private information, and success depends on beliefs about the trustworthiness of the speaker (see Austen-Smith and Feddersen, "Deliberation, Preference Uncertainty, and Voting Rules"). For an interesting effort to model deliberation as reasoning—arguing from premises to conclusions, where individuals can check the quality of the reasoning themselves—see Catherine Hafer and Dimitri Landa, "Deliberation as Self-Discovery and Institutions for Political Speech," *Journal of Theoretical Politics* 19, 3 (2007): 329–360.

12. Amy Gutmann and Dennis Thompson, *Why Deliberative Democracy?* (Princeton, NJ: Princeton University Press, 2004), 3.

13. Jon Elster, "Introduction," in *Deliberative Democracy*, 8.

14. John Dryzek, *Deliberative Democracy and Beyond* (Oxford: Oxford University Press, 2004), 31.

15. Ibid., 8.

16. Ibid., 167 and, in general, chap. 3.

17. I believe that Lynn Sanders was the first to raise this objection, in "Against Deliberation," *Political Theory* (1997): 347–376.

18. Archon Fung, *Empowered Participation: Reinventing Urban Democracy* (Princeton, NJ: Princeton University Press, 2004), chap. 4.

19. See Rebecca Abers, "Reflections on What Makes Empowered Participatory Governance Happen," in *Deepening Democracy*, 206, and, more generally, her *Inventing Local Democracy* (Boulder, CO: Lynne Rienner, 2000); Gianpaolo Baiocchi, *Militants and Citizens: The Politics of Participatory Democracy in Porto Alegre* (Stanford, CA: Stanford University Press, 2005).

20. In his critique of deliberative democracy, Posner is less hostile to locally focused discussion about the provision of public goods, perhaps for reasons of the kind noted in the text. See Richard A. Posner, *Law, Pragmatism, and Democracy* (Cambridge, MA: Harvard University Press, 2003).

21. Stephen Ansolabehere, Alan Gerber, and James M. Snyder, "Equal Votes, Equal Money: Court-Ordered Redistricting and the Distribution of Public Expenditure in the American States," *American Political Science Review* (August 2002): 767–777.

22. Raghabendra Chattopadhyay and Esther Duflo, "Women as Policy Makers: Evidence from a Randomized Policy Experiment in India," *Econometrica* 72, 5 (2004): 1409–1443.

23. Gianpaolo Baiocchi, "The Citizens of Porto Alegre," *Boston Review* 31, 2 (March–April 2006).

24. Lucio Baccaro, "The Construction of Democratic Corporatism in Italy," *Politics and Society* 30, 2 (June 2002): 327–357.

25. Cass Sunstein, "Group Judgments: Statistical Means, Deliberation, and Information Markets," *NYU Law Review* 80 (June 2005): 962–1049; and Tali Mendelberg's very instructive discussion of deliberation and small-group decision-making, in "The Deliberative Citizen: Theory and Evidence," in *Political Decision-Making, Deliberation, and Participation: Research in Micropolitics*, edited by Michael X. Delli Carpini, Leonie Huddy, and Robert Shapiro, vol. 6 (Greenwich, CT: JAI Press, 2002), 151–193.

26. See Cohen and Rogers, "Power and Reason."

27. See Cohen, "Deliberation and Democratic Legitimacy"; and Habermas, *Between Facts and Norms*, chap. 7.

28. Diana Mutz explores a different tension between deliberation and participation in her important book, *Hearing the Other Side: Deliberative Versus Participatory Democracy*

(Cambridge: Cambridge University Press, 2006). Mutz argues that deliberation among the diverse encourages greater toleration, but dampens participation because of a desire to avoid conflict with the people to whom one talks. Participation in turn is animated by a sense of passion that is dampened by deliberation. I am not sure that Mutz's results extend outside participation in highly competitive political settings. But the challenge she raises is deep and needs to be addressed.

29. See, for example, Derek Bell, "The Referendum: Democracy's Barrier to Racial Equality," *Washington Law Review* 54, 1 (1978): 1–29; and Yannis Papadopolous, "A Framework for Analysis of Functions and Dysfunctions of Direct Democracy: Top-Down and Bottom-Up Perspectives," *Politics and Society* 23 (1995): 421–448.

30. Habermas, *Between Facts and Norms*, chap. 8; John Rawls, *Political Liberalism* (New York: Columbia University Press, 1996), 14, 382–383.

31. Julia Abelson, Pierre-Gerlier Forest, John Eyles, Patricia Smith, Elisabeth Martin, and François-Pierre Gauvin, "Deliberations About Deliberative Methods: Issues in the Design and Evaluation of Public Participation Processes," *Social Science and Medicine* 57 (2003): 239–251; Ned Crosby, "Citizens' Juries: One Solution for Difficult Environmental Questions," in *Fairness and Competence in Citizen Participation: Evaluating Models for Environmental Discourse*, edited by O. Renn, T. Webler, and P. Wiedelmann (Boston: Kluwer Academic Press, 1995), 157–174; G. Smith and C. Wales, "The Theory and Practice of Citizens' Juries," *Policy and Politics* 27, 3 (1999): 295–308; John Gastil, *By Popular Demand* (Berkeley and Los Angeles: University of California Press, 2000).

32. For a sketch of polls and implications, see Bruce Ackerman and James Fishkin, *Deliberation Day* (New Haven, CT: Yale University Press, 2005), esp. chap. 3.

33. See Lucio Baccaro and Konstantinos Papadakis, "The Downside of Deliberative Public Administration" (unpublished).

34. For discussion of the issues sketched here, see Cohen and Sabel, "Directly Deliberative Polyarchy"; Cohen and Sabel, "Global Democracy?"; and Joshua Cohen and Charles Sabel, "Sovereignty and Solidarity in the EU," in *Governing Work and Welfare in a New Economy: European and American Experiments*, edited by Jonathan Zeitlin and David Trubek (Oxford: Oxford University Press, 2003), 345–375.

Discussion Questions: Democracy

1. If a computer could be programmed to render wise decisions about public policy, would democratic decision-making thereby be rendered unnecessary?
2. Why should those in the minority on an issue accept a policy passed by the majority?
3. Is public deliberation necessary to legitimate democratic decisions?

Part V

HUMAN RIGHTS

The history of political philosophy has focused on sovereign states and the individuals living within them. Much contemporary work, however, recognizes distinctive issues that concern relations between different states and citizens living in different parts of the world. Among the most pressing of these issues are the moral obligations among citizens of different nations.

Onora O'Neill raises several philosophical concerns about the idea of human rights, arguing that they are strange because they assign no definite obligations to particular agents. Thomas Pogge is concerned fundamentally with the questions of what governments and citizens of wealthy, resource-rich nations owe to persons living in impoverished nations. On Pogge's view the governments and citizens of the well-off nations in part cause poverty in other parts of the world and therefore are morally obligated to take appropriate steps to alleviate the situation. Finally, Martha Nussbaum calls attention to some unsettling empirical facts about gender and global poverty. She argues that a capabilities approach to justice is better able than competing theories to address international problems.

READING 13

The Dark Side of Human Rights

ONORA O'NEILL

In his *Reflections on the Revolution in France* Edmund Burke asks, "What is the use of discussing a man's abstract right to food or medicine? The question is upon the method of procuring and administering them. In that deliberation I shall always advise to call in the aid of the farmer and the physician rather than the professor of metaphysics."[1]

Burke's question is sharp. What is the point of having a right? More specifically, what is the point of having an abstract right unless you also have a way of securing whatever it is that you have a right to? Why should we prize natural or abstract rights if there is no way of ensuring their delivery? And if we need to secure their delivery, are not "the farmer and the physician" not merely of greater use than abstract or natural rights, but also of greater use than positive rights to claim food or medicine? For a hungry person, positive and justiciable rights to food are, to be sure, better than abstract rights that are not justiciable: but those who know how to grow, harvest, store, and cook food are more useful, and having the food is better still. When we are ill, positive and justiciable rights to health care are, to be sure, better than abstract rights that are not justiciable: but skilled doctors and nurses are more useful, and receiving their care is better still.

In a way it is surprising to find Burke discussing abstract rights to food or health care, for these presumed rights came to full prominence only in the late twentieth century. They are commonly called welfare rights, and contrasted with liberty rights. This, I think, is a misnomer. The salient feature of these rights is not that they contribute to the welfare of the recipient (although they are likely to do so), but that they are rights to goods or services. If there are to be rights to goods or services, those goods and services must be provided, and more specifically provided *by someone*—for example, by the farmer and the physician.

Most of the abstract rights against which Burke campaigned were the rights proclaimed in the *Declaration of the Rights of Man and of the Citizen* of 1789

(*Declaration of 1789*). They are what we now call liberty rights. The short list in Article 2 of the *Declaration* states succinctly, "The natural rights of man, which must not be prevented . . . are freedom, property, security and resistance to oppression."[2] Needless to say, the right to property is not to be understood as a right to some amount of property, but as a right to security of tenure of property: it too is a liberty right, not a right to any goods or services.[3] Much of the *Declaration of 1789* is concerned with the rights to process needed to make liberty rights justiciable: rights to the rule of law, to habeas corpus, to what we would now call accountable public administration. The rights of the *Declaration of 1789* are rights against *all* others and *all* institutions. Liberty rights are universal—and so are the corresponding obligations. They are compromised if *any* others are exempt from those counterpart obligations. If anyone may infringe my rights to freedom, property, and security, or to resist oppression, I have only incomplete and blemished rights of these sorts.

On closer consideration, matters have turned out to be rather more complicated. The institutions for securing and enforcing liberty rights require an allocation of certain obligations to specified others rather than to all others. First-order obligations to respect liberty rights must be universal, but second-order obligations to ensure that everyone respects liberty rights must be allocated. There is no effective rule of law without law enforcement, and law enforcement needs law enforcers who are assigned specific tasks; there is no effective accountability of public administration without institutions that allocate the tasks and responsibilities and hold specified officeholders to account. Nevertheless, the asymmetry between abstract liberty rights and abstract rights to goods and services is convincing: we can know who violates a liberty right without any allocation of obligations, but we cannot tell who violates a right to goods or services unless obligations have been allocated.

This well-known point has not impeded the rise of an international human rights culture that is replete with claims about abstract rights to goods and services, now seen as universal human rights, but often muddled or vague, or both, about the allocation of the obligations without which these rights not merely cannot be met, but remain undefined. The cornucopia of universal human rights includes both liberty rights and rights to goods and services, and specifically rights to food and rights to health care.[4] The right to food is proclaimed in Article II of the 1966 *International Covenant on Economic, Social, and Cultural Rights* (*CESCR*), which asserts "the right of everyone to an adequate standard of living for himself and his family, including adequate food, clothing and housing, and to the continuous improvement of living conditions" (the *continuous improvement* is a nice touch!).[5] Article II of *CESCR* has been adopted as a guiding principle of the Food and Agriculture Organization (FAO), which has made its mission "food security for all."[6] The right to health (to *health*, not just to *health care*: another nice touch!) is proclaimed in Article I2 of the *CESCR*, which recognizes "the right of everyone to the enjoyment of the highest attainable standard of physical and mental health."[7] Article 12 has been adopted as the guiding principle of the World Health Organisation (WHO).[8]

There is an interesting difference between Articles 11 and 12 of *CESCR*. The right to food is viewed as a right to *adequate food*, not to the *best attainable food*; the right to health is viewed as a right to the *highest attainable standard . . . of health*, and not as a *right to adequate health*. One can see why the drafters of the *Covenant* may have shrunk from proclaiming a *right to adequate health*, but in qualifying this right as a *right to the highest attainable standard of health* many questions were begged. Is this right only a right to the standard of health that a person can attain with locally available and affordable treatment—however meager that may be? Or is it a right to the highest standard available globally—however expensive that may be? The first is disappointingly minimal, and the latter barely coherent (how can everyone have a right to the best?). And what is required of the farmer, the physician, and others who actually have to provide food and health care? Uncertainties of this sort are unavoidable unless the obligations that correspond to rights to goods and services are well specified.

Norms, Aspirations, and Cynicism

Does any of this matter? Perhaps we should view the Declarations and Covenants that promulgate human rights as setting out noble aspirations, which are helpful to articulate and bear in mind when establishing institutions, programmes, policies, and activities that allocate obligations. In effect, we would concede that the rhetoric of universal human rights to goods or services was deceptive, but defend it as a noble lie that helps to mobilize support for establishing justiciable rights of great importance. There is something to be said for this view of human rights Declarations and Covenants as ideological documents that can help mobilize energy for action that makes a difference, but many would see this as cynical.

In any case, this interpretation of human rights claims would be wholly at odds with ordinary understandings of rights. Both liberty rights and rights to goods and services are standardly seen as *claim-rights or entitlements* that are valid against those with the counterpart obligations. Rights are seen as one side of a normative relationship between right-holders and obligation-bearers. We normally regard supposed claims or entitlements that nobody is obliged to respect or honour as null and void, indeed undefined. An understanding of the normative arguments that link rights to obligations underlies daily and professional discussion both of supposedly *universal* human rights, and of the *special* rights created by specific voluntary actions and transactions (treaty, contract, promise, marriage, etc.). There cannot be a claim to rights that are rights against nobody, or nobody in particular: universal rights will be rights against all comers; special rights will be rights against specifiable others.

Only if we jettison the entire normative understanding of rights in favour of a merely aspirational view can we break the normative link between rights and their counterpart obligations. If we take rights seriously and see them as normative rather than aspirational, we must take obligations seriously. If on the other hand we opt for a merely aspirational view, the costs are high. For then we would also have to accept that where human rights are unmet, there is no breach of obligation, nobody at fault, nobody who can be held to account, nobody to blame, and nobody who owes redress. We would in effect have to accept that human rights claims are not real claims.

Most advocates of human rights would be reluctant to jettison the thought that they are *prescriptive* or *normative* in favour of seeing them as merely *aspirational*.[9] We generally view human rights claims as setting out requirements from the standpoint of recipients, who are *entitled to* or *have a claim to* action or forbearance by others with corresponding obligations. From a normative or prescriptive view, the point of human rights claims would be eroded if nobody were required to act or forbear to meet these claims. A normative view of rights claims has to take obligations seriously, since they are the counterparts to rights; it must view them as articulating the normative requirements that fall either on all or on specified obligation-bearers. Few proponents of human rights would countenance the thought that there are human rights that nobody is obliged to respect. (The converse thought is unproblematic: there can be obligations even where no claimants are defined; such "imperfect" obligations are generally seen as moral obligations, but not as obligations of justice with counterpart rights.)

The claim that rights must have well-specified counterpart obligations is not equivalent to the commonplace piety that rights and responsibilities go together, which asserts only that right-holders are also obligation-bearers. This is often, but not always, true. Many agents—citizens, workers, students, teachers, employees—are both right-holders and obligation-bearers. But some right-holders—infants, the severely disabled, the senile—cannot carry obligations, so have no responsibilities. By contrast, the claim that rights must have counterpart obligations asserts the exceptionless logical point that where anyone is to have a right, there must be identifiable others (either all others or specified others) with accurately corresponding obligations. From a normative view of rights, obligations and claimable rights are two perspectives on a single normative pattern: without the obligations there are no rights. So while obligations will drop out of sight if we read human rights "claims" merely as aspirations rather than requirements, so too will rights, as they are usually understood. Unsurprisingly, aspirational readings of human rights documents are not popular. However, such readings at least offer an exit strategy if we conclude that claiming rights without specifying counterpart obligations is an unacceptable deception, and find that we can't develop an adequate normative account of obligations and rights.

Clearly it would be preferable to offer a serious account of the allocation of obligations that correspond to all human rights. But do Declarations and Covenants provide an account—or even a clue—to the allocation of the obligations that are the counterparts to rights to goods and services? This point was complicated at the birth of human rights by the unfortunately obscure drafting of the 1948 *UDHR*,[10] which gestures to the thought that certain obligations lie with states, then confusingly assigns them indifferently to nations, countries, and peoples as well as states. Not all of these have the integrated capacities for action and decision-making needed for agency, and so for carrying obligations. For present purposes I shall leave problems arising from this unfortunate drafting aside, and rely on the fact that in later documents, including *CESCR*, these ambiguities are apparently resolved in favour of assigning obligations to states party, that is, to the signatory states.

This approach has apparent advantages—and stings in its tail. The first sting is that states that do not ratify a Covenant will not incur the obligations it specifies: not a welcome conclusion to advocates of universal human rights, since these states thereby escape obligations to respect, let alone enforce, the rights promulgated. The second sting is sharper. The obligations created by signing and ratifying Covenants are *special*, not *universal* obligations. So the rights that are their corollaries will also be *special* or *institutional rights*, not *universal human rights*. Once we take a normative view of rights and obligations, they must be properly matched. If human rights are independent of institutional structures, if they are not created by special transactions, so too are the corresponding obligations; conversely if obligations are the creatures of convention, so too are the rights.

These unwelcome implications of taking the human rights documents at face value might be avoided in several ways. One well-known thought is that so long as we confine ourselves to liberty rights, there is no allocation problem, since these rights are only complete if *all* others are obliged to respect them. We can coherently see universal liberty rights as independent of institutions or transactions, and read the parts of instruments that deal with liberty rights as affirming rather than creating those rights (justifying such claims would be a further task). But the fact that liberty rights do not face an allocation problem (although enforcing them raises just that problem) offers small comfort to those who hope to show that rights to goods or services—for example, to food and medicine—are universal human rights rather than the creatures of convention. A normative view of human rights cannot view rights to food and medicine as preinstitutional while denying that there are any preinstitutional counterpart obligations or obligation-holders; it must take a congruent view of the counterpart obligations. But this suggests that such rights must be special, institutional rights rather than universal human rights. There is, of course, nothing wrong or problematic about conventional or institutional rights, but if Declarations and Covenants create rights to goods and services, claims that they are universal or human rights lack justification. Declarations and Covenants cannot show that some particular configuration of institutional rights and obligations is universally optimal or desirable, or even justifiable.

This dilemma might be fudged by allowing the idea of human rights to goods and services to drift between two interpretations. A view of rights to goods and services as independent of institutions and transactions could be cited as offering a basis for justifying some rather than other institutional arrangements. A view of rights to goods and services as the creatures of convention could fit with well-defined counterpart institutional obligations, but offers no claims about their justification other than the fact that (some) states have signed up to them. Equivocation is a desperate justificatory strategy. Yet this equivocation is disconcertingly common in discussions of human rights claims.

This dilemma within normative views of rights and obligations can be resolved in more than one way. We could conclude that liberty rights are fundamental and universal, and claim that they can be justified without reference to Covenants or institutions, but concede that rights to goods and services are special (institutional, positive) rights that can be justified only by appeal to specific transactions, such as signing and ratifying Covenants. We could try to justify a configuration of special rights and the institutional structures that secure them and their counterpart obligations. For example, we might argue that certain rights to goods and services and their counterpart obligations protect basic human needs or interests, or that they have utilitarian or economic justification. Or we could justify institutional structures that define and secure special rights and obligations more deeply by appealing to a theory of the good (moral realists) or a theory of duty (Kantians). The option that is closed is to claim that human rights and obligations are corollary normative claims, but that there are some universal rights without counterpart obligations. So there are plenty of possibilities—although each may raise its own difficulties. If none of these possibilities can be made to work, the default position would be to reject normative views of human rights and to see human rights claims as aspirational (noting that aspirations need justification too) and to treat the task of establishing institutions that allow for justiciable claims as a task to be guided in part by appealing to those aspirations. And then, it may seem, we in effect endorse a cynical reading of the human rights Declarations and Covenants.

State Obligations

These are awkward problems, but I think that others may lie deeper. The deepest problem may be that the obligations assigned to states by some of the most significant Declarations and Covenants are *not* the corollaries of the human rights that the documents proclaim. The Covenants do not assign states straightforward obligations to respect liberty rights (after all, liberty rights have to be respected by all, not only by states), but rather second-order obligations to *secure* respect for them. Equally, they do not assign states obligations to meet rights to goods and services, but rather second-order obligations to *ensure* that they are met. For example, Article 2 of the *CESCR* proclaims that "each State Party to the present Covenant undertakes to take steps, individually and through international assistance and co-operation, especially economic and technical, to the maximum of its available resources, with a view to achieving progressively the full realisation of the rights recognized in the present Covenant by all appropriate means, including particularly the adoption of legislative measures."[11]

"Achieving progressively the full realisation of . . . rights . . . by all appropriate means" is evidently not merely a matter of respecting the rights recognized in *CESCR*. It is a matter of ensuring that others—both individuals and institutions—carry out the obligations that correspond to those rights. Later comments by the Office of the High Commissioner for Human Rights spell out some of the obligations that states are taken to assume if they ratify the two Covenants.[12]

An immediate and encouraging thought might be that if the obligations assigned to states by the international Declarations and Covenants are *not* the counterparts of the human rights proclaimed, but second-order obligations to ensure or secure respect for such rights, then this may resolve the allocation problem for rights to goods and services. States party to a Covenant are seen as acquiring special obligations by signing and ratifying the instrument. It would then be clear that those special, second-order obligations did not have counterpart rights, let alone counterpart universal human rights. They are second-order obligations to secure some configuration of first-order rights and obligations. This thought may be helpful: since obligations without counterpart rights are normatively coherent (unlike rights without counterpart obligations), we can take a normative view of the obligations assumed by states that sign and ratify the Covenants, and can see them as setting requirements. Human rights enter into the Covenants only indirectly as aspects of the content of second-order state obligations.

But a second thought is far less congenial to those who would like to see human rights as normative. If the obligations that the Declarations and Covenants assign to states are *not* the counterparts of the human rights these instruments declare or recognize, then they also do not define the first-order obligations that are the counterparts of human rights. Rather the problem of giving a coherent normative instantiation of Declarations and Covenants is devolved to the states party, which may (or may not) set out to secure positive rights for their citizens. If the claims of the human rights documents have normative force, they must be matched by obligations; if they are not matched by obligations, they are *at best* aspirational.

As I suggested earlier, it may not be wholly a misfortune if the supposed rights declared in the Declarations and Covenants are seen as aspirations. Legal commentators might be willing to say that there is still substance in there, in that the states partly take on real obligations to realize these aspirations. Nonlawyers may habitually make the mistake of thinking that Declarations and Covenants claim that there are preinstitutional universal human rights, but their mistake is not necessary—although politically convenient—for progress towards the realisation of the underlying aspirations once states have signed up. This is a coherent position, but unlikely to be popular with those who seek to base ethical and political claims on appeals to human rights, which they see as normatively fundamental rather than as the creatures of the convention that are anchored in the Covenants that assign obligations to realize aspirations to states.

And there are further difficulties. If we read Declarations and Covenants as instruments by which states assume second-order obligations to define and allocate first-order obligations that correspond to certain human rights (now no longer seen as universal rights), why should all the obligations lie with states? A plausible answer would be that states, and only states, have the powers necessary to carry the relevant second-order obligations to define and allocate first-order obligations and rights to individuals and institutions. The story is told of a journalist who asked the bank robber Willie Sutton why he robbed banks and got the puzzled answer "That's where the money is." Similarly we might reply to anyone who wonders why Declarations and Covenants assign obligations that are to secure human rights to states by pointing out that that's where the power is.

But the thought that it makes sense to assign all second-order obligations to define and allocate obligations to states because they, and only they, have the power to discharge these obligations is often less than comforting. Many states violate rather than respect human rights. Assigning second-order obligations to define and allocate first-order obligations and rights to agents who do not even reliably respect the first-order obligations that correspond to those rights may be rather like putting foxes in charge of henhouses. It is true enough that those who are to achieve progressively the full realization of human rights must have capacities to do so—but it does not follow that those with (a good range of) the necessary capacities can be trusted to do so. Some states—not only those we think of as rogue states—disregard or override many of the Covenant rights. Some sign and ratify the relevant international instruments, but make limited efforts to work towards their full realization.

Other states lack the power to carry the obligations to "achieve progressively the full realisation of the rights recognized" in Declarations and Covenants. Weak states—failed states, quasi states—cannot carry such demanding obligations. Although they may not always violate them, they cannot secure their inhabitants' liberty rights; still less can they ensure that their inhabitants have effective entitlements to goods and services. It is an empty gesture to assign the obligations needed for human rights to weak states, comparable to the empty gesture made by town councils in Britain in the 1980s that proclaimed their towns nuclear-free zones. Indeed, even strong and willing states may find that they cannot "achieve progressively the full realisation of the rights recognized" in Declarations and Covenants. Strong states may have a monopoly of the legitimate use of force within their territories; but they seldom have a monopoly of the effective use of other forms of power. There are plenty of reasons for thinking carefully about the specific character of state power, and for questioning the assumption that powerful—let alone weak—states can carry the range of second-order obligations that they ostensibly take on in signing and ratifying human rights instruments.

Given these realities, it may be worth reconsidering whether all second-order obligations to secure human rights should lie with states. Perhaps some of them should lie with powerful nonstate actors, such as transnational corporations, powerful nongovernmental organizations, or major religious, cultural, professional, and educational bodies. The assumption that states and states alone should hold all the relevant obligations may reflect the extraordinary dominance of state power in the late twentieth century, rather than a timeless solution to the problem of allocating obligations to provide goods and services effectively. For present purposes, I shall leave these unsettling possibilities unexplored, but say a little more about some of the cultural and political costs that are linked to persistent confusion between normative and aspirational views of human rights.

Control and Blame

If human rights are not preconventional, universal rights, but are grounded in the special obligations assumed by states, then there is—at the very least—an awkward gap between reality and rhetoric. The second-order obligations of states are discharged by imposing first-order obligations on others and enforcing them. The reality is that state agency and state power, and that of derivative institutions, are used to construct institutions that (partially) secure rights, and that to do this it is necessary to control the action of individuals and institutions systematically and in detail. If states party are to discharge the second-order obligations they assume in signing and ratifying human rights Covenants, they must not only ensure that liberty rights are respected by all, but must assign and enforce first-order obligations whose discharge will deliver rights to goods and services to all. Human beings, it is evident, will not merely be the intended *beneficiaries* of these obligations, but will carry the intended *burdens.*

The system of control that states must impose to ensure that these obligations are discharged is likely to be dauntingly complex. Yet, as Burke pointed out, what we really need if we are to have food and medicine is the active engagement of "the farmer and the physician." Can that active engagement be secured or improved by imposing detailed and complex obligations on those who are to carry the relevant first-order obligations? There is much to consider here, and I offer very brief comments under four headings: complexity, compliance, complaint, and compensation.

Complexity

Detailed control is needed to "achieve progressively the full realization" of very complex sets of potentially conflicting rights, which must be mutually adjusted. It is no wonder that legislation in the age of human rights has become prolix and demanding. Those who frame it have to seek to ensure that individuals and institutions conform to a very large number of constraints in all activities, so have to set and enforce very detailed requirements.[13] It is now common in developed societies to find that legislation imposes highly complex procedures that bristle with duties to register, duties to obtain permission, duties to consult, rights to appeal, as well as proliferating requirements to record, to disclose, and to report. Such legislation is typically supplemented by copious regulation, relentless "guidance," prolix codes of good practice, and highly intrusive forms of accountability. These highly detailed forms of social control may be unavoidable in a public culture that aims to "achieve progressively the full realization" of an extraordinarily complex set of rights, so has to impose complex demands and burdens on all activities and all areas of life.

The results are demanding for the state agencies that are supposed to set the requirements and police the system. They can be dementing for the institutions and individuals that are to carry the first-order obligations—not least for the farmer and the physician. Complex controls risk stilling active engagement. Those of whom too much that is extraneous to their basic tasks—growing food, caring for the sick—is required are likely to resent the proliferating and time-consuming requirements to obtain permissions, to consult third parties, to record, to disclose, to report, and to comply with the demands of inspectors or regulators. These requirements for control and accountability impose heavy human and financial costs, and are often damaging to the performance of primary tasks. Those who face these burdens on their attempts to perform demanding substantive tasks—the farmer and the physician—may comply and resent (and sometimes engage in defensive practices); they may protest and complain; or they may withdraw from activities that have been made too burdensome. The costs of complex control systems are paid in increasing wariness and weariness, scepticism and resentment, and ultimately in less active engagement by "the farmer and the physician," and by others who come to see themselves primarily as obligation-bearers rather than as right-holders.

Compliance

Individuals who are subject to hyper-complex legislation, regulation, and control are offered two roles. As obligation-bearers their role is compliance; as right holders they are permitted and encouraged to seek redress and to complain when others fail to comply. The individuals and institutions on whom first-order obligations are imposed in the name of securing human rights are offered limited options: they can soldier loyally on in compliance with the obligations states impose; they can voice their discontent; they can exit from the tasks that have been made too burdensome by the excess complexity of legislation and regulation.[14] Loyal compliance becomes harder and more burdensome when the sheer number and complexity of requirements imposed damage the quality with which substantive tasks can be achieved. Voicing concern and objecting to these controls provide some, but limited, relief. Exit from the activities that have been made too burdensome may often be the most reasonable and the preferred option. For "the farmer and the physician," exit means giving up growing food and caring for the sick.

There may be ways of extending human rights that do not carry these costs, that use a "lighter touch," that achieve "better regulation."[15] But the jury is out on this matter. At present, and certainly in the UK, the juggernaut of human rights demands, at every stage of legislation and of the regulatory process, tends to increase complexity even when the costs for "the farmer and the physician," and the damage to the services they provide, are high and well known.

Complaint

First-order obligation-bearers are also right-holders, and it may be that the burdens their obligations impose are recompensed by the rights they enjoy as a result of others discharging their obligations. However, the experience of right-holders is not symmetric with that of obligation-bearers. Individuals act as right-holders only when something has gone awry. In that situation they may complain, seek redress and compensation. The legislation and regulation of states that take human rights seriously often provide a range of remedies—for those with the time, energy, courage (or foolhardiness) to pursue them. When complaints work, redress may be achieved and compensation may be secured. But often the experience of complainants is less than happy because the process of achieving redress is complex, exhausting, and frustrating, and the remedies less than would satisfy and assuage a sense of injury. Since the role of complainant is too often one that exhausts, demoralizes, and undermines active engagement, many who are wronged do not choose this course of action. For "the farmer and the physician" and for many others the choice is mainly between loyalty and exit: giving voice is not generally a positive experience, since it requires complainants to see themselves as victims rather than as actively engaged.

Compensation and Blame

The best outcome of the voice option is that, with luck and persistence, those who take on the role of victim or complainant achieve redress and compensation, or some opportunity for the dubious pleasures of casting blame. Compensation clearly has its positive side—although it may be hard to achieve, limited in amount, and is not always worth the struggle through the complexities of process. Blaming by contrast is a readily available and cheap pleasure—even for complainants whose case is not upheld. Those who cast blame can appropriate, enjoy, and prolong their role and status as victims, can enjoy indignation and a feeling of superiority, even if they cannot quite identify or demonstrate the failings of others. If it proves impossible to identify a blameworthy culprit, they can at least blame the system, that is to say the institutional framework that is failing to achieve "progressively the full realization of the rights recognized . . . by all appropriate means, including particularly the adoption of legislative measures."

There is a dark and tempting undercurrent of pleasure in blaming. Nobody has written about the psychology of blaming, or about its murky appeal and insidious psychological effects, more brilliantly and darkly than Nietzsche. Some of his comments are particularly apt to the realities of the farmer and the physician:

> Suffering people all have a horrible willingness and capacity for inventing pretexts for painful emotional feelings. They already enjoy their suspicions; they're brooding over bad actions and apparent damage. They ransack the entrails of their past and present, looking for dark and dubious stories, in which they are free to feast on an agonizing suspicion and to get intoxicated on their own poisonous anger. They rip open the oldest wounds; they bleed themselves to death from long-healed scars. They turn friends, wives, children, and anyone else who is closest to them into criminals. "I am suffering. Someone or other must be to blame for that."[16]

I do not wish to suggest that the human rights culture inevitably promotes this rancorous approach to life. But I do not think we should accept at face value the view that it is all about respect for persons and treating others as agents. Much of it is indeed about protecting the weak and vulnerable. But it is also about extending the power of states over nonstate actors and human individuals, about establishing systems of control and discipline that extend into the remotest corners of life, about running people's lives for them while leaving them with the consoling pleasures of blame. As Bernard Williams puts it, blame is "the characteristic reaction of the morality system" in which obligations and rights have become the sole ethical currency.[17]

We find it unsurprising that the ruling ideas of past eras have been superseded and modified, and we can hardly doubt that human rights are a central ruling idea of our age. Yet we do not find much current discussion of the likelihood that the idea of human rights may suffer the same fate. Public discourse is for the most part admiring, and often represents human rights as unquestionable truth and progress: we may question anything—except human rights. Indeed, unlike some earlier dominant ideologies, the human rights movement has acquired the beguiling feature of being an ideology not only of and for the ruling classes, but an ideology for—and increasingly of—the oppressed. This seems to me a good reason for thinking particularly carefully and critically about the internal structure of human rights claims, for trying to be less gestural about their basis and their limits, and for being more explicit about their costs as well as their benefits. The farmer and the physician, and others whose work and commitment are indispensable, are the key to securing a decent standard of life for all: their active enthusiasm and efforts are more valuable than their dour compliance with prescribed procedures, their resentful protest, let alone their refusal to contribute.

Notes

1. Edmund Burke, *Reflections on the Revolution in France*, edited by Conor Cruise O'Brien (London: Penguin Books, 1984), 151–152.

2. *Declaration of the Rights of Man and of the Citizen*, 1789, http://www.magnacartaplus.org/french-rights/1789.htm.

3. Note also Art. 17 of the *Declaration of 1789*: "Property, being an inviolable and sacred right, no one may be deprived of it; unless public necessity, legally investigated, clearly requires it, and just and prior compensation has been paid."

4. Set out in the *UN International Covenant on Civil and Political Rights*, 1966 (*CCPR*). This Covenant also "recognizes" various rights that are not liberty rights. See http://www.magnacartaplus.org/uno-docs/covenant.htm.

5. *CESCR*, Art. Ii. See http://www.unhchr.ch/html/menu3/b/a_cescr.htm.

6. See the FAO website: http://www.fao.org/UNFAO/about/index_en.html.

7. *CESCR*, Art. 12. The two Articles expand on rights proclaimed in Article 25 of the *Universal Declaration of Human Rights* of 1948 (*UDHR*), which runs, "Everyone has the right to a standard of living adequate for the health and well-being of himself and of his family, including food, clothing, housing and medical care and necessary social services, and the right to security in the event of unemployment, sickness, disability, widowhood, old age or other lack of livelihood in circumstances beyond his control." For the text of the UDHR, see http://www.bee-leaf.com/universaldeclarationhumanrights.html.

8. The WHO's objective, as set out in its Constitution, is "the attainment by all peoples of the highest possible level of health," defined expansively as "a state of complete physical, mental and social well-being and not merely the absence of disease or infirmity." See http://www.who.int/about/en/.

9. See James Griffin, "Discrepancies Between the Best Philosophical Account of Human Rights and the International Law of Human Rights," *Proceedings of the Aristotelian Society* 101 (2001): 1–28.

10. The text can be found at http://www.imcl/biz/docs/humanrights.pdf. For further comments on some confusions about obligations and agency in *UDHR*, see Onora O'Neill, "Agents of Justice," in *Global Justice*, edited by Thomas W. Pogge (Oxford: Blackwell, 2001), 188–203.

11. *CESCR*, Art. 2, at http://www.unhchr.ch/html/menu3/b/a_cescr.htm.

12. *The Nature of States Parties Obligations*, Art. 2, para i of the Covenant, Fifth Session, 1990, Office of the High Commissioner for Human Rights, *CESCR* General comment 3, http://www.unhchr.ch/tbs/doc.nsf/(symbol)/CESCR+General+comment+3.En?Open Document.

13. Michael Moran, *The British Regulatory State: High Modernism and Hyper-innovation* (Oxford: Oxford University Press, 2003). Moran argues that the new regulatory state is neither liberal nor decentralizing, despite its commitment to human rights. Rather it is both interventionist and centralizing in ways that colonize hitherto relatively independent domains of civil society—including those of the farmer and the physician.

14. See Albert O. Hirschmann, *Exit, Voice, and Loyalty: Responses to Decline in Firms, Organizations, and States* (Cambridge, MA: Harvard University Press, 1970), for a classic analysis of these options.

15. The United Kingdom government established a *Better Regulation Task Force* in 1997. It promotes the "five principles of better regulation," which are said to be Proportionality, Accountability, Consistency, Transparency, and Targeting (consistency is a nice touch!). See the task force's website at http:// www.brtf.gov.uk/.

16. Friedrich Nietzsche, *The Genealogy of Morals*, Part III, section 15. This translation, which draws on earlier received versions, can be found at *The Nietzsche Channel*'s website at http://www.geocities.com/thenietzschechannel/onthe3.htm#3ei5.

17. Bernard Williams, *Ethics and the Limits of Philosophy* (London: Fontana, 1985), 177.

READING

14

World Poverty and Human Rights

THOMAS POGGE

Despite a high and growing global average income, billions of human beings are still condemned to lifelong severe poverty, with all its attendant evils of low life expectancy, social exclusion, ill health, illiteracy, dependency, and effective enslavement. The annual death toll from poverty-related causes is around 18 million, or one-third of all human deaths, which adds up to approximately 270 million deaths since the end of the Cold War.[1]

This problem is hardly unsolvable, in spite of its magnitude. Though constituting 44 percent of the world's population, the 2,735 million people the World Bank counts as living below its more generous $2 per day international poverty line consume only 1.3 percent of the global product, and would need just 1 percent more to escape poverty so defined.[2] The high-income countries, with 955 million citizens, by contrast, have about 81 percent of the global product.[3] With our average per capita income nearly 180 times greater than that of the poor (at market exchange rates), we could eradicate severe poverty worldwide if we chose to try—in fact, we could have eradicated it decades ago.

Citizens of the rich countries are, however, conditioned to downplay the severity and persistence of world poverty and to think of it as an occasion for minor charitable assistance. Thanks in part to the rationalizations dispensed by our economists, most of us believe that severe poverty and its persistence are due exclusively to local causes. Few realize that severe poverty is an ongoing harm we inflict upon the global poor. If more of us understood the true magnitude of the problem of poverty and our causal involvement in it, we might do what is necessary to eradicate it.

That world poverty is an ongoing harm *we* inflict seems completely incredible to most citizens of the affluent countries. We call it tragic that the basic human rights of so many remain unfulfilled, and are willing to admit that we should do more to help. But it is unthinkable to us that we are actively responsible for this catastrophe. If we were, then we, civilized and sophisticated denizens of the developed countries, would be guilty of the largest crime against humanity ever committed, the death toll of which exceeds, every week, that of the recent tsunami and, every three years, that of World War II, the concentration camps and gulags included. What could be more preposterous?

But think about the unthinkable for a moment. Are there steps the affluent countries could take to reduce severe poverty abroad? It seems very likely that there are, given the enormous inequalities in income and wealth already mentioned. The common assumption, however, is that reducing severe poverty abroad at the expense of our own affluence would be generous on our part, not something we owe, and that our failure to do this is thus at most a lack of generosity that does not make us morally responsible for the continued deprivation of the poor.

I deny this popular assumption. I deny that the 955 million citizens of the affluent countries are morally entitled to their 81 percent of the global product in the face of three times as many people mired in severe poverty. Is this denial really so preposterous that one need not consider the arguments in its support? Does not the radical inequality between our wealth and their dire need at least put the burden on us to show why we should be morally entitled to so much while they have so little? In *World Poverty and Human Rights*, I dispute the popular assumption by showing that the usual ways of justifying our great advantage fail.[4] My argument poses three mutually independent challenges.

Actual History

Many believe that the radical inequality we face can be justified by reference to how it evolved, for example, through differences in diligence, culture, social institutions, soil, climate, or fortune. I challenge this sort of justification by invoking the common and very violent history through which the present radical inequality accumulated. Much of it was built up in the colonial era, when today's affluent countries ruled today's poor regions of the world: trading their people like cattle, destroying their political institutions and cultures, taking their lands and natural resources, and forcing products and customs upon them. I recount these historical facts specifically for readers who believe that even the most radical inequality is morally justifiable if it evolved in a benign way. Such readers disagree about the conditions a historical process must meet for it to justify such vast inequalities in life chances. But I can bypass these disagreements because the actual historical crimes were so horrendous, diverse, and consequential that no historical entitlement conception could credibly support the view that our common history was sufficiently benign to justify today's huge inequality in starting places.

Challenges such as this are often dismissed with the lazy response that we cannot be held responsible for what others did long ago. This response is true but irrelevant. We indeed cannot inherit responsibility for our forefathers' sins. But how then can we plausibly claim the *fruits* of their sins? How can we have been entitled to the great head start our countries enjoyed going into the postcolonial period, which has allowed us to dominate and shape the world? And how can we be entitled to the huge advantages over the global poor we consequently enjoy from birth? The historical path from which our exceptional affluence arose greatly weakens our moral claim to it—certainly in the face of those whom the same historical process has delivered into conditions of acute deprivation. They, the global poor, have a much stronger moral claim to that 1 percent of the global product they need to meet their basic needs than we affluent have to take 81 rather than 80 percent for ourselves. Thus, I write, "A morally deeply tarnished history must not be allowed to result in *radical* inequality."[5]

Fictional Histories

Since my first challenge addressed adherents of historical entitlement conceptions of justice, it may leave others unmoved. These others may believe that it is permissible to uphold any economic distribution, no matter how skewed, if merely it *could* have come about on a morally acceptable path. They insist that we are entitled to keep and defend what we possess, even at the cost of millions of deaths each year, unless there is conclusive proof that, without the horrors of the European conquests, severe poverty worldwide would be substantially less today.

Now, *any* distribution, however unequal, *could* be the outcome of a sequence of voluntary bets or gambles. Appeal to such a fictional history would "justify" anything and would thus be wholly implausible. John Locke does much better, holding that a fictional history can justify the status quo only if the changes in holdings and social rules it involves are ones that all participants could have rationally agreed to. He also holds that in a state of nature persons would be entitled to a proportional share of the world's natural resources. Whoever deprives others of "enough and as good"—either through unilateral appropriations or through institutional arrangements, such as a radically inegalitarian property regime—harms them in violation of a *negative* duty. For Locke, the justice of any institutional order thus depends on whether the worst-off under it are at least as well off as people would be in a state of nature with a proportional resource share.[6] This baseline is imprecise, to be sure, but it suffices for my second challenge: however one may want to imagine a state of nature among human beings on this planet, one could not realistically conceive it as involving suffering and early deaths on the scale we are witnessing today. Only a thoroughly organized state of civilization can produce such horrendous misery and sustain an enduring poverty death toll of 18 million annually. The existing distribution is then morally unacceptable on Lockean grounds insofar as, I point out, "the better-off enjoy significant advantages in the use of a single natural resource base from whose benefits the worse-off are largely, and without compensation, excluded."[7]

The attempt to justify today's coercively upheld radical inequality by appeal to some morally acceptable *fictional* historical process that *might* have led to it thus fails as well. On Locke's permissive account, a small elite may appropriate all of the huge cooperative surplus produced by modern social organization. But this elite must not enlarge its share even further by reducing the poor *below* the state-of-nature baseline to capture *more* than the entire cooperative surplus. The citizens and governments of the affluent states are violating this negative duty when we, in collaboration with the ruling cliques of many poor countries, coercively exclude the global poor from a proportional resource share and any equivalent substitute.

Present Global Institutional Arrangements

A third way of thinking about the justice of a radical inequality involves reflection on the institutional rules that give rise to it. Using this approach, one can justify an economic order and the distribution it produces (irrespective of historical considerations) by comparing them to feasible alternative institutional schemes and the distributional profiles they would produce. Many broadly consequentialist and contractualist conceptions of justice exemplify this approach. They differ in how they characterize the relevant affected parties (groups, persons, time slices of persons, and so on), in the metric they employ for measuring how well off such parties are (in terms of social primary goods, capabilities, welfare, and so forth), and in how they aggregate such information about well-being into an overall assessment (for example, by averaging, or in some egalitarian, prioritarian, or sufficientarian way). These conceptions consequently disagree about how economic institutions should be best shaped under modern conditions. But I can bypass such disagreements insofar as these conceptions agree that an economic order is unjust when it—like the systems of serfdom and forced labor prevailing in feudal Russia or France—foreseeably and avoidably gives rise to massive and severe human rights deficits. My third challenge, addressed to adherents of broadly consequentialist and contractualist conceptions of justice, is that we are preserving our great economic advantages by imposing a global economic order that is unjust in view of the massive and avoidable deprivations it foreseeably reproduces. "There is a shared institutional order that is shaped by the better-off and imposed on the worse-off," I contend. "This institutional order is implicated in the reproduction of radical inequality in that there is a feasible institutional alternative under which such severe and extensive poverty would not persist. The radical inequality cannot be traced to extra-social factors (such as genetic handicaps or natural disasters) which, as such, affect different human beings differentially."[8]

Three Notions of Harm

These three challenges converge on the conclusion that the global poor have a compelling moral claim to some of our affluence and that we, by denying them what they are morally entitled to and urgently need, are actively contributing to their deprivations. Still, these challenges are addressed to different audiences and thus appeal to diverse and mutually inconsistent moral conceptions.

They also deploy different notions of harm. In most ordinary contexts, the word "harm" is understood in a historical sense, either diachronically or subjunctively: someone is harmed when she is rendered worse off than she was at some earlier time, or than she would have been had some earlier arrangements continued undisturbed. My first two challenges conceive harm in this ordinary way, and then conceive justice, at least partly, in terms of harm: we are behaving unjustly toward the global poor by imposing on them the lasting effects of historical crimes, or by holding them below any credible state-of-nature baseline. But my third challenge does not conceive justice and injustice in terms of an independently specified notion of harm. Rather, it relates the concepts of *harm* and *justice* in the opposite way, conceiving harm in terms of an independently specified conception of social justice: we are *harming* the global poor if and insofar as we collaborate in imposing an *unjust* global institutional order upon them. And this institutional order is definitely unjust if and insofar as it foreseeably perpetuates large-scale human rights deficits that would be reasonably avoidable through feasible institutional modifications.[9]

The third challenge is empirically more demanding than the other two. It requires me to substantiate three claims. Global institutional arrangements are causally implicated in the reproduction of massive severe poverty. Governments of our affluent countries bear primary responsibility for these global institutional arrangements and can foresee their detrimental effects. And many citizens of these affluent countries bear responsibility for the global institutional arrangements their governments have negotiated in their names.

Two Main Innovations

In defending these three claims, my view on these more empirical matters is as oddly perpendicular to the usual empirical debates as my diagnosis of our moral relation to the problem of world poverty is to the usual moral debates.

The usual *moral* debates concern the stringency of our moral duties to help the poor abroad. Most of us believe that these duties are rather feeble, meaning that it isn't very wrong of us to give no help at all. Against this popular view, some (Peter Singer, Henry Shue, Peter Unger) have argued that our positive duties are quite stringent and quite demanding; and others (such as Liam Murphy) have defended an intermediate view according to which our institutional order plays in the persistence of severe poverty.

Thanks to the inattention of our economists, many believe that the existing global institutional order plays no role in the persistence of severe poverty, but rather that national differences are the key factors. Such "explanatory nationalism" appears justified by the dramatic performance differentials among developing countries, with poverty rapidly disappearing in some and increasing in others.[10] Cases of the latter kind usually display plenty of incompetence, corruption, and oppression by ruling elites, which seem to give us all the explanation we need to understand why severe poverty persists there.

But consider this analogy. Suppose there are great performance differentials among the students in a class, with some improving greatly while many others learn little or nothing. And suppose the latter students do not do their readings and skip many classes. This case surely shows that local, student-specific factors play a role in explaining academic success. But it decidedly *fails* to show that global factors (the quality of teaching, textbooks, classroom, and so forth) play no such role. A better teacher might well greatly improve the performance of the class by eliciting stronger student interest in the subject and hence better attendance and preparation.

Once we break free from explanatory nationalism, global factors relevant to the persistence of severe poverty are easy to find. In the WTO negotiations, the affluent countries insisted on continued and asymmetrical protections of their markets through tariffs, quotas, antidumping duties, export credits, and huge subsidies to domestic producers. Such protectionism provides a compelling illustration of the hypocrisy of the rich states that insist and command that their own exports be received with open markets.[11] And it greatly impairs export opportunities for the very poorest countries and regions. If the rich countries scrapped their protectionist barriers against imports from poor countries, the populations of the latter would benefit greatly: hundreds of millions would escape unemployment, wage levels would rise substantially, and incoming export revenues would be higher by hundreds of billions of dollars each year.

The same rich states also insist that their intellectual property rights—ever-expanding in scope and duration—must be vigorously enforced in the poor countries. Music and software, production processes, words, seeds, biological species, and drugs—for all these, and more, rents must be paid to the corporations of the rich countries as a condition for (still multiply restricted) access to their markets. Millions would be saved from diseases and death if generic producers could freely manufacture and market life-saving drugs in the poor countries.[12]

While charging billions for their intellectual property, the rich countries pay nothing for the externalities they impose through their vastly disproportional contributions to global pollution and resource depletion. The global poor benefit least, if at all, from polluting activities, and also are least able to protect themselves from the impact such pollution has on their health and on their natural environment (such as flooding due to rising sea levels). It is true, of course, that we pay for the vast quantities of natural resources we import. But such payments cannot make up for the price effects of our inordinate consumption, which restrict the consumption possibilities of the global poor as well as the development possibilities of the poorer countries and regions (in comparison to the opportunities our countries could take advantage of at a comparable stage of economic development).

More importantly, the payments we make for resource imports go to the rulers of the resource-rich countries, with no concern about whether they are democratically elected or at least minimally attentive to the needs of the people they rule. It is on the basis of effective power alone that we recognize any such ruler as entitled to sell us the resources of "his" country and to borrow, undertake treaty commitments, and buy arms in its name. These international resource, borrowing, treaty, and arms privileges we extend to such rulers are quite advantageous to them, providing them with the money and arms they need to stay in power—often with great brutality and negligible popular support. These privileges are also quite convenient to us, securing our resource imports from poor countries irrespective of who may rule them and how badly. But these privileges have devastating effects on the global poor by enabling corrupt rulers to oppress them, to exclude them from the benefits of their countries' natural resources, and to saddle them with huge debts and onerous treaty obligations. By substantially augmenting the perks of governmental power, these same privileges also greatly strengthen the incentives to attempt to take power by force, thereby fostering coups, civil wars, and interstate wars in the poor countries and regions—especially in Africa, which has many desperately poor but resource-rich countries, where the resource sector constitutes a large part of the gross domestic product.

Reflection on the popular view that severe poverty persists in many poor countries because they govern themselves so poorly shows, then, that it is evidence not for but against explanatory nationalism. The populations of most of the countries in which severe poverty persists or increases do not "govern themselves" poorly, but *are* very poorly governed, and much against their will. They are helplessly exposed to such "government" because the rich states recognize their rulers as entitled to rule on the basis of effective power alone. We pay these rulers for their people's resources, often advancing them large sums against the collateral of future exports, and we eagerly sell them the advanced weaponry on which their continued rule all too often depends. Yes, severe poverty is fueled by local misrule. But such local misrule is fueled, in turn, by global rules that we impose and from which we benefit greatly.

Once this causal nexus between our global institutional order and the persistence of severe poverty is understood, the injustice of that order, and of our imposition of it, becomes visible. "What entitles a small global elite—the citizens of the rich countries *and* the holders of political and economic power in the resource-rich developing countries—to enforce a global property scheme under which we may claim the world's natural resources for ourselves and can distribute these among ourselves on mutually agreeable terms?" I ask. "How, for instance, can our ever so free and fair agreements with tyrants give us property rights in crude oil, thereby dispossessing the local population and the rest of humankind?"[13]

Notes

1. World Health Organization, *World Health Report 2004* (Geneva: WHO, 2004), Annex Table 2, www.who.int/whr/2004.

2. For detailed income poverty figures, see Shaohua Chen and Martin Ravallion, "How Have the World's Poorest Fared Since the Early 1980s?," *World Bank Research Observer* 19, 2 (2004): 153, wbro.oupjournals.org/cgi/content/abstract/19/2/141 (reporting 2001 data). Ravallion and Chen have managed the World Bank's income poverty assessments for well over a decade. My estimate of the poor's share of the global product is justified in Thomas W. Pogge, "The First UN Millennium Development Goal: A Cause for Celebration?" *Journal of Human Development* 5, 3 (2004): 387. For a methodological critique of the World Bank's poverty statistics, see 381–385, based on my joint work with Sanjay G. Reddy, "How *Not* to Count the Poor," www.socialanalysis.org.

3. World Bank, *World Development Report 2003* (New York: Oxford University Press, 2003), 235 (giving data for 2001).

4. Thomas W. Pogge, *World Poverty and Human Rights: Cosmopolitan Responsibilities and Reforms* (Cambridge: Polity Press, 2002).

5. Ibid., 203.

6. For a fuller reading of Locke's argument, see ibid., chap. 5.

7. Ibid., 202.

8. Ibid., 199.

9. One might say that the existing global order is not unjust if the only feasible institutional modifications that could substantially reduce the offensive deprivations would be extremely costly in terms of culture, say, or the natural environment. I preempt such objections by inserting the word "reasonably." Broadly consequentialist and contractualist conceptions of justice agree that an institutional order that foreseeably gives rise to massive severe deprivations is unjust if there are feasible institutional modifications that foreseeably would greatly reduce these deprivations without adding other harms of comparable magnitude.

10. Pogge, *World Poverty and Human Rights*, 139ff.

11. Ibid., 15–20.

12. See Thomas W. Pogge, "Human Rights and Global Health," *Metaphilosophy* 36, 1–2 (2005): 182–209.

13. Pogge, *World Poverty and Human Rights*, 142.

READING

15

Capabilities and Social Justice

MARTHA NUSSBAUM

Women in much of the world lack support for fundamental functions of a human life. Unequal social and political circumstances give women unequal human capabilities. This essay critiques other approaches to these inequalities and offers a version of the capabilities approach. The central question asked by the capabilities approach is not "How satisfied is this woman?" or "How much in the way of resources is she able to command?" It is, instead, "What is she actually able to do and to be?" The core idea seems to be that of the human being as a dignified free being who shapes his or her own life, rather than being passively shaped or pushed around by the world in the manner of a flock or herd animal. The basic intuition from which the capabilities approach begins, in the political arena, is that human abilities exert a moral claim that they should be developed. Capability, not functioning, is the appropriate political goal.

> It will be seen how in place of the wealth and poverty of political economy come the rich human being and rich human need. The rich human being is . . . the human being in need of a totality of human life-activities.
>
> —Marx, *Economic and Philosophical Manuscripts of 1844*

> *I found myself beautiful as a free human mind.*
>
> —Mrinal, heroine of Rabindranath Tagore's "Letter from a Wife" (1914)

I. Development and Sex Equality

Women in much of the world lack support for fundamental functions of a human life. They are less well nourished than men, less healthy, more vulnerable to physical violence and sexual abuse. They are much less likely than men to be literate, and still less likely to have preprofessional or technical education. Should they attempt to enter the workplace, they face greater obstacles, including intimidation from family or spouse, sex discrimination in hiring, and sexual harassment in the workplace—all, frequently, without effective legal recourse. Similar obstacles often impede their effective participation in political life. In many nations women are not full equals under the law: they do not have the same property rights as men, the same rights to make a contract, the same rights of association, mobility, and religious liberty.[1] Burdened, often, with the "double day" of taxing employment and full responsibility for housework and child care, they lack opportunities for play and the cultivation of their imaginative and cognitive faculties. All these factors take their toll on emotional well-being: women have fewer opportunities than men to live free from fear and to enjoy rewarding types of love—especially when, as often, they are married without choice in childhood and have no recourse from a bad marriage. In all these ways, unequal social and political circumstances give women unequal human capabilities.

According to the *Human Development Report 1999* of the United Nations Development Programme (UNDP), there is no country that treats its women as well as its men, in areas ranging from basic health and nutrition to political participation and economic activity.

One area of life that contributes especially greatly to women's inequality is the area of care. Women are the world's primary, and usually only, caregivers for people in a condition of extreme dependency: young children, the elderly, those whose physical or mental handicaps make them incapable of the relative (and often temporary) independence that characterizes so-called normal human lives. Women perform this crucial work, often, without pay and without recognition that it is work. At the same time, the fact that they need to spend long hours caring for the physical needs of others makes it more difficult for them to do what they want to do in other areas of life, including employment, citizenship, play, and self-expression.[2]

My aim in this brief presentation will be first to indicate why I believe other approaches to these inequalities are not fully adequate and the capabilities approach is needed. Then I shall mention some very general features of the capabilities approach to show how it can handle the problems other approaches fail to handle.

II. Deficiencies of Other Approaches

Prior to the shift in thinking that is associated with the work of Amartya Sen,[3] and with the *Human Development Reports* of the UNDP,[4] the most prevalent approach to measuring quality of life in a nation used to be simply to ask about GNP per capita. This approach tries to weasel out of making any cross-cultural claims about what has value—although, notice, it does assume the universal value of opulence. What it omits, however, is much more significant. We are not even told about the distribution of wealth and income, and countries with similar aggregate figures can exhibit great distributional variations. (Thus South Africa always did very well among developing nations, despite its enormous inequalities and violations of basic justice.) Circus girl Sissy Jupe, in Dickens's novel *Hard Times*, already saw the problem with this absence of normative concern for distribution. She says that her economics lesson didn't tell her "who has got the money and whether any of it is mine."[5] So too with women around the world: the fact that one nation or region is in general more prosperous than another is only a part of the story; it doesn't tell us what government has done for women in various social classes, or how they are doing. To know that, we'd need to look at their lives. But then we need to specify, beyond distribution of wealth and income itself, what parts of lives we ought to look at—such as life expectancy, infant mortality, educational opportunities, health care, employment opportunities, land rights, political liberties. Seeing what is absent from the GNP account nudges us sharply in the direction of mapping out these and other basic goods in a universal way, so that we can use the list of basic goods to compare quality of life across societies.

A further problem with all resource-based approaches, even those that are sensitive to distribution, is that individuals vary in their ability to convert resources into functionings. (This is the problem that has been stressed for some time by Amartya Sen in his writings about the capabilities approach.) Some of these differences are straightforwardly physical. Nutritional needs vary with age, occupation, and sex. A pregnant or lactating woman needs more nutrients than a nonpregnant woman. A child needs more protein than an adult. A person whose limbs work well needs few resources to be mobile, whereas a person with paralyzed limbs needs many more resources to achieve the same level of mobility. Many such variations can escape our notice if we live in a prosperous nation that can afford to bring all individuals to a high level of physical attainment; in the developing world we must be highly alert to these variations in need. Again, some of the pertinent variations are social, connected with traditional hierarchies. If we wish to bring all citizens of a nation to the same level of educational attainment, we will need to devote more resources to those who encounter obstacles from traditional hierarchy or prejudice: thus women's literacy will prove more expensive than men's literacy in many parts of the world. If we operate only with an index of resources, we will frequently reinforce inequalities that are highly relevant to well-being. As my examples suggest, women's lives are especially likely to raise these problems; therefore, any approach that is to deal adequately with women's issues must be able to deal well with these variations.

If we turn from resource-based approaches to preference-based approaches, we encounter another set of difficulties.[6] Such approaches have one salient advantage over the GNP approach: they look at people, and assess the role of resources as they figure in improving actual people's lives. But users of such approaches typically assume without argument that the way to assess the role of resources in people's lives is simply to ask them about their satisfaction with their current preferences. The problem with this idea is that preferences are not exogenous, given independently of economic and social conditions. They are at least in part constructed by those conditions. Women often have no preference for economic independence before they learn about avenues through which women like them might pursue this goal; nor do they think of themselves as citizens with rights that were being ignored before they learn of their rights and are encouraged to believe in their equal worth. All of these ideas, and the preferences based on them, frequently take shape for women in programs of education sponsored by women's organizations of various types. Men's preferences, too, are socially shaped and often misshaped. Men frequently have a strong preference that their wives should do all the child care and all the housework—often in addition to working an eight-hour day. Such preferences, too, are not fixed in the nature of things: they are constructed by social traditions of privilege and subordination. Thus a preference-based approach typically will reinforce inequalities: especially those inequalities that are entrenched enough to have crept into people's very desires.

Once again, although this is a fully general problem, it has special pertinence to women's lives. Women have especially often been deprived of education and information, which are necessary, if by no means sufficient, to make preferences a reliable indicator of what public policy should pursue. They have also often been socialized to believe that a lower living standard is what is right and fitting for them, and that some great human goods (for example, education, political participation) are not for them at all. They may be under considerable social pressure to say they are satisfied without such things, and yet we should not hastily conclude that public policy should not work to extend these functions to women. In short, looking at women's lives helps us see the inadequacy of traditional approaches; and the urgency of women's problems gives us a very strong motivation to prefer a nontraditional approach.

Finally, let us consider the influential human rights approach. This approach has a great deal to say about these inequalities, and the language of rights has proven enormously valuable for women, both in articulating their demands for justice and in linking those demands to the earlier demands of other subordinated groups. And yet the rights framework is shaky in several respects. First, it is intellectually contested: there are many different conceptions of what rights are, and what it means to secure a right to someone. (Are rights prepolitical, or artifacts of laws and institutions? Do they belong to individual persons only, or also to groups? Are they always correlated with duties, and who has the duties correlated with human rights? And what are human rights rights to? Freedom from state interference primarily, or also a certain positive level of well-being and opportunity?) Thus to use the language of rights all by itself is not very helpful: it just invites a host of further questions about what is being recommended. Second, the language of rights has been associated historically with political and civil liberties, and only more recently with economic and social entitlements. But the two are not only of comparable importance in human lives, they are also thoroughly intertwined: the liberties of speech and association, for example, have material prerequisites. A woman who has no opportunities to work outside the home does not have the same freedom of association as one who does. Women deprived of education are also deprived of much meaningful participation in politics and speech. Third, the human rights approach has typically ignored urgent claims of women to protection from domestic violence and other abuses of their bodily integrity. It has also typically ignored urgent issues of justice within the family: its distribution of resources and opportunities among its members, the recognition of women's work as work. This neglect is not accidental, because the rights approach is linked with the tradition of liberal political philosophy that typically recognizes a distinction between the public and the private realms, and puts the family off-limits for purposes of state action. Fourth and finally, the rights approach is often linked with the idea of negative liberty, and with the idea of protecting the individual from state action. Although rights of course need not be understood in this way, their history, at least in the Lockean tradition, does lend itself to that sort of interpretation, and the focus on such areas of negative liberty has been a persistent obstacle to making progress for women in areas ranging from compulsory education to the reform of marriage.

III. Human Dignity and Human Capabilities

I shall now argue that a reasonable answer to all these concerns—capable of giving good guidance to governments establishing basic constitutional principles and to international agencies assessing the quality of life—is given by a version of the capabilities approach.

The central question asked by the capabilities approach is not "How satisfied is this woman?" or even "How much in the way of resources is she able to command?" It is, instead, "What is she actually able to do and to be?" Taking a stand for political purposes on a working list of functions that would appear to be of central importance in human life, users of this approach ask, "Is the person capable of this, or not?" They ask not only about the person's satisfaction with what she does, but also about what she does, and what she is in a position to do (what her opportunities and liberties are). They ask not just about the resources that are present, but also about how those do or do not go to work, enabling the woman to function.

To introduce the intuitive idea behind the approach, it is useful to start from this passage of Marx's 1844 *Economic and Philosophical Manuscripts*, written at a time when he was reading Aristotle and was profoundly influenced by Aristotelian ideas of human capability and functioning: "It is obvious that the *human* eye gratifies itself in a way different from the crude, non-human eye; the human *ear* different from the crude ear, etc. . . . The *sense* caught up in crude practical need has only a *restricted* sense. For the starving man, it is not the human form of food that exists, but only its abstract being as food; it could just as well be there in its crudest form, and it would be impossible to say wherein this feeding activity differs from that of *animals*."

Marx here singles out certain human functions—eating and the use of the senses, which seem to have a particular centrality in any life one might live. He then claims that there is something that it is to be able to perform these activities in a fully human way—by which he means a way infused by reasoning and sociability. But human beings don't automatically have the opportunity to perform their human functions in a fully human way. Some conditions in which people live—conditions of starvation, or of educational deprivation—bring it about that a being who is human has to live in an animal way. Of course what he is saying is that these conditions are unacceptable, and should be changed.

Similarly, the intuitive idea behind my version of the capabilities approach is twofold. First, that there are certain functions that are particularly central in human life, in the sense that their presence or absence is typically understood to be a mark of the presence or absence of human life. Second, and this is what Marx found in Aristotle, that there is something that it is to do these functions in a truly human way, not a merely animal way. We judge, frequently enough, that a life has been so impoverished that it is not worthy of the dignity of the human being, that it is a life in which one goes on living, but more or less like an animal, not being able to develop and exercise one's human powers. In Marx's example, a starving person just grabs at the food in order to survive, and the many social and rational ingredients of human feeding can't make their appearance. Similarly, the senses of a human being can operate at a merely animal level—if they are not cultivated by appropriate education, by leisure for play and self-expression, by valuable associations with others; and we should add to the list some items that Marx probably would not endorse, such as expressive and associational liberty, and the freedom of worship. The core idea seems to be that of the human being as a dignified free being who shapes his or her own life, rather than being passively shaped or pushed around by the world in the manner of a flock or herd animal.

At one extreme, we may judge that the absence of capability for a central function is so acute that the person isn't really a human being at all, or any longer—as in the case of certain very severe forms of mental disability, or senile dementia. But I am less interested in that boundary (important though it is for medical ethics) than in a higher one, the level at which a person's capability is "truly human," that is, *worthy* of a human being. The idea thus contains a notion of human worth or dignity.

Notice that the approach makes each person a bearer of value, and an end. Marx, like his bourgeois forebears, holds that it is profoundly wrong to subordinate the ends of some individuals to those of others. That is at the core of what exploitation is: to treat a person as a mere object for the use of others. What this approach is after is a society in which individuals are treated as each worthy of regard, and in which each has been put in a position to live really humanly.

I think we can produce an account of these necessary elements of truly human functioning that commands a broad cross-cultural consensus, a list that can be endorsed for political purposes by people who otherwise have very different views of what a complete good life for a human being would be. The list is supposed to provide a focus for quality-of-life assessment and for political planning, and it aims to select capabilities that are of central importance, whatever else the person pursues. They therefore have a special claim to be supported for political purposes in a pluralistic society.[7]

The list is, emphatically, a list of separate components. We cannot satisfy the need for one of them by giving people a larger amount of another one. All are of central importance, and all are distinct in quality. The irreducible plurality of the list limits the trade-offs that it will be reasonable to make, and thus limits the applicability of quantitative cost-benefit analysis.

The basic intuition from which the capability approach begins, in the political arena, is that human abilities exert a moral claim that they should be developed. Human beings are creatures such that, provided with the right educational and material support, they can become fully capable of these human functions. That is, they are creatures with certain lower-level capabilities (which I call "basic capabilities"[8]) to perform the functions in question. When these capabilities are deprived of the nourishment that would transform them into the high-level capabilities that figure on my list, they are fruitless, cut off, in some way but a shadow of themselves. If a turtle were given a life that afforded a merely animal level of functioning, we would have no indignation, no sense of waste and tragedy. When a human being is given a life that blights powers of human action and expression, that does give us a sense of waste and tragedy—the tragedy expressed, for example, in the statement made by Tagore's heroine to her husband, when she says, "I am not one to die easily." In her view, a life without dignity and choice, a life in which she can be no more than an appendage, was a type of death of her humanity.

IV. Functioning and Capability

I have spoken both of functioning and of capability. How are they related? Getting clear about this is crucial in defining the relation of the "capabilities approach" to our concerns about paternalism and pluralism. For if we were to take functioning itself as the goal of public policy, a liberal pluralist would rightly judge that we were precluding many choices that citizens may make in accordance with their own conceptions of the good. A deeply religious person may prefer not to be well nourished, but to engage in strenuous fasting. Whether for religious or for other reasons, a person may prefer a celibate life to one containing sexual expression. A person may prefer to work with an intense dedication that precludes recreation and play. Am I declaring, by my very use of the list, that these are not fully human or flourishing lives? And am I instructing government to nudge or push people into functioning of the requisite sort, no matter what they prefer?

It is important that the answer to this question is no. Capability, not functioning, is the appropriate political goal. This is so because of the very great importance the approach attaches to practical reason, as a good that both suffuses all the other functions, making them fully human, and also figures, itself, as a central function on the list. The person with plenty of food may always choose to fast, but there is a great difference between fasting and starving, and it is this difference that we wish to capture. Again, the person who has normal opportunities for sexual satisfaction can always choose a life of celibacy, and the approach says nothing against this. What it does speak against (for example) is the practice of female genital mutilation, which deprives individuals of the opportunity to choose sexual functioning (and indeed, the opportunity to choose celibacy as well).[9] A person who has opportunities for play can always choose a workaholic life; again, there is a great difference between that chosen life and a life constrained by insufficient maximum-hour protections and/or the "double day" that makes women unable to play in many parts of the world.

Once again, we must stress that the objective is to be understood in terms of *combined capabilities.* To secure a capability to a person, it is not sufficient to produce good internal states of readiness to act. It is necessary, as well, to prepare the material and institutional environment so that people are actually able to function. Women burdened by the "double day" may be *internally* incapable of play—if, for example, they have been kept indoors and zealously guarded since infancy, married at age six, and forbidden to engage in the kind of imaginative exploration of the environment that male children standardly enjoy. Young girls in poor areas of rural Rajasthan, India, for example, have great difficulty *learning* to play in an educational program run by local activists—because their capacity for play has not been nourished early in childhood. On the other hand, there are also many women in the world who are perfectly capable of play in the internal sense, but who are unable to play because of the crushing demands of the "double day." Such a woman does not have the *combined capability* for play in the sense intended by the list. Capability is thus a demanding notion. In its focus on the environment of choice, it is highly attentive to the goal of functioning, and instructs governments to keep it always in view. On the other hand, it does not push people into functioning: once the stage is fully set, the choice is theirs.

One might worry that any approach as committed as is the capabilities approach to identifying a number of substantive areas of state action, and urging the state to promote capability in all of these areas by affirmative and not just negative measures, would ride roughshod over citizens' liberties and preferences, and thus become ultimately an illiberal approach. There are several distinct ways in which my version of the capabilities approach tries to meet this concern. One way is by specifying the capabilities at a high level of generality and allowing a lot of latitude for different interpretations of a capability that suit the history and traditions of the nation in question. A free-speech right that works well for the U.S. may not be right for Germany, which has expressed a commitment to the prohibition of anti-Semitic literature and expression that seems entirely appropriate, given its history. A second way, as this example shows, is that the standard political and civil liberties figure prominently within the content of the capabilities list. But the most important way in which the approach protects diversity and pluralism, or so it seems to me, is that it aims at capability rather than actual functioning, at the empowering of citizens rather than at dragooning them into one total mode of life.

V. Capabilities and Care

Let me now return to the other approaches and briefly indicate how the capabilities approach goes beyond them. It appears superior to the focus on opulence and GNP, because it (a) treats each and every human being as an end, and (b) explicitly attends to the provision of well-being in a wide range of distinct areas of human functioning. It appears superior to resource-based approaches because it looks at the variable needs human beings have for resources and the social obstacles that stand between certain groups of people and the equal opportunity to function. It provides a rationale for affirmative measures addressing those discrepancies. It appears superior to preference-based approaches because it recognizes that preferences are endogenous, the creation of laws and institutions and traditions, and refuses to hold human equality hostage to the status quo. Finally, the approach is a close ally of the human rights approach and is complementary with some versions of it. But it has, I believe, a superior clarity in the way in which it defines both the goal of political action and its rationale. And it makes fully clear the fact that the state has not done its job if it simply fails to intervene with human functioning: affirmative shaping of the material and social environment is required to bring all citizens up to the threshold level of capability.

Finally, there is one salient issue on which, or so it seems to me, the capabilities approach goes well beyond all other approaches stemming from the liberal tradition: this is the issue of care and our need both to receive care and to give it. All human beings begin their lives as helpless children; if they live long enough, they are likely to end their lives in helplessness, whether physical or also mental. During the prime of life, most human beings encounter periods of extreme dependency; and some human beings remain dependent on the daily bodily care of others throughout their lives. Of course putting it this way suggests, absurdly, that "normal" human beings do not depend on others for bodily care and survival; but political thought should recognize that some phases of life, and some lives, generate more profound dependency than others.

The capabilities approach, more Aristotelian than Kantian, sees human beings from the first as animal beings whose lives are characterized by profound neediness as well as by dignity. It addresses the issue of care in many ways: under "life" it is stressed that people should be enabled to complete a "normal" human life span; under "health" and "bodily integrity" the needs of different phases of life are implicitly recognized; "sense," "emotions" and "affiliation" also target needs that vary with the stage of life. "Affiliation" is of particular importance, since it mentions the need for both compassion and self-respect, and it also mentions nondiscrimination. What we see, then, is that care must be provided in such a way that the capability for self-respect of the receiver is not injured, and also in such a way that the caregiver is not exploited and discriminated against on account of performing that role. In other words, a good society must arrange to provide care for those in a condition of extreme dependency without exploiting women as they have traditionally been exploited, and thus depriving them of other important capabilities. This huge problem will rightly shape the way states think about all the other capabilities.[10]

The capabilities approach has a great advantage in this area over traditional liberal approaches that use the idea of a social contract. Such approaches typically generate basic political principles from a hypothetical contract situation in which all participants are independent adults. John Rawls, for example, uses the phrase "fully cooperating members of society over a complete life."[11] But of course no human being is that. And the fiction distorts the choice of principles in a central way, effacing the issue of extreme dependency and care from the agenda of the contracting parties, when they choose the principles that shape society's basic structure. And yet such a fundamental issue cannot well be postponed for later consideration, since it profoundly shapes the way social institutions will be designed.[12] The capabilities approach, using a different concept of the human being, one that builds in need and dependency into the first phases of political thinking, is better suited to good deliberation on this urgent set of issues.

The capabilities approach may seem to have one disadvantage in comparison to some other approaches: it seems difficult to measure human capabilities. If this difficulty arises already when we think about such obvious issues as health and mobility, it most surely arises in a perplexing form for my own list, which has added so many apparently intangible items, such as development of the imagination, and the conditions of emotional health. We know, however, that anything worth measuring, in human quality of life, is difficult to measure. Resource-based approaches simply substitute something easy to measure for what really ought to be measured, a heap of stuff for the richness of human functioning. Preference-based approaches do even worse, because they not only don't measure what ought to be measured; they also get into quagmires of their own concerning how to aggregate preferences—and whether there is any way of doing that task that does not run afoul of the difficulties shown in the social choice literature. The capabilities approach as so far developed in the *Human Development Reports* is admittedly not perfect: years of schooling, everyone would admit, are an imperfect proxy for education. We may expect that any proxies we find as we include more capabilities in the study will be highly imperfect also—especially if it is data supplied by the nations that we need to rely on. On the other hand, we are at least working in the right place and looking at the right thing; and over time, as data-gathering responds to our concerns, we may expect increasingly adequate information, and better ways of aggregating that information. As has already happened with human rights approaches, we need to rely on the ingenuity of those who suffer from deprivation: they will help us find ways to describe, and even to quantify, their predicament.

Notes

1. For examples of these inequalities, see Martha Nussbaum, *Women and Human Development: The Capabilities Approach* (Cambridge: Cambridge University Press, 2000), chap. 3, my "Religion and Women's Human Rights," in *Religion and Contemporary Liberalism*, edited by Paul Weithman (Notre Dame, IN: University of Notre Dame Press, 1997), 93–137, and my *Sex and Social Justice* (New York: Oxford University Press, 1999).

2. See Eva Kittay, *Love's Labor: Essays on Women, Equality, and Dependency* (New York: Routledge, 1999); Nancy Folbre, "Care and the Global Economy," background paper for United Nations Development Programme, *Human Development Report 1999* (New York: Oxford University Press, 1999); Mona Harrington, *Care and Equality: Inventing a New Family Politics* (New York: Knopf, 1999); and Joan Williams, *Unbending Gender: Why Family and Work Conflict and What to Do About It* (New York: Oxford University Press, 1999).

3. The initial statement is in Amartya Sen, "Equality of What?" in *Tanner Lectures on Human Values*, edited by S. McMurrin, vol. 1 (Cambridge: Cambridge University Press, 1980), reprinted in Amartya Sen, *Choice, Welfare, and Measurement* (Oxford: Basil Blackwell, 1982; and Cambridge, MA: MIT Press, 1982). See also various essays by Amartya Sen in *Resources, Values, and Development* (Oxford: Basil Blackwell, 1984; and Cambridge, MA: Basil Blackwell and MIT Press, 1984), and *Commodities and Capabilities* (Amsterdam, the Netherlands: North-Holland, 1985). See also Amartya Sen, "Well-Being, Agency, and Freedom," The Dewey Lectures 1984, *Journal of Philosophy* 82 (1985): 169–221, "Capability and Well-Being," in *The Quality of Life*, edited by Martha Nussbaum and Amartya Sen (Oxford: Clarendon Press, 1993), 30–53, "Gender Inequality and Theories of Justice," in *Women, Culture, and Development*, edited by Martha Nussbaum and Jonathon Glover (Oxford: Clarendon Press, 1995), 153–198, and *Inequality Reexamined* (Oxford: Clarendon Press, 1995; and Cambridge, MA: Harvard University Press, 1992). See also Jean Drèze and Amartya Sen, *Hunger and Public Action* (Oxford: Clarendon Press, 1989), and *India: Economic Development and Social Opportunity* (Delhi, India: Oxford University Press, 1995).

4. United Nations Development Programme, *Human Development Reports: 1993, 1994, 1995, 1996* (New York: Oxford University Press, 1993, 1994, 1995, 1996). For related ap-

proaches in economics, see Partha Dasgupta, *An Inquiry into Well-Being and Destitution* (Oxford: Clarendon Press, 1993); Bina Agarwal, *A Field of One's Own: Gender and Land Rights in South Asia* (Cambridge: Cambridge University Press, 1994); Sabina Alkire, "Operationalizing Amartya Sen's Capability Approach to Human Development: A Framework for Identifying Valuable Capabilities," D.Phil. diss., Oxford University, 1999; S. Anand and C. Harris, "Choosing a Welfare Indicator," *American Economic Association Papers and Proceedings* 84 (1993): 226–249; Frances Stewart, "Basic Needs, Capabilities, and Human Development," in *In Pursuit of the Quality of Life*, edited by Avner Offer (Oxford: Oxford University Press, 1996); Prasanta Pattanaik, "Cultural Indicators of Well-Being: Some Conceptual Issues," in UNESCO, *World Culture Report: Culture, Creativity, and Markets* (Paris: UNESCO Publishing, 1998), 333–339; Meghnad Desai, "Poverty and Capability: Towards an Empirically Implementable Measure," Suntory-Toyota International Centre Discussion Paper No. 27 (London: London School of Economics Development Economics Research Program, 1990); and Achin Chakraborty, "The Concept and Measurement of the Standard of Living," Ph.D. diss., University of California at Riverside, 1996. For discussion of the approach, see K. Aman, ed., *Ethical Principles for Development: Needs, Capabilities, or Rights* (Montclair, NJ: Montclair State University Press, 1991); and K. Basu, P. Pattanaik, and K. Suzumura, eds., *Choice, Welfare, and Development: A Festschrift in Honour of Amartya K. Sen* (Oxford: Clarendon Press, 1995).

5. See the discussion of this example in Martha Nussbaum and Amartya Sen's "Introduction" to *The Quality of Life*.

6. Chapter 2 of my *Women and Human Development* gives an extensive account of economic preference-based approaches, arguing that they are defective without reliance on a substantive list of goals such as that provided by the capabilities approach. Again, this is a theme that has repeatedly been stressed by Sen in his writings on the topic (see note 3).

7. Obviously, I am thinking of the political more broadly than do many theorists in the Western liberal tradition, for whom the nation-state remains the basic unit. I am envisaging not only domestic deliberations but also cross-cultural quality-of-life assessments and other forms of international deliberation and planning.

8. See the fuller discussion in my *Women and Human Development*, chap. 1.

9. See my *Sex and Social Justice*, chaps. 3 and 4.

10. See my "The Future of Feminist Liberalism," a Presidential Address to the Central Division of the American Philosophical Association, April 22, 2000, *Proceedings and Addresses of the American Philosophical Association* 74, 2 (November 2000): 47–79.

11. A frequent phrase. See John Rawls, *Political Liberalism* (New York: Columbia University Press, 1993), 20, 21, 183, and elsewhere. For detailed discussion of Rawls's views on this question, see my "Rawls and Feminism," in *The Cambridge Companion to Rawls*, edited by Samuel Freeman (Cambridge: Cambridge University Press, 2002). See also my "The Future of Feminist Liberalism."

12. See the excellent argument in Kittay, *Love's Labor*.

Discussion Questions: Human Rights

1. Do rights exist in the absence of institutions to enforce them?
2. Is any person's poverty a violation of human rights?
3. Can human rights conflict with one another?

ABOUT THE CONTRIBUTORS

Elizabeth S. Anderson is Arthur F. Thurnau Professor and John Rawls Collegiate Professor of Philosophy and Women's Studies at the University of Michigan.

Richard Arneson is Professor of Philosophy at the University of California, San Diego.

Ian Carter is Associate Professor of Political Philosophy at the University of Pavia.

Thomas Christiano is Professor of Philosophy and Law at the University of Arizona.

John Christman is Professor of Philosophy, Political Science, and Women's Studies at Pennsylvania State University.

G. A. Cohen (1941–2009) was Chichele Professor of Social and Political Theory, All Souls College, Oxford University.

Joshua Cohen is Martha Sutton Weeks Professor of Ethics in Society and Professor of Political Science, Philosophy, and Law at Stanford University.

Ronald Dworkin is Frank Henry Sommer Professor of Law and Philosophy at New York University and Emeritus Professor of Jurisprudence at University College London.

David Miller is Professor of Political Theory at Nuffield College, Oxford University.

Martha Nussbaum is Ernst Freund Distinguished Service Professor of Law and Ethics at the University of Chicago.

Onora O'Neill is Professor of Philosophy at Cambridge University.

Philip Pettit is Laurance S. Rockefeller University Professor of Politics and Human Values at Princeton University.

Thomas Pogge is Professor of Philosophy and International Affairs at Yale University.

Amartya Sen is Lamont University Professor and Professor of Economics and Philosophy at Harvard University.

Kok-Chor Tan is Associate Professor of Philosophy at the University of Pennsylvania.

SOURCE CREDITS

Ronald Dworkin, "Equality": Reprinted by permission of the publisher from JUSTICE FOR HEDGEHOGS by Ronald Dworkin, pp. 351–364, Cambridge, Mass.: The Belknap Press of Harvard University Press, Copyright © 2011 by Ronald Dworkin.

Elizabeth S. Anderson, "What is the Point of Equality": Adapted from "What Is the Point of Equality?" *Ethics* 109, no. 2 (1999): 287–337. Copyright © 1999 by University of Chicago Press. Reprinted with permission of The University of Chicago Press. Article edited by Elizabeth Anderson.

Kok-Chor Tan, "A Defense of Luck Egalitarianism": *CV*, no. 11 (2008): 665–690. Reprinted with permission.

G. A. Cohen, "Rescuing Justice from Constructivism and Equality from the Basic Structure Restriction": COHEN, G.A.; *ON THE CURRENCY OF EGALITARIAN JUSTICE, AND OTHER ESSAYS IN POLITICAL PHILOSOPHY.* Princeton University Press. Reprinted by permission of Princeton University Press.

David Miller, "Justice and Boundaries" *Politics, Philosophy, and Economics* 8, no. 3 (2009): 291–309. Copyright © 2009 by Sage Publications. Reprinted by Permission of Sage.

Amartya Sen, "Capabilities and Resources": Reprinted by permission of the publisher from THE IDEA OF JUSTICE by Amartya Sen, pp. 253–268, Cambridge, Mass.: The Belknap Press of Harvard University Press, Copyright © 2009 by Amartya Sen.

Philip Pettit, "The Instability of Freedom as Noninterference": Adapted from "The Instability of Freedom as Noninterference: The Case of Isaiah Berlin" *Ethics* 121, no. 4 (2011): 693–716 . © 2011 by The University of Chicago Press. Reprinted with permission of University of Chicago Press. Article edited by Philip Pettit.

John Christman, "Can Positive Freedom Be Saved?": Adapted from "Saving Positive Freedom" in *Political Theory* 33, no. 1 (2005): 79–88. Copyright © 2005 by Sage Publications. Reprinted by Permission of SAGE Publications. Article edited by John Christman.

Ian Carter, "The Myth of 'Merely Formal Freedom'": Previously published as "Debate: The Myth of 'Merely Formal Freedom'" *Journal of Political Philosophy* 19, no. 4 (2011): 1–10. Copyright © 2011 by John Wiley and Sons. Reprinted with permission.

Richard Arneson, "Democracy Is Not Intrinsically Just": from *Justice and Democracy: Essays for Brian Berry*, ed. by Keith Dowding, Robert E. Goodin, and Carole Pateman (Cambridge University Press, 2004), pp. 40–58. Copyright © 2004 Cambridge University Press. Reprinted with the permission of Cambridge University Press.

Thomas Christiano, "The Authority of Democracy": *Journal of Political Philosophy* 12, no. 3 (2004): 266–290. Copyright © 2004 by John Wiley and Sons. Reprinted with permission.

Joshua Cohen, "Reflections on Deliberative Democracy": *Philosophy, Politics, Democracy,* Harvard (2009): 326–347. Copyright © 2009 John Wiley and Sons. Reprinted with permission.

Onora O'Neill, "The Dark Side of Human Rights": *International Affairs* 81, no. 2 (2005): 427–439. Copyright © 2005 by John Wiley and Sons. Reprinted with permission.

Thomas Pogge, "World Poverty and Human Rights": *Ethics and International Affairs* 19, no. 1 (2005): 1–7. Copyright © 2005 Carnegie Council for Ethics in International Affairs. Reprinted with the permission of Cambridge University Press.

Martha Nussbaum, "Capabilities and Social Justice": *International Studies Review* 4, no. 2 (2002): 123–135. Copyright © 2002 by John Wiley and Sons. Reprinted with permission.

INDEX